IMPLICIT MEMORY
AND
METACOGNITION

Carnegie Mellon Symposia
on Cognition

David Klahr, Series Editor

IMPLICIT MEMORY
AND
METACOGNITION

Edited by

LYNNE M. REDER
Carnegie Mellon University

LEA LAWRENCE ERLBAUM ASSOCIATES, PUBLISHERS
1996 Mahwah, New Jersey

A-28085

Lawrence Erlbaum Associates, Inc., Publishers
10 Industrial Avenue
Mahwah, New Jersey 07430

Cover design by Kristin L. Alfano

Library of Congress Cataloging-in-Publication Data

Implicit memory and metacognition / edited by Lynne M. Reder.
    p.   cm. — (Carnegie Mellon symposia on cognition).
    Papers presented at the Twenty-seventh Carnegie Symposium on
Cognition, held 1994 at Carnegie-Mellon University.
    Includes bibliographical references and indexes.
    ISBN 0-8058-1859-6 (cloth : alk. paper). — ISBN 0-8058-1860-X
(pbk. : alk. paper).
    1. Implicit memory—Congresses. 2. Explicit memory—Congresses.
3. Metacognition—Congresses. 4. Memory—Congresses. I. Reder,
Lynne M. II. Carnegie Symposium on Cognition (27th : 1994 :
Carnegie-Mellon University). III. Series.
BF378.I55I46 1996
153.1'2—dc20
                                      96-29383
                                        CIP

Printed in the United States of America
10 9 8 7 6 5 4 3 2 1

To my parents,
Edna and Melvin Reder

Contents

Preface

This book is a collection of the papers presented at the 27th Carnegie Symposium on Cognition. The focus of this symposium was on metacognition and its relationship to implicit memory. Metacognition is a term that spans many subareas in psychology, and it means different things to different people. A dominant view has been that metacognition involves the monitoring of performance in order to control cognition; however, it seems reasonable (as Reder & Schunn argue in their chapter) that much of the control of cognitive processes runs *implicitly*; that is, without awareness. Newer still is the field of implicit memory, and likewise it has different connotations to different subgroups. Nevertheless, I take it to mean that a prior experience affects behavior without the individual's appreciation (ability to report) that such a prior event affected that behavior.

These two areas of memory research, implicit memory and metacognition, seem to be at two opposite ends of the spectrum—one seemingly conscious and control-oriented, the other occurring without subjects' awareness. Do these processes relate to each other in interesting ways, or do they operate independently without reference to each other? The relatively novel conjecture that much of the control of cognition operates at an implicit level sparked my desire to explore the interrelations between the two fields—metacognition and implicit memory.

Both fields are very new, having been developed in the last two decades, and they generate a lot of excitement and research interest. When I decided to organize this symposium I went to the library, looked for articles on metacognition, and found that there were hundreds. The same was true for implicit memory. However, my final search found *zero* entries on the two in combination. In other words, *Metacognition and Implicit Memory* is the first book attempting to integrate what ought to be closely linked efforts in the study of cognitive science. It is gratifying that a number of chapters in this volume clearly indicate the connections between the two areas. For example, Kelley and Jacoby state in their introduction that they were initially convinced that implicit memory and metacognition were not related (other contributors said as much to me privately), but as they began to think about it further, they concluded that "metacognition and implicit memory are so similar as not to be separate topics" (p. 287). As should be clear from a number of the contributions to this volume, not everyone believes the two areas are identical, but many offer reasons to believe that these two sets of processes are heavily interdependent. It is my hope that this volume will be the springboard for future synergistic work between these two areas.

Quite simply, the chapters and commentaries are arranged in the order that they were presented at the conference. Kihlstrom, Shames, and Dorfman provide an intriguing discussion that links intimations of knowledge to metacognition and implicit memory. It is exciting to see formulations taking constructs typically considered "fuzzy," such as intuitions, and placing them within an information processing framework. Whereas Kihlstrom and his colleagues show how implicit knowledge can affect metacognitive judgments, P. Graf and Birt lay out how different metacognitive activities are brought to bear on implicit and explicit processing. They highlight the importance of different aspects of the rememberer and test situation and how these can influence performance. Reder and Schunn offer a mechanistic account of how implicit memory can produce metacognitive judgments. They also argue that control of strategy choice operates primarily at an implicit level. Siegler, Adolph, and Lemaire are also concerned with the mechanisms driving strategy choice behavior, offering data from a wide range of domains which support the general view that strategy selection is adaptive. They show the consistent variability in strategy use from infants to the elderly. Anderson, in his commentary, compares the theoretical perspectives of all these chapters to his view represented in ACT–R and gives examples of ACT–R productions that could be written to explain the various phenomena described in these chapters. He further argues that people can behave optimally without needing to report the contents of their memories.

The chapter by Narens, A. Graf, and Nelson uses their metacognitive framework to understand the processes involved in explicit and implicit memory tasks. They conducted experiments attempting to meld the paradigms used in their own metacognitive research with the paradigms used to test implicit memory. Funnell, Metcalfe, and Tsapkini describe a unique clinical patient having a high verbal receptive vocabulary but not the ability to produce words on demand (production anomic). Contrasting his performance with normal college subjects is informative, in that he has strong feelings of knowing for almost every queried word, explicit knowledge of the targets, and an excellent ability to provide self-reflective, conscious inspection of his knowledge. Loftus, Coan, and Pickrell describe their important work, arguing that so-called recovery of repressed memories frequently may be confabulated without the previously "repressed" person's awareness of any fabrication. That is, they argue convincingly and provide experimental evidence that it is fairly easy to lead people to "remember" and believe an event from years earlier that never happened. Dawes' commentary highlights some of the important implicit assumptions underlying each of these chapters and points out that sometimes we confuse labels for constructs.

Norman and Schacter discuss the relationship between metacognitive and implicit memory functions and how the brain might implement these processes. They present evidence from clinical cases and PET studies that help refine our understanding of frontal lobe functioning in metacognition. Shimamura reviews a wide range of literature demonstrating the role of the prefrontal cortex in monitoring and controlling memory processes. He also suggests that implicit memory processes may be located in another region of the brain (i.e., posterior cortical regions), and then offers a theoretical conjecture on the interrelation of these two sets of processes. In his commentary, McClelland relates the cognitive neuroscientific approaches of Funnell et al., Norman and Schacter, and Shimamura to computational modeling efforts in this area using the PDP framework.

Kelley and Jacoby review their work on misattribution effects. These illustrate very clearly how their work can exemplify the intersection of implicit memory and metacognition. Benjamin and Bjork introduce the idea of "retrieval fluency" that supplements the notion of "perceptual fluency" introduced by Jacoby and his collaborators. Their construct of retrieval fluency does an excellent job of integrating results from the fields of metacognition and implicit memory. Simon, in his commentary, provides an overall perspective on the conference and the issues discussed. In addition to offering insight on the various ideas developed in many of the chapters, he relates the contributors' ideas to his own framework and compares his theoretical perspective, embodied in EPAM, with other cognitive architectures such as ACT and PDP.

This conference was made possible with support from the Office of Naval Research and the Carnegie Mellon Department of Psychology. Lisa Kouvolo deserves recognition for doing a heroic job in arranging this, her first, symposium. Lisa had never attended such a symposium before, but she learned this task while juggling her regular duties. Margaret Kinsky deserves praise for being cool and efficient in dealing with fires as they arose. Thanks also go to the Psychology department staff and students for pitching in. I want to give a special thank you to Betty Boal who, until this one, single-handedly organized every symposium for three decades, devoting herself to them full time. Despite the fact that she was recovering from knee surgery, Betty remained available for consultation, gave generously of her advice and time, and managed to come over to help out on the day of the symposium. We are all grateful to her for her kindness and great spirit.

Jason Wyse was responsible for actually getting this book together. He took charge of the chapters, making sure that we had everything and reformatting the chapters so that we could give a clean, coherent set to the publishers. Without him, the book would have taken much longer to produce. I owe him a great debt.

—Lynne M. Reder

Chapter 1

Intimations of Memory and Thought

John F. Kihlstrom
Yale University

Victor A. Shames
University of Arizona

Jennifer Dorfman
University of Memphis

> *Poe dismissed the methods of both Bacon and Aristotle as the paths to certain knowledge. He argued for a third method to knowledge which he called imagination; we now call it intuition. . . . [Intuition] lets the classification start so that the successive iterations, back and forth between the empirical and the rational, hone the product until it eventually conforms to nature. . . . Simply start, and like Poe, trust in the imagination.*
> —Allan Sandage and John Bedke
> *Cambridge Atlas of Galaxies*, 1994

In *The Art of Thought*, Wallas (1926) decomposed human problem solving into a series of discrete stages, depicted in Fig. 1.1. In the *preparation* stage, the thinker accumulates declarative and procedural knowledge within the domain of the problem. Preparation requires awareness that there is a problem to be solved; it entails the adoption of a problem-solving attitude, and the deliberate analysis of the problem itself. Sometimes, the thinker solves the problem at this point. This is especially the case, Wallas thought, with what we would now call routine problems, in which the systematic application of a well-known algorithm will eventually produce the correct solution. If so, the thinker moves immediately from preparation to the *verification* stage, in which the provisional solution is confirmed and refined or discovered to be incorrect after all.[1]

At other times, however, the deliberate cognitive effort deployed during the preparation stage fails, and the thinker falls short of solving the problem.

---

[1]For a review of Wallas' analysis in light of modern research on thinking and problem solving, see Seifert, Meyer, Davidson, Patalano, and Yaniv (1995).

The Stages of Thought

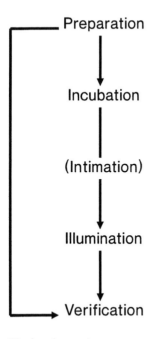

Preparation

Incubation

(Intimation)

Illumination

Verification

FIG. 1.1. The stages of thought.
Adapted from Wallas (1926).

Under these circumstances, Wallas (1926) argued that thinkers often switch to an *incubation* stage, in which deliberate, conscious problem-solving activity is suspended. The thinker may shift his or her attention to some other problem, or take a break and not think of any problem at all. In either case, Wallas believed, problem-solving activity continued at or beyond the fringes of consciousness. That this was the case was demonstrated (at least to Wallas's satisfaction) by the fact that the incubation period often ends in a "flash" of insight in which the solution to the problem suddenly appears in the consciousness of the thinker. This newfound insight is then subject to verification, just as before. As Wallas described it:

> The Incubation stage covers two different things, of which the first is the negative fact that during Incubation we do not voluntarily or consciously think on a particular problem, and the second is the positive fact that a series of unconscious and involuntary (or foreconscious and forevoluntary) mental events may take place during that period. (p. 86)

* * *

> [T]he final "flash," or "click" . . . is the culmination of a successful train of association, which may have lasted for an appreciable time, and which has probably been preceded by a series of tentative and unsuccessful trains. (pp. 93–94)

* * *

[T]he evidence seems to show that both the unsuccessful trains of association, which might have led to the "flash" of success, and the final and successful train are normally either unconscious, or take place (with "risings" and "fallings" of consciousness as success seems to approach or retire), in that periphery or "fringe" of consciousness which surrounds the disk of full luminosity. (p. 94)

The risings of consciousness as success seems to approach: Wallas was quite clear that, during the incubation stage at least (and, for that matter, perhaps during the preparation stage as well), there comes a time when the thinker knows that the solution is forthcoming, even though he or she does not know what that solution is. He used the term *intimation* to refer to: "that moment in the Illumination stage when our fringe-consciousness of an association-train is in the state of rising consciousness which indicates that the fully conscious flash of success is coming" (p. 97). In other words, Wallas's intimations are *intuitions* (Bowers, 1984, 1994; Bowers, Farvolden, & Mermigis, 1995).

Intuitions, in turn, are a special form of *metacognition* (Flavell, 1979; Nelson & Narens, 1994; for reviews, see Metcalfe & Shimamura, 1994; Nelson, 1992). Metacognitions reflect people's knowledge or beliefs about their cognitive states and processes. In the context of problem solving, they are exemplified by feelings of warmth (FOWs; Newell, Simon, & Shaw, 1962/1979), where thinkers believe they are close to a solution, even though they are not aware of what that solution is. In the context of remembering, they are exemplified by feelings of knowing (FOKs; Hart, 1965), where rememberers believe that they know something, even though they are not aware of what they know.

In this chapter, we draw attention to some parallels between FOWs and FOKs on the one hand, and implicit memory on the other. In implicit memory, the person's experience, thought, and action is affected by past events which he or she cannot consciously remember (Graf & Schacter, 1985; for reviews, see Graf & Masson, 1993; Lewandowki, Dunn, & Kirsner, 1989; Roediger & McDermott, 1993; Schacter, 1987, 1995). Similarly, in FOWs and FOKs, the person's experience, thought, and action is affected by the solutions to problems which he or she has not yet consciously solved, or by knowledge which he or she has not yet consciously retrieved. In the remainder of this chapter, we argue that these intimations of memory and thought—FOKs and FOWs—share underlying mechanisms with implicit memory—or, at least, can have their origins in a priming process that is something like implicit memory.[2]

---

[2]For other discussions of priming effects in problem solving, see Lockhart and Blackburn (1993) and Mandler (1994).

INTIMATIONS OF THOUGHT

The role played by intuitions in problem solving is admittedly controversial. Newell and Simon (1973), in their work on the General Problem Solver, suggested that intuitions, in the form of FOWs, are produced by a representation in short-term memory of the distance between the problem solver's current state and the ultimate goal state. In a series of studies, however, Metcalfe (1986a, 1986b; Metcalfe & Wiebe, 1987) found that FOWs are not necessarily accurate predictors of problem-solving success. Specifically, Metcalfe has argued that FOWs are accurate when problems are solved by memory retrieval, inasmuch as they reflect the gradual accumulation of problem-relevant information; but they are not accurate, and may even be misleading, when problems are solved by insight, inasmuch as insight requires restructuring the problem itself. Nevertheless, it does not seem that the two categories of problems—those that are solved by memory retrieval and those that are solved by restructuring—are mutually exclusive. In any event, it is clear that problems which can be solved by memory retrieval can still generate the "Aha!" experience that is the phenomenological essence of insight (Simon, 1986/1989).

Consider a particular type of word problem popularized by Mednick (1962; Mednick & Mednick, 1967) in the Remote Associates Test (RAT). The subject is presented with a set of three words, and the problem is to come up with a fourth word that is an associate of all three. A popular example is:

> Democrat
> Girl
> Favor,

to which the solution is *party*. Smith (1995) has proposed a simple algorithm for solving RAT items:

1. select a test word;
2. retrieve an associate to that test word;
3. select a second test word;
4. test whether the associate retrieved in Step 2 is also an associate of the test word selected in Step 3;
   if so, proceed to Step 5;
   if not, return to Step 1;
5. select the third test word;
6. test whether the associate retrieved in Step 2 is also an associate of the test word selected in Step 5;
   if so, that associate is the solution;
   if not, return to Step 1.

A process like this does not have much of the character of an insight problem: It looks more like a matter of pure, brute-force memory retrieval. In fact, however, when people address RAT problems, they often have the "Aha!" experience as they achieve insight into the problem and its solution. If they do not achieve the solution on their own, then they may well have an "Aha!" experience when someone else tells them what the solution is. Both forms of "getting it" have the qualities of insight.

For present purposes, however, it is more important to note that people also have intuitions about these problems, in advance of their solution. Bowers and his colleagues (Bowers et al., 1995; Bowers, Regehr, Balthazard, & Parker, 1990) have developed a variant of the RAT called the Dyads of Triads (DOT) test, in which subjects are presented with two RAT-like items, one of which (the *coherent* item) is soluble, the other (the *incoherent* item) not:

	Playing	Still	
	Credit	Pages	
(Card)	Report	Music	*(none)*

Subjects are asked to inspect the items and generate the answer to the coherent one; if they fail to do so, they are asked to indicate which triad is, in fact, soluble. Bowers et al. (1990) found that subjects are able to distinguish coherent from incoherent triads at better than chance levels, even though they are not able to solve the coherent triad. Figure 1.2 presents the results from five different samples of subjects who went through this procedure. The unsolved DOT items are classified in terms of the subjects' confidence that their choices were correct. In each sample, overall, the choices were correct significantly more often than would be expected by chance. This was especially the case when subjects were at least moderately confident of their choices.

It is of interest to note that Bowers et al. (1990) distinguished between two types of coherent triads. In *semantically convergent* triads, such as:

> Goat
> Pass
> Green   (Mountain)

the solution word preserves a single meaning across the three elements. In semantically *divergent* triads, such as:

> Strike
> Same
> Tennis   (Match),

the solution word has a different meaning in association with each element. Interestingly, the accuracy with which subjects can identify coherent triads is greater for convergent than for divergent ones.

Intuitions on the
Dyads of Triads Task

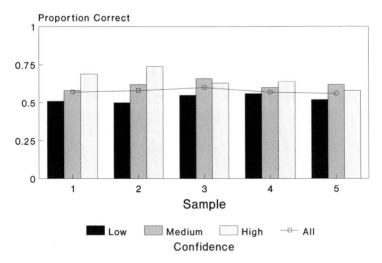

FIG. 1.2. Accuracy of classification of RAT items in the DOT test, by confidence level. Chance performance = .5. Adapted from Bowers et al. (1990).

Bowers et al. (1990; see also Bowers et al., 1995) suggested that these intuitions in problem solving reflect the automatic activation (Anderson, 1983) of knowledge stored in semantic memory—in other words, they suggested that intuitions were based on priming effects similar to those familiar in the study of implicit memory. In this respect, the proposal of Bowers et al. picks up on an earlier suggestion by Yaniv and Meyer (1987) that priming lies at the bottom of another metacognitive phenomenon, FOKs in semantic memory.

Yaniv and Meyer (1987) presented subjects with the definitions of uncommon words, and asked them to generate the word itself:

LARGE BRIGHT COLORED HANDKERCHIEF; BRIGHTLY COLORED SQUARE OF SILK MATERIAL WITH RED OR YELLOW SPOTS, USUALLY WORN AROUND THE NECK.

If the subjects could produce an answer, they were asked to rate their confidence that they were correct. If they could not do so, they made "tip of the tongue" (TOT) and FOK judgments. In any case, each trial ended with a lexical-decision task, in which the subjects saw six items, among which was the answer to the word-definition problem that had been presented just before. For example:

SPENDING
DASCRIBE
BANDANNA
TRINSFER
ASTEROID
UMBRELLA.

In their first experiment, the lexical-decision task was presented immediately after the rare-word definition. In their second experiment, a period of about 4 minutes intervened between them. Yaniv and Meyer's (1987) general finding was that subjects showed priming on the lexical decision concerning the word targeted by the definition, regardless of whether they were able to produce the answer in the first place. Interestingly, the extent of priming was correlated with the experience of the TOT state and the magnitude of FOK ratings—what they called *latent accessibility*. The priming effect only occurred when the target was in a state of high latent accessibility. Yaniv and Meyer suggested that priming formed the basis of the TOT and FOK judgments to begin with. However, the level of activation involved is subthreshold: large enough to produce palpable priming effects, but less than that required for conscious retrieval of the item from semantic memory. In other words, subjects can be influenced by levels of activation that are lower than those required for conscious awareness.

We are aware of some criticism of Yaniv and Meyer's conclusion. For example, Connor, Balota, and Neely (1992) found that items receiving high TOT and FOK ratings also showed priming when the lexical-decision task preceded the word-generation task by a week—an outcome that is difficult to explain by persistent subthreshold activation. Nevertheless, Shames (1994; see also Shames, Forster, & Kihlstrom, 1995) adapted the Yaniv and Meyer procedure to the RAT task studied by Bowers et al. (1990). The idea is that if Bowers et al. are right, and unsolved (but solvable) RAT items activate semantic memory representations of their solutions, this activation should produce priming on the lexical-decision task.

In his doctoral dissertation, Shames (1994) presented subjects with single RAT items (not the DOTs employed by Bowers et al., 1990). In his basic experiment (Shames, 1994, Experiment 1), the subjects were given 5 seconds to produce the single associate common to all three RAT cues—except that, instead of requiring the subjects to produce the actual remote associates, they were simply asked to indicate whether they knew the answer. In fact, given the difficulty of the items and the short interval for thought, the subjects' responses were negative on most of the trials. Immediately after responding on each trial, six items were presented for lexical decision, following the procedure of Yaniv and Meyer. Comparing response latencies to target and control items, both item and subject analyses revealed a significant priming effect (Fig. 1.3). That is, response latencies were shorter when making lexical decisions about RAT items compared to controls. However, this was only the case for the *unsolved* RAT items: Items that had been successfully solved during the 5-second interval produced smaller, nonsignificant priming effects. When Shames repeated his experiment, using a larger set of RAT items (Experiment 5), he observed priming for both solved and unsolved items. However, in other studies he generally confirmed the original effect, priming for unsolved but not solved items, or at least more priming for solved than for unsolved. For example, in another experiment Shames (Experiment 6) decided not to rely on subjects' verbal reports of success and failure in solving RAT items, and simply compared items classified on the basis of the performance of a normative group. Those items that were very difficult (i.e., those that were unlikely to have been solved in the time allotted) showed priming, whereas those that were somewhat easier (i.e., those that were more likely to have been solved) did not.

Still, the fact that 5 seconds elapsed between the presentation of the RAT items and the lexical-decision task raises the possibility that correct solutions occur after the 5-second interval, over the course of the lexical-

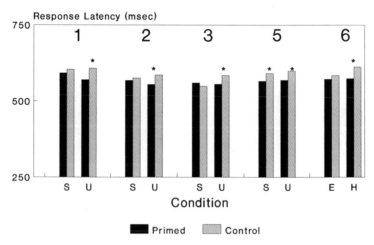

Lexical-Decision Priming in the Remote-Associates Test

FIG. 1.3. Priming effects on lexical decision of solved and unsolved RAT items in Experiments 1–3 and 5–6 of Shames (1994; see also Shames et al., 1995). S = solved, U = unsolved items; E = easy, H = hard items. An asterisk (*) indicates a significant priming effect. Adapted from Shames (1994).

decision task itself. Thus, for example, the priming effect might reflect the subject's recognition that an item presented for lexical decision is also the solution to the previous RAT item. This does not seem to be the case. When subjects are asked to inspect the six items presented for lexical decision, and decide whether each is the answer to the preceding RAT item, response latencies are about a second longer than when the subjects perform the lexical-decision task (Shames, 1994, Experiment 4). Therefore, the priming effect is emerging before the subjects recognize the target as the solution to an unsolved RAT item.

The difference in priming between solved and unsolved problems is interesting, and has been replicated twice more in experiments discussed here later (Shames, 1994, Experiments 2 and 3; see Fig. 1.3). It may be a form of the Zeigarnik (1927) effect. In the present chapter, however, we want to focus on the priming effects of the unsolved items.

What about the Connor et al. (1992) critique of the Yaniv and Meyer (1987) procedure? Connor et al. suggested that the priming observed by Yaniv and Meyer was due to the general familiarity of information in the cue definitions, rather than any subthreshold activation of the target words, or to a postlexical checking process in which the relation between target and cue facilitated response. We believe that Shames's results are not just item effects, or effects of the RAT cues as opposed to the answers, but rather seem to reflect actual problem-solving activity. Evidence for this comes from another experiment, in which subjects studied RAT items in a recognition-memory paradigm. In other words, they were presented with RAT items to memorize, not to solve. Under these circumstances, there was no priming of the solutions to the RAT task (Shames, 1994, Experiment 2). We find this interesting, because it suggests that activation does not spread automatically from the RAT cues to the corresponding RAT solutions; if it did, the item would prime the solution regardless of the task posed to the subject.

Another piece of evidence against an automatic activation hypothesis is provided by another experiment (Shames, 1994, Experiment 3), in which subjects worked on incoherent RAT items consisting of two related cues, and one unrelated one. In this instance, there was no priming of the common associate to the two related cues. Therefore, the spread of activation toward the item common to the related cues seems to be controlled by the nature of the third cue.

Thus, there are at least two aspects of Shames's data which cast doubt on a cue-familiarity interpretation. First, priming is observed only when subjects perform the RAT task with coherent items, not when they perform a memory task, or when the items are incoherent. Thus, the priming effects cannot be produced by general familiarity with the cues. Second, it takes subjects about a second longer to decide that a target is the solution to an RAT item than to decide that it is a word, so postlexical checking will not help the subjects in this instance. Therefore, Shames (1994) really does seem to have evidence for subthreshold priming by RAT items after all. As Bowers et al. (1990, 1995) have argued, this subthreshold priming of the answers may well form the basis for subjects' intuitions about which RAT items are soluble in the Dyads of Triads task.

INTIMATIONS OF MEMORY

Now let us consider the role of intuitions in memory—by which we mean episodic memory, memory for past events. Most work on intuitions of memory is concerned with FOKs in *semantic* memory tasks, such as answering general-information questions or generating words from their definitions (for early examples, see Brown & McNeil, 1966; Hart, 1965; see also Nelson, Gerler, & Narens, 1984; Reder & Ritter, 1992). Thus, subjects who cannot recall the answer are more or less accurate in predicting whether they will recognize the answer when they see it. In the semantic-memory context, therefore, FOKs are intuitions about what people know. We want to know whether there are similar intuitions about what happened in the past—*feelings of familiarity* (FOFs), perhaps, as opposed to feelings of knowing?

A variety of experiments on episodic metamemory suggest that there are such feelings (Hart, 1967; Nelson, Leonesio, Shimamura, Landwehr, & Narens, 1982; Schacter, 1983). Consider a prototypical experiment in which subjects are asked to study a list of paired associates, and then to recall the response terms when presented with the stimulus terms as cues. Where they fail to do so, they are asked to predict whether they will be able to identify the response terms when presented with them later. It turns out that such intuitions are relatively accurate. Moreover, FOFs rise and fall as a function of the same sorts of encoding, storage, and retrieval variables that affect recall and recognition. Of course, in the paired-associate case, it could be that FOFs reflect the subject's conscious recollection of the stimulus term, rather than any preconscious intuition about the response term. That is, if you recognize the stimulus term from the study list, it is a reasonable bet that you will recognize the response term as well. However, evidence indicates that FOFs are based on information about the forgotten target, not just about the remembered cue. For example, subjects can often recall partial information about the attributes of the response term, even if they cannot reconstruct it completely.

We have been interested in another aspect of people's intuitions about the past. Our thinking in this domain is grounded in Mandler's (1980) two-process theory of recognition memory (see also Atkinson & Juola,

1973; Jacoby & Dallas, 1981). Mandler began by defining recognition as a *judgment of prior occurrence*. In this way, he reminded us, along with Bartlett (1932), that all remembering is problem-solving activity—a task in which the problem is to reconstruct a mental representation of the past. If so, then it is reasonable to expect that we will have feelings of warmth as we come closer to solving the problem of reconstructing the past. Anyway, Mandler (1980) argued that two quite different mental processes contribute to judgments of recognition. The first of these processes, *retrieval*, entails the actual recovery of an episodic memory trace; it is the conscious recollection of an event, including information about the event itself, the spatio-temporal context in which the event occurred, and the self as the agent or patient, stimulus or experiencer, of the event (Kihlstrom, 1996). The second of these processes, *familiarity*, involves the activation of trace information, but not the recovery of contextual information. Recognition-by-familiarity is exemplified by the common experience when a name, or face, or voice "rings a bell": We have a feeling we have met the person before, but we do not know where or when that encounter happened. We are not even sure it happened at all, but if we had to bet, we would say it did. It is a little like that old Rodgers and Hart song (Hart & Rodgers, 1937/1993):

> Some things that happen for the first time,
> Seem to be happening again.
> And so it seems that we have met before,
> And laughed before, and loved before,
> But who knows where or when!

It seems to Mandler, and it also seems to us, that these two recognition processes are differentially related to explicit and implicit memory. Recognition-by-retrieval is obviously explicit, because it entails the conscious recollection of a past event. By contrast, recognition-by-familiarity has something of the character of implicit memory: a change in the individual's experience, thought, or action that is attributable to a past event, in the absence of conscious recollection of that event. Perhaps the activation of memory representations produces what Jacoby and Dallas (1981) called perceptual *fluency*, and this salience underlies both priming effects and the feeling of familiarity.

If so, then we would have an explanation for a puzzling observation in some forms of amnesia, which is that amnesics can sometimes recognize events that they cannot recall. This observation was first made by Huppert and Piercy (1977), and later confirmed by Hirst and his colleagues (Hirst et al., 1986; Hirst, Johnson, Phelps, & Volpe, 1988). It has long been a puzzle, because recognition should not happen under many theories of amnesia. Thus, it has been proposed that amnesia disrupts episodic but not semantic memory (Schacter & Tulving, 1982); or declarative, but not procedural (or at least nondeclarative), memory (Cohen & Squire, 1980; Squire & Knowlton, 1995); or explicit, but not implicit, memory (Tulving & Schacter, 1990). The problem is that both recall and recognition are explicit, declarative, episodic memory tasks. But are they really? We know by now, particularly from the work of Jacoby and his colleagues (e.g., Jacoby, 1991), that there are no pure tests, and every memory task has both explicit and implicit components. This seems to be especially true for recognition. According to Mandler's analysis, recognition-by-retrieval is definitely related to explicit memory, but recognition-by-familiarity is more closely related to implicit memory. If implicit memory is preserved, amnesics might strategically use priming, or perceptual salience, to make recognition judgments by familiarity.

We now know that implicit memory *is* preserved in amnesia, or at least some forms of priming are. However, until recently it was in doubt that implicit memory could support performance on an explicit memory task. Despite the fact that priming and recognition share many common properties (for a review, see Dorfman, Kihlstrom, Cork, & Misiaszek, 1995), Squire and his colleagues (Squire, Shimamura, & Graf, 1985) have argued that the recognition displayed by amnesics is unrelated to priming. Further, they have implied that when recognition occurs it is because the amnesic patients are not densely enough amnesic to abolish all explicit, declarative, episodic memory. Squire et al. buttressed their argument with a study of depressed patients receiving electroconvulsive therapy (ECT)—a treatment that produces both retrograde and anterograde amnesia (for a review, see Squire, 1984). Their focus was on the anterograde component. In the experiment, patients studied three separate word lists, 45, 65, and 85 minutes following a dose of (bilateral or unilateral) ECT, and received tests of word-stem completion and three-alternative forced-choice recognition 15 minutes after each study trial. The bilateral patients showed a profound recognition impairment compared to the unilateral patients and untreated controls, and their performance improved with time as the effects of the ECT remitted. However, the bilateral patients showed no impairment in stem completion at any time. Squire et al. (1985) claimed that recognition was dissociated from stem completion (the former impaired, the latter spared; the former improved over time, the latter did not). Therefore, priming could not form a basis for recognition.

Well, maybe. One problem with the Squire et al. (1985) study is that we do not know what the subjects' criteria for recognition were. If subjects are required to be certain (or think they are), they are most likely to depend on retrieval processes, and to ignore, or discount, feelings of familiarity. However, if subjects are encouraged to guess (or do so anyway), they may capitalize on feelings of familiarity, and their recognition performance might well be related to priming.

It is quite clear that subjects can indeed adopt different criteria for recognition judgments, and that these different criteria yield different outcomes. Subjects can be very conservative, requiring certainty before saying "yes" to a test item; or they can be more liberal, saying "yes" to lots of probes, even when they do not consciously remember them. Of course, we know from the theory of signal detection, if not from common sense, that random guesses will produce lots of false alarms: Hits may go up, but false alarms will go up too, and when we take these into account we may find that recognition does not really improve after all. However, if the feeling of familiarity reflects priming from a previous study episode, false alarms will not go up—or, at least, they will not go up as much. This is because the subjects' guesses are not random, but rather are influenced by experiences of perceptual salience or familiarity; put another way, their guesses are *informed* guesses. They are more like Wallas's (1926) intimations, only in the context of episodic memory, and if subjects rely on these intuitions, their hunches will be right more often than they are wrong.

So, here is the hypothesis:

if priming produces a feeling of familiarity in response to a cue,

and

if subjects are allowed, or encouraged, to make strategic use of that feeling,

then

recognition levels will be genuinely improved over those observed when subjects are discouraged in this respect,

but

this improvement will occur only if implicit memory is spared in the first place.

It should be clear that in some respects this situation represents the bright side of Jacoby's process-dissociation argument, and its associated method of opposition (Jacoby, 1991; see also Toth, Reingold, & Jacoby, 1994). In his research Jacoby seeks to eliminate conscious influences on test performance, providing an uncontaminated estimate of the extent of unconscious influences. By contrast, asking subjects to shift their criteria for recognition is specifically intended to maximize unconscious influences on task performance.

Let us give you an example from some data on recognition in posthypnotic amnesia. In this phenomenon, subjects cannot remember the events and experiences that transpired while they were hypnotized; in that minority of the population which achieves extremely high scores on the standard hypnotic susceptibility scales (a group known to hypnosis researchers as *hypnotic virtuosos*), this amnesia can be very dense indeed. However, it has long been known (Kihlstrom, 1980) that posthypnotic amnesia spares implicit memory. To illustrate, consider the following results from a study reported by Dorfman and Kihlstrom (1995). Hypnotized subjects memorized a list of words, and then received a suggestion for posthypnotic amnesia worded as follows, after which hypnosis was terminated:

> After you open your eyes, you will not remember the words you have learned, or that you learned any words, until I say to you, *"Now you can remember everything!"* You will not remember anything until then.

A control group memorized the list without being hypnotized, and received no suggestion for amnesia. For the explicit memory test, the subjects were presented with words of which the list items were close associates, as well as an equal number of words associated with nonlist items; for each cue, the subjects were asked to recall a related item from the memorized word list. For the implicit memory test, the subjects were presented with the same sorts of items, and were asked to produce three free associates to each cue (everything was counterbalanced). This procedure revealed a double dissociation between explicit and implicit memory: Hypnotic subjects performed worse than controls on explicit cued recall, but better than controls on implicit free association. Postexperimental interviews, as well as a follow-up study employing Jacoby's method of opposition, strongly suggested that the controls, who remembered the memorized word list perfectly well, consciously suppressed list items that occurred to them as free associates—a suggestion which we are currently pursuing in new research. The important point is that the amnesic subjects showed clear priming on the test of free association. Because implicit memory was preserved in these subjects, we would expect them to show good recognition when encouraged to capitalize on the feeling of familiarity that comes with priming.

We did not have a test of recognition in this study, but we do have relevant data from another series of studies (Kihlstrom, Dorfman, & Tataryn, 1995). In our first study, a group of highly hypnotizable subjects was hypnotized, memorized a list of 16 items, and received a suggestion for amnesia before hypnosis was terminated. Recognition of targets and lures (which were counterbalanced across subjects) was by means of confidence judgments employing a four-point rating scale:

1—You are *certain* that the item was not on the list;
2—You *think* that the item *was not* on the list, but you're not sure;
3—You *think* that the item *was* on the list, but you're not sure; and
4—You are *certain* that the item was on the list.

Such a four-point scale yields three criteria for recognition:

strict—counting only items that receive a rating of "4";
moderate—counting items that receive ratings of "3" as well; and
liberal—counting even those items that receive ratings of "2."

If we plot hits and false alarms, we see that hits rose appreciably as we loosened the criterion for recognition (Fig. 1.4). False alarms also increased somewhat, but not commensurately, so if we calculate d' (from the pooled data), we get increasing values of d' for the strict, moderate, and liberal criteria, respectively. We think that this improvement in recognition comes

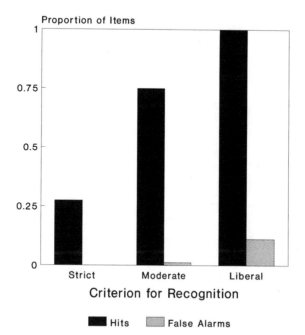

FIG. 1.4. Recognition memory under three criteria during posthypnotic amnesia. Adapted from Kihlstrom, Dorfman, and Tataryn (1995).

from priming, which creates a feeling of familiarity, or an experience of perceptual salience, without the retrieval of contextual information; put another way, priming informs the subject's recognition judgments.

We have other studies of recognition in posthypnotic amnesia that yield substantially the same results, but we wanted to have an experiment in which we could look at priming and recognition in the same subjects; and we also wanted to test our ideas in another form of amnesia. For this purpose, Dorfman et al. (1995) took a leaf from Squire et al. (1985), and reexamined priming and recognition in ECT-induced amnesia. Their experiment was modeled after that of Squire et al., but examined retrograde rather than anterograde amnesia. The patients studied a list of items 10–30 minutes prior to receiving a dose of bilateral ECT, and their memory was tested 50–60 minutes later in the recovery room. The list items were divided into four sets (counterbalanced), each of which was subject to a different form of memory test. Explicit memory for one set of items was tested by stem-cued recall, implicit memory for a second set by stem completion.

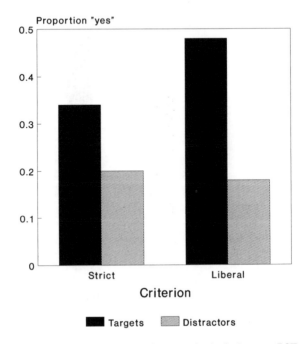

FIG. 1.5. Recognition memory under two criteria during post-ECT retrograde amnesia. Adapted from Dorfman et al. (1995).

The subjects showed very poor stem-cued recall, compared to a control group, but performance on stem completion was unimpaired. Recognition memory for the third and fourth sets of items was tested by a yes/no procedure: For the third group, the subjects were instructed to adopt a strict criterion for recognition, saying "yes" only when they were certain that the item was on the list; for the fourth group, they were instructed to adopt a liberal criterion, saying "yes" if they thought that the item was old, even if they were not sure. Figure 1.5 shows the results. The strict criterion showed the expected impairment; under the liberal criterion, hits went up, but false alarms did not, so that there was actually an increase in d' with the shift in criterion. The important point is that recognition was spared, to at least some degree, when priming was spared—provided that subjects were allowed, or encouraged, to capitalize on the feeling of familiarity that comes with priming.

To sum up, these experiments reveal something interesting about the relations between metacognition and implicit memory. Metacognition, as reflected in subjects' intuitions about which items *might* have been on the list, was clearly associated with priming, a classical expression of implicit memory. We think this is the same sort of priming that Shames (1994) observed, which in turn lies at the basis of the problem-solving intuitions captured by Bowers and his colleagues (Bowers et al., 1990, 1995)—thus bringing us full circle.

INTIMATIONS, INTUITIONS, AND IMPLICIT THOUGHT

What Wallas called intimations, Bowers (1994) called *intuitions*. They reflect the person's feeling that a decision, judgment, or solution is correct, in the absence of supporting evidence, or even in the face of evidence to the contrary. Intuitions of this sort have not received much attention from cognitive psychologists: Two recent historical surveys of thinking and problem solving (Dominowski & Bourne, 1994; Ericsson & Hastie, 1994) make no reference to the term at all.[3] The term *intuition* does not appear in the index to a comprehensive, and otherwise excellent, textbook on thinking and problem solving (Sternberg, 1994)—although in his contribution to that volume, Hunt (1994) does speak of the transition "From Intuitions to Problem Spaces" (p. 216)—as if the former have been abandoned in favor of the latter. Modern research on thinking and problem solving has a strongly analytic flavor to it, what with its emphasis on mental representation and computation, hypotheses and strategies, and knowledge and

---

[3]For a systematic analysis of intuitions, written as modern research on thinking was only just beginning, see Westcott (1968).

skill. As Bowers (1994; Bowers et al., 1995) has noted, the very notion of intuitions seems antithetical to the information-processing approach—too right-hemisphere, too warm and fuzzy, too touchy-feely, too—well, too California. By contrast, we wish to argue that intuitions are very *Pittsburgh*— that they can be understood in terms of activation, priming, and other concepts that are part and parcel of modern information-processing theory. Intuitions are not beyond the pale.

Bowers (1994) has noted that "intuition is often tainted by an implication of irrationality, illogicality, or mental laziness" (p. 613). This identification of the intuitive with the irrational underlies Ross's (1977) classic paper on "The Intuitive Psychologist and His Shortcomings," Nisbett and Wilson's (1977) essay "On Telling More Than We Can Know," and many applications of the heuristics approach to judgment and decision making (e.g., Nisbett & Ross, 1980). Just because intuitions are sometimes wrong, however, does not mean that we should not have them, or that we should not use them. In fact, because thinking generally proceeds from partial information to complete information (Newell & Simon, 1973), intuitions must play a central role in thinking, reasoning, and problem solving.

Presentation of a problem, or a retrieval cue, activates and integrates relevant preexisting knowledge structures, and in the course of solving the problem, or remembering the event, the cognitive system builds on these structures, accruing new information and gradually approaching a solution. These activation and elaboration processes are one basis for implicit memory (Dorfman, 1994), so it should not be surprising that they are revealed in phenomena such as priming. In the final analysis, intuitions form part of the motivational backdrop for problem solving, remembering, and thinking in general, because our sense that a problem is soluble, that some fact resides in our mental storehouse of knowledge, or that a past event happened, provides us with reasons for persevering at the task at hand when we might otherwise give up. Andrew Wiles, the mathematician who has apparently proved Fermat's last theorem, would never have devoted 7 years of his life to the task if he had not had the intuition that the path to success was through the Taniyama–Shimura conjecture.

Moreover, as Bowers (1994) has argued, intuitions represent our tendency, as intelligent problem solvers, to go beyond the information given by a problem or a retrieval cue. If that journey sometimes leads us astray, it also sometimes leads us in profitable new directions. Thus, intuitions are an important part of the creative process. As Ferris (1995) has noted in his comments on the passage from Sandage and Bedke (1994) that forms the epigram to this chapter, intuitions are the way out of the closed cognitive loop of induction and deduction.

From the experiments described in this chapter, it appears that the processes underlying intuitions closely resemble those which underlie implicit memory. In recognition, people's intuitions about the past—the feeling of familiarity, in the absence of full recollection—seem to be based on the perceptual fluency that comes with priming. Here, we have a case in which people can strategically capitalize on implicit memory in order to perform an explicit memory task. Priming can also underlie people's intuitions in more traditional problem-solving situations as well. These intuitions are not exactly implicit memories, because they are not representations of past events. Nor are they implicit percepts (Kihlstrom, Barnhardt, & Tataryn, 1993), because they are not representations of current environmental stimuli. We actually think of these mental states as *implicit thoughts* (Kihlstrom, 1987, 1990): instances in which an idea or image influences experience, thought, or action in the absence of conscious awareness of what that idea or image is. Having thoughts, and even knowing that we have thoughts, but yet not knowing what those thoughts are, is a metacognitive puzzle that further research on implicit memory and related phenomena should help us to solve.

For the present, however, it is clear that problem solutions, like memories, are not discontinuous, all-or-none affairs, remaining entirely unconscious until they emerge full-blown into the full light of consciousness. There is a point, as they approach and cross what Wallas (1926), following William James (1890), called the "fringe" of consciousness, when we know they are coming, even when we do not know what they are. This is the point, between preparation and insight, where intuitions occur.

ACKNOWLEDGMENTS

For additional coverage of problems of intuition, incubation, and insight, see Dorfman, Shames, and Kihlstrom (1994). Preparation of this chapter was supported by Grant MH–35856 from the National Institute of Mental Health to John F. Kihlstrom, a Minority Graduate Research Fellowship from the National Science Foundation to Victor A. Shames, and a postdoctoral fellowship from the National Institute of Mental Health to Jennifer Dorfman. Thanks to John Anderson, Mahzarin Banaji, Talia Ben-Zeev, Robert Crowder, Marilyn Dabady, Isabel Gauthier, William Hayward, Katherine Krause, Elizabeth Phelps, Lynne Reder, Robert Sternberg, Michael Tarr, and Heidi Wenk, Pepper Williams for their comments. Kenneth S. Bowers died on July 4, 1996.

REFERENCES

Anderson, J. R. (1983). A spreading activation theory of memory. *Journal of Verbal Learning & Verbal Behavior, 22,* 261–295.

Atkinson, R. C., & Juola, J. F. (1973). Factors influencing speed and accuracy of word recognition. In S. Kornblum (Ed.), *Attention and performance IV* (pp. 583–612). New York: Academic Press.

Bartlett, F. C. (1932). *Remembering: A study in experimental and social psychology.* Cambridge, England: Cambridge University Press.

Bowers, K. S. (1984). On being unconsciously influenced and informed. In K. S. Bowers & D. Meichenbaum (Eds.), *The unconscious reconsidered* (pp. 227–272). New York: Wiley–Interscience.

Bowers, K. S. (1994). Intuition. In R. J. Sternberg (Ed.), *Encyclopedia of intelligence* (pp. 613–617). New York: Macmillan.

Bowers, K S., Farvolden, P., & Mermigis, L. (1995). Intuitive antecedents of insight. In S. M. Smith, T. M. Ward, & R. A. Finke (Eds.), *The creative cognition approach* (pp. 27–52). Cambridge, MA: MIT Press.

Bowers, K. S., Regehr, G., Balthazard, C. G., & Parker, K. (1990). Intuition in the context of discovery. *Cognitive Psychology, 22,* 72–110.

Brown, R., & McNeil, D. (1966). The "tip of the tongue" phenomenon. *Journal of Verbal Learning & Verbal Behavior, 5,* 325–337.

Cohen, N. J., & Squire, L. R. (1980). Preserved learning and retention of pattern-analyzing skill in amnesia: Dissociation of "knowing how" and "knowing that." *Science, 210,* 207–209.

Connor, L. T., Balota, D. A., & Neely, J. H. (1992). On the relation between feeling of knowing and lexical decision: Persistent subthreshold activation or topic familiarity? *Journal of Experimental Psychology: Human Learning & Memory, 18,* 544–554.

Dominowski, R. L., & Bourne, L. E. (1994). History of research on thinking and problem solving. In R. J. Sternberg (Ed.), *Thinking and problem solving* (pp. 1–35). San Diego: Academic Press.

Dorfman, J. (1994). Sublexical components in implicit memory for novel words. *Journal of Experimental Psychology: Learning, Memory, & Cognition, 20,* 1108–1125.

Dorfman, J., & Kihlstrom, J. F. (1995). *Implicit memory in posthypnotic amnesia.* Manuscript in preparation, University of Memphis, Memphis, TN.

Dorfman, J., Kihlstrom, J. F., Cork, R. C., & Misiaszek, J. J. (1995). Priming and recognition in ECT-induced amnesia. *Psychonomic Bulletin & Review, 2,* 244–248.

Dorfman, J., Shames, V. A., & Kihlstrom, J. F. (1994). Intuition, incubation, and insight: Implicit cognition in problem solving. In G. Underwood (Ed.), *Implicit cognition.* Oxford, England: Oxford University Press.

Ericcson, K. A., & Hastie, R. (1994). Contemporary approaches to the study of thinking and problem solving. In R. J. Sternberg (Ed.), *Thinking and problem solving* (pp. 1–79). San Diego: Academic Press.

Ferris, T. (1995, May 15). Minds over matter. *New Yorker,* pp. 46–50.

Flavell, J. (1979). Metacognition and cognitive monitoring: A new area of cognitive-developmental inquiry. *American Psychologist, 34,* 906–911.

Graf, P., & Masson, M. E. J. (1993). *Implicit memory: New directions in cognitive development and neuropsychology.* Hillsdale, NJ: Lawrence Erlbaum Associates.

Graf, P., & Schacter, D. L. (1985). Implicit and explicit memory for new associations in normal subjects and amnesic patients. *Journal of Experimental Psychology: Learning, Memory, & Cognition, 11,* 501–518.

Hart, J. T. (1965). Memory and the feeling-of-knowing experience. *Journal of Educational Psychology, 56,* 208–216.

Hart, J. T. (1967). Memory and the memory-monitoring process. *Journal of Verbal Learning & Verbal Behavior, 6,* 685–691.

Hart, L., & Rodgers, R. (1993).Where or when" [from *Babes in Arms*]. Milwaukee, WI: Hal Leonard. Original work published 1937

Hirst, W., Johnson, M. K., Kim, J. K., Phelps, E. A., Risse, G., & Volpe, B. T. (1986). Recognition and recall in amnesics. *Journal of Experimental Psychology: Learning, Memory, & Cognition, 12,* 445–451.

Hirst, W., Johnson, M. K., Phelps, E. A., & Volpe, B. T. (1988). More on recognition and recall with amnesia. *Journal of Experimental Psychology: Learning, Memory, & Cognition, 14,* 758–762.

Hunt, E. (1994). Problem solving. In R. J. Sternberg (Ed.), *Thinking and problem solving.* In E. C. Carterette & M. P. Friedman (Eds.), *Handbook of Perception and Cognition* (2nd ed.). San Diego, CA: Academic Press.

Huppert, F. A., & Piercy, M. (1977). Recognition memory in amnesic patients: A defect in acquisition? *Neuropsychologia, 15,* 643–652.

Jacoby, L. L. (1991). A process dissociation framework: Separating automatic from intentional uses of memory. *Journal of Memory & Language, 30,* 513–541.

Jacoby, L. L., & Dallas, M. (1981). On the relationship between autobiographical memory and perceptual learning. *Journal of Experimental Psychology: Learning, Memory, & Cognition, 110,* 306–340.

James, W. (1890). *Principles of psychology* [2 vols.]. New York: Holt.

Kihlstrom, J. F. (1980). Posthypnotic amnesia for recently learned material: Interactions with "episodic" and "semantic" memory. *Cognitive Psychology, 12,* 227–251.

Kihlstrom, J. F. (1987). The cognitive unconscious. *Science, 237,* 1445–1452.

Kihlstrom, J. F. (1990). The psychological unconscious. In L. A. Pervin (Ed.), *Handbook of personality: Theory and research* (pp. 445–464). New York: Guilford.

Kihlstrom, J. F. (1996). Consciousness and me-ness. In J. Cohen & J. Schooler (Eds.), *Scientific approaches to the question of consciousness* (pp. 451–468). Mahwah, NJ: Lawrence Erlbaum Associates.

Kihlstrom, J. F., Dorfman, J., & Tataryn, D. J. (1995). *Free recall, cued recall, and recognition during posthypnotic amnesia.* Manuscript in preparation, Yale University, New Haven, CT.

Lewandowsky, S., Dunn, J. C., & Kirsner, K. (Eds.). (1989). *Implicit memory: Theoretical issues.* Hillsdale, NJ: Lawrence Erlbaum Associates.

Lockhart, R. S., & Blackburn, A. B. (1993). Implicit processes in problem solving. In P. Graf & M. E. J. Masson (Eds.), *Implicit memory: New directions in cognitive development and neuropsychology* (pp. 95–115). Hillsdale, NJ: Lawrence Erlbaum Associates.

Mandler, G. (1980). Recognizing: The judgment of previous occurrence. *Psychological Review, 87,* 252–271.

Mandler, G. (1994). Hypermnesia, incubation, and mind-popping: On remembering without really trying. In C. Umilta & M. Moscovitch (Eds.), *Attention and performance XV: Conscious and nonconscious information processing* (pp. 3–33). Cambridge, MA: MIT Press.

Mednick, S. A. (1962). The associative basis of the creative process. *Psychological Review, 69,* 220–232.

Mednick, S. A., & Mednick, M. T. (1967). *Examiner's manual: Remote Associates Test.* Boston: Houghton Mifflin.

Metcalfe, J. (1986a). Feeling of knowing in memory and problem solving. *Journal of Experimental Psychology: Learning, Memory, & Cognition, 12,* 288–294.

Metcalfe, J. (1986b). Premonitions of insight predict impending error. *Journal of Experimental Psychology: Learning, Memory, & Cognition, 12,* 623–634.

Metcalfe, J., & Shimamura, A. P. (Eds.). (1994). *Metacognition: Knowing about knowing.* Cambridge, MA: MIT Press.

Metcalfe, J., & Wiebe, D. (1987). Intuition in insight and noninsight problem solving. *Memory & Cognition, 15,* 238–246.

Nelson, T. O. (Ed.). (1992). *Metacognition: Core readings.* Needham Heights, MA: Allyn & Bacon.

Nelson, T. O., Gerler, D., & Narens, L. (1984). Accuracy of feeling-of-knowing judgments for predicting preceptual identification and relearning. *Journal of Experimental Psychology: General, 113,* 282–300.

Nelson, T. O., Leonesio, R. J., Shimamura, A. P., Landwehr, R. F., & Narens, L. (1982). Overlearning and the feeling of knowing. *Journal of Experimental Psychology: Learning, Memory, & Cognition, 8,* 279–288.

Nelson, T. O., & Narens, L. (1994). Why investigate metacognition? In J. Metcalfe & A. P. Shimamura (Eds.), *Metacognition: Knowing about knowing* (pp. 1–26). Cambridge, MA: MIT Press.

Newell, A., & Simon, H. A. (1973). *Human problem solving.* Englewood Cliffs, NJ: Prentice-Hall.

Newell, A., Simon, H. A., & Shaw, J. C. (1979). The process of creative thinking. In H. A. Simon (Ed.), *Models of thought* (pp. 144–174). New Haven, CT: Yale University Press. (Original work published 1962)

Nisbett, R. E., & Ross, L. (1980). *Human inference: Strategies and shortcomings in social judgment.* Englewood Cliffs, NJ: Prentice-Hall.

Nisbett, R. E., & Wilson, T. D. (1977). Telling more than we can know: Verbal reports on mental processes. *Psychological Review, 84,* 231–259.

Reder, L. M., & Ritter, F. E. (1992). What determines initial feeling of knowing? Familiarity with question terms, not with the answer. *Journal of Experimental Psychology: Learning, Memory, & Cognition, 18,* 435–452.

Roediger, H. L., & McDermott, K. B. (1993). Implicit memory in normal human subjects. In F. Boller & J. Grafman (Eds.), *Handbook of neuropsychology* (Vol. 8, pp. 63–131). Amsterdam: Elsevier.

Ross, L. (1977). The intuitive psychologist and his shortcomings: Distortions in the attribution process. In L. Berkowitz (Ed.), *Advances in experimental social psychology* (Vol. 10, pp. 173–200). New York: Academic Press.

Sandage, A., & Bedke, J. (1994). *Cambridge atlas of galaxies* [2 vols.]. Washington, DC: Carnegie Institution of Washington.

Schacter, D. L. (1983). Feeling of knowing in episodic memory. *Journal of Experimental Psychology: Learning, Memory, & Cognition, 9,* 39–54.

Schacter, D. L. (1987). Implicit memory: History and current status. *Journal of Experimental Psychology: Learning, Memory, & Cognition, 13,* 501–518.

Schacter, D. L. (1995). Implicit memory: A new frontier for cognitive neuroscience. In M. Gazzaniga (Ed.), *The cognitive neurosciences* (pp. 815–824). Cambridge, MA: MIT Press.

Schacter, D. L., & Tulving, E. (1982). Memory, amnesia, and the episodic/semantic distinction. In R. L. Isaacson & N. E. Spear (Eds.), *The expression of knowledge* (pp. 33–65). New York: Plenum.

Seifert, C. M., Meyer, D. E., Davidson, N., Patalano, A. L., & Yaniv, I. (1995). Demystification of cognitive insight: Opportunistic assimilation and the prepared-mind perspective. In R. J. Sternberg & J. E. Davidson (Eds.), *The nature of insight* (pp. 65–124). Cambridge, MA: MIT Press.

Shames, V. A. (1994). *Is there such a thing as implicit problem solving?* Unpublished doctoral dissertation, University of Arizona, Tucson, AZ.

Shames, V. A., Forster, K. I., & Kihlstrom, J. F. (1995). *Implicit problem solving.* Manuscript in preparation, University of Arizona, Tucson, AZ.

Shimamura, A. P., & Squire, L. R. (1984). Paired associate learning and priming effects in amnesia: A neuropsychological study. *Journal of Experimental Psychology: General, 113,* 556–570.

Simon, H. A. (1989). The information-processing explanation of Gestalt phenomena. In H. A. Simon (Ed.), *Models of thought* (Vol. 2, pp. 481–493). New Haven, CT: Yale University Press. (Original work published 1986)

Smith, S. M. (1995). Fixation, incubation, and insight in memory and creative thinking. In S. M. Smith, T. B. Ward, & R. A. Finke (Eds.), *The creative cognition approach* (pp. 135–156). Cambridge, MA: MIT Press.

Squire, L. R. (1984). ECT and memory dysfunction. In B. Lerer, R. D. Weiner, & R. H. Balmaker (Eds.), *ECT: Basic mechanisms* (pp. 156–163). London: John Libbey.

Squire, L. R., & Knowlton, B. J. (1995). Memory, hippocampus, and brain systems. In M. Gazzaniga (Ed.), *The cognitive neurosciences* (pp. 825–837). Cambridge, MA: MIT Press.

Squire, L. R., Shimamura, A. P., & Graf, P. (1985). Independence of recognition memory and priming effects: A neuropsychological analysis. *Journal of Experimental Psychology: Learning, Memory, & Cognition, 11*, 37–44.

Sternberg, R. J. (Ed.). (1994). *Thinking and problem solving*. In E. C. Carterette & M. P. Friedman (Eds.), *Handbook of Perception and Cognition* (2nd ed.). San Diego: Academic Press.

Toth, J. P., Reingold, E. M., & Jacoby, L. L. (1994). Toward a redefinition of implicit memory: Process dissociations following elaborative processing and self-generation. *Journal of Experimental Psychology: Learning, Memory, & Cognition, 20*, 290–303.

Tulving, E., & Schacter, D. L. (1990). Priming and human memory systems. *Science, 247*, 301–306.

Wallas, G. (1926). *The art of thought*. New York: Franklin Watts.

Westcott, M. R. (1968). *Toward a comprehensive psychology of intuition: A historical, theoretical, and empirical inquiry*. New York: Holt, Rinehart & Winston.

Yaniv, I., & Meyer, D. E. (1987). Activation and metacognition of inaccessible stored information: Potential bases for incubation effects in problem solving. *Journal of Experimental Psychology: Learning, Memory, and Cognition, 13*, 187–205.

Zeigarnik, B. (1927). Das Behalten von erledigten und unerledigten Handlungen. *Psychologie Forschung, 9*, 1–85.

Chapter 2

Explicit and Implicit Memory Retrieval: Intentions and Strategies

Peter Graf
Angela R. Birt
University of British Columbia

The domain of metacognition is loosely defined as those aspects of knowledge and cognition that are *about* cognition (cf. Brown, 1987; Kluwe, 1987; Metcalfe & Shimamura, 1994). According to Brown (1987), "Knowledge about cognition [metaknowledge] refers to the stable, statable, often fallible, and often late developing information that human thinkers have about their own cognitive processes" (pp. 67–68) or about the cognitions of others. In his seminal writings on the topic, Flavell (1979, 1987) explained that metaknowledge can be about different things, most notably about tasks and strategies. Task knowledge includes an understanding of how attributes such as familiarity of materials, availability of cues, or speed instructions influence the manner in which a task might be carried out, or knowledge about the likelihood of being successful on the task. Knowledge of strategies includes an appreciation of their resource requirements and their effectiveness, as well as an understanding of which one might be most suitable for a particular situation. To the extent that such types of knowledge are statable or accessible to conscious awareness, they can be used to reflect on cognitive processing, to select optimal processing strategies, or to make decisions about the course of a mental activity (e.g., whether to start or terminate memory retrieval).

This chapter is about the metacognitive difference between intending to remember versus not intending to remember, and the difference between intending to learn and not intending to learn. The difference between implicit and explicit memory retrieval maps onto the first of these contrasts. According to Graf and Schacter (1985), "Implicit memory is revealed when performance on a task is facilitated in the absence of conscious recollection of previous experiences" (p. 501), and later, they stated that "Explicit memory is revealed by intentional recollection from a specific previous episode, whereas implicit memory is revealed when performance on a task is facilitated without deliberate recollection from a specific learning episode" (Graf & Schacter, 1987, p. 45).

One goal of this chapter is to probe into the different strategies that subjects engage for memory retrieval in these different intentional states. What is already known about the particular strategies that are engaged for implicit and explicit memory retrieval? We "dissect" these strategies in order to highlight their individual properties—for example, the fact that they differ by being aimed at different knowledge domains or neighborhoods (Fisher & Craik, 1977; Nelson, 1989), and the fact that they may also differ in terms of domain size; that is, by implicating larger or smaller memory search sets (Anderson, 1983; Nelson, 1981). Our second goal is to inquire into how different intentions at the time of learning influence subjects' mental activities. Different learning intentions are likely to influence subjects' selection of a task appropriate processing strategy, or they might change the probability of engaging a particular strategy, and in turn, these activities determine subsequent performance on implicit and explicit memory tests.

PREVIOUS ENCOUNTERS

Only a small number of previous investigations on implicit versus explicit memory test performance have been directly concerned with metacognitive issues, and in several recent reviews metacognition was mentioned only a few times and was never the main topic of discussion (Engelkamp & Wippich, 1995; Graf & Masson, 1993; Schacter, Chiu, & Ochnser, 1993; Richardson-Klavehn, Gardiner, & Java, 1996; Roediger & McDermott, 1993). Similarly, in our previous work with implicit and explicit memory tests, metacognitive issues were not the primary concern, except for one such issue that arose in connection with the manner in which implicit and explicit memory retrieval are usually operationalized (see Buchner, Erdfelder, & Vaterrodt-Plünnecke, 1995; Graf, 1995; Graf & Komatsu, 1994; Jacoby, 1991; Jacoby, Lindsay, & Toth, 1992; Komatsu, Graf, & Uttl, 1995).

In the vast majority of previous experiments, implicit and explicit memory retrieval have been operationalized in terms of performance on different kinds of memory tests that were defined by cues, instructions, and the environment. The validity of this operationalization has been questioned, however, on the grounds that memory tests are imprecise instruments which do not completely control subjects' cognitive activity (Dunn & Kirsner, 1988), and as a consequence, test performance cannot be interpreted as a pure index of a particular kind of strategic processing. Consider what could happen on an implicit word stem completion test in which written word stems, such as *int____*, are shown and the task is to respond with the first completions that come to mind. While doing the test, a subject may become aware of the fact that words generated as stem completions had been in a previously studied list, and in turn, this awareness could lead to a shift in retrieval strategy, perhaps making it more like the strategy that is required for explicit memory tests.

Researchers tend to employ a variety of methods in order to prevent, or at least reduce, the likelihood of such retrieval strategy shifts. They tend to arrange events and distractor tasks so as to disguise the episodic-memory aspects of the implicit test, and they use various cover tasks for inducing the appropriate mental set for each test (see Graf & Mandler, 1984; Schacter & Graf, 1986). Schacter and his colleagues (Bowers & Schacter, 1990; Schacter, Bowers, & Booker, 1989) and others (McAndrews & Moscovitch, 1990; Richardson-Klavehn, Gardiner, & Java, 1996, cited in Roediger & McDermott, 1993) have also used specific questionnaires for identifying, and for subsequently "weeding out," subjects whose implicit memory test performance might be confounded by intentional memory retrieval. Despite these efforts, we do not yet have (and do not claim to have) tests that are strategy pure, but by using convergent methods (for discussion see Roediger & McDermott, 1993) we have accumulated an extensive body of observations that shows in a variety of different ways how implicit and explicit memory retrieval differ from each other.

In order to gain further theoretical insight into this body of findings, we zoom in on the specific strategies used for each kind of memory test and ask, what are the specific strategy properties or features that distinguish implicit from explicit memory test performance? We ask this question because clearly, if two strategies differ by more than one property, it will be crucial to identify which of them are necessary for explaining the findings in the literature.

FROM INTENTIONS TO STRATEGIES

Explicit and implicit memory tests have been defined in terms of different conscious intentions that guide memory retrieval (Graf & Schacter, 1985). In following through on their intentions, subjects are likely to evaluate the memory test requirements, to consult their knowledge of such tasks and to review what resources are available, and then they select or construct a particular kind of processing approach or strategy (Brown, 1987; Kluwe, 1987; Nelson & Narens, 1990). According to a two-volume set by Pressley and

Levin (1983a, 1983b), the word strategy has been used in a variety of ways, including to mean a set of "cognitive operations over and above the processes that are natural consequences of carrying out a task, ranging from one such operation to a sequence of interdependent operations" (Pressley, Forrest-Pressley, Elliott-Faust, & Miller, 1985, p. 4). Particularly worth noting is that the origin of a strategy—whether it is subject-initiated or experimenter-supplied (cf. Craik, 1986)—is not part of the definition, and similarly, the attentional resource demands of a strategy—whether it runs off automatically or depends on conscious control—are also not a defining characteristic (Pressley et al., 1985). In short, a strategy appears to be a mental construct or plan, more or less familiar, practiced and automatized, that is engaged for organizing and guiding the cognitive processes required for a task. More important, this definition of strategy highlights and captures, at a metacognitive level, the difference between implicit and explicit memory test processing, and it extends to many previous investigations on the effects of learning intentions and strategies.

Strategies for Learning

Rote Rehearsal. Rehearsal, or the simple activity of turning things over in the mind, is probably the most extensively investigated learning strategy, but to our knowledge, until now no one has specifically explored how this strategy influences subsequent implicit and explicit memory retrieval. Nevertheless, a brief review of empirical and theoretical work on rehearsal is instructive by illuminating how subjects' intentions to learn can be converted and forged into specific strategies. We turned to this literature in order to determine whether an intention to learn influences the probability of engaging in rehearsal, or whether it changes either the amount of rehearsal or the type of rehearsal.

Much of the original work on rehearsal was motivated by early information processing models of human memory (Atkinson & Shiffrin, 1968; Waugh & Norman, 1965) according to which this type of activity served two basic functions: to maintain information in short-term memory, and to transfer it to long-term memory. The rehearsal strategy, more specifically the number of times each to-be-remembered (TBR) target was rehearsed and the order in which subjects organized retrieval, was invoked to explain various phenomena, including the serial position curve, the finding that free-recall test performance was higher after slow than fast study-list presentation, and the fact that a rehearsal preventing activity immediately following list presentation reduced or eliminated the recency component of the serial position curve (see Crowder, 1976; Kausler, 1974; Murdock, 1974). More directly relevant to our central topic, many investigations manipulated subjects' intentions at the time of learning, for example, by instructing some of them (i.e., subjects in the intentional learning condition) to anticipate a memory test while keeping other subjects (i.e., subjects in the incidental learning condition) ignorant of the test. The evidence shows that subjects are more likely to rehearse TBR targets in the intentional than incidental learning condition (Eysenck & Eysenck, 1982; Flavell & Wellman, 1977). More generally, it appears that when the goal is to remember a specific list of targets, intending versus not intending to learn increases the probability or the frequency of rehearsal, or both, and rehearsal is positively correlated with explicit recall and recognition test performance under some but not all study/test conditions (see Rundus, 1971, versus Craik & Watkins, 1973; Woodward, Bjork, & Jongeward, 1973).

In addition to shaping the probability or frequency of rehearsal, study-phase intentions also seem to influence subject's choice of one from among a set of alternative strategies that could be engaged for a particular task. Consider research on the development of human memory which has revealed, first, that strategic rehearsal tends not to occur spontaneously in preschool children, but second, that once acquired the use of this strategy increases rapidly across the school-age years (Flavell & Wellman, 1977; Hagen & Kingsley, 1968; Hagen & Stanovich, 1977; Keeney, Cannizzo, & Flavell, 1967). More relevant is the additional developmental finding that when children first begin to rehearse—engage in strategic study-phase processing—they tend to focus more on sensory and perceptual aspects of TBR targets, in contrast to older children and adults who tend to focus more on meaning (Kail, 1979; Swanson, 1983). (A similar preference in favor of sensory attributes also is obtained when children from different age groups are instructed to sort items that "are the same." Young children tend to sort by color, shape or size, whereas older children are more likely to group by meaning or by conceptual-category membership.) Experiments comparing young and old adults point to a comparable difference in list-learning strategy, showing that young adults tend to process TBR words mainly in terms of their meaning, whereas old adults focus processing at lower level, more physical (e.g., sound, visual appearance) properties of TBR targets (Craik & Jennings, 1992).

Developmental changes in the type of processing are interesting, in part, because they underscore the availability of different kinds of meta-cognitive strategies for learning and remembering. Because alternative learning strategies are available, subjects must select among them and this selection is a meta-activity that is shaped by subjects' intentions, by their evaluation of the anticipated memory testing conditions, by their knowledge of alternative strategies, and by the availability of attentional resources (Brown, 1987; Flavell, 1979; Nelson & Narens, 1990).

Intentions With Levels of Processing. A wealth of evidence from experiments that followed the introduction of the levels of processing framework seems to conflict with the conclusion that study-phase intentions are critical in shaping (quantitatively or qualitatively) the processing strategies engaged for a task. Levels experiments illustrate that at least in one type of situation study-phase intentions seem to have no effect on the manner in which TBR targets are processed. Levels of processing (Craik & Lockhart, 1972; Craik & Tulving, 1975; Craik & Watkins, 1973) is a framework for memory research that emphasizes the distinction between two different kinds of rehearsal called elaborative and maintenance rehearsal, respectively (Craik & Watkins, 1973; Woodward et al., 1973; for reviews see Eysenck, 1978; Lockhart & Craik, 1990; Postman, 1975). Maintenance rehearsal (or what was simply called rehearsal in the previous paragraph) refers to the activity of repeating or recycling exactly one's processing of a target, whereas elaborative rehearsal is the activity of processing a target further; for example, by examining its relationship with other targets and with the context in which it is presented. Craik and Lockhart (1972) applied this framework by presenting each TBR target (e.g., ball) together with a question (e.g., Does it rhyme with hall? Is it a toy?), and they guided and controlled study-phase processing by requiring subjects to answer these questions. Subsequent performance on recall and recognition tests was consistently higher after study questions that focused processing on the meaning rather than the sound or visual appearance of TBR targets (Eysenck, 1978; Lockhart & Craik, 1990; Postman, 1975). More immediately relevant to our central topic, a number of experiments also have varied study-phase intentions by informing some subjects (in the intentional learning condition) but not other subjects (in the incidental learning condition) about the fact that memory for the TBR targets would be assessed (e.g., Neill, Beck, Bottalico, & Molloy, 1990). The results from recall and recognition memory tests showed no influence due to such intention manipulations, but as expected they did reveal consistent and strong effects due to the levels manipulation (see Cermak & Craik, 1979; Postman, 1975).

The contrast between the levels findings and those from the preceding section is also instructive. On one hand, it suggests that when subjects are left to fend for themselves (i.e., when no specific type of processing is required for or indicated by the task), an intention to learn is translated into a strategy for processing (strategic rehearsal, in the present case) the TBR targets, and at least with adults the use of this strategy tends to facilitate later explicit memory test performance. On the other hand, when the experimenter specifies the manner in which targets are to be processed, either by means of study tasks (as in levels experiments) or by means of instructions, an intention to learn has no effect. The null effect may occur because the requirements of the given task tax the available processing resources and thereby prevent subjects from engaging in additional, strategically guided processing over and above that indicated by the study task and by the instructions. An alternative possibility is that subjects operate according to a satisfying strategy (Simon, 1967) and elect not to develop their own strategy when some type of processing is already specified by the experiment, especially if the act of selecting or constructing a processing strategy is resource demanding.

Learning Intention Effects on Implicit and Explicit Memory Tests. Researchers have only recently turned to investigate and compare directly the influence of study-phase intentions on later implicit and explicit memory test performance (Greene, 1986; Neill et al., 1990). An experiment by Greene (1986) compared the effects of intentional versus incidental learning on a word-stem completion test and on a cued recall test. For the critical manipulation, subjects were required to repeat words out loud in a filler task that was inserted between presenting and recalling different series of digits, and in one condition (the intentional learning condition), subjects were forewarned that memory for the words would be tested whereas no mention of this test was made in the incidental learning condition. The results showed higher cued recall test performance in the intentional than incidental condition, and performance was also higher when a large (10 s) versus only a small (2 s) amount of time was allowed for rehearsal. These findings, which have been replicated by Neill et al. (1990), show the same pattern of explicit memory test performance as was found in previous experiments in which study trial processing also was not experimenter determined. By contrast, word-stem completion test baseline performance and priming were similar across the intentional and incidental learning conditions, and neither was affected by the amount of time allowed for rehearsal. The findings suggest that priming and implicit memory retrieval are not under direct intentional or strategic control.

In a second experiment, however, Neill et al. (1990) found a different pattern of effects due to intention to learn. In contrast to the method of Greene (1986) and that employed for their own Experiment 1, Neill et al.'s Experiment 2 gave subjects more precise instructions that defined exactly how memory would be assessed (i.e., either with a word recognition or fragment completion test) and subjects also were given practice on each test. With this type of preparation, the results showed that intentional learning instructions facilitated performance on both test types. Neill et al. also reported that exposure duration (1, 3, or 6.5 s per TBR word) only benefited recognition performance, thereby replicating the explicit memory test results from their Experiment 1 as well as those from Greene. In interpreting the findings, Neill et al. speculated that intentions have comparable influences on implicit and explicit memory retrieval, but only when subjects are provided sufficient information (and when tests are equally familiar, equally easy, etc.) that permits them to construct an appropriate strategy for each test. An alternative possibility which can accommodate the findings from Neill et al.'s Experiment 1 and those reported by Greene is that by giving more precise instructions and by including a test-practice session, the subjects became aware of the memory testing purpose of the fragment completion test, and in turn, this awareness induced them to rely on intentional retrieval even on the stem-completion test. Further research will be required to choose between these possibilities.

Sequence Learning. The role of study-phase intentions has been investigated for a long time under the umbrella label *implicit learning* (see Nissen & Bullemer, 1987; Reber, 1967, 1989; Seger, 1994; Shanks & St. John, 1994). In contrast to research on implicit versus explicit memory retrieval, experiments on implicit learning are concerned with *performance while learning*, and the goal is to identify trial-to-trial changes in performance that occur when intending versus not intending to learn. Implicit learning can be explored with numerous tasks (see Seger, 1994), and one of these, the serial reaction time (SRT) task, involves presenting subjects a series of trials in which a signal appears in one of several (e.g., four, five, six) different locations on a computer screen. The subjects' task is to respond by pressing a key corresponding to the location in which the signal appears and the dependent variable is accuracy (was the right key pressed?) and the time (in ms) required for responding. The SRT can be structured or regulated in several different ways, but the usual approach is to make the order in which signals appear in the different locations follow some kind of repeating pattern or other rule. For example, a simple series of locations can be repeated cyclically (e.g., Nissen & Bullemer, 1987; Stadler, 1992), or a sequence of locations can be constructed according to various probabilistic constraints (Cleeremans & McClelland, 1991; Stadler, 1992). Learning is usually revealed by comparing performance (speed and accuracy) across blocks of trials on the repeating sequence to a control condition in which the sequence is random. Nissen and Bullemer (1987) found that learning, indexed by reaction time, improved more rapidly with a repeating sequence than with a random sequence. Moreover, when subjects in the repeating sequence condition were shifted from a repeating to a random sequence, their reaction time increased dramatically. This combination of findings, the interaction between type of sequence and amount of practice and the effect due to shifting from a repeating to a random sequence, are proof that subjects learned something about sequential regularity.

Recently, a study by Stadler (1989) provided evidence which suggests that this kind of learning does not depend on consciously controlled processing. In this study, subjects performed an SRT task with different patterns, each with 7 trials or locations (i.e., a sequence of 7 lights appearing on different locations). After 11 blocks of training, the patterns were changed so that a target—defined as the ith location signal in the sequence—no longer appeared at the predicted location. When this was done, the time required to react to the signals increased dramatically. In addition, subjects were also given a prediction task in which they performed the first 6 trials of the sequence as during training, but on Trial 7 they were shown a stimulus display without a target and were asked to predict where, according to what they knew and had learned, the target should appear. Subjects' performance on this explicit memory task was no better than would be expected by chance, and there was no other evidence that they were aware of the sequential structure of the task. This combination of findings complements those reported by Greene (1986) and Neill et al. (1990; Experiment 1) by suggesting that intentional, strategic processing is not required for learning complex sequences. Like the findings we reviewed earlier, sequence learning also seems not to be under direct intentional or strategic control, at least not under the limited circumstances that have so far been investigated (for recent reviews see Seger, 1994; Shanks & St. John, 1994).

Directed Forgetting. Research on directed forgetting is relevant to whether or not encoding processes can be stopped, canceled, or both under strategic control. In a typical directed-forgetting experiment (see Bjork, 1972, and Epstein, 1972, for early reviews), the presentation of each item in a study list is followed by an instruction to remember or to forget that item. Prior to study, subjects are told that they will be tested on only those items accompanied by a remember instruction; however, at test they are required to remember both the remember and forget words. Experiments with this procedure have shown markedly better memory for the remember words as indexed by performance on both recall and recognition tests.

More recent studies have compared the influence of directed forgetting manipulations on explicit as well as implicit memory tests (e.g., Basden, Basden, & Gargano, 1991; MacLeod, 1989; Paller, 1990). To illustrate, Paller found that free recall and cued recall were better for words associated with *remember* instruction, whereas no such advantage for *remember* words was found on the stem completion test (i.e., priming effects were comparable for remember and forget words). To explain this finding, Paller suggested that remember words must have been encoded more elaboratively than forget words—consistent with previous claims and evidence that study-trial elaborative processing facilitates recall and recognition test performance (e.g., Craik & Lockhart, 1972; Postman, 1975)—and this difference in processing had no effect or only a minimal effect on priming (e.g., Graf, 1994; Graf & Mandler, 1984; Mandler, 1980). This pattern of findings indicates that the intention to remember or not to remember is translated into a specific encoding strategy, or in Paller's case, perhaps into two qualitatively or quantitatively different strategies for remember and forget words, respectively. The fact that priming is not influenced by remem-

ber/forget manipulations suggests that once launched, the memory encoding processes which are required for priming operate ballistically; they
cannot be stopped and their consequences cannot be undone by a simple
strategy shift.

Summary. This section was intended only as a superficial sketch of how
different intentions can influence subjects' learning phase activities. Even
this sketch is sufficient, however, to reveal that different learning intentions
may affect the quantity and quality of cognitive activities, but that the
mapping of intentions onto strategies and learning activities depends on
many factors, including subjects' age, knowledge, and skill levels, as well as
the availability of experimenter supplied instructions and strategies. So far,
only a tiny portion of previous investigations has explored how different
learning strategies influence priming versus explicit memory test performance. We know from the sequence learning literature that implicit (or
unintended) learning can occur even in the absence of explicit memory for
studied sequences, but to our knowledge, empirical work in this area has not
yet investigated whether different intentions or learning strategies have the
same or different effects on priming versus explicit memory performance.
However, the message from the direct forgetting literature is clearer and
indicates that the cognitive processes required for priming are not under
the direct control of learning intentions and their associated strategies.

Strategies for Retrieval

In this section, we focus on differences between explicit and implicit memory
retrieval, which as a topic area, is the test-phase complement of the preceding
section. In order to learn about the strategies that guide implicit and explicit
memory retrieval, we could proceed as in the last section, and explore, for
example, under what circumstances different retrieval strategies are used,
or how their use develops with age. Instead of using this approach, however,
we "dissect" the strategies in order to uncover their individual properties; for
example, the fact that they differ by virtue of being aimed at different
knowledge domains or neighborhoods. What other properties distinguish
the retrieval strategies engaged for implicit versus explicit memory tests? If
multiple distinctive properties exist, which ones are defining of the implicit
versus explicit retrieval distinction?

Retrieval Strategies, Domains, and Specificity. It is difficult to correctly
identify and describe the difference in cognitive activity when intending to
versus when not intending to recollect a recently studied list of targets, but
at least the following strategy properties spring to mind as potential differences: the novelty, familiarity, or automaticity of the strategy used to initiate

and guide processing, the domain of memory that is to be searched, and the size of the to-be-searched memory domain. Consistent with the broad-stroke manner in which implicit and explicit memory retrieval are usually defined (see Graf & Schacter, 1985, 1987), until now no one seems to have distinguished among such strategy properties and thus we cannot say how each contributes to the difference between priming and explicit memory test performance.

Some researchers (e.g., Jacoby, 1991; Jacoby, Lindsay, & Toth, 1992; but see Graf & Komatsu, 1994) have proceeded as if the first of these properties—the degree of automaticity of the different retrieval strategies—is the most crucial factor that explains performance dissociations between explicit and implicit tests. According to another theoretical orientation, however, the memory domain (see later discussion) seems to be more crucial for explaining, for example, amnesic patients' ability to show normal priming effects together with severely impaired performance on recall and recognition tests (reviewed in Squire & Butters, 1992). Many findings are consistent with both of these perspectives, and yet both may be premature, and we will not know the answer until researchers uncouple the effects due to one strategy property from those due to other, confounded strategy properties.

James (1890/1962) explained that we "make search in our memory for a forgotten idea, just as we rummage our house for a lost object. In both cases, we visit what seems to us the probable neighborhood of that which we miss" (p. 297). The same basic spatial search metaphor is part of many modern views of memory which specify that retrieval is a goal-directed process which involves selective access to particular domains of knowledge (e.g., Humphreys, Bain, & Pike, 1989; Nelson, 1989; Raaijmaker & Shiffrin, 1981; Seidenberg & McClelland, 1989; Shiffrin, 1970). The appropriate search domain for a memory task is typically specified by instructions, test cues (e.g., word fragments), contextual cues and response requirements, and implicit and explicit memory tests are designed to target different domains. For explicit memory tests, the search domain is memory for *a specific set of recently encountered events or experiences* (i.e., episodic memory), whereas it is *knowledge, facts, or skills* (i.e., semantic or procedural memory) for implicit memory tests. These two test types differ also in terms of the size of their memory search sets. Search set size refers to the number of alternative responses that are in a specified memory domain. Both implicit and explicit tests involve a limited memory search domain, albeit with domains of different size (or specificity); the former stipulates a specific spatial/temporal context that constrains the number of legitimate responses, whereas for implicit memory tests no such criteria are given, or the criteria are far more general, like the ones that govern language use in other situations.

These reflections on search set size, domain, and automaticity of strategy serve to underscore the fact that implicit and explicit memory retrieval, as they are usually operationalized, implicate cognitive strategies that could differ in terms of at least three different properties. Consequently, in order to achieve a clearer understanding of how performance dissociations between implicit and explicit memory tests can and do arise, it is crucial that the causal role of strategy familiarity or automaticity, for example, be distinguished from other factors, such as effects due to different memory search domains or different search set sizes. Consider that the size of the memory-search set can vary substantially across different tasks, and this strategy property is known to have a profound and predictable effect on test performance (see Anderson, 1976, 1983; Watkins & Watkins, 1975). In relative terms, the retrieval domain for standard explicit recall test seems narrow (e.g., the usual task is to recollect the words from a specific previously studied list), but it could be made even narrower, for example, by asking only for recall of the first few items from the TBR list or only for recall of the written words after studying both written and spoken words (e.g., Jacoby, 1991; Komatsu et al., 1995). By contrast, in an autobiographical memory experiment (e.g., Howes & Katz, 1992), the instruction to recall (with or without cues) any personal episodes or experiences defines a much broader domain. The size of the search set for implicit memory tests can also be very large, as when subjects are required to free associate to cues with any word that comes to mind (Shimamura & Squire, 1989); it is much narrower, however, when subjects are required to generate appropriate exemplars in response to a specific cue such as animal names or the first letters of words (Graf, Shimamura, & Squire, 1985; Bolla & Lindgren, 1990), and even narrower when required to find words corresponding to word fragments that have only one possible completion (e.g., Tulving, Schacter, & Stark, 1982). Elsewhere, we have suggested that search set-size differences may explain differences in the persistence of priming effects across delays (see Graf & Mandler, 1984).

The influence of search size on explicit memory test performance has been targeted by many previous investigations (e.g., Anderson, 1976, 1983; Nelson, Bajo, & Casanueva, 1985; Watkins & Watkins, 1975). Nelson et al. (1985) showed that recall is lower for target words that have more rhyme associates than for targets with fewer rhyme associates. Similarly, reaction time studies have found that subjects are slower to recognize a previously studied target or fact after having acquired a large as opposed to a small set of additional concepts that are associated with the same target or fact (Anderson, 1976, 1983; Lewis & Anderson, 1976). In general, it appears that as knowledge about a particular topic increases, there is a corresponding decrease in the ability to retrieve a particular recently acquired fact about that same topic, a phenomenon generally known as the *fan effect*

(Anderson, 1976, 1983). In contrast to this evidence, however, related research has shown that domain size effects can be reduced or eliminated, or they can be positively correlated with explicit memory test performance; for example, under study conditions that focus processing on specific associations between targets and their respective superordinate "fan node" (e.g., Nelson, Gee, & Schreiber, 1992; Reder & Ross, 1983). Here we do not address these apparently conflicting findings; instead, we list them in order to illustrate the complex influence due to search set size on explicit memory test performance. It seems plausible to us that similar types of influences due to search set size may also occur on implicit memory test performance, thereby providing one more reason for why future work must attempt to uncouple implicit/explicit performance dissociations due to this factor (i.e., search set-size differences) from those due to retrieval domain and strategy automaticity.

A Preliminary Experiment

We have recently initiated a research program in this area, and briefly report a preliminary experiment. The specific topic of the experiment was the influence on implicit and explicit memory test performance due to different search set sizes, whether a search set-size manipulation would have the same effects on both test types or whether this particular strategy property contributes (i.e., acts as a confound) in some way to the observed performance differences between implicit and explicit memory tests.

In the experiment, university students were shown a list of 24 common words, with two words drawn from each of 12 different categories such as fruits or transportation means. All words were atypical instances from their respective categories (e.g., avocado as a type of fruit, carriage as a means of transportation). At the time of study, half of these target words were presented with a semantic task that required rating them in terms of pleasantness, whereas the others were given with a nonsemantic encoding task (i.e., counting the number of completely enclosed spaces in each word) that directed subjects' attention to the surface characteristics of the written targets. Memory was assessed either with an explicit cued recall test or with an implicit category production test, and the same written cues—category labels—were used for both tests. For the explicit test, subjects were instructed to think back to the previous studied list and to recall instances belonging to each category, whereas for the implicit test, they were directed to generate instances belonging to each category and there was no mention of the previous study list. For the critical search set-size manipulation, the instruction directed subjects either to recall/produce *any instances* belonging to each category (large search set) or to recall/produce *only instances that are typical* members of each category (smaller search set). Consistent with previous findings with explicit memory tests, we anticipated that cued recall would be higher in the semantic than nonsemantic study task condition (Craik & Lockhart, 1972), and because the instruction to recall only typical instances defines a smaller search set than the instruction to recall any instances, we expected higher perform- ance in the former condition. More critical, on the assumption that search set size has the same influence on implicit as on explicit memory retrieval, we expected the same pattern of effects in priming. Finally, previous work has shown that on tasks like category production, priming tends to show an effect due to levels of processing manipulations (Roediger & McDer- mott, 1993), and we also expected to replicate this finding.

The findings, which are reproduced in Fig. 2.1 are preliminary because the experiment had relatively few subjects per memory test condition (N

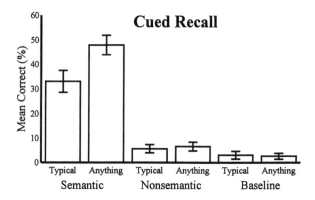

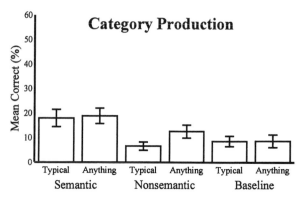

FIG. 2.1.   Mean (*sem* shown in brackets) percentage of targets produced on the explicit cued-recall test and on the category production test, as a function of level of processing at study and of test instruction manipulation.

= 38) and baseline performance was too low and likely confounded with serious floor effects. Despite these reservations, however, the findings were thought provoking. As expected, the levels of processing study-task manipulation had a much larger influence (in terms of effect size units) on cued recall (1.95) than on priming (0.55), thereby replicating findings reviewed by Roediger and McDermott (1993). More interesting, the means from each test point to an interaction between search set size and the levels manipulation. These findings are only preliminary and must be interpreted cautiously, especially in light of previously discussed concerns. Ongoing work is designed to replicate the critical interaction with different test types. In the meantime, we regard the findings in Fig. 2.1 to be like a promissory note, and we expect that by continuing our efforts, we will find evidence that the search set size variable contributes to dissociations between implicit and explicit memory test performance.

Implications

Memory test performance is a product of many variables, some of which "belong" to the remember and others to the task or situation, as illustrated by Fig. 2.2. In response to information from the instructions, the study test cues, and the context, the remember selects or creates and then follows a strategy that "orchestrates" processing. The nature of this strategy also depends on many remember variables or properties, such as knowledge of the task at hand, practice with routines or skills, and the

CONSTRAINTS ON PROCESSING

Remember	Test/Task
Cognitive Apparatus	**Cues**
Sensory Skills & Procedures	Types
Working Memory & Attentional Resources	Format Attributes
Problem Solving & Reasoning Skills & Strategies	Availability
Episodic Memories	
Knowledge	**Instructions**
Language Skills	Novelty or Familiarity
Motor Skills	Domain
	Set Size
Brain	
	Context
	Local, Global
	Response Type

FIG 2.2.   A map of different aspects of the remember and of the situation that can influence the cognitive activity that occurs (or is possible) in any study or test condition. Previous research has targeted only a few of the items that are listed, whereas others remain unexplored.

availability of attentional resources. Memory research has a long tradition of asking about intentions and strategies, primarily questions about the strategies engaged for learning (e.g., What kinds are there, In what situation are they used, Are some more attention demanding, Can they be stopped?) and how they influence recall and recognition test performance. The first section of this chapter outlined a few prominent examples from this literature. By contrast, recent research with implicit and explicit memory tests has focused more attention on retrieval strategies.

Our current knowledge of implicit and explicit retrieval strategies comes from research efforts that can be pigeonholed according to the various entries in Fig. 2.2. Cognitive psychology's efforts have focused primarily on topics or task properties appearing under *cues* (i.e., the specific materials made available for study or at test). For example, they have asked about how word frequency, the modality of presentation, or the type of test cue (e.g., complete words, word fragments) influence implicit and explicit memory test performance. Smaller scale efforts have been made to learn about the role of study and test contexts (e.g., happy vs. sad, verbal vs. pictorial), and about influences due to specific modes of responding (e.g., speed vs. accuracy). By contrast, developmentally oriented investigations and studies with various neuropsychological patients have tended to focus attention more on attributes of the remember (e.g., familiarity with different learning strategies, individual differences in processing resources).

Our objective in this chapter was to provide insight into those aspects of implicit and explicit memory retrieval that fit into Fig. 2.2 under the *instructions* heading. Instructions to subjects are critical and often the only variable manipulated to bring about implicit and explicit memory retrieval, and for this reason, we turned the spot light to properties of strategies that are selected or created in response to instructions. The results of our exercise suggest that novelty (subjects' familiarity with the instructions), search domain (the to-be-searched memory space), and search set size should be entered as features of instructions, and that future research must disentangle the effect of each of them on implicit and explicit memory tests.

ACKNOWLEDGMENTS

Preparation of this chapter was funded by a research grant to Peter Graf and a graduate studentship to Angela R. Birt, both from the Natural Sciences and Engineering Research Council of Canada. Correspondence concerning this chapter should be addressed to Peter Graf, Department of Psychology, University of British Columbia, 2136 West Mall, Vancouver, B.C., V6T 1Z4. Email: pgraf@cortex.psych.ubc.ca.

REFERENCES

Anderson, J. R. (1976). *Language, memory, and thought*. Hillsdale, NJ: Lawrence Erlbaum Associates.

Anderson, J. R. (1983). A spreading activation theory of memory. *Journal of Verbal Learning and Verbal Behavior, 22*, 261–295.

Atkinson, R. C., & Shiffrin, R. M. (1968). Human memory: A proposed system and its control processes. In K. W. Spence & J. T. Spence (Eds.), *The psychology of learning and motivation II* (pp. 89–195). New York: Academic Press.

Basden, B. H., Basden, D. R., & Gargano, G. J. (1991). Directed forgetting in implicit and explicit memory tests: A comparison of methods. *Journal of Experimental Psychology: Learning, Memory, and Cognition, 19*, 603–616.

Bjork, R. A. (1972). Theoretical implications of directed forgetting. In A. W. Melton & E. Martin (Eds.), *Coding processing in human memory* (pp. 217–235). Washington, DC: Winston.

Bolla, K. I., & Lindgren, K. N. (1990). Predictors of verbal fluency (FAS) in the healthy elderly. *Journal of Clinical Psychology, 46*, 623–628.

Bowers, J. S., & Schacter, D. L. (1990). Implicit memory and test awareness. *Journal of Experimental Psychology: Learning, Memory, and Cognition, 16*, 404–416.

Brown, A. (1987). Metacognition, executive control, self-regulation and other more mysterious mechanisms. In F. E. Weinert & R. H. Kluwe (Eds.), *Metacognition, motivation, and understanding* (pp. 65–116). Hillsdale, NJ: Lawrence Erlbaum Associates.

Buchner, A., Erdfelder, E., & Vaterrodt-Plünnecke, B. (1995). Toward unbiased measurement of conscious and unconscious memory processes within the process dissociation framework. *Journal of Experimental Psychology: General, 124*, 137–160.

Cermak, L. S., & Craik, F. I. M., (Eds.). (1979). *Levels of processing in human memory*. Hillsdale, NJ: Lawrence Erlbaum Associates.

Cleeremans, A., & McClelland, J. L. (1991). Learning the structure of event sequences. *Journal of Experimental Psychology: General, 120*, 235–253.

Craik, F. I. M. (1986). A functional account of age differences in memory. In F. Klix & H. Hagendorf (Eds.), *Human memory and cognitive capabilities: Mechanisms and performances* (pp. 409–422). New York: Elsevier.

Craik, F. I. M., & Jennings, J. M. (1992). Human memory. In Fergus I. M. Craik & Timothy A. Salthouse (Eds.), *Handbook of aging and cognition* (pp. 51–110). Hillsdale, NJ: Lawrence Erlbaum Associates.

Craik, F. I. M., & Lockhart, R. S. (1972). Levels of processing: A framework for memory research. *Journal of Verbal Learning and Verbal Behavior, 11*, 671–684.

Craik, F. I. M., & Tulving, E. (1975). Depth of processing and the retention of words in episodic memory. *Journal of Experimental Psychology: General, 104*, 268–294.

Craik, F. I. M., & Watkins, M. J. (1973). The role of rehearsal in short-term memory. *Journal of Verbal Learning and Verbal Behavior, 12*, 599–603.

Crowder, R. G. (1976). *Principles of learning and memory*. Hillsdale, NJ: Lawrence Erlbaum Associates.

Dunn, J. C., & Kirsner, K. (1988). Discovering functionally independent mental processes: The principle of reversed association. *Psychological Review, 95*, 91–101.

Engelkamp, J., & Wippich, W. (1995). Current issues in implicit and explicit memory. *Psychological Research, 57*, 143–144.

Epstein, W. (1972). Mechanisms of directed forgetting. In G. H. Bower (Ed.), *The psychology of learning and motivation* (Vol. 6, pp. 147–191). New York: Academic Press.

Eysenck, M. W. (1978). Levels of processing: A critique. *British Journal of Psychology, 68*, 157–169.

Eysenck, M. W., & Eysenck, M. C. (1982). Effects of incentive on cued recall. *Quarterly Journal of Experimental Psychology: Human Experimental Psychology, 34A*, 489–498.

Fisher, R. P., & Craik, F. I. M. (1977). Interaction between encoding and retrieval operations in cued recall. *Journal of Experimental Psychology: Human Learning and Memory, 3,* 701–711.

Flavell, J. H. (1979). Metacognition and cognitive monitoring: A new area of cognitive-developmental inquiry. *American Psychologist, 34,* 906–911.

Flavell, J. H. (1987). Speculations about the nature and development of metacognition. In F. E. Weinert & R. H. Kluwe (Eds.), *Metacognition, motivation, and understanding* (pp. 21–29). Hillsdale, NJ: Lawrence Erlbaum Associates.

Flavell, J. H., & Wellman, H. M. (1977). Metamemory. In R. V. Kail & J. W. Hagen (Eds.), *Perspectives on the development of memory and cognition* (pp. 3–33). Hillsdale, NJ: Lawrence Erlbaum Associates.

Graf, P. (1994). Explicit and implicit memory: A decade of research. In C. Umiltà & M. Moscovitch (Eds.), *Attention and performance XV: Conscious and nonconscious information processing* (pp. 681–696). Cambridge, MA: Bradford.

Graf, P. (1995). Defining the opposition procedure: A reply to Toth, Reingold, and Jacoby's (1995) response to Graf and Komatsu (1994). *European Journal of Cognitive Psychology, 7,* 225–231.

Graf, P., & Komatsu, S. (1994). Process dissociation procedure: Handle with caution. *European Journal of Cognitive Psychology, 6,* 113–129.

Graf, P., & Mandler, G. (1984). Activation makes words more accessible but not necessarily more retrievable. *Journal of Verbal Learning and Verbal Behavior, 23,* 553–568.

Graf, P., & Masson, M. E. J. (Eds.). (1993). *Implicit memory: New directions in cognition, development, and neuropsychology.* Hillsdale, NJ: Lawrence Erlbaum Associates.

Graf, P., & Schacter, D. L. (1985). Implicit and explicit memory for new associations in normal and amnesic subjects. *Journal of Experimental Psychology: Learning, Memory, and Cognition, 11,* 501–518.

Graf, P., & Schacter, D. L. (1987). Selective effects of interference on implicit and explicit memory for new associations. *Journal of Experimental Psychology: Learning, Memory, and Cognition, 13,* 45–53.

Graf, P., Squire, L. R., & Mandler, G. (1984). The information that amnesic patients do not forget. *Journal of Experimental Psychology: Learning, Memory, and Cognition, 10,* 164–178.

Greene, R. L. (1986). Word stems as cues in recall and completion tasks. *Quarterly Journal of Experimental Psychology: Human Experimental Psychology, 38,* 663–673.

Hagen, J. W., & Kingsley, P. R. (1968). Labeling effects in short-term memory. *Child Development, 39,* 113–121.

Hagen, J. W., & Stanovich, K. G. (1977). Memory: Strategies of acquisition. In R. V. Kail & J. W. Hagen (Eds.), *Perspectives on the development of memory and cognition* (pp. 89–111). Hillsdale, NJ: Lawrence Erlbaum Associates.

Howes, J. L., & Katz, A. N. (1992). Remote memory: Recalling autobiographical and public events from across the lifespan. *Canadian Journal of Psychology, 46,* 92–116.

Humphreys, M. S., Bain, J. D., & Pike, R. (1989). Different ways to cue a coherent memory system: A theory for episodic, semantic, and procedural tasks. *Psychological Review, 96,* 208–233.

Jacoby, L. L. (1991). A process dissociation framework: Separating automatic from intentional uses of memory. *Journal of Memory and Language, 30,* 513–541.

Jacoby, L. L., Lindsay, D. S., & Toth, J. P. (1992). Unconscious influences revealed: Attention, awareness, and control. *American Psychologist, 47,* 802–809.

James, W. (1962). *Psychology: Briefer course.* New York: Collier. (Original work published 1890)

Kail, R. (1979). *The development of memory in children.* San Francisco: Freeman.

Kausler, D. H. (1974). *Psychology of verbal learning and memory.* New York: Academic Press.

Keeney, F. J., Cannizzo, S. R., & Flavell, J. H. (1967). Spontaneous and induced verbal rehearsal in a recall task. *Child Development, 38,* 953–966.

Kluwe, R. H. (1987). Executive decisions and regulation of problem solving behavior. In F. E. Weinert & R. H. Kluwe (Eds.), *Metacognition, motivation, and understanding* (pp. 31–64). Hillsdale, NJ: Lawrence Erlbaum Associates.

Komatsu, S., Graf, P., & Uttl, B. (1995). Process dissociation procedure: Core assumptions fail, sometimes. *European Journal of Cognitive Psychology, 7,* 19–40.

Lewis, C. H., & Anderson, J. R. (1976). Interference with real world knowledge. *Cognitive Psychology, 7,* 311–355.

Lockhart, R. S., & Craik, F. I. M. (1990). Levels of processing: A retrospective commentary on a framework for memory research. *Canadian Journal of Psychology, 44,* 87–112.

Mandler, G. (1980). Recognizing: The judgment of previous occurrence. *Psychological Review, 87,* 252–271.

MacLeod, C. M. (1989). Directed forgetting affects both direct and indirect tests of memory. *Journal of Experimental Psychology: Learning, Memory, and Cognition, 15,* 13–21.

McAndrews, M. P., & Moscovitch, M. (1990). Transfer effects in implicit tests of memory. *Journal of Experimental Psychology: Learning, Memory, and Cognition, 16,* 772–788.

Metcalfe, J., & Shimamura, A. P., (Eds.). (1994). *Metacognition: Knowing about knowing.* Cambridge, MA: MIT Press.

Murdock, B. B., Jr. (1974). *Human memory: Theory and data.* Hillsdale, NJ: Lawrence Erlbaum Associates.

Neill, W. T., Beck, J. L., Bottalico, K. S., & Molloy, R. D. (1990). Effects of intentional versus incidental learning on explicit and implicit tests of memory. *Journal of Experimental Psychology: Learning, Memory, and Cognition, 16,* 457–463.

Nelson, D. L. (1981). Many are called but few are chosen: The influence of context on the effects of category size. In C. H. Bower (Ed.), *The psychology of learning and motivation* (Vol. 15, pp. 129–162). New York: Academic Press.

Nelson, D. L. (1989). Implicitly activated knowledge and memory. In C. Izawa (Ed.), *Current issues in cognitive psychology: The Tulane Flowerree Symposium on Cognition* (pp. 369–387). New York: Lawrence Erlbaum Associates.

Nelson, D. L., Bajo, M. T., & Casanueva, D. (1985). Prior knowledge and memory: The influence of natural category size as a function of intention and distraction. *Journal of Experimental Psychology: Learning, Memory, and Cognition, 11,* 94–105.

Nelson, D. L., Gee, N. R., & Schreiber, T. A. (1992). Sentence encoding and implicitly activated memories. *Memory and Cognition, 20,* 643–654.

Nelson, T. O., & Narens, L. (1990). Metamemory: A theoretical framework and new findings. In G. H. Bower (Ed.), *The psychology of learning and motivation* (Vol. 26, pp. 125–173). New York: Academic Press.

Nissen, M. J., & Bullemer, P. (1987). Attentional requirements of learning: Evidence from performance measures. *Cognitive Psychology, 19,* 1–32.

Paller, K. A. (1990). Recall and stem-completion priming have different electrophysiological correlates and are modified differentially by directed forgetting. *Journal of Experimental Psychology: Learning, Memory, and Cognition, 16,* 1021–1032.

Postman, L. (1975). Verbal learning and memory. *Annual Review of Psychology, 26,* 291–334.

Pressley, M., & Levin, J. R. (1983a). *Cognitive strategy research: Educational applications.* New York: Springer.

Pressley, M., & Levin, J. R. (1983b). *Cognitive strategy research: Psychological foundations.* New York: Springer.

Pressley, M., Forrest-Pressley, D. J., Elliot-Faust, D. J., & Miller, G. E. (1985). Children's use of cognitive strategies, how to teach strategies, and what to do if they can't be taught. In M. Pressley & C. J. Brainerd (Eds.), *Cognitive learning and memory in children* (pp. 1–47). New York: Springer.

Raaijmaker, J. G. W., & Shiffrin, A. M. (1981). Search of associative memory. *Psychological Review, 88,* 93–134.

Reber, A. S. (1967). Implicit learning of artificial grammars. *Journal of Verbal Learning and Verbal Behavior, 65,* 855–863.

Reber, A. S. (1989). Implicit learning and tacit knowledge. *Journal of Experimental Psychology: General, 118,* 219–235.

Reder, L. M., & Ross, B. H. (1983). Integrated knowledge in different tasks: Positive and negative fan effects. *Journal of Experimental Psychology: Learning, Memory, and Cognition, 9,* 55–72.

Richardson-Klavehn, A., Gardiner, J. M., & Java, R. I. (1996). Memory: Task dissociations, process dissociations, and dissociations of consciousness. In G. Underwood (Ed.), *Implicit cognition* (pp. 85–158). Oxford, UK: Oxford University Press.

Roediger, H. L., & McDermott, K. B. (1993). Implicit memory in normal human subjects. In F. Boller & J. Grafman (Eds.), *Handbook of neuropsychology* (Vol. 8, pp. 63–131). New York: Elsevier.

Rundus, D. (1971). Analysis of rehearsal processes in free recall. *Journal of Experimental Psychology, 89,* 63–77.

Schacter, D. L., Bowers, J. S., & Booker, J. (1989). Intention, awareness, and implicit memory: The retrieval intentionality criterion. In S. Lewandowsky, J. C. Dunn, & K. Kirsner (Eds.), *Implicit memory: Theoretical issues* (pp. 47–65). Hillsdale, NJ: Lawrence Erlbaum Associates.

Schacter, D. L., Chiu, C. Y., & Ochsner, K. N. (1993). Implicit memory: A selective review. *Annual Review of Neuroscience, 16,* 159–182.

Schacter, D. L., & Graf, P. (1986). Effects of elaborative processing on implicit and explicit memory for new associations. *Journal of Experimental Psychology: Learning, Memory, and Cognition, 12,* 432–444.

Seger, C. A. (1994). Implicit learning. *Psychological Bulletin, 115,* 163–196.

Seidenberg, M. S., & McClelland, J. L. (1989). A distributed, developmental model of word recognition and naming. *Psychological Review, 96,* 523–568.

Shanks, D. R., & St. John, M. F. (1994). Characteristics of dissociable human learning systems. *Behavioral & Brain Sciences, 17,* 367–447.

Shiffrin, R. M. (1970). Memory search. In D. A. Norman (Ed.), *Models of human memory* (pp. 375–447). New York: Academic Press.

Shimamura, A. P., & Squire, L. R. (1989). Impaired priming of new associations in amnesia. *Journal of Experimental Psychology: Learning, Memory, and Cognition, 15,* 721–728.

Simon, H. A. (1967). Motivational and emotional controls of cognition. *Psychological Review, 74,* 29–39.

Squire, L. R., & Butters, N. (1992). *Neuropsychology of memory* (2nd ed.). New York: Guilford.

Stadler, M. A. (1989). On learning complex procedural knowledge. *Journal of Experimental Psychology: Learning, Memory, and Cognition, 15,* 1061–1069.

Stadler, M. A. (1992). Statistical structure and implicit serial learning. *Journal of Experimental Psychology: Learning, Memory, and Cognition, 18,* 318–327.

Swanson, H. L. (1983). Relations among metamemory, rehearsal activity and word recall of learning disabled and non-disabled readers. *British Journal of Educational Psychology, 53,* 186–194.

Tulving, E., Schacter, D. L., & Stark, H. A. (1982). Priming effects in word-fragment completion are independent of recognition memory. *Journal of Experimental Psychology: Learning, Memory, and Cognition, 8,* 336–342.

Watkins, O. C., & Watkins, M. J. (1975). Buildup of proactive inhibition as a cue overload effect. *Journal of Experimental Psychology: Human Leaning and Memory, 1,* 442–452.

Waugh, N. C., & Norman, D. A. (1965). Primary memory. *Psychological Review, 72,* 89–104.

Woodward, A. E., Bjork, R. A., & Jongeward, R. H. (1973). Recall and recognition as a function of primary rehearsal. *Journal of Verbal Learning and Verbal Behavior, 13,* 608–617.

Chapter 3

Metacognition Does Not Imply Awareness: Strategy Choice Is Governed by Implicit Learning and Memory

Lynne M. Reder
Christian D. Schunn
Carnegie Mellon University

Metacognition means different things to different people and is generally acknowledged to include a wide range of phenomena. Nonetheless, there are two core meanings of the term metacognition to which most researchers using that label often refer: monitoring and control of cognitive processes. Monitoring of cognitive processes can include awareness of the component steps in cognitive processes as well as awareness of various features of these steps including their duration and their successfulness. For example, one might be aware of the steps one goes through in serving a tennis ball, as well as the successfulness of the serve.

Monitoring typically refers to awareness of the features of the current behavior. In contrast, control of cognitive processes refers to the processes that modify behavior, such as the selection of a strategy for performing a task. For example, deciding whether to search for a phone number in memory or search for it in a phone book, as well as deciding how long to search memory before giving up, are instances of control processes. In this chapter we focus on the relationship between monitoring and control of cognition in a special way: We argue that some aspects of metacognition typically called monitoring, and therefore implying awareness, actually operate without much awareness. Moreover, the control processes that operate to affect strategy choice are frequently influenced by implicit processes.

The relationship between the two forms of metacognition is particularly interesting. One possibility is that control of cognitive processes occurs through explicit monitoring of cognitive processes. Although this assumption is not frequently stated explicitly, it is clearly a very commonly held assumption—the very justification for studying metacognitive monitoring is that it is believed to be necessary for control. Further, this view has been clearly articulated by several of the main researchers of metacognitive behavior. For example, Nelson and Narens (1994) described people as "systems containing self-reflective mechanisms for evaluating (and reevaluating) their progress and for changing their ongoing processing" (p. 7). Similarly, Metcalfe (1994) noted that, "Most researchers agree that the human episodic memory system requires, for its optimal functioning, a subsidiary monitoring and control system" (p. 137). These assumptions can also be found in more developmentally oriented work on metacognition. For example, Davidson, Deuser, and Sternberg (1994) stated that, "Metacognition, or knowledge of one's own cognitive processes, guides the problem-solving process and improves the efficiency of this goal-oriented behavior" (p. 207).

In contrast to this commonly shared assumption about the relationship between monitoring and control, we believe that the opposite is true. That is, we believe that the control of cognitive processing is not achieved through explicit monitoring. Instead, we believe that the control of cognitive processing is primarily achieved through *implicit learning* and *implicit memory*.

We define *implicit learning* to be changes in behavior based on past experience for which the individual has no reportable awareness of such learning (cf. A. S. Reber, 1989; this is not to say that there was no memory or awareness of the events during which learning occurred). For example, in a probability learning experiment by A. S. Reber and Millward (1971), subjects learned to anticipate the changing probabilities of events in the experiment without any explicit awareness of these changing probabilities. In their experiment, subjects were given a training phase in which they observed 1,000 events at the rate of 2 per second. During this training phase, the probability that a certain event would occur changed gradually in a cyclical fashion every 50 trials. Subjects learned to anticipate these shifts: In the test phase they were quite successful at predicting the changing probability of these events over time. However, subjects were unaware of this shifting probability. Similar results of learning without the ability to report what was learned or any awareness that there was learning have been obtained by Berry and Broadbent (1984), and Lewicki, Hill, and Bizot (1988). In our view, this phenomenon of implicit learning extends to control of cognitive processing such as strategy selection. That is, we believe that strategy choice is influenced by past experience and that the individual is frequently unaware of these influences.[1]

---

[1]Our intention is not to develop a philosophical argument concerning the nature of consciousness. Nonetheless, our definition of nonconscious or implicit learning/memory does involve lack of reportability. We do not wish to imply, however, that an organism that is somehow incapable of ever reporting an event is incapable of having conscious awareness. Rather, we mean to imply that for someone generally capable of reporting events, the inability to report an event is evidence that it was not explicitly learned.

Like implicit learning, we define *implicit memory* to be changes in behavior that are based on past experience for which the individual has no awareness of such influence. The distinctions between implicit learning and memory are that (a) the experiences influencing memory tend to be discrete or even unitary (as opposed to continuous) events and there tend not to be interdependencies or contingencies among these events, and (b) the behavior that is affected in implicit memory is also something typically ascribed to declarative memory rather than procedural memory (Anderson, 1976; Cohen & Squire, 1980). For example, in an experiment by Warrington and Weiskrantz (1970), amnesics and controls were given two tests of explicit memory (free recall and recognition) and two tests of implicit memory (word fragment identification and word stem completion). As expected, they found that the amnesics performed much worse on the explicit memory tests. However, the amnesics performed at equal levels with the controls on the implicit memory tests, indicating that there could be intact memory without awareness. Subsequent experiments with normals have found other demonstrations of dissociations between implicit and explicit memory. For example, Jacoby (1983) found when subjects *generate* a to-be-remembered item (say "cold" when asked for the opposite of *hot*), their retention on explicit tests is better than when they merely study the word (read the word COLD); however, implicit tests did not show that advantage. Testing the issue of awareness more directly in normals, Bowers and Schacter (1990) divided normal subjects by their self- reports of whether they noticed any relationship between the words they produced on the target perceptual identification task and the words studied earlier. They found that there were equal levels of priming across the two groups of subjects (although there were other differences in types of responses made) indicating that the priming effect could occur without awareness.

It is important to distinguish between the strategy-selection processes and the strategies themselves. Although we argue that people are unaware of what causes them to select one strategy rather than another, we make no claims about their awareness of the results of the strategy selections. People are often aware of the strategy that they execute. For example, people might not be aware of what led them to decide to use a calculator, but usually they are aware that they decided to use the calculator. On the other hand, when the processes or strategies are executed rapidly, it is quite possible that people are even unaware of the strategy that was selected.

Contrary to commonly held assumptions concerning metacognition, we will show that important aspects of metacognition are implicit. In particular, this chapter focuses on the implicit nature of strategy selection. Previous research has shown (e.g., Lovett & Anderson, in press; Miner & Reder, 1994; Reder, 1987, 1988) that two types of variables influence strategy selection: features contained in the question or problem, and variables outside the problem or question. These influences are sometimes referred to as *intrinsic* and *extrinsic* variables. An example of an intrinsic variable is the familiarity with terms in a problem. Task instructions and what strategy has been working recently are examples of extrinsic variables.

This chapter is organized around the distinction between intrinsic and extrinsic variables, summarizing empirical evidence for the implicit nature of each kind of variable. In the case of intrinsic variables, we describe a computational model that implements these variables using implicit processes. We also consider the evidence that suggests that people may be completely unaware of the entire strategy selection process. Finally, we discuss why strategy selection is driven by implicit processes. This issue is especially important given the general intuition that control of cognitive processes should be the result of the monitoring of cognitive processes.

INTRINSIC METACOGNITIVE VARIABLES AFFECTING STRATEGY CHOICE

It is generally accepted that superficial features of a problem influence the strategy that is chosen to solve the problem. The work of Hinsley, Hayes, and Simon (1977) described in an earlier Carnegie Symposium showed that people will be influenced to select a particular strategy to solve an algebra word problem when features of the problem prime the particular strategy or problem solving schema even though in fact it is an incorrect schema. More recently, Ross (1984, 1989; Blessing & Ross, 1996) has shown in many experiments that "remindings" will influence the method selected to solve statistics problems and various other tasks. Similarly, Lovett and Anderson (in press) have shown that strategy selection is influenced by features in the problem.

On the other hand, the claim that people select a question-answering strategy prior to executing any strategy, specifically prior to searching for the answer (Reder, 1982) has not been generally accepted (e.g., LeFevre, Greenham, & Waheed, 1993; Siegler, 1989; Siegler & Jenkins, 1989; Siegler & Shrager, 1984). Even more controversial has been the claim that one of the criteria used in the decision of whether to search for the answer is a rapid "feeling-of-knowing" and that this rapid feeling-of-knowing depends *only* on features of the question and not at all on partial retrievals of the answer (Reder, 1987, 1988; Reder & Ritter, 1992).

The early evidence for this position came from experiments using a "gameshow" paradigm where subjects were told to imagine that they were competing against another contestant and that in order to have an opportunity to answer questions, they had to respond as rapidly as possible with an immediate impression of whether or not they knew the answer to the question. Subjects were able to make this assessment of their knowledge very quickly and accurately. Importantly, subjects' impressions of whether or not they knew the answer could be subverted by making pairs of terms from the question spuriously familiar—some question terms had been part of an earlier rating task that was nominally unrelated to the gameshow task. Although exposure to the terms increased the tendency to think that the answer was known, it did not influence the ability to produce the correct answer.

In a subsequent series of arithmetic gameshow experiments, we explored this phenomenon more carefully, controlling for prior knowledge, and tracked how learning and feeling-of-knowing changed as a function of exposure to problems (Reder & Ritter, 1992). Arithmetic problems that people were unlikely to know before the experiment (e.g., 37 * 23) were used as stimuli. Subjects were exposed to problems over and over (up to 28 times in one experiment; in others, up to 20 times) and each time made a very rapid assessment of whether they knew the answer. The subjects indicated their assessment by pressing one key if they thought they could retrieve the answer, and a different key if they thought they had to calculate the answer. This quick assessment took place in about a half second and was too little time to actually retrieve the answer. Subjects were allowed to study the answer to the problem after each trial and were given incentives to learn the answers and to select retrieve. However, there were disincentives for selecting retrieve if the answer was not known. *Know* was operationally defined as giving the correct answer within one second *after* selecting retrieve.

Evidence that these first impressions were based on aspects of the question, and not a partial retrieval of the answer, came from several results of the experiments. First, time to give the rapid first impression (where subjects choose retrieve or calculate) was affected by practice with the task, but not by practice with a specific problem. In other words, the practice with a specific problem that led to faster answers did not lead to faster preliminary judgments. The second result came from operator switch problems—some of the problems were distorted such that the operator was switched so that the two operands had appeared together before but not with that operator. For example, if 21 + 35 was presented earlier, then 21 * 35 could appear as a special operator switch trial. For such a problem, the subject could not know the answer because it had not been previously presented, and its answer was unrelated to the answer of the original problem. However, such a problem would still look familiar as a first impression. In fact, it was operand co-occurrence that predicted retrieve judgments, not how often the exact problem had been seen. In other words, subjects were as likely to think they knew the answer to a problem that they had never seen before as one that they had seen 20 times, provided that only the operator had been switched. By contrast, problems where the order of operands was inverted (e.g., 28 + 13 → 13 + 28), to which subjects consequently still knew the answer, were much less likely to be selected for retrieve than novel, operator-switch problems, for which they did not know the answer (Reder & Ritter, 1992).

A third result that supports the view that a rapid feeling-of-knowing is a function of exposure to the problem and not of knowledge of the answer comes from Experiment 1 of Schunn, Reder, Nhouyvanisvong, Richards, and Stroffolino (in press). In this experiment sometimes subjects were exposed to problems without getting a chance to actually answer the problem (either by calculation or retrieval) and without having the opportunity to study the answer. This manipulation was done for only a subset of the problems, called *infrequently-answered problems*. As one would expect, speed and accuracy in producing the answers were affected by how often subjects studied and answered the questions; on the other hand, tendency to select retrieve was not affected by those variables, but was affected by exposure to the problem itself. In other words, when we controlled for exposure time to the problem and decoupled exposure to the problem with exposure to the answer, the former predicted feeling-of-knowing and the latter predicted actual knowing. Figure 3.1 displays the percentage use of the retrieval strategy as a function of the total exposure to the problem.[2]

An Activation-Based Model for Rapid Feeling-of-Knowing

There have been a number of other results, both ours and others' (e.g., Metcalfe, Schwartz, & Joaquim, 1993; Schwartz & Metcalfe, 1992), that support the claim that feeling-of-knowing is influenced exclusively by terms in the question. Our claim, however, focuses on feeling-of-knowing as it affects strategy selection, and is restricted to the rapid feeling-of-knowing that precedes execution of the retrieval strategy. Given that feeling-of-knowing, like strategy selection, tends to be thought of as the essence of a metacognitive strategy, it is important to defend our claim that this rapid feeling-of-knowing is actually an *implicit process* rather than an *explicit process*.

There are several arguments that can be made for this claim. One of these is that the process model that we use to account for this phenomenon has an implicit quality to it. The decision-making process involves rapid and automatic flow of activation rather than slow and controlled decision making about discrete features in the environment. This type of model is arguably just the type of model that can also account for other memory phenomena that are typically described as aspects of implicit memory (e.g., false fame judgments, subliminal priming causing spurious word recognition [Reder &

---

[2]The last three points for the infrequently-answered problems are unstable because they have a mean of 19 observations per point, whereas the preceding points have a mean of 150 observations per point.

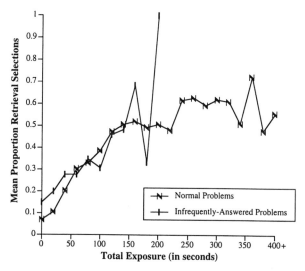

FIG. 3.1. The mean percentage of retrieval strategy selections as a function of total exposure to the problem (in seconds) for Experiment 1 of Schunn et al. (in press). Adapted from Schunn et al. (in press). Adapted with permission.

Gordon, in press]). Below, we describe an activation-based model that can account for these results.

The SAC Model

Reder's model which stands for *Source of Activation Confusion* was developed to account for misattributions and cognitive illusions (Reder & Gordon, 1996; see also Kamas & Reder, 1994). The model bears a family resemblance to Anderson's (1983, 1993) ACT model, although SAC is concerned primarily with declarative memory, and makes slightly different representational and processing assumptions. The representation used by SAC can be thought of as a rather generic semantic network model of declarative memory. The representation consists of interassociated nodes representing concepts and varying in long term strength. For the simulations described here, there are nodes that represent numbers (e.g., 5, 17, 31), nodes that represent operators (e.g., +, /, *), and nodes that represent whole problems (e.g., 17 + 31). The nodes representing whole problems connect the operands and operators to the answers. Nodes that represent numbers may serve as operand nodes for some problems and answer nodes for other problems (e.g., 31 is an operand in the problem 23 * 31, and is also the answer to 14 + 17). Examples of this representation scheme can be seen in Fig. 3.2.

The strength of a node represents the history of exposure to that concept, with more exposure producing greater strengthening. Nodes that

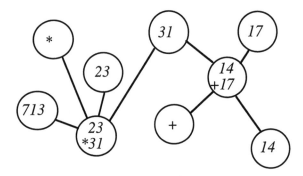

FIG. 3.2. Example nodes in the SAC network.

represent arithmetic problems such as *27 * 34* would start out weak at the
beginning of the experiment, as these problems were initially unfamiliar
to the subjects. By contrast, nodes for familiar problems such as *12 * 12*
would be strong even at the beginning of the experiment. However, we
did not use problems that were likely to have pre-experimental familiarity,
and the simulations presented here assume that all problem nodes are
created for the first time during the experiment.

Strength can also be thought of as the baseline or resting activation
level of a node. Increases and decreases in this baseline strength change
according to a power function:

$$B = c \, \Sigma \, t_i^{-d} \tag{1}$$

where B is the base-level activation, c and d are constants, and t_i is the
time since the ith presentation. This function captures both power law
decay of memories with time, and power law learning of memories with
practice.[3] The central feature of power law decay is that memories decay
quickly initially and then much more slowly at increasing delays. Similarly,
the central feature of power law learning is that first exposures to an item
contribute more than do subsequent exposures. That is, the incremental
contributions of each new exposure decreases with increasing numbers of
exposures.

The base or resting activation level of a node should be distinguished
from the *current activation* values of a node. The current level of a node
will be higher than its baseline whenever it receives stimulation from the
environment; that is, when the concept is mentioned or perceived, or
when the concept receives activation from other nodes. Whereas baseline

---

[3]See Anderson and Schooler (1991) for a discussion of the evidence for this function in
learning and retention phenomena.

strength decays according to a power function (i.e., first quickly and then slowly), *current* activation decays rapidly and exponentially toward the base level. Let A represent the current level of activation and B represent the base level of activation. Then, the decrease in *current* activation will be:

$$\Delta A = -\rho \, (A - B) \tag{2}$$

such that, after each trial, the current activation will decrease for every node by the proportion ρ times that node's current distance from its base-level activation. In all of our simulations, we used a value of 0.8 for ρ. To present a concrete example, suppose after a trial, a node's base-level activation was 20 and its current activation was 60. Then after just one trial, the current activation would drop to 28; that is, $60 - .8 * (60 - 20)$. After three trials, the current activation would have dropped to 20.3, not significantly different than the resting activation of 20. Thus, current activation drops quite rapidly, and only has noticeable effects on the trial on which it became activated, and perhaps the trial immediately thereafter.

Activation spreads between nodes via links. Links connect nodes that are associated through conceptual relations. For example, links connect nodes that represent the components of a problem to the node that represents the entire problem. Links also connect the nodes that represent the entire problem with nodes that represent the answer. These links will vary in strength depending on how often the two concepts have been thought of at the same time. Strength of links also depends on the delay between exposures. Specifically, we assume a power function given by:

$$S_{s,r} = \Sigma \, t_i^{\, -d_L} \tag{3}$$

where $S_{s,r}$ is the strength of the link from the node s to node r, t_i is the time since the ith coexposure, and d_L is the decay constant for links.

We said earlier that the current activation level of a node can rise from environmental stimulation or from associated nodes that send activation to it. How much activation is sent depends on the activation level of the source (sending) node and on the strength of the link from the source node to the receiving node, relative to all competing links out of the same source node. The change in activation of some node r is computed by summing the spread of activation from all source nodes s connected to node r according to the equation:

$$\Delta A_r = \Sigma(A_s * S_{s,r} / \Sigma S_{s,i}) \tag{4}$$

where ΔA_r is the change in activation of the receiving node r, A_s is the activation of each source node s, $S_{s,r}$ is strength of the link between nodes s and r, and $\Sigma S_{s,i}$ is sum of the strengths of all links emanating from node s. The effect of the ratio $S_{s,r}/\Sigma S_{s,i}$ is to limit the total spread from a node s to all connected nodes to be equal to the node s's current activation A_s.[4] For example, if a node had three connections emanating from it with link strengths of 1, 2, and 3, then the activation spread along those links would be, respectively, 1/6, 1/3 (i.e., 2/6), and 1/2 (i.e., 3/6) of the node's current activation level.

With these few assumptions, we can provide an account of the rapid feeling-of-knowing responses if we also assume that feeling-of-knowing monitors intersection of activation from two source nodes. Specifically, when two terms in a question send out activation to associated concepts and an intersection of activation is detected by bringing an intermediate node over threshold, a person will have a feeling-of-knowing response (cf. Dosher & Rosedale, 1989, 1990; Glucksberg & McCloskey, 1981; Ratcliff & McKoon, 1988; Reder, 1979, 1987, 1988, for related treatments of intersection of activation).

For present purposes, we assume that the nodes corresponding to the operands and the operator in the problem are activated when the problem is presented (e.g., 17, 31, and +). Activation spreads from these nodes to the node that represents the entire problem (e.g., 17 + 31). The extent of activation that accumulates at the problem node affects the likelihood of selecting retrieve as the strategy of choice.

Implementational Details: Generating Predictions From the Model

This model can be used to predict feeling-of-knowing decisions (i.e., deciding between retrieval and computation). It can also predict which answers are retrieved from memory, and the speed with which the answers are retrieved. In this chapter, we focus on the feeling-of-knowing, or retrieve/compute, decisions.

In this spreading activation model, feeling-of-knowing judgments are based on the activation level of a problem node in memory after a problem has been presented. When a problem is presented, all the nodes representing the components are activated. For example, in the problem 23 * 37, the nodes representing 23, *, and 37 are all activated. Activation then spreads to the node representing 23 * 37, in addition to other problem nodes connected to the nodes representing 23, *, and 37. Feeling-of-knowing judgments are based on the activation of the most activate problem node.

---

[4]This feature gives the model the ability to simulate fan effects (Anderson, 1974, 1976, 1983; Reder & Anderson, 1980; Reder & Ross, 1983), an important feature of declarative memory.

The computer simulation is given as input the same problems presented to the subjects. Because each subject received a different set of problems in a random order, a separate simulation was conducted for each subject. This was important because on a given trial the expected activation level for a problem would vary depending on the exact sequence of trials: For any subject on a given trial, the number of links, the current activation, and strengths would be different from any other subject's values. The simulation output is a probability of selecting to retrieve on each trial. We now step through the process by which that probability is determined.

At the start of the experiment, the representation of memory for the simulation is identical regardless of the experimental stimuli to be seen. Nodes for the operands and operators are assumed to already exist, whereas nodes for the problem components are assumed not to exist (i.e., the problems are novel). For simplicity, the initial base level strengths of the operand nodes (numbers used in the problems) and operator nodes are set to a constant amount. When problems are seen for the first time, a problem node is created, as are the links from the component operand and operator nodes to the novel problem node. The initial base level strengths of the problem nodes and of the links is simply determined by the equations determining power-law growth and decay—the selection of initial strength values requires no extra constants.

We assume that on each trial, all the nodes representing the problem components are activated to some constant amount. We assume that a basic perceptual process activates these nodes, and that all the problem components (e.g., the operators and the operands) used in these experiments were familiar entities. For example, when the problem 23 * 37 is presented, the three nodes representing 23, *, and 37 are activated. Activation then spreads along the links emanating from nodes representing each of the problem components to other associated nodes. Activation only spreads to directly connected nodes at this point, and is not yet carried forward beyond the first layer of receiving nodes.

Once the activation has spread across these links, activation of the problem nodes can be used to make a strategy selection between retrieve and calculate (a feeling-of-knowing judgment). The activation value of the most active problem node is used. Again, these values are affected by aspects of the simulation such as those represented in Equation 4. Rather than making a binary choice, the simulation predicts a probability of choosing retrieve based on this activation value. This means that if the activation value of the most active node is low, the probability of selecting retrieve is very low; conversely, when the activation value of a node is very high, the probability of selecting retrieval is high, but not necessarily unity. This probability of choosing retrieve is calculated by assuming a normal distribution of activation values with a fixed variance and activation threshold for selecting retrieve. This probability is reflected in the formula:

$$P = N[(A - T)/Sd] \qquad (5)$$

where A is the activation of the highest problem node, T is the subject's threshold, Sd is the standard deviation, and N[x] is the area under the normal curve to the left of x for a normal curve with mean = 0, and standard deviation = 1.

After each trial, all the strengths and activations are updated. It is at this point that if a new problem has been presented for the first time, that a new node representing that problem is created, and links are created connecting the component nodes to the problem node.

The simulation just described involves seven parameters, enumerated in Table 3.1. The table lists the values that were used and reviews the equations mentioned earlier. With the exception of the threshold parameter, which varied by subject, all of these parameter values were held constant across subjects and across experiments that we tested (4 data sets in all). The threshold parameter was allowed to vary across subjects because it was obvious from the data that subjects differed greatly in how often they decided to select retrieve. Although the subjects might have differed on other dimensions as well, there were no other obvious differences (with the exception of the one mentioned later), and so, for parsimony's sake, the other six parameters were held constant across subjects.

We fit the experiment using these seven parameters and also using an eighth parameter. This eighth parameter was simply a binary value by subject reflecting whether the subject had a predilection not to choose retrieve for a particular operator. We decided to include this parameter

TABLE 3.1
SAC Model Parameter Descriptions and Values, and the Model Equations

Parameter Name	Function	Value
input-activation	Input current activation for component nodes	50
r	Exponential decay constant for current activation	0.8
c	Power-law growth constant for base level activation	5
d	Power-law decay constant for base level activation	0.175
d_L	Power-law decay constant for link strength	0.12
T	Retrieve/compute decision threshold	30–200
Sd	Retrieve/compute decision standard deviation	45
never-retrieve	Does subject decide to never retrieve for one of the operators?	T/F

Equations

(1) $B = c \, \Sigma \, t_i^{-d}$
(2) $\Delta A = -\rho \, (A - B)$
(3) $S_{s,r} = \Sigma \, t_i^{-d_L}$
(4) $\Delta A_r = \Sigma (A_s * S_{s,r}/\Sigma S_{s,i})$
(5) $P = N[(A - T)/Sd]$

because we found that some subjects had a strong aversion to choosing retrieve for a particular operator. For example, a few subjects never chose retrieve for problems involving the operator *sharp* (a novel operator that involved a combination of addition and multiplication). Perhaps they did not want to memorize problems that involved a fake operator. A few other subjects were found to never retrieve for multiply although they chose retrieve for *sharp* problems. These subjects may have been bothered by the modular arithmetic that was used in Reder and Ritter (1992) and in Schunn, Reder, et al. (in press) and did not want to memorize the wrong answers to multiply problems. Whatever subjects' reasons for choosing to never retrieve for an operator, we found that the eighth parameter was useful for simulating these subjects—those that seemed to use a metarule for making their decisions, in which they refused to retrieve for one of the operators.

To model these subjects, we had the simulation put the probability of choosing retrieve at zero for the operator in question. The criterion for a subject to be put in this class of having a metarule was choosing retrieve less than 5% of the time for a given operator. It should be noted that this rule was invoked only 8 times out of 58 subjects modeled. We felt it was better to use this metarule than to assign separate thresholds for problems of each operator type. Not only would this give us too many degrees of freedom, it was hardly necessary: Except for these few subjects using this metarule, the correlation between the rate of selecting retrieval for problems involving of each operator type was quite high across subjects. Finally, it is important to note that although we believe that some subjects actually employed this metarule, this feature of the simulation is not necessary to fit the data. Therefore, the fits to data without the use of this feature are also presented.

To compare the model's predictions to subjects' actual retrieve/compute decisions, we used an aggregation procedure developed by Anderson (1990). For each trial, for each subject, the model produced a probability of choosing retrieve based on the calculated activation values resulting from the trial history for that subject. That is, the probability reflected the model's experience with the exact same problems given to the subject. This probability was also based on the particular subject's threshold. Because subjects made binary decisions on each trial and the simulation produced probabilities, it was necessary to aggregate trials. That is, all trials for a given subject in which the simulation predicted that the probability of selecting retrieve would fall between 0 and 10% were grouped together; all trials where the probability fell between 10 and 20% were grouped together and so on. Next, we tabulated the actual proportion of retrieval strategy selections that were made by that subject for the exact same trials in each probability range. This was done for all probability ranges. The ranges were made sufficiently

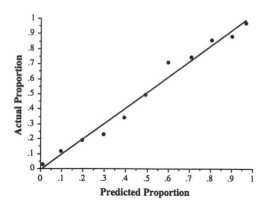

FIG. 3.3. Predicted vs. actual proportion of retrieval strategy selections in
Reder and Ritter, grouped by predicted proportion for all problems.

large such that at least 5 data points would be collected in each range—
thereby ensuring stable proportions. The fit of the model was tested by
plotting mean actual proportion of retrieval strategy selections against mean
expected percent retrievals. A perfect fit would be a straight line with a slope
of 1 and a y-intercept of 0 (i.e., predicted = actual).

The model fit the data quite well, producing a Pearson's r of .990 (see Fig.
3.3).[5] The slope of the best fitting line was not significantly different from 1
(slope = 1.03, $t(9) = 0.61$, $p > .5$), nor was the intercept significantly different
from 0 (intercept = -0.004, $t(9) = 0.15$, $p > .8$). Without the never-retrieve
rule, the model's overall fit was just as good (Pearson's r of .990).

A key result of Reder and Ritter (1992) was that subjects were as likely
to select retrieve for operator-switch problems as for training problems.
The model predicts this effect because operators are associated with a
large number of problems (i.e., they have a very large fan) and the amount
of activation spread from a node along any one link is inversely related to
the number of links emanating from that node (see Anderson, 1983, for
a more complete discussion of the fan effect). Thus, the model predicts
that there will be little impact of switching operators on retrieve/compute
decisions because the activations of the problem nodes are not significantly
affected. Verifying this prediction, the fit of the model to the operator-
switch retrieve data is quite good ($r = .981$). Figure 3.4 presents this fit.[6]
Again, the slope of the best fitting line was not significantly different from
1 (slope = 1.15, $t(4) = 1.35$, $p > .25$), nor was the intercept significantly
different from 0 (intercept = 0.014, $t(4) = 0.2$, $p > .8$).

---

[5]Plots of individual subject values can be found in Schunn et al. (in press).

[6]Fewer groupings were used in this analysis because there were relatively few operator-
switch problems.

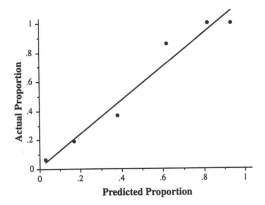

FIG. 3.4. Predicted vs. actual proportion of retrieval strategy selections in Reder and Ritter, grouped by predicted proportion, for the operator-switch problems only.

Fitting the Model to Other Data Sets

The extraordinarily good fits of the model to the data might be partially caused by searching the parameter space to find the best values of the parameters to fit the data. For this reason it seemed important to use the same parameter estimates on several other data sets and see whether comparable fits could be obtained without searching the parameter space. We therefore fit three other data sets using the same values.

Earlier in the chapter, we referred to an experiment (Experiment 1 of Schunn et al.) that showed that rapid first impressions (i.e., rapid decisions to retrieve) were based on familiarity with the problem rather than strength of association to the answer. To review, in Experiment 1 we did not switch the operator to show this effect; rather, for some problems exposure to the problem was decoupled from learning the answer by frequently denying the subject an opportunity to solve the problem or study the answer with the problem. That experiment confirmed that the conclusions of Reder and Ritter (1992) were not based on a less than perfect encoding of the problem. That is, a possible alternative interpretation of Reder and Ritter was that subjects failed to encode the operator and just assumed that it was the operator usually seen with the operands. Because there were no operator switch problems, that possibility was ruled out. Subjects still based their decision on whether or not to retrieve on the amount of exposure to the problem, not the answer.

As noted earlier, the same parameter values were used across all the fits of the individual subjects in the Reder and Ritter (1992) experiment, with the exception of the individual subject thresholds. These same parameter values were used to fit the subject strategy choices in Experiment

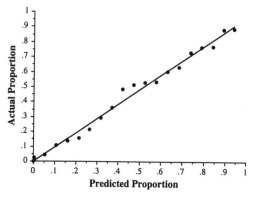

FIG. 3.5. Predicted vs. actual proportion of retrieval strategy selections in Experiment 1, grouped by predicted proportion, for all problems.

1 of Schunn et al. (in press) where the only parameter values to change were again the subject thresholds. The fit of the simulation's predictions to the subject performance is shown in Fig. 3.5. The fit to each individual subject's data is comparable and may be seen in Schunn et al. We accounted for as much experimental variance as in the first experiment that we attempted to fit. The correlation between predicted use of retrieve and actual use was $r = .994$. Without the never retrieve rule, the correlation was also excellent, $r = .971$.

In another experiment (Experiment 2 of Schunn et al.), we performed a replication of the Reder and Ritter experiments (with the operator swap) except that we had subjects come back 24 hours later. On the first day, there were no operator swaps; the second day was the same experiment as the first day, but with all new problems (novel combinations of operands used on Day 1) and some operator swap problems. The operator swap problems used operand pairs from the second day and from the first day. In other words, there were operator swap problems for both Day 1 and Day 2 problems, but all operator swap problems occurred on Day 2. Again we used the same parameter values as we had in the other model fitting efforts. In this case, we also used the same individual threshold value for a given subject on both Day 1 and Day 2. We used the same decay rate parameter to account for forgetting over 1 hour and to account for forgetting over 24 hours.[7] The fits for the Day 1, Day 2 data and the operator swap data for Day 1 and Day 2 problems are shown in Fig. 3.6. The correlation between the observed and predicted use of the retrieval strategy was .994, .986, 1.0, and .971 for these respective data sets.

---

[7]Specifically, we estimated passage of time by number of intervening trials in the original experiments. To remain consistent, we estimated the number of intervening trials for 24 hours. There were 300 trials in 90 minutes, so we estimated 4,800 trials in 24 hours and used that value for the 24-hour delay condition.

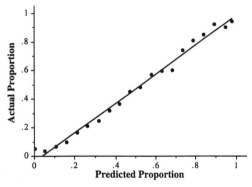

FIG. 3.6a. Predicted vs. actual proportion of retrieval selections in Experiment 2 of Schunn et al. (in press), grouped by predicted proportion, for Day 1 problems only.

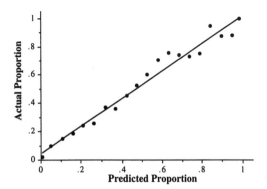

FIG. 3.6b. Predicted vs. actual proportion of retrieval selections in Experiment 2 of Schunn et al. (in press), grouped by predicted proportion, for Day 2 training problems only.

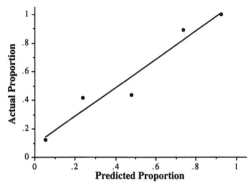

FIG. 3.6c. Predicted vs. actual proportion of retrieval selections in Experiment 2 of Schunn et al. (in press), grouped by predicted proportion, for same day operator-switch test problems only.

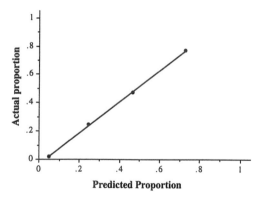

FIG. 3.6d. Predicted vs. actual proportion of retrieval selections in Experiment 2 of Schunn et al. (in press), grouped by predicted proportion, for previous day operator-switch test problems only.

Summary of Model Fitting Enterprise

The experiments clearly showed that rapid feelings of knowing are made based on familiarity with pairs of terms from the question and are not based on partial retrieval of the answer. The SAC model seems to do an excellent job of capturing this process, fitting four data sets extremely well using only a few constant parameter values. This enterprise involved 58 subjects, each with between 250 and 500 trials to predict. Given that there were 6 parameter values that remained constant across all experiments and were estimated for only the first experiment, these fits are especially impressive. It is worth noting that the same parameter value for decay was retained even when we started fitting data that involved a 24-hour delay from acquisition to test.

Reder's SAC model also answered the computational conundrum of how people can make a rapid preliminary evaluation of whether or not it is fruitful to search memory before actually engaging in such a search: In our model, activation converges on the problem node from elements in the question; this logically precedes retrieval of the answer. Therefore, a person would easily have the opportunity to make a decision about strategy preference before execution on retrieval could begin.[8]

How general are the conclusions? It is conceivable that the heuristic used to make a rapid feeling-of-knowing is idiosyncratic to the task employed. That

---

[8]Although beyond the scope of the simulation, we believe that when people choose to retrieve, they simply wait for activation to continue to spread from the activated problem node to the node representing the answer. When people choose to calculate, they then shift their focus of attention to the calculation process. However, even in this case, the spread of activation to the answer nodes is not stopped; it is merely attenuated, and the activation of nodes involved in the calculation process will dominate in terms of overall activation levels.

is, we used artificial arithmetic problems and a forced deadline. On the other hand, this same finding has been shown before with general knowledge questions for which subjects are not given a specific deadline for responding. In that case, too, subjects made feeling-of-knowing judgments (estimates of whether they could answer the question) faster than they could retrieve the answer and those feelings of knowing were equally susceptible to distortions from prior exposure to terms in the question.

There are other reasons to think that the rapid feeling-of-knowing is part of the normal question-answering process. In that general knowledge experiment, there was a second group of subjects who were asked to give the answer as quickly as they could (rather than estimate whether or not they knew the answer). These subjects were affected by the spurious priming just like the estimate group, but for these subjects, the priming led to longer search times before responding "don't know." In other words, the answer group was not asked to give a rapid feeling-of-knowing and therefore the manipulation that inflated feeling-of-knowing judgments for the estimate group instead caused them to initiate more or longer searches. Another reason to think that this rapid first impression is part of the normal question answering procedure is that the total time to estimate whether they knew the answer and then retrieve the answer (measured separately and then summed) was equivalent to the total time to indicate that the answer was found (without first providing an explicit estimate) and then to speak it.

THE IMPLICIT CHARACTER
OF FEELING-OF-KNOWING

Now that we have shown how the SAC model can account for rapid feeling-of-knowing, we are left with the task of justifying why we believe rapid feeling-of-knowing to be a largely implicit process. Of course, part of the argument depends on the definition of implicit process, and by that we mean processes that are "not reportable," "not open to inspection," or that are "involved in tasks generally considered to be implicit memory tasks." Kihlstrom, Shames, and Dorfman (chapter 1, this volume) make an eloquent case for the similarity between implicit processes and feeling-of-knowing. We agree with their view that "the person's experience, thought, and action is affected by . . . [aspects] . . . which he or she has not remembered" (p. 3).

Although we agree that this rapid feeling-of-knowing is based on something unreportable, we differ as to the nature of that which is unreportable or implicit. Kihlstrom et al. are referring to subthreshold activation of the answer, and for their task, that may well be the case. However, for the task that we explore (i.e., rapid feelings of knowing), impressions are not based on a *subthreshold* activation of the *answer*. Rather, the judgments are based on a *suprathreshold* activation of the *problem node*. We call the process implicit because the subject does not know why the answer seems available. The subject uses a heuristic that generally works, but high activation of a problem node does not guarantee that there is an answer associated to it nor does it guarantee that the *correct* problem node was activated.[9] That subjects can have their heuristic subverted by prior exposure to terms in the question or familiarity with critical parts of the problem is evidence for the implicit nature of the process. It is a seat-of-the-pants heuristic, a gut feeling that cannot be explained by the subject. The important point is that the subject is *unaware* of why the answer seems available. If the subject realized that it was because pieces of the question were familiar, the subject would not make these positive feeling-of-knowing judgments.

Indeed, one of the hallmarks of manipulations that affect implicit memory is that when subjects become aware of the manipulations, they make different attributions about their memories. For example, Jacoby and Whitehouse (1989) have found an increase in the tendency to say "old" to a word when, just prior to it, there was a brief exposure to the same word. However, this influence of a brief flash only occurred when the subjects were *unaware* of the flash. Likewise, an earlier exposure to non-famous names will tend to increase the probability that these names will later be judged famous, provided that the subject does not remember the context in which the name was seen earlier. When the person is aware of the brief flash or remembers studying the name earlier, the attribution of familiarity changes and the subject no longer has an increased tendency to respond "old" or to judge the name as famous.

In a similar vein, the gameshow experiment of Reder (1987, Experiment 6) demonstrated that subjects try to counteract experimental manipulations that affect their implicitly driven (i.e., activation-based) judgments. In this experiment, general knowledge questions had been primed by having pairs of terms from the questions rated for co-occurrence in everyday life. This earlier exposure to those terms caused subjects to have a spurious feeling-of-knowing, despite the fact that subjects seemed aware of this manipulation at least some of the time. For the more difficult the questions, the subjects were more likely to think they knew the answer if it had been primed (see Table 3.2). However, for just the easiest questions, subjects were appreciably *less* likely to judge that they knew the answer to the question if it had been primed. We take this as evidence that subjects used the strategy of raising their criterion for saying that they knew the answer when they recognized that terms in the question had been primed. However, this attempt to counter the spurious feeling-of-knowing was only partially successful. That

---

[9]Nonetheless, this mechanism is an excellent heuristic, giving d's of over 2.0 and gammas (Nelson, 1984, 1986) over .8. Those values are calculated over trials that include the operator switch problems (that lead people astray), so clearly this heuristic works well overall.

TABLE 3.2
The Proportion of Questions Attempted at Each Difficulty Level for
Primed and Unprimed Questions in Experiment 6 of Reder (1987)

Question Difficulty	Unprimed	Primed
Easy	0.82	0.76
Moderate	0.50	0.52
Hard	0.24	0.31

Note. Adapted from Reder (1987). Adapted with permission.

is, despite the correction in threshold, there was still a residual influence of the spurious priming when the answer was not known. The strategy to counteract the spurious familiarity only served to *reduce* the number of positive feeling-of-knowing responses when the answer *was* known.

Some definitions of implicit memory focus on the notion that there is no intention to remember or retrieve. However, there are many phenomena that might be considered products of implicit memory that may involve intentional inspections of memory. Some of these have been called *illusions of memory*, and contain some inaccurate components of metamemory. For example, the false-fame results of Jacoby and his associates (Jacoby, Kelley, Brown, & Jasechko, 1989; Jacoby, Woloshyn, & Kelley, 1989), and the inaccurate judgments of learning of Dunlosky and Nelson (1992) share a quality: In all cases, subjects were influenced by prior experiences and misinterpreted memory traces when making judgments. Benjamin and Bjork (chapter 14, this volume) illustrate how people can misattribute current familiarity with a memory trace to long-term learning of the trace and vice versa. Of course, showing the lack of accuracy in metamemorial judgments such as those described by Narens, Nelson, and their colleagues is not direct support for the position that strategy choice is based on implicit memory. Nonetheless, we contend that it is the current activation level of the memory trace, which can come about by recent priming or earlier exposure, that drives the inference processes that are used for these judgments. We believe that implicit memory processes are just that—the availability heuristic (Kahneman & Tversky, 1973) driven by current activation levels (cf. Kamas & Reder, 1994).

EXTRINSIC METACOGNITIVE VARIABLES AFFECTING STRATEGY CHOICE

A primary extrinsic variable that has been shown to influence strategy selection is the strategies' past history of success. This effect was first demonstrated by Luchins (1942) in what he termed the Einstellung Effect, in which recent success with one strategy caused subjects to overlook a much easier strategy. The principles of operant conditioning (Watson, 1925) describe a more general version of the influence of success on strategy use. That is, it was hypothesized that positive reinforcement (e.g., success) leads to increased occurrence of a behavior (e.g., a strategy), and negative reinforcement (e.g., failure) leads to decreased occurrence of a behavior. More recently the importance of prior history of success has been demonstrated anew. For example, Lovett and Anderson (in press) used a problem-solving task analogous to the classic water-jug task of Luchins (1942). They found that subjects were guided in their strategy preference not only by features of the problem, but also by the recent history of success of the various strategies.

Another illustration of the adaptiveness of strategy choice to the apparent success of the strategy are the data of Rudnicky (1990). His task allowed for the use of alternative strategies to perform operations within a spreadsheet: Subjects could use either a relative movement (arrow key) to get around in a spreadsheet in order to perform a required task, or they could use an absolute movement (a *go to* command). Their preference for these two commands for performing the tasks depended on the system delay (e.g., the arrow key was not popular when there was an appreciable system delay after each keystroke) and the distance to be traversed in the spreadsheet (e.g., *go to*'s were used more often for longer distance traversals). The most remarkable aspect of the data was that the tendency to adopt a given strategy was extremely well tuned to minimize the expected wait time. Subjects used the expected total duration for an action to choose the most efficient strategy; however, it is unlikely that subjects could explicitly calculate the optimal use of these strategies in "real time."

Of course, a strategy's history of success is not the only extrinsic variable that influences strategy choice. For example, although subjects do not necessarily select the strategy that corresponds with the official task demands, task instructions nonetheless have an impact on strategy preference even when accuracy does not depend on a specific strategy (Reder, 1987, Experiment 2). Likewise, explicit advice about which strategy is likely to prove successful in a given context does not guarantee that the suggested strategy will work, but it does influence preference (Reder, 1987, Experiment 3). Our interest in the success of a strategy is that we believe that subjects are frequently *unaware* of which strategy is most successful or that they are being influenced by strategy successfulness. In the case of the Rudnicky (1990) task, it seems unlikely that subjects were in fact making conscious decisions of strategy use. Hernnstein (1990) found that even pigeons were precisely tuned to the success base rate of particular choices, so there is reason to believe that subjects can be influenced without conscious awareness. Next, we review data that support this view.

Implicit Monitoring of the Extrinsic Variables

The extrinsic variable on which we focus our attention is the history of success with the strategy. It is of interest to us because its influence has been so frequently studied and has evidence relevant to the issue of awareness. Although it has been found that people are sometimes exquisitely sensitive to the probability of success or the relative usefulness of the various available strategies, we have reason to believe that this sensitivity is not in conscious awareness.

Three quite different experiments (Lemaire & Reder, 1996; Reder, 1987; Zbrodoff & Logan, 1986) illustrate subjects' adaptive use of strategies without even any awareness of the use of one of the strategies, let alone the relative use (proportional use) of the strategies. In Zbrodoff and Logan's experiment, subjects were given addition problems to verify or reject, such as 8 + 4 = 13. Subjects made many errors when given problems in which the answer was the correct answer to the corresponding multiplication problem, such as 8 + 4 = 32. The subjects' tendency to make these errors depended on the relative proportion of such foils: The greater the proportion of foils, the less the number of errors. That subjects are sensitive to the relative proportion of such foils is not terribly noteworthy for this chapter except to note that subjects were totally unaware that they were especially prone to making these kinds of errors!

In Experiment 1 of Reder (1987), subjects were extremely adaptive to the relative proportion of statements to be verified that had actually been presented as part of the previously read stories, yet totally oblivious to these proportions or even the strategies that they were using. In that experiment, subjects read a series of stories and were asked to make plausibility judgments for statements about the story. For one group of subjects, there was an 80% probability that a statement to be verified had been presented earlier as part of the story. In the case of false statements, it was an 80% probability that the exact contradiction of the statement had been presented earlier in the story. This condition was called the Direct Retrieval Bias condition because direct retrieval was likely to work. For another group of subjects, the probabilities were 20% instead of 80%. This condition was called the Plausibility Bias condition because most answers could only be made using plausibility. After reading six stories and answering questions after each story, the ratio of previously-presented to not-previously-presented statements became 50% for both groups (where previous presentation was not predictive of truth because the exact contradiction also counts as a previous presentation). Figure 3.7 illustrates subjects' sensitivity to the probability of success with a strategy. The y-axis plots the difference in latency between statements that had been previously presented or not, or in other words, the relative advantage of having seen the statement

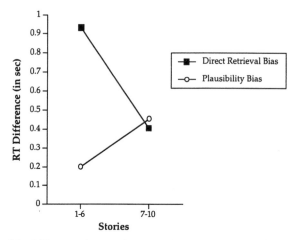

FIG. 3.7. Difference in reaction time between stated and nonstated statements (collapsed over plausibility) as a function of strategy bias, when bias imposed (Stories 1–6) and not imposed (Stories 7–10) for Experiment 1 of Reder (1987).

earlier. We take this difference as an index of the proportional use of the retrieve strategy as opposed to the plausibility strategy. Note that the size of the difference is much larger for the group where the retrieval strategy would work 80% of the time. The size of the difference becomes comparable for the two groups when the proportions become the same for the two groups.

Again, like in the Zbrodoff and Logan (1986) experiment, what makes these results especially noteworthy is that subjects were totally unaware of which strategy they were using more often, what the base-rate frequency was of presented statements in the story, whether that proportion changed during the experiment, or in which direction. Yet despite this inability to report these frequencies or to appreciate what strategies they were using, the data clearly indicate that they were very adaptive in their strategy use.

Lemaire and Reder (1996) have also found this dissociation between influence of the manipulation and awareness of the manipulation. Subjects were given multiplication problems to verify or reject, such as 8 * 4 = 33. Subjects' latencies to reject incorrect answers were slower the closer in value the answer to the correct answer, with one important qualification: Subjects were faster to reject problems that violated the parity rule. For example, 8 * 4 = 33 violates parity because the product of operands that are even must be even. The relative RT advantage of violations compared to incorrect nonviolations of the parity rule depended on the proportion of wrong answers that were consistent or inconsistent with the parity rule. When 80% of the incorrect answers violated the parity rule, the RT *advantage* for violations over nonviolations was five times larger than when there were only 20% violations among the incorrect facts to reject. There were also more errors (false acceptance) for nonviolation inequalities when most of the problems did violate the parity rule. However, when asked to guess what percentage of the problems were parity consistent problems, the subjects' responses did not differ for the conditions in which the parity did differ. In other words, the subjects seemed not to have explicit access to the relevant proportions. Furthermore, when asked about the parity rule, many subjects reported being unaware of the rule!

The notion that strategy use should be optimal without conscious awareness seems controversial from the perspective of metacognition; however, there is considerable work in the field of implicit learning that has already established this point quite clearly. Research under the title of implicit learning performed by Berry and Broadbent (1984), Lewicki et al. (1988), and A. S. Reber (1989) have shown a dissociation between subjects' performance and subjects' ability to report the rules that seem to guide their performance. For example, on a given trial in the experiments of Berry and Broadbent, a subject was told the output of a hypothetical sugar factory in tons and asked to choose the number of workers for the next month so that the output of the factory would remain within a specified range. The relationship between the tonnage and the number of workers was not obvious, yet subjects became proficient at controlling the factory's output. When asked to state the rule, subjects could not do this and claimed to make their responses on the basis of some sort of intuition or because the response *seemed* correct.

CONNECTIONS BETWEEN IMPLICIT LEARNING
AND IMPLICIT MEMORY

Given the similarity of the two words—learning and memory—and both starting with the modifier "implicit," one might think that the terms "implicit memory" and "implicit learning" are synonyms and therefore find the heading here silly or nonsensical. However, these two terms do in fact refer to two distinct subdisciplines where there exist few examples of papers where one literature cites the other literature. That is, it is almost as if the two approaches are being conducted without an awareness or interest in the other. Ignoring the obvious similarity in names, these two disciplines are still highly interrelated. Consider, for example, the work of P. J. Reber (1993; P. J. Reber & Kotovsky, 1992) on implicit learning: Similarity or even formal isomorphism between two different problems affected subjects' ability to solve the second problem, such that they were much faster to solve the second problem; however, subjects were unaware of this formal similarity and attributed the improvement on the second problem to it having an easier solution. This result is reminiscent of the finding on implicit memory of Jacoby, Allan, Collins, and Larwill (1988), in which subjects rated the loudness of aurally presented sentences that were embedded in white noise. Sentences that had been previously presented were rated as significantly louder than those that had not. Similarly, Warton and Lange (1994) found that subjects' ratings of the comprehensibility of written passages increased when they had previously read a passage with similar underlying themes. Jacoby et al.'s and Warton and Lange's subjects failed to appreciate that the perception of loudness or comprehensibility was due to temporary effects on their memory trace, just as Reber's subjects failed to recognize that the ease of solution was actually due to learning from performing a similar task earlier.

WHY SHOULD METACOGNITIVE PROCESSES BE IMPLICIT?

We began this chapter with the somewhat counterintuitive claim that many of the processes that are considered prototypically metacognitive are not in fact open to conscious awareness (i.e., are not reportable). This seemed counterintuitive because it is typically assumed that metacognition is the one aspect of cognition that is mostly likely to be conscious. Indeed, we have argued that even the monitoring processes are frequently occurring without conscious awareness. Given that metacognition has been long thought to be the essence of the conscious aspects of cognitive processing, why should it be that these processes too are largely occurring without conscious awareness?

Again, we should review what we mean by conscious awareness. We mean that the information is reportable (see footnote 1). So perhaps we should rephrase our question to be, *Why do the processes that are typically considered metacognitive largely occur without the ability to report or verbalize the nature of these processes?* Perhaps the answer is that strategy selection is implicit because the very task of attempting to verbalize or make conscious the processes is interfering with the task at hand. Berry and Broadbent (1984) reported that performance degraded when subjects attempted to verbalize what was going on in the implicit learning tasks, especially when the rule underlying the task was not transparent. Smith, Haviland, Reder, Brownell, and Adams (1976) found that when subjects were consciously aware of the choices involved in a perception task, performance was significantly worse. The explanation put forward there too was that the conscious process interfered with the normal, automatic process of perception. This notion that automatic processes are interfered with by verbal processing has been most clearly articulated by Schooler (e.g., Schooler & Engstler-Schooler, 1990; Schooler, Ohlsson, &

Brooks, 1993; Schooler, Ryan, & Reder, in press; Wilson & Schooler, 1991). In these papers, he has demonstrated that performance is qualitatively different, and, more importantly, quantitatively worse when subjects attempt to give verbal reports. One interpretation of these results is that the act of verbalizing or trying to come up with a verbal representation uses processing capacity in a limited capacity system. Because we do not normally attempt to verbalize these processes, the act of verbalization is especially taxing and disruptive to the relatively automatic processes.

Another possible explanation for why strategy selection occurs implicitly is that it may not be worth the extra computational effort to consider the strategy selections explicitly. In many of the experiments that we reviewed in this chapter, subjects demonstrated very impressive sensitivities to various factors, and were well calibrated in their strategy selections. Thus, if the human architecture is so adept at making strategy selections implicitly, the small room for improvement may render an explicit strategy selection process inefficient.

There is considerable evidence that some of the processes which underlie these metacognitive tasks occur automatically, and are basic cognitive processes. For example, Hasher and Zacks (1979), Hintzman (1988), and others have demonstrated that people automatically register frequency information. This ability does not degrade with age (Hertzog & Dixon, 1994), nor with multitasking; however, if subjects are asked to be conscious of how they are making their decisions, they may well not use this automatically registering frequency information and base their judgments on some other process. For example, the literature on base-rate neglect (e.g., Kahneman & Tversky, 1973; Tversky & Kahneman, 1974) has found that people often do not use base rates in their decision making when they are presented the base-rate information in a verbal summary format. By contrast, when people are allowed to experience the base-rate information in a nonverbal problem-solving context, they are quite sensitive to base-rate information (Koehler, 1993; Spellman, 1993).

IMPLICATIONS FOR EDUCATION

In considering the implications of these findings for educational practice, one must be careful in distinguishing between strategy selection and learning of new strategies. Our main thesis is that the processes which select between strategies in the current repertoire are independent of explicit monitoring, and that attempts to make those processes explicit results in degraded performance. For this case, the educational implications are clear: The implicit strategy selection processes should be left implicit, and attempts to tune them through explicit instructions will fail.

By contrast, the case of learning new strategies may be entirely differ-ent—it may well be that the process by which new strategies are learned is an explicit one and amenable to explicit interventions. Demonstrations of improving task performance by explicitly teaching new, more effective strategies are fairly common. For example, much of primary and secondary education consists of learning new skills via explicit teaching. Of course, these demonstrations do not prove that explicit teaching methods are better than more implicit teaching methods (e.g., learning by examples or learning by doing). However, studies by Chi and colleagues (Chi, Bassok, Lewis, & Reimann, 1989; Chi & VanLehn, 1991) provide suggestive evi-dence on this issue. They found that the ability to provide good self-explanations was important for learning physics problem-solving skills. Similarly, Crowley (1994) found that children acquired and transferred new strategies much more effectively when forced to provide explanations.

Given these findings, one can speculate about the next task for educa-tional researchers: to determine whether poor performance on a task is due to incorrect strategy selection among an existing repertoire or lack of knowledge of the appropriate strategy. If the appropriate strategy is missing, then explicit teaching methods are likely to be best. However, if the ap-propriate strategy is known but simply not selected, then more implicit methods of teaching are required. For example, one might structure the environment such that student receives much success feedback with the desired strategy or much failure with undesired strategies.

CAVEATS

Of course, we do not claim that strategy selection cannot be done explicitly, nor that it is not occasionally influenced by explicit factors. For example, Reder (1987) has shown that subjects' strategy selections can be influenced by explicit instructions. However, it is also true, much to experimenters' chagrin, that subjects frequently ignore explicit instructions (e.g., Mynatt, Doherty, & Tweney, 1978; Wason & Johnson-Laird, 1972).

There are also other cases in which people have been shown to have explicit knowledge of strategy effectiveness. For example, Crowley and Siegler (1993) found that young children were able to judge the effectiveness of a strategy even before they started using it. However, that people occasionally have explicit knowledge of strategy effectiveness does not necessarily imply that they use this explicit knowledge in making strategy selections.

Our conclusions may seem incongruous with our readers' own intro-spections that they are frequently aware of the variables affecting strategy choice. We have two responses: (a) of course there are times when people are aware of all the variables that affect their choice behavior; (b) however, sometimes people may *attribute* reasons for actions (strategy choices) that are plausible reasons that have no basis in fact. That is, people are frequently conscious of the strategy (behavior) selected, and from those observations inferences are made about why the strategy was selected. Nisbett and Wilson (1977) have made a strong case that our verbal reports for why we behave the way we do are not always accurate.

Earlier we described cases in which explicit awareness had negative impact on performance. However, awareness need not always influence performance negatively; it could also simply have no effect. For example, in Experiment 2 of Schunn et al. (in press), subjects were asked during the debriefing whether they were aware of the operator-swap manipulation. We hypothesized that if awareness had helped performance, then the aware subjects would have been less likely to be fooled by the operator-swap manipulation (like Jacoby and Whitehouse's subjects); if awareness had hurt, then the aware subject would have been more likely to be fooled by the operator-swap manipulation. However, awareness of this manipulation had no influence on the subjects' tendency to be fooled (i.e., select retrieve and then give the answer to the original problem), $F(1, 21) < 1$. In this case, awareness neither helped nor hurt the subjects.

CONCLUSIONS

We conclude this chapter as we began, namely with the bold conjecture that much of the processing that is called metacognitive typically operates at an implicit level; that is, without conscious awareness. Many of the tasks that are called monitoring are also operating without conscious awareness—people cannot veridically report what they have perceived and acted on. Furthermore, when people make efforts to change the nature of the task so that they are conscious and can report what they are doing, they run the risk of fundamentally changing their performance in non-optimal ways.

ACKNOWLEDGMENTS

Preparation of this chapter was supported by a grant from the Office of Naval Research N00014-95-1-0223 to the first author. The authors wish to thank P. Stroffolino for development of the original SAC simulations and D. Richards for conducting the original fits of the simulation to the empirical data.

REFERENCES

Anderson, J. R. (1974). Retrieval of propositional information from long-term memory. *Cognitive Psychology, 6,* 451–474.

Anderson, J. R. (1976). *Language, memory, and thought.* Hillsdale, NJ: Lawrence Erlbaum Associates.

Anderson, J. R. (1983). *The architecture of cognition.* Cambridge, MA: Harvard University Press.

Anderson, J. R. (1990). *The adaptive character of thought.* Hillsdale, NJ: Lawrence Erlbaum Associates.

Anderson, J. R. (1993). *Rules of the mind.* Hillsdale, NJ: Lawrence Erlbaum Associates.

Anderson, J. R., & Schooler, L. J. (1991). Reflections of the environment in memory. *Psychological Science, 2,* 396–408.

Berry, D. C., & Broadbent, D. E. (1984). On the relationship between task performance and associated verbalizable knowledge. *Quarterly Journal of Experimental Psychology, 36A,* 209–231.

Blessing, S. B., & Ross, B. H. (1996). Context effects in problem categorization and problem solving. *Journal of Experimental Psychology: Learning, Memory, and Cognition, 22,* 792–810.

Bowers, J. S., & Schacter, D. L. (1990). Implicit memory and test awareness. *Journal of Experimental Psychology: Learning, Memory, and Cognition, 16,* 404–416.

Chi, M. T., Bassok, M., Lewis, M. W., & Reimann, P. (1989). Self-explanations: How students study and use examples in learning to solve problems. *Cognitive Science, 13*(2), 145–182.

Chi, M. T., VanLehn, K. A. (1991). The content of physics self-explanations. *Journal of the Learning Sciences, 1*(1), 69–105.

Cohen, N. J., & Squire, L. R. (1980). Preserved learning and retention of pattern analyzing skills in amnesia: Dissociation of knowing how and knowing that. *Science, 210,* 207–210.

Crowley, K. (1994). *How children learn from examples: A developmental study of explanation-based learning.* Unpublished doctoral dissertation, Carnegie Mellon University, Pittsburgh, PA.

Crowley, K., & Siegler, R. S. (1993). Flexible strategy use in young children's tic-tac-toe. *Cognitive Science, 17*(4), 531–651.

Davidson, J. E., Deuser, R., & Sternberg, R. J. (1994). The role of metacognition in problem solving. In J. Metcalfe & A. P. Shimamura (Eds.), *Metacognition: Knowing about knowing* (pp. 207–226). Cambridge, MA: Bradford.

Dosher, B. A., & Rosedale, G. (1989). Integrated retrieval cues as a mechanism for priming in retrieval from memory. *Journal of Experimental Psychology: General, 118,* 191–211.

Dosher, B. A., & Rosedale, G. (1990, November). *Dual cues in item recognition: An ensemble model of priming.* Paper presented at the Thirty-First Annual Meeting of the Psychonomics Society, New Orleans, LA.

Dunlosky, J., & Nelson, T. O. (1992). Importance of the cue for judgment of learning JOLs and the delayed-JOL effect. *Memory and Cognition, 204,* 374–380.

Glucksberg, S., & McCloskey, M. (1981). Decisions about ignorance: Knowing that you don't know. *Journal of Experimental Psychology: Human Learning and Memory, 7,* 311–325.

Hasher, L., & Zacks, R. T. (1979). Automatic and effortful processes in memory. *Journal of Experimental Psychology: General, 108,* 356–388.

Hernnstein, R. J. (1990). Rational choice theory. *American Psychologist, 45,* 356–367.

Hertzog, C., & Dixon, R. A. (1994). Metacognitive development in adulthood and old age. In J. Metcalfe & A. P. Shimamura (Eds.), *Metacognition: Knowing about knowing* (pp. 227–251). Cambridge, MA: Bradford.

Hinsley, D. A., Hayes, J. R., & Simon, H. A. (1977). From words to equations: Meaning and representation in algebra word problems. In P. A. Carpenter & M. A. Just (Eds.), *Cognitive processes in comprehension* (pp. 89–106). Hillsdale, NJ: Lawrence Erlbaum Associates.

Hintzman, D. L. (1988). Judgments of frequency and recognition memory in a multiple-trace memory model. *Psychological Review, 95,* 528–551.

Jacoby, L. L. (1983). Remembering the data: Analyzing interactive processes in reading. *Journal of Verbal Learning and Verbal Behavior, 22,* 485–508.

Jacoby, L. L., Allan, L. G., Collins, J. C., & Larwill, L. K. (1988). Memory influences subjective experience: Noise judgments. *Journal of Experimental Psychology: Learning, Memory, and Cognition, 14,* 240–247.

Jacoby, L. L., Kelley, C., Brown, J., & Jasechko, J. (1989). Becoming famous overnight: Limits on the ability to avoid unconscious influences of the past. *Journal of Personality and Social Psychology, 56,* 326–338.

Jacoby, L. L., & Whitehouse, K. (1989). An illusion of memory: False recognition influenced by unconscious perception. *Journal of Experimental Psychology: General, 118*(2), 126–135.

Jacoby, L. L., Woloshyn, V., & Kelley, C. (1989). Becoming famous without being recognized: Unconscious influences of memory produced by dividing attention. *Journal of Experimental Psychology: General, 118,* 115–125.

Kahneman, D., & Tversky, A. (1973). On the psychology of prediction. *Psychological Review, 80,* 237–251.

Kamas, E., & Reder, L. M. (1994). The role of familiarity in cognitive processing. In E. O'Brien & R. Lorch (Eds.), *Sources of coherence in text comprehension: A festschrift in honor of Jerome L. Myers.* Hillsdale, NJ: Lawrence Erlbaum Associates.

Koehler, J. J. (1993). *The base rate fallacy myth* [On-line]. Available: psyc.4.49.base-rate.1. koehler.

LeFevre, J., Greenham, S. L., & Waheed, N. (1993). The development of procedural and conceptual knowledge in computational estimation. *Cognition and Instruction, 11*(2), 95–132.

Lemaire, P., & Reder, L. M. (1996). *Is the strategy selection process biased: A case study (or the example) of arithmetic product verification?* Manuscript submitted for publication.

Lewicki, P., Hill, T., & Bizot, E. (1988). Acquisition of procedural knowledge about a pattern of stimuli that cannot be articulated. *Cognitive Psychology, 20,* 24–37.

Lovett, M. C., & Anderson, J. R. (in press). History of success and current context in problem solving: Combined influences on operator selection. *Cognitive Psychology.*

Luchins, A. S. (1942). Mechanization in problem solving. *Psychological Monographs, 54*(Whole No. 248).

Metcalfe, J. (1994). A computational modeling approach to novelty monitoring, metacognition, and frontal lobe dysfunction. In J. Metcalfe & A. P. Shimamura (Eds.), *Metacognition: Knowing about knowing* (pp. 137–156). Cambridge, MA: Bradford.

Metcalfe, J., Schwartz, B. L., & Joaquim, S. G. (1993). The cue-familiarity heuristic in metacognition. *Journal of Experimental Psychology: Learning, Memory, and Cognition, 19,* 851–864.

Miner, A., & Reder, L. M. (1994). A new look at feeling-of-knowing: Its metacognitive role in regulating question answering. In J. Metcalfe & A. P. Shimamura (Eds.), *Metacognition: Knowing about knowing* (pp. 47–70). Cambridge, MA: Bradford.

Mynatt, C. R., Doherty, M. E., & Tweney, R. D. (1978). Consequences of confirmation and disconfirmation in a simulated research environment. *Quarterly Journal of Experimental Psychology, 30,* 395–406.

Nelson, T. O. (1984). A comparison of current measure of the accuracy of feeling-of-knowing predictions. *Psychological Bulletin, 95,* 109–133.

Nelson, T. O. (1986). ROC curves and measures of discrimination accuracy: A reply to Swets. *Psychological Bulletin, 100,* 128–132.

Nelson, T. O., & Narens, L. (1994). Why investigate metacognition? In J. Metcalfe & A. P. Shimamura (Eds.), *Metacognition: Knowing about knowing* (pp. 1–25). Cambridge, MA: Bradford.

Nisbett, R. E., & Wilson, T. D. (1977). Telling more than we can know: Verbal reports on mental processes. *Psychological Review, 84,* 231–259.

Ratcliff, R., & McKoon, G. (1988). A retrieval theory of priming in memory. *Psychological Review, 95*(3), 385–408.

Reber, A. S. (1989). Implicit learning and tacit knowledge. *Journal of Experimental Psychology: General, 118,* 219–235.

Reber, A. S., & Millward, R. B. (1971). Event tracking in probability learning. *American Journal of Psychology, 84,* 85–99.

Reber, P. J. (1993). *Working memory, learning and transfer of nonverbalizable knowledge: Solving the balls and boxes puzzle.* Unpublished doctoral dissertation, Department of Psychology, Carnegie Mellon University, Pittsburgh, PA.

Reber, P. J., & Kotovsky, K. (1992). Learning and problem solving under a memory load. In *Proceedings of the 14th Annual Conference of the Cognitive Science Society* (pp. 1068–1073). Hillsdale, NJ: Lawrence Erlbaum Associates.

Reder, L. M. (1979). The role of elaborations in memory for prose. *Cognitive Psychology, 11,* 221–234.

Reder, L. M. (1982). Plausibility judgments versus fact retrieval: Alternative strategies for sentence verification. *Psychological Review, 89,* 250–280.

Reder, L. M. (1987). Strategy selection in question answering. *Cognitive Psychology, 19,* 90–137.

Reder, L. M. (1988). Strategic control of retrieval strategies. In G. H. Bower (Ed.), *The psychology of learning and motivation* (Vol. 22, pp. 227–259). San Diego: Academic Press.

Reder, L. M., & Anderson, J. R. (1980). A partial resolution of the paradox of interference: The role of integrating knowledge. *Cognitive Psychology, 12,* 447–472.

Reder, L. M., & Gordon, J. S. (1996). Subliminal perception: Nothing special cognitively speaking. In J. Cohen & J. Schooler (Eds.), *Cognitive and neuropsychological approaches to the study of consciousness.* Mahwah, NJ: Lawrence Erlbaum Associates.

Reder, L. M., & Ritter, F. E. (1992). What determines initial feeling of knowing? Familiarity with questions terms, not with the answer. *Journal of Experimental Psychology: Learning, Memory, and Cognition, 18,* 435–451.

Reder, L. M., & Ross, B. H. (1983). Integrated knowledge in different tasks: The role of retrieval strategy on fan effects. *Journal of Experimental Psychology: Learning, Memory, and Cognition, 9,* 55–72.

Ross, B. H. (1984). Remindings and their effects in learning a cognitive skill. *Cognitive Psychology, 16,* 371–416.

Ross, B. H. (1989). Distinguishing types of superficial similarities: Different effects on the access and use of earlier problems. *Journal of Experimental Psychology: Learning, Memory, and Cognition, 15,* 456–468.

Rudnicky, A. I. (1990, April). *System response delay and user strategy selection.* Invited poster given at the 1990 Conference on Human Factors in Computing System, Seattle, WA.

Schooler, J. W., & Engstler-Schooler, T. Y. (1990). Verbal overshadowing of visual memories: Some things are better left unsaid. *Cognitive Psychology, 17,* 36–71.

Schooler, J. W., Ohlsson, S., & Brooks, K. (1993). Thoughts beyond words: When language overshadows insight. *Journal of Experimental Psychology: General, 122,* 166–183.

Schooler, J. W., Ryan, R. S., & Reder, L. (in press). The costs and benefits of verbally rehearsing memory for faces. In D. Herrmann, M. Johnson, C. McEvoy, C. Hertzog, & P. Hertel (Eds.), *Basic and applied memory: New findings.* Hillsdale, NJ: Lawrence Erlbaum Associates.

Schunn, C. D., Reder, L. M., Nhouyvanisvong, A., Richards, D. R., & Stroffolino, P. J. (in press). To calculate or not calculate: A source activation confusion (SAC) model of problem-familiarity's role in strategy selection. *Journal of Experimental Psychology: Learning, Memory, and Cognition.*

Schwartz, B. L., & Metcalfe, J. (1992). Cue familiarity but not target retrievability enhances feeling-of-knowing judgments. *Journal of Experimental Psychology: Learning, Memory, and Cognition, 18,* 1074–1083.

Siegler, R. S. (1989). How domain-general and domain-specific knowledge interact to produce strategy choices. *Merrill–Palmer Quarterly, 35,* 1–26.

Siegler, R. S., & Jenkins, E. A. (1989). *How children discover new strategies.* Hillsdale, NJ: Lawrence Erlbaum Associates.

Siegler, R. S., & Shrager, J. (1984). Strategy choices in addition and subtraction: How do children know what to do? In C. Sophian (Ed.), *Origins of cognitive skills* (pp. 229–293). Hillsdale, NJ: Lawrence Erlbaum Associates.

Smith, E. E., Haviland, S. E., Reder, L. M., Brownell, H., & Adams, N. (1976). When preparation fails: Disruptive effects of prior information on perceptual recognition. *Journal of Experimental Psychology: Human Perception and Performance, 2,* 151–161.

Spellman, B. (1993). Implicit learning of base rates: Commentary on Koehler on base-rate [On-line]. Available: psyc.4.61.base-rate.4.spellman.

Tversky, A., & Kahneman, D. (1974). Judgment under uncertainty: Heuristics and biases. *Science, 185,* 1124–1131.

Warrington, E. K., & Weiskrantz, L. (1970). Amnesic Syndrome: Consolidation or retrieval? *Nature, 228,* 629–630.

Wason, P. C., & Johnson-Laird, P. N. (1972). *Psychology of reasoning: Structure and content.* Cambridge, MA: Harvard University Press.

Watson, J. B. (1925). *Behaviorism.* New York: Norton.

Wharton, C., & Lange, T. E. (1994). Analogical transfer through comprehension and priming. In *Proceedings of the Sixteenth Annual Conference of the Cognitive Science Society* (pp. 934–939). Hillsdale, NJ: Lawrence Erlbaum Associates.

Wilson, T. D., & Schooler, J. W. (1991). Thinking too much: Introspection can reduce the quality of preferences and decisions. *Journal of Personality and Social Psychology, 60,* 181–192.

Zbrodoff, N. J., & Logan, G. D. (1986). On the autonomy of mental processes: A case study of arithmetic. *Journal of Experimental Psychology: General, 115,* 118–130.

Chapter 4

Strategy Choices
Across the Life Span

Robert S. Siegler
Karen E. Adolph
Patrick Lemaire
Carnegie Mellon University

One of the most striking characteristics of human cognition is its variability. Both children and adults often possess multiple strategies, rules, concepts, and theories that they use to think about a given phenomenon or solve a given type of problem. For example, in such diverse domains as arithmetic, spelling, serial recall, and moral reasoning, children know and use multiple strategies. Recent trial-by-trial analyses have shown that the variability is present even in domains that have given rise to classic stage theories. Thus, when 5-year-olds are presented number conservation problems, they not only judge on the basis of the relative lengths of the rows, as stated in Piaget's theory and virtually all developmental psychology textbooks, but also sometimes rely on the type of transformation and other times rely on the results of counting (Siegler, 1995).

This variability is not just a cognitive curio, something that is true but without further ramifications. Rather, it appears to influence both performance and learning. With regard to performance, the greater the number of relevant rules, strategies, or conceptualizations that an individual can apply to a task, the more finely the person can fit the one they use on a particular occasion to task and situational demands. For example, in a study of preschoolers' arithmetic, children who already occasionally used the min strategy (counting from the larger addend) were able to solve more challenging problems than they had previously encountered (e.g., 2 + 21), whereas children who had not yet discovered the strategy were unable to adapt to the challenges posed by such problems and simply said they couldn't solve them (Siegler & Jenkins, 1989). Similarly, possessing multiple ways of thinking about a task correlates positively with ability to learn more about it (Graham & Perry, 1993; Siegler, 1995).

Although cognitive variability can potentially enhance performance and learning, the degree to which it does so depends on how well children choose among the alternative strategies. If children know a faster strategy and a slower, more accurate one, they will benefit only if they choose the faster strategy when speed is most important and choose the more accurate one when accuracy is. Selecting randomly will yield worse performance than always using the approach that on average yields the better outcome. Thus, the benefits of cognitive variability depend on the quality of choices among alternatives.

How adaptive are these choices? Those interested in children's strategy choices have tended to reach quite negative conclusions. They have focused on findings that children who have been taught new strategies often do not use them later when they are free to choose (Ghatala, Levin, Pressley, & Goodwin, 1986; Keeney, Cannizzo, & Flavell, 1967), that children frequently choose alternatives with lower expected values over ones with higher values (Klayman, 1985), and that children who have been encouraged to plan commonly fail to do so (Scholnick & Friedman, 1987). This has led to conclusions such as the following:

> Certainly one of the lessons from research across many areas of cognition is that children often do not use their available knowledge . . . A child might know that rehearsal is a good strategy for remembering a list of chores that need to be done, but not rehearse because he or she lacks time, energy, capacity, or motivation to exert the effort. (Flavell, Miller, & Miller, 1993, p. 261)

Despite these pessimistic impressions, an increasing body of evidence indicates that children's strategy choices are usually highly adaptive. The choices respond in reasonable ways both to inherent problem characteristics and to fluctuating situational demands. For example, children most often adopt particular strategies on problems in which those strategies are most advantageous. They also choose strategies in ways that respond to concerns of both speed and accuracy. Moreover, they respond appropriately to situational incentives to use one strategy rather than another. Table 4.1 lists some of the types of choices on which children have been found to choose adaptively and the domains in which they have been found to make them.

Research on the adaptiveness of children's strategy choices has focused almost entirely on children between 4 and 12 years of age. Related work on the adaptiveness of adults' strategy choices has focused almost entirely on the adaptiveness of the choices of college students and other youthful

TABLE 4.1
Types of Adaptive Choices and Domains in Which They
Have Been Documented in Children's Strategy Choices

1. **Adaptation to problem difficulty**
   Infant locomotion (Adolph, 1993)
   Arithmetic (Cooney, Swanson, & Ladd, 1988; Geary & Burlingham-Dubree, 1989;
     Hubbard, LeFebre, & Greenham, 1994)
   Memory strategies (DeLoache, 1994)
   Decision making (Klayman, 1985)
   Causal reasoning (Schultz et al., 1986)
2. **Adaptation to episodic success of strategies**
   Memory strategies (McGilly & Siegler, 1989)
3. **Adaptation to changing competence**
   Arithmetic (Lemaire & Siegler, 1995)
4. **Adjusting to task instructions**
   Tic-tac-toe (Crowley & Siegler, 1993)
   Planning (Gardner & Rogoff, 1990)
5. **Adjusting to demands on cognitive resources**
   Decision making (Klayman, 1985)
   Memory strategies (Guttentag, 1984)
6. **Balancing immediate and long-term goals**
   Tic-tac-toe (Crowley & Siegler, 1993)
   Reading (Goldman & Saul, 1991)
7. **Balancing concerns of speed and accuracy**
   Reading (Brent & Routh, 1978)
   Tic-tac-toe (Crowley & Siegler, 1993)

adults. However, Siegler (1995), among others, has claimed that the adaptiveness of strategy choices reflects basic features of human cognition, and
that adaptive choices should therefore be evident in all age groups from
infancy to old age. The goal of the present chapter is to test this hypothesis
through examining strategy choices not only among children and young
adults but also among infants and older adults.

The chapter is divided into four main parts. The first describes five basic
phenomena regarding strategy choice, and illustrates them with examples
from research on 4- to 12-year-old children. The second part describes a
computer simulation, ASCM, that embodies a set of hypotheses about the
mechanisms that underlie these five phenomena. Relying entirely on implicit knowledge, ASCM generates highly adaptive choices, similar to those
that children make. The third part of the chapter focuses on the strategy
choices of infants who need to go down ramps of varying steepness; many of
the same basic phenomena emerge as with older children and the simulation
model. The fourth part focuses on the strategy choices of senior citizens
asked to solve mental multiplication problems; again, many of the same
phenomena emerge. The overall objective is to show that throughout the
life span, people choose adaptively among alternative strategies.

BASIC PHENOMENA RELEVANT
TO STRATEGY CHOICES

Variability

Innumerable studies have depicted cognitive development in terms of a 1:1 correspondence between children's age and their way of thinking. Young children are said to think in one way, somewhat older children in a somewhat more sophisticated way, yet older children in a yet more sophisticated way. Contrary to this standard depiction, however, recent trial-by-trial analyses indicate that children of a single age often think about a given problem, concept, or phenomenon in a variety of ways.

One task in which such cognitive variability has been observed is elementary school children's strategies for solving single-digit addition problems. Examination of both videotaped records of ongoing behavior and immediately retrospective self-reports reveals five relatively common strategies (each used on between 3% and 36% of trials among the kindergartners, first graders, and second graders in Siegler, 1987a). Sometimes children use the *sum strategy*, in which they count from one; to solve 3 + 6, a child using the sum strategy might put up three fingers, then six more, then count from one to nine. Other times children use the *min strategy*, which involves counting from the larger addend the number of times indicated by the smaller addend. Here, they would solve 3 + 6 by counting "6, 7, 8, 9" or "7, 8, 9." On other occasions, they use *decomposition*, which involves translating the problem into an easier form and then making the necessary adjustment. A child solving 3 + 6 via decomposition might think, "3 + 7 = 10, 6 is 1 less than 7, so 3 + 6 = 9." Still other times, they use *retrieval* or *guessing* to generate an answer.

These diverse strategies are not artifacts of one child consistently using one strategy and another child consistently using a different one. The majority of kindergartners, first graders, and second graders use at least three of the five strategies; a substantial minority use more (Siegler, 1987a). This multiple strategy use is apparent within classes of similar problems, and even on the same problem presented to the same child on consecutive days. In two studies, one on addition (Siegler & Shrager, 1984) and one on time telling (Siegler & McGilly, 1989), fully one-third of children used different strategies on the identical problem on two successive days. Only a small part of this day-to-day variability could be explained by learning, because the progression of strategies was not consistently from less to more advanced. For example, in the study of addition, almost as many children retrieved the answer on the first day and used the sum strategy on the second as did the reverse.

This strategy diversity is not limited to any particular domain. Consider just findings from our own studies. To multiply, 8- to 10-year-olds sometimes repeatedly add one of the multiplicands, sometimes write the problem and then recognize the answer, sometimes write and then count groups of hatch marks that represent the problem, and sometimes retrieve the answer from memory (Lemaire & Siegler, 1995). To tell time, 7- to 9-year-olds sometimes count forward from the hour by ones, fives, or both, sometimes count backwards from the hour by ones and/or fives, sometimes count from reference points such as the half hour, and sometimes retrieve the time that corresponds to the clock hands' configuration (Siegler & McGilly, 1989). To spell words, 7- and 8-year-olds sometimes sound out words, sometimes look them up in dictionaries, sometimes write out alternative forms and try to recognize which is correct, and sometimes recall the spelling from memory (Siegler, 1986). To serially recall lists of unrelated stimuli, 5- to 8-year-olds sometimes repeatedly recite the names of items within the list during the delay period, sometimes recite the names once and stop, and sometimes just wait (McGilly & Siegler, 1989, 1990).

Similar strategy diversity has been observed by other investigators in children's arithmetic (Cooney, Swanson, & Ladd, 1988), causal reasoning (Shultz, Fisher, Pratt, & Rulf, 1986), scientific reasoning (Schauble, 1990), spatial reasoning (Ohlsson, 1984), referential communication (Kahan & Richards, 1986), language use (Kuczaj, 1977), and motor activity (Goldfield, 1994). The diverse strategies have been observed among adults as well as children, and in Japan and China as well as in North America and Europe (Geary, Fan, & Bow-Thomas, 1992; Kuhara-Kojima & Hatano, 1989). It has been observed in the order with which strategies are considered as well as in the strategies that are used (Reder, 1982, 1988; Reder & Ritter, 1992). These studies alone call into serious question the typical description that at Age N, children are in Stage X, have rule X, have theory X, use strategy X; at age N + n they are in stage Y, have rule Y, have theory Y, use strategy Y; and so on.

Adaptive Strategy Choices

Children's strategy choices have been shown to be adaptive in several ways. One involves their choice of whether to state a retrieved answer or to use a *backup strategy* (any approach other than retrieval, such as the sum and min strategies in addition). The more difficult a problem, the more often children use backup strategies to solve it. This pattern of strategy choice is adaptive because it enables children to use the faster retrieval approach most often on problems where it yields correct answers and to use the slower backup strategies most often on problems where they are necessary to produce accurate performance. Consistent with this analysis, forcing children to retrieve on all trials by imposing a very short time limit produces a sharp falloff in accuracy, with the falloff largest on the problems on which children most often use backup strategies when they are allowed to choose freely (Siegler & Robinson, 1982).

This pattern of choices between retrieval and backup strategies has been found to be extremely general across populations and domains. It holds true with problem difficulty defined either by percentage of errors or by length of solution times; with high achieving and low achieving students; with suburban White and inner city Black children; and with addition, subtraction, multiplication, time telling, spelling, and word identification (Geary & Burlingham-Dubree, 1989; Geary & Wiley, 1991; Kerkman & Siegler, 1993; Lemaire & Siegler, 1995; Siegler, 1986, 1988a, 1988b).

Children also choose adaptively among alternative backup strategies. For example, when choosing between the min and sum strategies, children most often select the min strategy on problems where differences between addends are large and where the smaller addend is small (Siegler, 1987a). Thus, when solving single-digit addition problems, they are most likely to use the min strategy on problems such as 9 + 2. Problems with large differences between addends are the ones on which the min strategy produces the greatest savings in amount of counting, relative to the main alternative approach, the sum strategy. Complementarily, the easiest problems on which to execute the min strategy correctly are ones on which the smaller addend is small. It makes sense for children to use the min strategy most often on problems where its advantages over alternative strategies are greatest.

Change

Four main changes in children's strategy use occur with age and experience: acquisition of new strategies, changing frequency of use of existing strategies, improved efficiency of execution of strategies, and more adaptive choices among strategies (Lemaire & Siegler, 1995).

First consider acquisition of new strategies. Even after children know strategies that consistently yield correct performance on a class of problems, they continue to invent new strategies for solving them. For example, children who competently solve simple addition problems by using the sum strategy or retrieval go on to discover the min strategy (Siegler & Jenkins, 1989).

Above and beyond new strategies being added, there are substantial shifts in the relative frequency of strategies that are used to varying degrees throughout the period. For example, in 5- to 7-year-olds' single-digit addition, three strategies tend to be present throughout the period: retrieval, the sum strategy, and guessing. Frequency of the first approach steadily increases from kindergarten to second grade, whereas that of the second and third steadily decreases (Siegler, 1987a).

Changes also are evident in the skill with which each strategy is executed. With practice, children become both faster and more accurate in their execution of strategies. For example, in Siegler (1987a), mean time to execute the min strategy decreased from 6 sec among kindergartners to 4 sec among second graders, and percent correct when using the strategy increased from 71% to 93%.

Finally, with problem-solving experience, choices among strategies become increasingly adaptive. Examination of French second graders at three points during their learning of single-digit multiplication illustrated this point (Lemaire & Siegler, 1995). At the time of the first observation, in the first 10 days of the children's learning, choices were already moderately attuned to problem difficulty. However, the correlations between problem difficulty and frequency of use of backup strategies were higher after 2 months of studying multiplication and still higher after four months of studying it.

Generalization

Observation of children in the weeks after they first discover a new strategy indicates that their generalization of it to new problems often takes a long time, at least when children possess other effective strategies (Kuhn, Schauble, & Garcia-Mila, 1992; Schauble, 1990; Siegler & Jenkins, 1989). However, generalization of new strategies can be considerably hastened if children encounter conditions that highlight the new strategy's advantages over previous approaches. For example, in a study of 4- and 5-year-olds' discovery of the min strategy (Siegler & Jenkins, 1989), in the initial sessions after the discoveries, children used the new approach only occasionally. As long as typical single digit problems were being presented, even children who had given excellent explanations of the advantages of the new strategy (e.g., "You don't have to count all those numbers"), continued more often to count from one. However, presentation of problems such as 3 + 22, on which the min strategy worked far better than alternative approaches, led children who had previously discovered the strategy to use it much more often and then to generalize it to single-digit problems as well. Thus, although generalization of new strategies is usually slow, it can be facilitated if problems are presented on which alternative approaches do not work and on which the new strategy does.

Individual Differences

Recognizing the variability of strategy use within individuals raises the issue of whether strategy use also varies in interesting ways among individuals. Although research on broad cognitive styles has not identified many strong consistencies in strategy use (Kogan, 1983; Sternberg, 1985), studies of more narrowly defined strategy choices have yielded more encouraging results. For example, examination of the choice between stating a retrieved answer and using a backup strategy has revealed consistent individual patterns in first graders' addition, subtraction, and word identification (Kerkman & Siegler, 1993; Siegler, 1988b). The research indicates three characteristic patterns: the good student, not-so-good student, and perfectionist patterns. Good students are children who usually rely on retrieval and who generally answer quickly and accurately. Not-so-good students sometimes use retrieval but generally execute both it and backup strategies quite slowly and inaccurately. Perfectionists are fairly fast and very accurate, but use retrieval even less often than the not-so-good students; instead, they rely heavily on backup strategies.

These patterns of individual differences in addition, subtraction, and word identification have been found in four different experiments, some involving high-SES, predominantly White, suburban populations and others involving low-SES, predominantly Black, inner-city populations. They also have proved predictive of standardized test scores and of future classroom placements: On the standardized tests, not-so-good students score significantly lower than the other two groups, are more likely to be classified as learning disabled, and are more likely to need to repeat a grade (Kerkman & Siegler, 1993; Siegler, 1988b). Thus, the differences between not-so-good students and the other two groups are of the type that are detected by standard psychometric tests. However, the differences between the strategy choices of good students and perfectionists are not apparent on these tests; they are more akin to differences in cognitive style.

Summary

The present perspective brings to center stage a different set of phenomena than are emphasized in traditional accounts of development. Rather than focusing on *the* problem solving approach that children use at each age, the perspective focuses on the *set of approaches* that children use. Highlighting this variability brings into the spotlight how children choose among the alternative approaches and what adaptive purposes the choices serve. The perspective also calls attention to several different types of changes: acquisition of new approaches, changes in the frequency of use of existing approaches, changes in the effectiveness with which these approaches are used, and increasingly adaptive choices among alternatives. The perspective also highlights how strategies are generalized beyond their initial contexts and how individuals vary in their strategy choices. We now describe a model aimed at accounting for these phenomena.

ASCM: A MODEL OF STRATEGY CHOICE

Children's strategies first became a major topic of research in the mid-1960s (e.g., Flavell, Beach, & Chinsky, 1966; Keeney, Cannizzo, & Flavell, 1967). The early research documented large changes in memory strategies between ages 5 and 8 years. Five-year-olds were said to rarely use strategies such as rehearsal and organization; 8-year-olds were said to consistently use them. Especially interesting were the results of efforts to teach such strategies to 5- and 6-year-olds who did not spontaneously use them. Such children often learned the strategies, and their performance improved when they used them. Despite these benefits, the children usually did not continue to use the strategies later, even in quite similar situations.

This puzzle was an important impetus for initial thinking about children's strategy choices—the metacognitive approach. It was labeled "metacognitive" because it focused on how knowledge about cognition might control cognitive activities. The fundamental assumption was that young children's failure to use new strategies reflected their limited understanding of their own cognitive capacities and of why the new strategies were needed.

It is important to note that the metacognitive models that were originally proposed focused on explicit, rationally derived, conscious metacognitive knowledge. The term *metacognitive* also at times has been used to refer to processes that are implicit, not derived from rational consideration, and unconscious. Greeno, Riley, and Gelman's (1984) planning networks, Van Lehn's (1983) repair models, and Halford's (1993) mental models, like our own model of strategy choice, fit this category. In the present context, however, the term metacognitive is used only in its original sense of explicit, rationally derived, conscious knowledge.

Metacognitive approaches assume that strategy choices are made through the cognitive system's explicit knowledge of its own workings. This knowledge is often said to be used by an "executive processor," which decides what the cognitive system should do (Case, 1978; Kluwe, 1982; Sternberg, 1985). Schneider and Pressley (1989) described the executive processor as follows:

> This executive is aware of the system's capacity limits and strategies. The executive can analyze new problems and select appropriate strategies and attempt solutions. Very importantly, the executive monitors the success or failure of ongoing performance, deciding which strategies to continue and which to replace with potentially more effective and appropriate routines. In addition, the efficient executive knows when one knows and when one does not know, an important requirement for competent learning. (p. 91)

Such metacognitive approaches are useful for pointing to one way in which, in principle, intelligent strategy choices could be generated. However, they also have a number of weaknesses, both theoretical and empirical (Brown & Reeve, 1986; Cavanaugh & Perlmutter, 1982; Siegler, 1988a). As statements of theory, they are all too reminiscent of the homunculus that sits atop the rest of the cognitive system and tells it what to do. Not unrelated to this problem, such metacognitive approaches have been vague about the mechanisms that produce the phenomena of interest. Do people make explicit judgments about their intellectual capacities, available strategies, and task demands every time they face a task they could perform in multiple ways? If not, how do they decide when to do so? Do they consider every strategy they could use on the task or only some of them? If only a subset, how do they decide which ones? How do people know what their cognitive capacity will be on a novel task or what strategies they could apply to it? The apparent simplicity of the metacognitive models masks a world of complexity.

Empirical evidence has raised questions about the fundamental assumption that underlies the models. Relations between explicit, verbalizable metacognitive knowledge and cognitive activity have proven weaker than originally expected (Cavanaugh & Perlmutter, 1982; Schneider 1985; Schneider & Pressley, 1989). This has cast doubt on whether explicit metacognitive knowledge in fact plays a central role in children's strategy choices.

Consider an empirical study of the role of metacognitive knowledge in children's arithmetic. The implicit causal pathway to strategy choices suggested by metacognitive models is:

Problem difficulty → Metacognitive judgments of problem difficulty → Strategy choices

To test whether children choose arithmetic strategies in this manner, Siegler and Shrager (1984) obtained measures of each of the three constructs. Problem difficulty was assessed in terms of children's percent correct on each of 25 simple addition problems. Metacognitive judgments of problem difficulty were obtained by asking the same children whether each problem was very hard (2 points), kind of hard (1 point), or easy (0 points). Strategy use was assessed by trial-by-trial analyses of videotapes of each child solving each addition problem.

The results indicated some relation between the children's metacognitive judgments and the other two measures. Actual difficulty of each problem correlated $r = .47$ with children's judgments of the difficulty of the problem. Judgments of the difficulty of each problem correlated $r = .51$ with percentage of trials on which children used backup strategies on the problem. Both of these correlations were significant. However, they were not nearly strong enough to account for the very strong correlation ($r = .91$) between actual difficulty of each problem and strategy choices on the problem. Thus, young children's metacognitive knowledge might contribute to their extremely adaptive strategy choices, but could not account for them. This perspective motivated development of a series of models that demonstrated how highly adaptive strategy choices could arise out of implicit strategy choice mechanisms (Siegler, 1987b, 1988b; Siegler & Shrager, 1984). The most advanced of these is ASCM, a model described more fully in Siegler and Shipley (1995). The particulars of the model concern development of single-digit addition skills between ages 4 and young adulthood, but its basic structure is intended to model strategy choices more generally.

The Model's Basic Structure

Figure 4.1 illustrates ASCM's overall organization. Strategies operate on problems to generate answers. The solution process yields information not only about the answer to the particular problem (e.g., 3 + 5), but also about the time required to solve the problem using that strategy and the accuracy of the strategy in answering the problem. This information is used to modify the database regarding the strategy, the problem, and their interaction.

The Database. The type of information that gets entered into the database is illustrated in Fig. 4.2. Through their experience solving problems, children gain knowledge of both strategies and problems. Knowledge of each strategy can be divided into knowledge based on actual data and knowledge based on projections (inferences) from that data.

The actual database includes *global data*—that is, data about each strategy's past speed and accuracy aggregated over all problems that the system

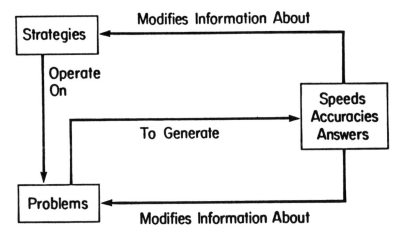

FIG. 4.1. An overview of the organization of ASCM.

Organization of database

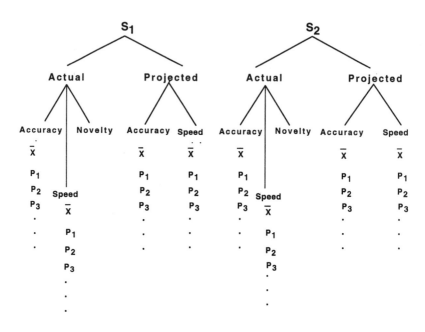

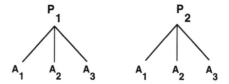

FIG. 4.2. The organization of ASCM's database in which information about past performance is linked to the strategy that produced the performance and the problem on which the performance occurred.

has encountered; *featural data*—that is, data on the strategy's speed and accuracy on all problems that it has encountered that have a particular feature (e.g., tie problems such as $4 + 4$ or $5 + 5$); *problem-specific data*—that is, data on the strategy's speed and accuracy on each particular problem; and *novelty data*—that is, data on the newness of the strategy.

The roles of the first three types of information should be easy to comprehend, but that of the novelty data may require some explanation.

Inclusion of the novelty data was motivated by an attempt to answer the question: How do new strategies ever come to be used in situations in which existing strategies work well? In the context of young children's addition, if a child can consistently solve a problem by using the sum strategy, why would the child ever try the min strategy on the problem? ASCM deals with this issue by assigning novelty points to newly discovered strategies. These novelty points temporarily add to the strength of new strategies, and thus allow the new strategies to be tried even when they have little or no track record.

With each use of a new strategy, some of its novelty strength is lost, but information about its speed and accuracy is gained. This leads to the strategy's probability of use increasingly being determined by the database on its effectiveness. The idea of novelty being a kind of strength was suggested by the observation that people (especially children) are often interested in exercising newly acquired cognitive capabilities (Piaget, 1970) and by the realization that without a track record, a newly acquired strategy might never be chosen, especially if reasonably effective alternatives were available.

Whenever ASCM is presented a problem, it uses these speed, accuracy, and novelty data to project how well each strategy is likely to do in solving the problem. If a strategy has never been used on a particular problem, ASCM's projections are based solely on global and featural data. If the strategy has never been used on the particular problem or on any problem with that feature, only global data are used to derive the projection.

The Model's Operation. ASCM is implemented as a running computer simulation. Its working can be summarized as follows:

1. At the beginning of its run, ASCM knows only the two addition strategies that are common among 4-year-olds—retrieval and the sum strategy—and basic procedures for choosing strategies, collecting data on the outcomes they generate, and projecting their future usefulness. These latter competencies are hypothesized to be basic properties of the human information processing system and to be present from birth.

2. During the learning phase, the simulation is repeatedly presented the 81 basic addition facts formed by all possible combinations of addend values 1–9 inclusive. The problems are presented equally often. In the absence of data on presentation rates over the large age range being modeled, this seemed the most conservative assumption.

3. After a number of exposures to each problem (60 trials/problem in the simulation runs reported here), the min strategy is added to those initially available. This is done to correspond to the time, usually sometime during first grade, when children add the min strategy to their repertoire. The process of strategy discovery is not yet modeled.

4. Strategy choices are based on the projected strength of each strategy. Projected strength is a function of the strategy's past speed and accuracy on problems as a whole, on problems with features in common with the current one, and on the particular problem being solved. For new strategies, the strategy's novelty boosts its strength beyond what its past performance alone would justify.

5. A logistic equation weights these sources of data according to the amount of information they reflect. When a strategy has rarely been used on a particular problem, global and featural data are weighted most heavily. As more information becomes available about how well the strategy works on the problem, problem-specific information receives increasing weight, eventually exercising the largest influence. The reasoning is that data derived from a few uses of a strategy are inherently noisy, but that problem-specific information based on a substantial data base ultimately is the best predictor of a strategy's future effectiveness on that problem. A similar logistic equation is used to weight data according to how recently they were generated. The reasoning underlying this decision was similar: Recent performance on a problem is given greater weight because it is likely to better predict future performance on the problem.

6. Each time a problem is presented, these weighted sources of information provide the input to a stepwise regression equation, which computes the projected strength of each strategy on the problem.

7. Probability of choosing a particular strategy is proportional to that strategy's projected strength relative to that of all strategies combined. The simulation attempts to execute whichever strategy is chosen.

8. If retrieval is chosen, three variables determine whether it can be executed to completion: the confidence criterion, the search length, and the associative strength of the retrieved answer. The confidence criterion is a threshold indicating how sure the child must be to state an answer. The search length indicates the number of efforts the child will make before ending attempts at retrieval. Both the confidence criterion and the search length vary randomly from trial to trial—they are associated neither with the strategy nor with the problem.

The associative strength of each answer, incorrect as well as correct, reflects the frequency with which that answer has been generated in the past (which in turn is a function of the frequency with which the problem has been presented, the probability of generation of each answer in the past, and interference from related problems; see Siegler and Shrager, 1984, for a detailed account of how this retrieval mechanism operates). The probability of each answer being retrieved is proportional to its associative strength relative to the associative strengths of all of the answers. If the associative strength of the retrieved answer exceeds the confidence criterion, that answer is stated; if not, but the search length has not been reached, retrieval is attempted again.

9. If retrieval does not yield a statable answer in the allotted number of searches, the model returns to the strategy choice phase and chooses among the backup strategies. The process is the same as at the beginning of the trial, except that retrieval is excluded from consideration (because it has already been tried). Thus, the probability of a given backup strategy being chosen at this point reflects its projected strength relative to that of all backup strategies.

10. Any strategy can generate either a correct answer or an error. Probabilities of errors using the sum and min strategies are proportional to the number of counts required to execute the strategy on that problem. The errors arise through double counting or skipping an object in the representation of the problem. Each count entails a probability of error; thus, the greater the number of counts, the more likely that an error will be made. On retrieval trials, errors arise through an incorrect answer being retrieved and having sufficient associative strength to be stated.

11. Solution times on backup strategy trials are proportional to a constant multiplied by the number of counts that are executed. The constant is smaller for the sum than for the min strategy, because children take less time per count in counting from one than in counting from other numbers (Siegler, 1987a). Solution times on retrieval trials reflect a constant multiplied by the number of searches prior to locating a statable answer. This constant is much smaller than those used with the backup strategies, reflecting the fact that retrieval is much faster than the sum or min strategies.

12. Each time an answer is advanced, ASCM increases the association between that answer and the problem and adds information regarding the speed and accuracy with which the answer was generated to the database for the strategy.

13. Each execution of a backup strategy also brings an increase in the strategy's speed and a decrease in its probability of generating an error. Thus, strategy execution improves with practice.

The Model's Performance

The tests of ASCM's performance involved a *learning phase* of a given length and a *test phase* that indicated the performance generated by the simulation after that amount of experience. During the learning phase, performance on each trial altered the data base regarding strategies, problems, and answers. The analogy was to experience that children would have had prior to entering the experimental situation. During the test phase, in contrast,

the database remained constant. The analogy was to children's performance in the experimental situation, after their having had a given amount
of preexperimental experience.

ASCM can be understood in terms of its treatment of the five basic
phenomena described earlier: variability, choice, change, generalization,
and individual differences.

Variability. ASCM uses diverse strategies both within and between problems. It tends to use strategies most often on the problems where they
work best, but strategies that work less well also are sometimes used.

Adaptive Strategy Choices. ASCM generates strong correlations (r's >
.90) between problem difficulty and frequency of backup strategy use on
the problem. This is true both when problem difficulty is measured by
percent errors on each problem and when problem difficulty is measured
by mean solution time on the problem. The model's pattern of choices
also is much like those of children. Siegler and Shipley (1995) correlated
ASCM's choices with those of 120 children who were finishing first grade.
After 750 trials/problem, the simulation's percent use of backup strategies
on each problem correlated $r = .93$ with that of the children. The best
predictors of its performance, size of the smaller addend and differences
between its addends, also were the same as those of the children.

Change. Perhaps the single most essential property of a simulation of
acquisition of arithmetic knowledge is that it progress from the relatively
inaccurate performance characteristic of children just beginning to add
to the virtually perfect performance that characterizes children by fifth or
sixth grade. ASCM met this test; after a learning phase of 60 trials/problem,
its performance was 31% correct, whereas after a learning phase of 1,250
trials/problem, its performance was 99% correct.

As shown in Fig. 4.3, ASCM's changes in frequency of use of the three
strategies also paralleled children's. At first, the simulation used only the
sum strategy and retrieval (the only strategies it knew), with the sum strategy
being employed on the large majority of trials. After the min strategy was
added, it became the most frequently used strategy, with the sum strategy
and retrieval also being used on substantial numbers of trials. This corresponds to children's performance at around first grade. Beyond this point,
use of both the sum and the min strategies decreased, and retrieval became
increasingly dominant. After a learning phase of 1,250 trials/problem,
retrieval was used on 95% of trials.

A third key type of progress involved decreases in solution times. The
overall decrease in times was produced by two factors: shifts from the
slower backup strategies to the faster retrieval approach, and faster execu-

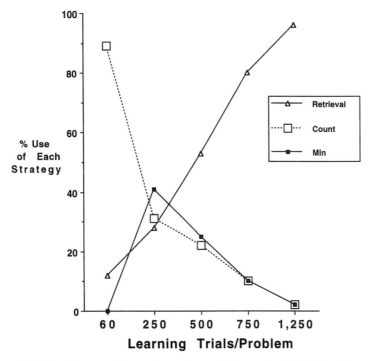

FIG. 4.3. Changes with experience in percent use of sum strategy, min strategy, and retrieval.

tion of each strategy. More interestingly, it went through the same sequence of variables that best predicted mean solution times. With short learning phases, its mean solution time on each of the 81 problems, like those of children, were best predicted by the sum of the addends on that problem (because the sum strategy was used most often). With longer learning phases, its mean time on each problem, again like that of children, was best predicted by the difference between the addends and the size of the smaller addend on the problem (because the min strategy was used most often). With still longer learning phases, its mean time on each problem, again like that of children, was best predicted by the product of the addends (a predictor believed to reflect use of retrieval; see Geary, 1994).

Finally, parallel to the results of Lemaire and Siegler (1995), the adaptiveness of ASCM's choices increased over trials until ceiling effects on accuracy and floor effects on percent use of backup strategies began to reduce the correlations at the end of its run. In particular, the correlations between percent of backup strategy use on each problem and percent errors steadily increased with increasing experience solving the problems. The correlations between percent backup strategy use on each problem and mean solution time on the problem showed similar increases with practice.

Generalization. As noted earlier, a key requirement for a realistic model of arithmetic is that it be able to generalize its knowledge of strategies to new problems. To test ASCM's ability to generalize, Siegler and Shipley (1995) presented it with 50 learning-phase exposures to each of 10 single-digit problems and then, during the test phase, examined its strategy choices on the other 71 problems. The procedure was repeated with 500 learning-phase trials/problem for each of the 10 problems, to see if generalization improved with experience. We were particularly interested in whether ASCM would choose the min strategy most often on problems where it was easiest to execute (i.e., where it could be executed with the fewest counts), where its advantage in reduced counting over the sum strategy was greatest, or both. For example, we wanted to know whether it would choose the min strategy especially often on $9 + 1$, a problem that has both of these properties.

ASCM showed exactly this pattern of generalization. On the 71 problems that had not been presented in the learning phase, the best predictor of percentage of trials on which the min strategy was used was the difference between the addends. The differentiation between problems on which the min strategy was more and less helpful increased with learning; differences between the addends was a better predictor of amount of generalization of the min strategy after a learning phase of 500 trials/problem than after one of 50 trials/problem. This made sense, because the model was obtaining increasingly valid data about each strategy's effectiveness on different problems.

Individual Differences. As noted earlier, Siegler (1988b) found substantial individual differences in children's approaches to addition, subtraction, and word identification tasks. The children could be classified into three distinct groups: the good students, the not-so-good students, and the perfectionists. As the names suggest, the good students were both more accurate and more likely to retrieve answers than the not-so-good students. The perfectionists were as accurate as the good students, but used retrieval even less often than the not-so-good students.

ASCM suggested a simple means through which the three individual difference groups could arise: parametric variation in peakedness of the distributions of associations and in confidence criteria. *Peakedness* refers to the degree to which the associative strength of answers to a problem is concentrated in a single answer (ordinarily the correct one). The more peaked the distribution of associations, the more likely that the correct answer will be retrieved, and the more likely that its associative strength will exceed the confidence criterion, leading to statement of the answer. The confidence criterion is a kind of threshold; the higher it is, the greater the associative strength of the retrieved answer must be to exceed it, and therefore, the fewer retrieved answers will be stated.

This view suggests an interpretation of each group's pattern of performance. The good-student pattern would arise from a combination of peaked distributions of associations and a wide range of confidence criteria. This would lead to both high accuracy and frequent use of retrieval, because the highly peaked distributions would result in frequent retrieval of the correct answer, which would have enough associative strength to exceed most confidence criteria and therefore be stated. The not-so-good-student pattern would arise from flat distributions of associations and low confidence criteria. This would generate inaccurate performance and medium amounts of retrieval, because incorrect answers would often be retrieved and would sometimes have sufficient associative strength to exceed the low confidence criteria and be stated. The perfectionist pattern would arise from peaked distributions and very high confidence criteria. This would lead to accurate performance but to low amounts of retrieval, because only the most peaked distributions would have correct answers with enough associative strength to exceed the very high confidence criteria.

To test this interpretation, Siegler and Shipley (1995) created three variants of the simulation. They differed only in their values of the two parameters hypothesized to underlie the individual differences: probability of correct execution of backup strategies (which largely determines the peakedness of distributions that are formed) and range of confidence criteria. The simulation of the not-so-good students' performance executed backup strategies less accurately than did the simulations of the perfectionists' and good students' performance, which were identical to each other in accuracy of execution of these strategies. The confidence criteria of the not-so-good students were consistently low (.10–.50), those of the perfectionists consistently high (.50–.90), and those of the good students included both low and high values (.10–.90). Other than these two parameter values, the simulations of the three groups were identical.

The variations in these two parametric values were sufficient to account for the observed pattern of individual differences. ASCM's simulation of the not-so-good students produced lower percentages correct than its simulations of the good students and perfectionists, which did not differ. Also as with children, ASCM's "good student" simulation produced the greatest amount of retrieval, its "not-so-good student" simulation the next most, and its "perfectionist" simulation the least. The simulations thus illustrated how qualitatively different patterns of performance can arise through parametric variations within the same basic processing system.

Implications

Within ASCM, the capacity to generate highly adaptive strategy choices is viewed as a basic part of human cognition. All mechanisms within it are believed to be present from extremely early in development and to remain present throughout the life span. This view implies that the types of adaptive strategy choices described earlier also should be present throughout the life span. In the next two sections, we describe data that share striking parallels with children's addition: variable strategy use, adaptive strategy choice, gradual change, generalization beyond the particular problems that have been encountered, and individual differences in style as well as competence. The first section focuses on the strategy choices of infants, the second on the strategy choices of old people.

HOW INFANTS SELECT STRATEGIES FOR ASCENDING AND DESCENDING SLOPES

Infants' first strategies are geared toward homely, everyday problems—resisting gravity, reaching and grasping, exploring objects, and locomoting independently around the environment. Traditionally, researchers described the development of motor skills as a progression of stages, in which infants discarded less mature strategies for more mature ones at each stage (e.g., Gesell & Thompson, 1938; McGraw, 1945). For example, when a small sugar pellet was placed in front of infants of varying ages, the youngest infants were reported to rake at it with their hands, older babies to scoop it into their hands, and still older ones to use a pincer grip to grasp it between thumb and forefinger. Younger infants were reported to begin crawling by pushing backward, older babies to inch forward on their bellies, even older infants to crawl on hands and knees, and still older ones to crawl on hands and feet.

More recently, researchers have begun to analyze infants' strategies in greater detail (e.g., Adolph, Eppler, & Gibson, 1993b; Gibson, 1988; Thelen, 1995). They have found greater variability in infants' repertoires at a single age or developmental level than previously indicated (e.g., Goldfield, 1994). For example, infants often reach unimanually on one trial and bimanually on the next for the same size toy (Corbetta & Thelen, in press). Babies often use multiple patterns of interlimb coordination to crawl a few feet along a flat path, even demonstrating variability from cycle to cycle (Veriejken et al., 1995). Such observations of variability raise the question of whether young infants select strategies adaptively to cope with practical motor problems.

Investigators working within a very different functional framework—the ecological approach (J. J. Gibson, 1979)—have found that older children and adults precisely match their action strategies to the changing exigencies of the physical environment. For example, adults and school children switch from walking on two feet to climbing on all fours to ascend stairs with risers higher than a constant proportion of their leg lengths (Mark, 1987; Pufall & Dunbar, 1992; Warren, 1984). Adults shift from walking head on to turning their bodies sideways to pass through apertures narrower than a constant proportion of their shoulder widths (Warren & Whang, 1987). Preschoolers adjust their speed and step length to cope with walking over balance beams of various widths and heights (Adolph, Ruff, Cappazolli, & Kim, 1994). To examine whether very young infants also select locomotor strategies adaptively, Adolph and colleagues challenged babies with a novel locomotor task—going up and down steep and shallow slopes (Adolph, 1995; Adolph, Eppler, & Gibson, 1993a).

The Slope Task

Slopes are an ideal venue for studying infants' strategy choices for two reasons. First, slopes are novel, allowing firsthand observation of how infants learn to cope with them. Most babies have few if any opportunities to learn about slanted surfaces in everyday situations. Parents typically limit children's exposure to ascent and descent throughout their first year of life by gating household stairs and closely monitoring their babies after the babies discover how to clamber on and off furniture. Second, because ability to locomote successfully on slopes depends on their steepness and on whether the goal is to go up or down, the task allows straightforward measurement of the degree of adaptiveness of the strategy choices. The role of steepness is obvious, but the effects of direction of movement may require some explanation. Biomechanically, going uphill is easier than going down, because infants can support their weight on a fully extended limb, and their hands are in a good position to stop a fall. Crawling and walking downhill require infants to support body weight and maintain balance on a bent arm or leg as the other limb swings forward, necessitating more strength and control as infants resist the pull of gravity. Both crawling and walking downhill place infants' hands in an awkward position to break a fall, thus adding to the difficulty of controlling the movement (Adolph, 1995; Adolph et al., 1993a).

A Study of Infants' Locomotor Strategy Choices. Adolph (1995) examined locomotor strategy choices in 14-month-old walking infants. Toddlers had different amounts of locomotor experience (ranging from 10 to 137 days) and skill, but all could walk at least 10 steps independently. The basic plan was to compare infants' strategy choices on safe slopes, where walking was possible, with their strategy choices on risky (i.e., steep) slopes, where they needed to use an alternative method of locomotion to avoid falling.

Materials and Procedure. Infants were tested on a large, carpeted walkway with a slope that could be set at angles ranging from 0° to 36° in 2° increments. The shallowest hills were safe for all babies; the steeper hills were increasingly risky. Each trial began with babies perched upright on the starting platform, facing the slope from their typical vantage point.

Parents stood at the far end of the walkway urging their babies to come up or down, offering Cheerios and attractive toys as enticements. An experimenter followed alongside the infants to ensure their safety.

In each test session, the experimenter used a psychophysical staircase procedure to identify the boundary between safe and risky slopes (described in Adolph, 1995). Slope boundaries were the steepest hills on which infants could walk up or down. These slope boundaries provided an index of the infants' physical abilities, as well as a way to compare strategy choices across infants relative to each baby's current level of walking skill.

The experimenter coded each trial online as *success* (walked safely), *failure* (tried to walk but fell), or *refusal* (slid down, climbed up, or avoided going). For the purpose of estimating slope boundaries, failures and refusals were treated as equivalent, unsuccessful outcomes. Success on a trial led to presentation of a steeper slope on the next trial; failure or refusal led to presentation of a shallower slope. The process continued until the experimenter identified a slope boundary according to a 67% criterion (the steepest hill on which the infant walked successfully on at least ⅔ of trials and failed or refused on at least ⅔ of trials at the next 2° increment and all steeper hills). To maintain infants' interest, easy baseline slopes (0° to 6°) were interspersed with the more challenging ones.

There was a wide range in infants' abilities. Some toddlers could manage only very shallow hills; others could walk over terrifically steep ones. Infants who were more proficient walking on flat ground (indexed by the length and width of their steps) and who had more days of walking experience were also more skillful walking up and down slopes, supporting the reliability of estimates of slope boundaries. As in earlier research (Adolph et al., 1993a), infants had steeper boundaries walking uphill than downhill (Fig. 4.4). Together, these results mean that a safe hill for a proficient walker is risky for a less skilled child and that hills safe for ascent are risky when going down.

The "GO Ratio." The critical question was whether infants' adapted their strategy choices to their current walking prowess on slopes. Infants' typical method of locomotion for travel over flat ground (walking) could be viewed as a sort of backup or default strategy. Presumably, if the surface appeared tractable, infants should walk up or down the hill, without shifting from the position in which the experimenter placed them on the starting platform. On the other hand, if infants decided the slope was risky, they should resort to a more effortful backup strategy: going up or down on all fours; sliding down head first, prone like Superman; sliding down while sitting on their bottoms; or scooting down on their bellies, feet first. A final backup strategy was to avoid going, which presumably indicated that they considered the slope too steep for either their typical method or available alternatives.

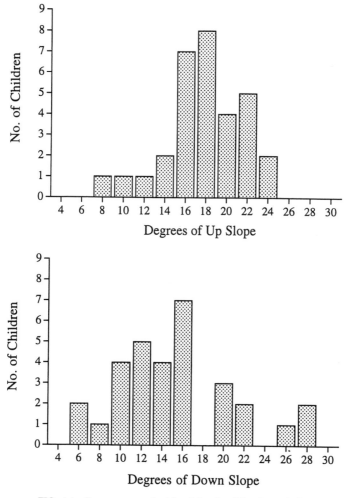

FIG. 4.4. Fourteen-month-old toddlers' walking boundaries.

The "GO ratio" provided an index of the adaptiveness of infants' strategy choices. It was defined as the percentage of trials on which infants attempted to walk over the slopes at various increments steeper and shallower than the slope boundary: (successes + failures)/(successes + failures + refusals). Success is rare on hills steeper than infants' slope boundaries, by definition; therefore, GO ratios on risky hills primarily reflect the ratio of failures to refusals. Likewise, failures are by definition rare on hills shallower than infants' slope boundaries, so that GO ratios on safe hills primarily reflect the ratio of successes to refusals.

At the slope boundary, the GO ratio is ≥ .67, by definition. However, the ratio can vary freely from 0 to 1 on slopes shallower and steeper than the boundary. Maximally adaptive strategy choices would imply two patterns: (a) a high GO ratio on safe hills—that is, ones shallower than the slope boundary, where probability of success is high; and (b) a low GO ratio on risky hills—that is, ones steeper than the slope boundary, where probability of falling is relatively high. Infants might err on the side of caution with a low ratio on perfectly safe slopes, or they might err on the side of boldness with a high ratio on hills too steep for them to traverse safely by walking.

Variability

On uphill trials, babies had few options—walking, crawling up on all fours, or avoiding. Variability in strategy choice for ascent was limited to only two of the three options. Infants always walked up safe hills. On risky hills, all 31 babies attempted their typical walking strategy on some trials, and most infants (24) also tried to climb up on hands and knees. Toddlers never refused to go at all on uphill trials. Similarly, in an earlier experiment with 14-month-old walkers tested on 10°, 20°, 30°, and 40° slopes, nearly all toddlers walked up shallower slopes, most crawled up steeper ones, and only 2 babies avoided ascent (Adolph et al., 1993a). Eight- to 9-month-old crawling infants pitted against the same four upward slopes showed similar compression of variability. They all attempted upward slopes on hands and knees and only 3 of 28 crawlers avoided ascent.

Babies had several options for descending slopes: walking, crawling, sliding prone, sitting, backing, or avoiding. Strategic variability was much greater on downhill trials, particularly downhill trials on risky slopes. Toddlers used a mean of 1.03 strategies for descending safe hills versus a mean of 2.23 strategies for descending risky hills. On safe hills, 30 toddlers used solely their typical walking strategy and only 1 baby walked and also crawled. Although any single backup strategy would have been sufficient to descend on risky hills, many infants used multiple methods. On risky hills, 1 infant used 3 backup strategies, 10 toddlers used 2 backup strategies, and 14 babies used only 1 backup strategy (2 reckless infants never used backup strategies and instead attempted to walk down every slope). Sliding in a sitting position and backing down feet first were used most often, followed by crawling, sliding prone and refusing to go at all. Variability was even more impressive in Adolph et al.'s (1993a) study where toddlers had only 4 descending trials in total, one trial each at 10°, 20°, 30°, and 40°. Eleven toddlers used 2 backup strategies, 10 used only 1 backup method and 2 intransigent infants attempted to walk down every hill. Eighteen toddlers used a backup sliding strategy rather than avoidance on at least one of the four descent trials. Variability was sharply reduced in the sample of 8.5-month-old crawling infants. Although every infant demonstrated the physical ability to execute all of the sliding positions, the only backup strategy used by crawlers was avoidance (14 Ss). As predicted by ASCM, there were changes in frequency of strategy use with age and locomotor experience, but no stage-like transitions from one strategy to another.

Adaptive Strategy Choices

The most stringent test of the adaptiveness of strategy choices was the difference between GO ratios on safe and risky hills. The ideal pattern of judgments would be high GO ratios on safe hills, where probability of successful walking was high, and low GO ratios on risky hills, where probability of successful walking was low. In addition, to the degree that choices were adaptive, the difference between GO ratios on safe and risky hills was expected to be higher on descent trials. On such trials, falling was relatively aversive, and the experimenter had to rescue infants to prevent injury. In contrast, on ascent trials, failures were relatively inconsequential, because the babies could catch themselves if they started to fall.

Consistent with this perspective, GO ratios were high on safe slopes and decreased steadily on risky hills, from .99 to .23 for uphill and from .94 to .11 for downhill (see top panel of Fig. 4.5). At each slope increment steeper than toddlers' slope boundaries, GO ratios were nearly twice as high on ascent trials as on descent ones. Toddlers' strategy choices were remarkably consistent. If they refused to walk over a particular slope increment, they also slid or avoided all steeper increments.

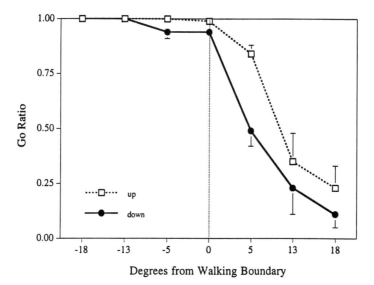

FIG. 4.5. GO ratios adapted to slopes steeper and shallower than slope boundary. GO ratios are proportion of trials where infants attempted to walk. Slope boundaries are steepest hills on which infants can walk without falling on at least ⅔ of trials.

On ascent trials, toddlers' strategy choices (walking versus climbing on all fours) were based on a brief glance before starting up. As in earlier research (Adolph et al., 1993a), infants hurled themselves forward onto upward slopes, trial after trial, with virtually no hesitation or prior haptic exploration. The story was very different on descent trials. As in the previous study, infants were more wary about going down. Exploratory activity on the starting platform precisely mirrored infants' perceptual judgments. Infants hesitated, looked, touched, and tested alternative sliding positions before starting down hills on which they used backup strategies (see bottom panel of Fig. 4.5). The evidence suggests that adaptive strategy choice is an essential and pervasive aspect of learning perceptual-motor skills (e.g., Adolph et al., 1993b; Gibson, 1979), as well as skills traditionally viewed as cognitive.

Change

Results of Adolph and colleagues' studies (Adolph, 1995; Adolph et al., 1993a) indicated the endpoints of an interesting developmental progression. Fourteen-month-old walking infants in these studies carefully adapted their locomotor strategies to the slant of steep and shallow slopes. They walked down safe hills within the limits of their physical abilities and used backup strategies on risky hills steeper than their walking abilities. In contrast, the strategy choices of younger crawling infants, 8.5-month-olds, were indiscriminate. More than half of the crawlers plunged headlong down every hill, falling on consecutive trials at 10°, 20°, 30°, and 40°, requiring rescue by the experimenter.

A recent longitudinal study tracking infants from their very first weeks of crawling until months after they began walking (Adolph, 1993) indicates that the increase in adaptive strategy choices from crawling to walking was not due to a stage-like transition resulting from maturation (the walkers in both studies were 6 months older than the crawlers), or the increased balance requirements of standing on two feet after walking onset (walking is more tipsy than crawling). Instead, change was due to everyday experience traveling around in infants typical method of locomotion. When infants first began crawling, regardless of age, they behaved like the crawlers in Adolph et al.'s (1993a) study. Most attempted risky hills and fell headlong. Strategy choices became increasingly adaptive over weeks of crawling until, by their last week of crawling, judgments were nearly perfect. This means that infants made sound and adaptive judgments for coping with slopes, despite continuous change in their crawling abilities on slopes. Surprisingly, there was no transfer from crawling to walking. In their first week of walking, infants attempted to walk down hills far beyond their capabilities. Again, errors decreased steadily as infants gained experience with that type of movement and posture. By 14 months of age, most infants

had several weeks of walking experience and their GO ratios were comparable to the infants in the Adolph (1995) study.

ASCM predicts that when people have little or no local and featural
information, their strategy choices are made primarily on the basis of
global information about each strategy. Consistent with this prediction,
new crawlers and walkers were at first biased toward their typical method
of locomotion but with weeks of experience, they became less biased in
this direction. Early in their experience, they relied heavily on their default
locomotor strategy (crawling or walking) on all trials, regardless of whether
they were ascending or descending and regardless of the slope of the hill.
Over weeks of crawling and walking, infants increasingly often used a
backup strategy for coping with the risky downhill slopes, while continuing
to rely on their usual locomotor approach on hills where it was effective.

Generalization

Specific experiences with descent were not related to toddlers' GO ratios
or use of backup strategies (Adolph, 1995). There were no differences
between infants encountering slopes for the first time and babies who had
experience going down playground slides or household stairs. Ten children
had gone down a small playground slide independently, but their GO
ratios were distributed in the same patterns as children without prior experience descending steep slopes. Fourteen toddlers had gone down a
short flight of stairs independently using the backing strategy; only 10 of
these infants used the backing strategy to descend slopes, and 6 infants
without experience backing down stairs used this strategy spontaneously
to cope with slopes. Three children had experienced falls resulting in
serious injuries while attempting to go down stairs, but they were no more
cautious on slopes than children who had never experienced a serious fall.
Similarly, of the 12 toddlers reported to back down stairs in Adolph et
al.'s (1993a) study, only 8 backed down slopes. Of the 11 toddlers who
had never backed down stairs, 4 babies used this strategy for the first time
on slopes.

Even more striking evidence of generalization from everyday locomotor
experience to strategy choice in the novel slope task was provided by
Adolph's (1993) recent longitudinal study. Adolph included a control
group to assess effects of practice in the slope task. Slope boundaries and
GO ratios were similar between control babies tested only three times on
slopes and experimental infants tested every three weeks on slopes. Both
groups improved, but the rates of improvement and the absolute levels of
performance were similar. The data suggest that learning resulted from
everyday locomotor experience in infants' homes and play yards, rather
than from experience in the experimental situation.

Individual Differences

Toddlers' behavior in the slope task revealed consistent individual differences, suggesting differences in their confidence criteria as well as differences in their ability to discriminate safe from risky hills (Fig. 4.6). Seventeen of the 31 14-month-olds in Adolph (1995) walked down safe hills and slid down nearly all risky ones (Group A). Their GO ratios averaged .90 at the slope boundary, .10 on slightly steeper hills (2–8 degrees beyond the boundary), and 0 on all steeper slopes. Among these 17 children, 7 showed perfect step functions, walking on all hills with less than a certain slope, using backup strategies on all steeper ones. These children's data indicate that they underestimated their abilities; they used backup strategies even on hills that they might have been able to traverse successfully using their usual locomotor approach. Like the "perfectionists" solving addition problems, they may have set extremely high confidence criteria for walking down the hill. The other 10 babies in the subgroup of 17 behaved like Siegler's (1988b) "good students." Their thresholds for use of a default strategy were high enough to thwart serious errors, but low enough that they pushed their outer window of possibilities for learning.

Two of the 31 children in the cross-sectional sample exhibited slightly more lenient response criteria (Group B). Their GO ratios were high until they encountered slopes of intermediate difficulty (10–16 degrees steeper than their boundaries), where ratios decreased sharply and remained at 0. Eight additional children seemed to have an extremely lenient response criteria (Group C). Their GO ratios were near 1.0 until they encountered impossibly steep hills (at least 18 degrees steeper than boundary). Together these 10 babies resembled the "not-so-good students" described in Siegler (1988b), in that they seemed to set very low confidence criteria and therefore to use their usual approach even where it was unlikely to succeed.

The remaining four infants in this cross-sectional sample responded indiscriminately (Group D). Their GO ratios never decreased below .50 on any slope. Like the two babies in the Adolph et al. (1993a) sample, they behaved as though they had no fear of hills. Their recklessness may reflect confidence that the experimenter would rescue them (they were indeed caught on every risky trial!), or it may reflect more serious difficulties in perceptual-motor learning. In summary, it does not take long for individual differences in strategy choices to become apparent; they can be seen even around children's first birthdays.

STRATEGY CHOICES OF YOUNG AND OLD ADULTS

In many situations, the strategies used by older adults differ considerably from those used by younger ones. This has been documented in such varied domains as memory strategies (Cimbalo & Brink, 1982), searching for

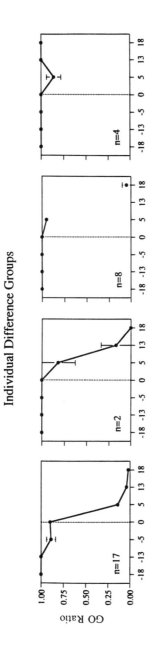

FIG. 4.6. Individual differences in infants' response criteria for downhill slopes.

locations on maps (Thomas, 1985), story recall (Adams, Labouvie-Vief, Hobart, & Dorosz, 1990), arithmetic (Geary & Wiley, 1991), question answering (Reder, Wible, & Martin, 1986), and chess playing (Charness, 1981).

Much less is known, however, about the adaptiveness of the choices that old people make. The only two studies of which we are aware (Geary, Frensch, & Wiley, 1993; Geary & Wiley, 1991) reported that old people's frequency of use of backup strategies in addition and subtraction vary significantly with characteristics of the problems, in particular with the sum of the addends and the size of the number being subtracted. In the case of addition, the magnitude of the correlation ($r = .80$) was comparable to those typically observed with children and younger adults; in the case of subtraction, the magnitude was much weaker ($r = .37$). Thus, it was unclear whether elderly adults choose strategies as adaptively as children and younger adults.

To compare as precisely as possible the adaptiveness of the strategy choices of younger and older adults, Siegler and Lemaire (in press) developed a new method for assessing adaptiveness. Past studies of strategy choices have measured adaptiveness of choices primarily by relating percent use of a given type of strategy (e.g., backup strategies) to problem difficulty, usually as measured by percent errors or mean solution time on each problem. Usually, these estimates of problem difficulty have been obtained from performance in choice conditions, in which subjects could use any strategy they chose. This method works well for most purposes, but can artifactually inflate or deflate the apparent adaptiveness of the choices. For example, if people are more accurate in using backup strategies than retrieval, the method will artifactually deflate the correlation obtained (because subjects will compensate for the differences in problem difficulty by using the more accurate backup strategies more often on more difficult problems).

The other method that sometimes has been used is to estimate problem difficulty solely from performance when only retrieval is allowed. This avoids the aforementioned confounding, but leads to problem difficulty being estimated solely by difficulty when retrieval is used. If problem difficulty differs when different strategies are used, then this procedure yields an incomplete picture of problem difficulty when multiple strategies are available.

Thinking about how ASCM works suggested a promising alternative approach to measuring the adaptiveness of strategy choices, the *choice/no-choice design*. Recall that within ASCM, predicted use of each strategy is a function of the strength of that strategy relative to that of alternative strategies. This implies that use of a given strategy should be a function of the difference between the strengths of the strategies. To obtain estimates of this difference requires determining how difficult each problem would be using each available strategy, and then testing how well their choices are predicted by the differences between or among the difficulties.

Siegler and Lemaire (in press) used this method in two experiments. In the *two-strategy experiment*, the choice being studied was whether to solve multiplication problems using a calculator or via mental arithmetic. Both college students and elderly adults made these choices. In the *three-strategy experiment*, the choice was whether to solve the problems via mental arithmetic, calculator, or pencil and paper. Only elderly subjects participated in this experiment.

The reason for comparing these particular age groups on these particular strategy choices was curiosity about whether the sociohistorical changes introduced by new technology influence the strategy choice process. For current college students, calculators have been widely available throughout the time they were learning multiplication. In contrast, for current elderly adults, calculators did not exist when they initially learned multiplication, and they continued to be rare for many years thereafter. A great many old people continue either never to use them or only to use them occasionally, preferring to solve problems either with no external aid or with pencil and paper. Contrasting the choices made by undergraduates and by old people, and contrasting the choices of old people who have had more or less experience with calculators, promised to shed light on how the choice process is influenced by such sociohistorical changes.

In both the two-strategy experiment and the three-strategy experiment, subjects first solved a set of problems using whichever strategy they wanted (*the choice condition*); then, in the *no-choice conditions*, they solved comparable sets of problems needing either to use mental multiplication (no other tools present), or needing to use a calculator (they had to punch the buttons and get the answer even if they could retrieve the answer), or, in the three-strategy experiment, needing to use pencil and paper (again they needed to write out the problem and get the answer even if they could retrieve it). This design eliminated the biases in estimates of problem difficulty introduced by nonrandom assignment of which strategies were used and which subjects used them on each problem. It also allowed a direct test of whether the difference in the strengths of the strategies was the best predictor of how often each approach was used, as predicted by ASCM.

The college students, all of whom participated in the two-strategy experiment, were undergraduates at Carnegie Mellon. The elderly subjects in the two-strategy experiment averaged 66 years (range = 61–73 years). They were recruited from a senior citizen's center. The elderly subjects in the three-strategy experiment averaged 75 years (range = 60–95), and were recruited from among the attendees of a different senior citizens' center. Members of both elderly groups had occupied a wide range of occupations when they worked, including hair dresser, mail clerk, music teacher, bookkeeper, cashier, food-service worker, statistician, secretary, and maintenance worker. Both the undergraduates and the two elderly samples were predominantly female (79% of the undergraduates; 87% and 97% of the two elderly samples).

In both procedures, subjects were presented four types of multiplication problems: N * 10 (e.g., 8 * 10), NN * 10 (e.g., 27 * 10), N * NN (e.g., 8 * 14), and NN * NN (e.g., 14 * 17). In the two-strategy experiment, a set of 72 problems was divided into three subsets of 24 problems each. The difficulty of problems was matched across the three sets, by equating mean product sizes as well as the types of problems within the sets. In the three-strategy experiment, comparable matching was done for a slightly different set of 72 problems divided into four subsets of 18 problems each. Presentation of the problem sets was counterbalanced in both experiments, so that each problem set appeared equally often in each condition.

Variable Strategy Use

As in previous studies, virtually all subjects, both younger and older, used multiple strategies. In the choice condition of the two-strategy experiment, 47 of 48 undergraduates and 59 of 60 elderly adults used both strategies. In the choice condition of the three-strategy experiment, 59 of 60 elderly adults also used at least 2 strategies, with 21 of 60 using all 3. Specifically, 1 subject only used mental arithmetic, 22 used mental arithmetic and the calculator, 16 used mental arithmetic and pencil and paper, and 21 used mental arithmetic, the calculator, and pencil and paper.

Adaptive Strategy Choice

Siegler and Lemaire (in press) examined three aspects of the adaptiveness of strategy choices, all of which pointed to similarly adaptive choices in younger and older adults.

Having a Choice Enhanced Speed and Accuracy. One test of the adaptiveness of choices involved examining whether being able to choose among alternative strategies yielded faster and more accurate performance than would have occurred if subjects had used the strategies in the same proportions but had assigned them randomly to problems. This test involved comparing speed and accuracy under no-choice and choice conditions. Each subject's speed and accuracy in the no-choice conditions was weighted by that subject's percent use of that strategy in the choice condition. Thus, for each subject's latency, the projected RT in the no-choice condition of the two-strategy experiment was (Mean RT in calculator-required condition * Percent use of calculator in choice condition) + (Mean RT in mental-arithmetic-required condition * Percent use of mental arithmetic in choice

TABLE 4.2
Mean Latencies (in Sec.) in Younger and Older Adults' Arithmetic

	10s Problems		No-10 Problems	
	Free Choice	Forced Choice[a]	Free Choice	Forced Choice[a]
	Two-Strategy Experiment			
Younger adults				
RTs	1.9	2.8	5.2	7.2
% errors	1	1	6	1.4
Older adults				
RTs	4.9	6.1	10.2	11.6
% errors	4	5	9	20
	Three-Strategy Experiment			
RTs	4	5.4	8.5	10.5
% errors	2	1	10	21

[a]Data in the forced-choice columns are a weighted average of performance in the mental-arithmetic-required condition and calculator-required conditions in the two-strategy experiment and over them and the pencil-and-paper-required condition in the three-strategy experiment. The weighting variable is percent use of each strategy in the free-choice condition of each experiment.

condition). This comparison was performed both for all problems and separately for problems with and without 10 as a multiplicand.

As shown in Table 4.2, having a choice led to faster and more accurate performance than would have been projected solely from percent use of each strategy. Speed was greater for both problems that included 10 as a multiplicand and problems that did not. Accuracy was greater for problems that did not have 10 as a multiplicand; it was essentially perfect on problems with 10 as a multiplicand regardless of how it was computed. The pattern was identical for undergraduates and for elderly adults, and identical in both the two-strategy and the three-strategy experiment.

Differences Between Performance Yielded by Strategies Predicts Their Frequency of Use. ASCM predicts that the difference between the speeds and accuracies of alternative strategies should be a better predictor of their frequency of use than should any structural variable, such as the size of the product or the number of digits in the problem. To test this prediction, Siegler and Lemaire (in press) ran stepwise regression analyses of percent use of mental arithmetic on each problem. For the two-strategy experiment, the two predictor variables that would be expected to be especially predictive of percent use of each strategy were (a) difference between mean RT for each problem when it was presented in the mental-arithmetic-required and calculator-required conditions; (b) difference between mean percent errors for each problem when it was presented in the mental-arithmetic-required and calculator-required conditions. The structural predictors that were included in the regression analyses were the sizes of the first multiplicand, second multiplicand, product, whether the problem included 10 as a multiplicand, and the number of digits in the problem.

In the analysis of college student's performance, three factors independently contributed to the percentage of variance accounted for in percent use of mental arithmetic on each problem: (a) difference between mean RT in the mental-arithmetic-required and calculator-required conditions on the problem ($R^2 = .72$); (b) whether 10 was a multiplicand (partial $R^2 = .14$); and (c) difference between mean percent errors in the mental-arithmetic-required and calculator-required condition on the problem (partial $R^2 = .01$). Overall, the three-term model explained 87% of the variance in frequency of use of mental arithmetic on each problem.

Similar results emerged in the two-strategy experiment with older adults. Three factors independently contributed to the percentage of variance accounted for in percent use of mental arithmetic on the problem: (a) difference between mean RT in the mental-arithmetic-required condition and the calculator-required condition on the problem ($R^2 = .61$); (b) whether one of the multiplicands was 10 (partial $R^2 = .18$); and (c) number of digits in the problem (partial $R^2 = .04$). Overall, the three-term model accounted for 83% of the variance. As with the undergraduates, most of the variance in the old people's frequency of use of mental arithmetic on the 72 problems was accounted for by the difference for each problem between performance yielded by the alternative strategies.

The analysis of the elderly people's percent use of mental arithmetic in the three-strategy experiment was slightly different, because here there were two alternatives to mental arithmetic. This led to Siegler and Lemaire including as a predictor not only the differences on each problem between speeds and accuracies generated by mental arithmetic and the calculator but also between those generated by mental arithmetic and pencil and paper. The same basic pattern of results emerged. Once again, the best predictor of percent use of mental arithmetic on each problem was a difference in performance between two strategies—in this case, the difference between percent errors on each problem generated using mental arithmetic and the calculator ($R^2 = .72$). Again problem characteristics added significant independent variance: number of digits (partial $R^2 = .07$) and whether 10 was a multiplicand (partial $R^2 = .06$). And once more, the three-term model accounted for a high percentage of total variance, in this case 85% of the variance in percent use of mental arithmetic on each of the 72 problems.

Thus, in accord with ASCM's predictions, the differences in speed and accuracy generated by the strategies on each problem was an excellent predictor of the frequency with which the strategies were chosen on that problem. It predicted well in absolute terms, accounting for between 61% and 72% of the variance in the younger and older adults' frequency of choices of the mental arithmetic strategy, and also predicted more accurately than any of the structural features of the problems. By eliminating selection artifacts from estimates of the speed and accuracy generated by each strategy on each problem, the choice/no-choice design demonstrated just how closely strategy choices are attuned to the relative performance yielded by different strategies.

Strategy Choices Were Almost Unbiased. The choice/no-choice design also allowed independent estimates of bias in the strategy choices. This estimate was provided by the intercept term of the regression equations of predictors of strategy use. Even if percent use of mental arithmetic were perfectly correlated with the difference between the time required to solve the problem via mental arithmetic or a calculator, subjects might not split their choices evenly on problems on which the two strategies took equally long to execute. They might instead split them evenly when the times favored one strategy or the other by several seconds, thus indicating a bias toward that strategy. For example, they might have a constant bias of 5 seconds for the calculator, but alter their percent choice of the calculator by a constant 10% for every 1 second deviation from this bias. Thus, they would use the calculator on 40% of problems on which mental arithmetic was 4 seconds faster, 50% on which it was 5 seconds faster, and 60% on which it was 6 seconds faster. This analysis raised the possibility that even though the choices of elderly adults were just as systematic as those of younger ones, and predicted by almost identical variables, their choices might be more biased. In particularly, given their limited experience with calculators, they might be more biased toward use of mental arithmetic.

In the two-strategy experiment, the intercept of both the undergraduates and the elderly adults differed significantly from 0, indicating that both groups of subjects were somewhat biased in their strategy choices. The bias in the two groups turned out to be in the same direction—in favor of mental arithmetic. It also proved to be almost identical in magnitude. The college students used each strategy on about 50% of trials when using the calculator yielded solutions about 1.5 sec faster than using mental arithmetic; the corresponding figure for older adults was 1.6 sec. Seen from a different perspective, on problems on which times were approximately equal (within 1 sec.) college students used mental arithmetic on 58% of trials, older adults on 59%. Thus, the biases of older and younger adults were no different.

Change

ASCM points to four main sources of strategic change: acquisition of new strategies, changing frequency of use of existing strategies, changing efficiency of execution of strategies, and changing adaptiveness of choices among strategies (Lemaire & Siegler, 1995). As described earlier, the present study did not examine discovery of new strategies, and both frequency of use of each strategy and degree of adaptiveness in the choices were highly similar for the younger and older adults. However, substantial changes with age were evident in efficiency of execution of the strategies.

To test changes in execution of each strategy, independent of differences in how often the strategies were used and which subjects used them, Siegler and Lemaire (in press) compared the speed and accuracy of younger and older adults in the no-choice condition of the two-strategy experiment.

Speed. Averaged across strategies and types of problems, younger adults were considerably faster than older adults (5.8 vs. 9.8 sec). They were faster both when they used mental arithmetic (7.3 vs. 11.1 sec) and when they used calculators (4.3 vs. 8.4 sec). The differences were greatest on the hardest problems (NN * NN) in the mental arithmetic condition. The undergraduates took an average of 13.3 sec to solve such problems, whereas the older adults required an average of 19.7 sec.

Accuracy of execution also was greater among the younger adults. The overall difference was 91% versus 86% correct. The difference was concentrated on the mental arithmetic problems (83% vs. 75% correct); both groups solved almost all problems correctly when they used the calculator. Somewhat surprisingly, differences in mental arithmetic accuracy were present on the NN * 10 problems (99% vs. 88% correct) as well as on the problems that did not include 10 as an addend. The fact that both speed and accuracy were greater among the younger adults indicated that the differences could not be attributed to speed–accuracy tradeoffs.

In summary, comparisons between younger and older adults revealed that (a) older adults were generally slower and less accurate than younger ones, but (b) the two groups used each strategy on comparable percentages of trials in the choice condition. This is consistent with several other studies of cognitive effects of aging, which have reported similar frequency of use of different strategies but less efficient execution of the strategies by older than by younger adults (e.g., Belmore, 1981; Cohen & Faulkner, 1983).

Individual Differences

In the three-strategy experiment, Siegler and Lemaire (in press) presented subjects with questionnaires concerning their past and present use of calculators and their attitudes toward the calculators, toward mental arithmetic, and toward solving problems via pencil and paper. Individual differences in these experiential and attitudinal variables were then related to individual differences in performance in the experimental situation.

As shown in Table 4.3, 33% of the elderly adults had no experience using calculators, 23% had occasional experience (less than once per month during both their working days and since), and the other 44% had more frequent experience. Degree of experience proved to be related to both how often and how efficiently subjects used the calculator. Percent use of the calculator increased from 19% for the elderly adults who never had used a calculator before the experiment to 30% among those who had used it more than once per month in either their work or current life. Even more striking were the changes with experience that occurred between choices of the calculator versus pencil and paper. Elderly adults who had never previously used a calculator used it on 40% of trials on which they used either a calculator or pencil and paper; those who had used it less than once per month chose it on 52% of trials on which they used one of the backup strategies, and those who had used it more than once per month chose it on 67% of trials on which they used one of the backup strategies.

CONCLUSIONS

As implied by ASCM, basic strategy choice phenomena seem to be present throughout the life span and in domains not usually thought of as cognitive, as well as ones that are. In particular, the experiments on infants' locomotion and older adults' multiplication indicated the same five phenomena as had previously been observed with children on standard cognitive tasks such as arithmetic, time telling, and memory strategies: cognitive variability, adaptive strategy choice, gradual change in strategy use, generalization of knowledge to new problems, and individual differences in style as well as expertise.

Cognitive variability was particularly evident in the infants' strategies for going down risky hills. Sometimes they tried to walk down, sometimes they tried to crawl down, sometimes they slid down on their bellies face first, sometimes they slid down feet first, sometimes they slid down on their bottoms, sometimes they refused to go down at all. Similarly, almost all older adults, like almost all younger adults, used both mental arithmetic and calculators when those were the options. When pencil and paper was also an option, almost all older adults used at least two of the three approaches and 35% used all three.

Adaptive strategy choices were similarly apparent in both infants and older adults. Infants varied their GO ratios with their walking boundaries.

TABLE 4.3

Individual Differences in Older Adults' Arithmetic as a Function of Prior Experience With Calculators (Three-Strategy Experiment)

	Percent Use (Free-Choice Condition)			Latencies (Forced-Choice Conditions)			Accuracy (Forced-Choice Conditions)		
	Mental Arithmetic (MA)	Calculator (CA)	Pencil-and-Paper (PP)	MA	CA	PP	MA	CA	PP
Use of calculator:									
None (N = 20)	52	19	29	10.7	9.9	9.4	29	3	7
< 1/month (N = 14)	44	29	27	11.1	7.6	7.5	26	1	8
> 1/month (N = 26)	55	30	15	8.5	6.9	6.7	23	1	8

They almost always would try their usual mode of locomotion on hills they could successfully traverse, but greatly decreased their reliance on this approach as the hills became increasingly difficult for them to navigate in that way. Older adults showed similarly adaptive strategy choices. The more that considerations of speed and accuracy favored use of a given strategy, the more often they relied on that strategy in the choice condition. These adaptive choices also led to their speed and accuracy being greater in the choice conditions than in the no-choice ones.

Gradual changes in strategy use and strategy choice were also apparent in both infants and elderly people. With age and locomotor experience, infants progressively decreased their GO ratios on risky slopes, although not on safe slopes. This allowed them to decrease their frequency of falling on slopes where that was a danger, whereas maintaining the ease of their usual approach when the danger of falling was minimal. Similarly, older adults with more calculator experience used calculators on a greater percentage of backup strategy trials than did adults with little or no such experience. Even the older adults with the greatest calculator experience, however, still relied on pencil and paper on one-third of backup strategy trials, indicating that their changeover to that approach was sufficiently gradual as to be incomplete after many years of use.

The infants showed generalization of locomotor experience in their strategy choices for descending down risky slopes. Even though both older and younger infants had little if any experience going down risky slopes, the older infants nonetheless progressively decreased their GO ratios on the risky slopes while maintaining them near ceiling level on slopes that were at or below their walking boundary. Similarly, the older adults generalized from their experience of how to choose between using mental arithmetic or pencil and paper to how to choose between using mental arithmetic or a calculator.

Finally, individual differences were present along stylistic as well as competence dimensions. Infants differed not just in their walking boundaries— a measure of competence—but also in their degree of recklessness. Some infants would resort to backup strategies even on slopes that were only slightly beyond their walking boundaries; others would attempt to walk down even slopes that were well beyond their abilities. Similarly, older adults who had never previously used a calculator differed not only in their skill at mental arithmetic—a measure of competence—but also in their willingness to try calculators. Some of them never used the calculator when they had the option of using pencil and paper; others, equally unfamiliar with calculators, used calculators more often than the familiar pencil-and-paper approach. Thus, these five phenomena—variable strategy use, adaptive choices among strategies, gradual change, generalization of knowledge to unfamiliar problems, and individual differences in style as well as competence—seem to be basic human characteristics present in infancy, childhood, young adulthood, and old age.

REFERENCES

Adams, C., Labouvie-Vief, G., Hobart, C. J., & Drosz, M. (1990). Adult age group differences in story recall style. *Journal of Gerontology: Psychological Sciences, 45,* 17–25.

Adolph, K. E. (1993). *Perceptual-motor development in infants' locomotion over slopes.* Unpublished doctoral dissertation, Emory University, Atlanta, GA.

Adolph, K. E. (1995). Psychophysical assessment of toddlers' ability to cope with slopes. *Journal of Experimental Psychology: Human Perception and Performance, 21,* 734–750.

Adolph, K. E., Eppler, M. A., & Gibson, E. J. (1993a). Crawling versus walking infants' perception of affordances for locomotion over sloping surfaces. *Child Development [Special section on developmental biodynamics], 64,* 1158–1174.

Adolph, K. E., Eppler, M. A., & Gibson, E. J. (1993b). Development of perception of affordances. In C. Rovee-Collier & L. P. Lipsett (Eds.), *Advances in infancy research* (Vol. 8, pp. 51–98). Norwood, NJ: Ablex.

Adolph, K. E., Ruff, H. A., Cappozoli, M. C., & Kim, D. R. (1994, November). *Preschoolers' strategies for allocating attention: Individual differences and task constraints.* Poster presented to the Psychonomic Society, St. Louis, MO.

Belmore, S. M. (1981). Age-related changes in processing explicit and implicit language. *Journal of Gerontology, 36,* 316–322.

Brent, D. E., & Routh, R. K. (1978). Response cost and impulsive word recognition errors in reading-disabled children. *Journal of Abnormal Child Psychology, 6,* 211–219.

Brown, A. L., & Reeve, R. (1986). Reflections on the growth of reflection in children. *Cognitive Development, 1,* 405–416.

Case, R. (1978). Intellectual development from birth to adulthood: A neo-Piagetian interpretation. In R. S. Siegler (Ed.), *Children's thinking: What develops?* (pp. 37–72). Hillsdale, NJ: Lawrence Erlbaum Associates.

Cavanaugh, J. C., & Perlmutter, M. (1982). Metamemory: A critical examination. *Child Development, 53,* 11–28.

Charness, N. (1981). Aging and skilled problem solving. *Journal of Experimental Psychology: General, 110,* 21–38.

Cimbalo, R. S., & Brink, L. (1982). Aging and the Von Restorff isolation effect in short-term memory. *Journal of General Psychology, 106,* 69–76.

Cohen, G. C., & Faulkner, B. A. (1983). Age differences in performance on two information-processing tasks: Strategy selection and processing efficiency. *Journal of Gerontology, 38,* 447–454.

Cooney, J. B., Swanson, H. L., & Ladd, S. F. (1988). Acquisition of mental multiplication skill: Evidence for the transition between counting and retrieval strategies. *Cognition and Instruction, 5,* 323–345.

Corbetta, D., & Thelen, E. (in press). The developmental origins of bimanual coordination: A dynamic perspective. *Journal of Experimental Psychology: Human Perception and Performance.*

Crowley, K., & Siegler, R. S. (1993). Flexible strategy use in young children's tic-tac-toe. *Cognitive Science, 17,* 531–561.

DeLoache, J. S. (1984). Oh where, oh where: Memory-based searching by very young children. In C. Sophian (Ed.), *Origins of cognitive skills.* Hillsdale, NJ: Lawrence Erlbaum Associates.

Flavell, J. H., Beach, D. R., & Chinsky, J. M. (1966). Spontaneous verbal rehearsal in a memory task as a function of age. *Child Development, 37,* 283–299.

Flavell, J. H., Miller, P. H., & Miller, S. A. (1993). *Cognitive development* (3rd ed.). Englewood Cliffs, NJ: Prentice-Hall.

Gardner, W. P., & Rogoff, B. (1990). Children's deliberateness of planning according to task circumstances. *Developmental Psychology, 26,* 480–487.

Geary, D. C. (1994). *Children's mathematical development.* Washington, DC: American Psychological Association.

Geary, D. C., & Burlingham-DuBree, A. Q. (1989). External validation of the strategy choice model for addition. *Journal of Experimental Child Psychology, 47,* 175–192.

Geary, D. C., Fan, L., & Bow-Thomas, C. C. (1992). Numerical cognition: Loci of ability differences comparing children from China and the United States. *Psychological Science, 3,* 180–185.

Geary, D. C., Frensch, P. A., & Wiley, J. G. (1993). Simple and complex mental subtraction: Strategy choice and speed-of-processing differences in young and elderly adults. *Psychology and Aging, 8,* 242–256.

Geary, D. C., & Wiley, J. G. (1991). Cognitive addition: Strategy choice and speed-of-processing differences in young and elderly adults. *Psychology and Aging, 6,* 474–483.

Gesell, A., & Thompson, H. (1938). *The psychology of early growth including norms of infant behavior and a method of genetic analysis.* New York: Macmillan.

Ghatala, E. S., Levin, J. R., Pressley, M., & Goodwin, D. (1986). A componential analysis of the effects of derived and supplied strategy-utility information on children's strategy selection. *Journal of Experimental Child Psychology, 41,* 76–92.

Gibson, E. J. (1988). Exploratory behavior in the development of perceiving, acting and the acquiring of knowledge. *Annual Review of Psychology, 39,* 1–41.

Gibson, J. J. (1979). *The ecological approach to visual perception.* Boston: Houghton Mifflin.

Goldfield, E. C. (1994). Dynamic systems in development: Action systems. In L. B. Smith & E. Thelen (Eds.), *A dynamic systems approach to development: Applications* (pp. 51–70). Cambridge, MA: MIT Press.

Goldman, S. R., & Saul, E. U. (1991). Flexibility in text processing: A stategy competition model. *Learning and Individual Differences, 2,* 181–219.

Graham, T., & Perry, M. (1993). Indexing transitional knowledge. *Developmental Psychology, 29,* 779–788.

Greeno, J. G., Riley, M. S., & Gelman, R. (1984). Conceptual competence and children's counting. *Cognitive Psychology, 16,* 94–143.

Halford, G. S. (1993). *Children's understanding: The development of mental models.* Hillsdale, NJ: Lawrence Erlbaum Associates.

Hubbard, K. E., LeFevre, J., & Greenham, S. L. (1994, June). *Procedure use in multiplication by adolescents.* Paper presented at the Annual meeting of the Canadian Society for Brain, Behavior, and Cognitive Science, Vancouver.

Kahan, L. D., & Richards, D. D. (1986). The effects of context on children's referential communication strategies. *Child Development, 57,* 1130–1141.

Keeney, F. J., Cannizzo, S. R., & Flavell, J. H. (1967). Spontaneous and induced verbal rehearsal in a recall task. *Child Development, 38,* 953–966.

Kerkman, D. D., & Siegler, R. S. (1993). Individual differences and adaptive flexibility in lower-income children's strategy choices. *Learning and Individual Differences, 5,* 113–136.

Klayman, J. (1985). Children's decision strategies and their adaptation to task characteristics. *Organizational Behavior and Human Decision Processes, 35,* 179–201.

Kluwe, R. H. (1982). Cognitive knowledge and executive control: Metacognition. In D. Griffin (Ed.), *Animal mind-human mind* (pp. 201–224). New York: Springer.

Kogan, N. (1983). Stylistic variation in childhood and adolescence: Creativity, metaphor, and cognitive styles. In P. H. Mussen (Ed.), *Handbook of child psychology, Vol. III, Cognitive development* (pp. 630–706). New York: Wiley.

Kuczaj, S. (1977). The acquisition of regular and irregular past tense forms. *Journal of Verbal Learning and Verbal Behavior, 16,* 589–600.

Kuhara-Kojima, K., & Hatano, G. (1989). Strategies for recognizing sentences among high and low critical thinkers. *Japanese Psychological Research, 31,* 1–19.

Kuhn, D., Schauble, L., & Garcia-Mila, M. (1992). Cross-domain development of scientific reasoning. *Cognition and Instruction, 9,* 285–327.

Lemaire, P., & Siegler, R. S. (1995). Four aspects of strategic change: Contributions to children's learning of multiplication. *Journal of Experimental Psychology: General, 124,* 83–97.

Mark, L. S. (1987). Eyeheight-scaled information about affordances: A study of sitting and stair climbing. *Journal of Experimental Psychology: Human Perception and Performance, 13,* 361–370.

McGilly, K., & Siegler, R. S. (1989). How children choose among serial recall strategies. *Child Development, 60,* 172–182.

McGilly, K., & Siegler, R. S. (1990). The influence of encoding and strategic knowledge on children's choices among serial recall strategies. *Developmental Psychology, 26,* 931–941.

McGraw, M. (1945). *The neuromuscular maturation of the human infant.* New York: Columbia University Press.

Ohlsson, S. (1984). Induced strategy shifts in spatial reasoning. *Acta Psychologica, 57,* 47–67.

Piaget, J. (1970). Piaget's theory. In P. H. Mussen (Ed.), *Carmichael's manual of child psychology: Vol. 1* (pp. 703–732). New York: Wiley.

Pufall, P. B., & Dunbar, C. (1992). Perceiving whether or not the world affords stepping onto and over: A developmental study. *Ecological Psychology, 4,* 17–38.

Reder, L. M. (1982). Plausibility judgments vs. fact retrieval: Alternative strategies for sentence verification. *Psychological Review, 89,* 250–280.

Reder, L. M. (1988). Strategic control of retrieval strategies. In G. H. Bower (Ed.), *The psychology of learning and motivation, Vol. 22* (pp. 227–259). San Diego, CA: Academic Press.

Reder, L. M. & Ritter, F. E. (1992). What determines initial feeling of knowing? Familiarity with question terms, not with the answer. *Journal of Experimental Psychology: Learning, Memory, and Cognition, 18,* 435–451.

Reder, L. M., Wible, C., & Martin, J. (1986). Differential memory changes with age: Exact retrieval versus plausible inference. *Journal of Experimental Psychology: Learning, Memory, and Cognition, 12,* 72–81.

Schauble, L. (1990). Belief revision in children: The role of prior knowledge and strategies for generating evidence. *Journal of Experimental Child Psychology, 49,* 31–57.

Schneider, W. (1985). Developmental trends in the metamemory-memory behavior relationship: An integrative review. In D. L. Forrest-Pressley, G. E. MacKinnon, & T. G. Waller (Eds.), *Cognition, metacognition, and human performance* (pp. 57–109). New York: Academic Press.

Schneider, W., & Pressley, M. (1989). *Memory development between 2 and 20.* New York: Springer.

Scholnick, E. K., & Friedman, S. L. (1987). The planning construct in the psychological literature. In S. L. Friedman, E. K. Scholnick, & R. R. Cocking (Eds.), *Blueprints for thinking: The role of planning in cognitive development* (pp. 3–38). Cambridge, England: Cambridge University Press.

Schultz, T. R., Fisher, G. W., Pratt, C. C., & Rulf, S. (1986). Selection of causal rules. *Child Development, 57,* 143–152.

Siegler, R. S. (1986). Unities in thinking across domains in children's strategy choices. In M. Perlmuter (Ed.), *Perspective on intellectual development.* Minnesota symposium on child development (Vol. 19, pp. 1–48). Hillsdale, NJ: Lawrence Erlbaum Associates.

Siegler, R. S. (1987a). The perils of averaging data over strategies: An example from children's addition, *Journal of Experimental Psychology: General, 106,* 250–264.

Siegler, R. S. (1987b). Strategy choices in subtraction. In J. Sloboda & D. Rogers (Eds.), *Cognitive processes in mathematics* (pp. 81–106). Oxford, England: Oxford University Press.

Siegler, R. S. (1988a). Strategy choice procedures and the development of multiplication skills. *Journal of Experimental Psychology: General, 117,* 258–275.

Siegler, R. S. (1988b). Individual differences in strategy choice: Good students, not-so-good students, and perfectionists. *Child Development, 59,* 833–851.

Siegler, R. S. (1995). How does change occur: A microgenetic study of number conservation. *Cognitive Psychology, 28,* 225–273.

Siegler, R. S., & Jenkins, E. A. (1989). *How children discover new strategies.* Hillsdale, NJ: Lawrence Erlbaum Associates.

Siegler, R. S., & Lemaire, P. (in press). Older and younger adults' strategy choices in multiplication: Testing predictions of ASCM via the choice/no-choice method. *Journal of Experimental Psychology: General.*

Siegler, R. S., & McGilly, K. (1989). Strategy choices in children's time-telling. In I. Levin & D. Zakay (Eds.), *Time and human cognition: A life span perspective* (pp. 185–218). New York: Elsevier Science.

Siegler, R. S., & Robinson, M. (1982). The development of numerical understandings. In H. W. Reese & L. P. Lipsitt (Eds.), *Advances in child development and behavior* (Vol. 16, pp. 241–312). New York: Academic Press.

Siegler, R. S., & Shipley, C. (1995). Variation, selection, and cognitive change. In G. Halford & T. Simon (Eds.), *Developing cognitive competence: New approaches to process modeling* (pp. 31–76). Hillsdale, NJ: Lawrence Erlbaum Associates.

Siegler, R. S., & Shrager, J. (1984). Strategy choices in addition and subtraction: How do children know what to do? In C. Sophian (Ed.), *Origins of cognitive skills* (pp. 229–293). Hillsdale, NJ: Lawrence Erlbaum Associates.

Sternberg, R. J. (1985). *Beyond IQ: A triarchic theory of human intelligence.* New York: Cambridge University Press.

Thelen, E. (1995). Motor development: A new synthesis. *American Psychologist, 50,* 79–95.

Thomas, J. L. (1985). Visual memory: Adult age differences in map recall and learning strategies. *Experimental Aging Research, 11,* 93–95.

Van Lehn, K. (1983). On the representation of procedures in repair theory. In H. P. Ginsburg (Ed.), *The development of mathematical thinking* (pp. 197–252). New York: Academic Press.

Veriejken, B., Adolph, K. E., Denny, M. A., Fadl, Y., Gill, S. V., & Lucero, A. A. (1995). Development of infant crawling: Balance constraints on interlimb coordination. In G. Bardy, R. J. Bootsma, & Y. Guiard (Eds.), *Studies in perception and action III* (pp. 255–258). Hillsdale, NJ: Lawrence Erlbaum Associates.

Warren, W. H. (1984). Perceiving affordances: Visual guidance of stair climbing. *Journal of Experimental Psychology: Human Perception and Performance, 10,* 683–703.

Warren, W. H., & Whang, S. (1987). Visual guidance of walking through apertures: Body-scaled information for affordances. *Journal of Experimental Psychology: Human Perception and Performance, 13,* 371–383.

Chapter 5

Implicit Memory and Metacognition: Why Is the Glass Half Full?

John R. Anderson
Carnegie Mellon University

This chapter is a commentary on four others in this volume (Kihlstrom, Shames, & Dorfman, Chapter 1; Reder & Schunn, Chapter 3; Siegler, Adolph, & Lemaire, Chapter 4; Graf & Birt, Chapter 2), which all address quite directly the relationship between implicit memory and metacognition. The first three are concerned with the role of implicit memory in metacognitive judgments, whereas the last is concerned with metacognitive processes in implicit memory and learning tasks. As will become clear, I am very much in sympathy with the ideas set forth in each of these chapters because my own ACT–R theory (Anderson, 1993) paints a very similar picture of human cognition. Rather than simply writing a laudatory commentary, it would be useful to compare and contrast each of the works with this theory. The many similarities serve to emphasize the growing consensus in the field. The differences, which I do not try to resolve, serve to indicate issues for further research. Before commenting on the chapters, I discuss the relationship between implicit memory and metacognition in the ACT–R theory; these considerations serve as the basis for my comments.

THE IMPLICIT-EXPLICIT DISTINCTION

There are all sorts of definitions of what is meant by implicit versus explicit cognitive processes, but the most straightforward is simply that explicit processes are those that are potentially reportable and implicit processes are those that are not. This definition runs into some difficulties with respect to situations where things are not reportable "for no fault of their own" such as when we lack the appropriate verbal labels or in the case of someone who might have paralyzed vocal musculature. This points to the fact that any such operational definition is only an approximation to the underlying mental state it is trying to capture.

Ericsson and Simon (1984) argued that the potentially reportable knowledge corresponds to the contents of working memory. In Anderson (1993) I described what the Ericsson-Simon criterion would mean in terms of the ACT–R architecture. This architecture divides knowledge into declarative and procedural knowledge and working memory corresponds to the active contents of declarative memory. Declarative knowledge can be reported by production rules that constitute the procedural knowledge of ACT–R. For instance, consider the task of doing multicolumn addition. There are production rules for performing the task such as:

Add-Column
IF the goal is to add digits n1 and n2 in the column
   and n1 + n2 = n3
THEN set as subgoal to write n3 in the column.

the condition "n1 + n2 = n3" could match some declarative fact such as "3 + 4 = 7." In this case, this would result in the subgoal to write out 7, which might involve both things like processing a carry into the column and the actual motor process of executing the writing of the answer. If this declarative fact was active (perhaps because it had just been retrieved by the preceding production) it could be accessed by a reporting production of the form:

Report-Fact
IF the goal is to provide a verbal report of what one is doing
   and there is a highly active fact
THEN set as a subgoal to report this fact.

This would set the subgoal to generate some utterance that described the fact. It could be that the system lacked the vocabulary or the vocal capacity to actually report the fact. However, within the ACT–R theory, the critical thing is that the subgoal can be set to report the fact that "3 + 4 = 7" and not whether it was actually reported. This is what is meant by "potentially reportable."

What is interesting is how much knowledge in ACT–R is not reportable by this criterion. Among the things not potentially reportable are the production rules themselves that guide the processing, the states of activation of the declarative elements, and information about which path to take when different production rules call for distinct actions in the same situation.

Although it might seem strange to some that so much knowledge in ACT–R is not reportable (and recent literature suggests a real fascination with what is not reportable in humans) what is stranger to me is that any of this knowledge should be reportable. As a cognitive modeler I have developed cognitive models of many processes. Getting models that adequately do the task they are supposed to do can be quite a demanding goal. To add the constraint the knowledge they use be represented in a form that can be reported poses a considerable additional burden. In fact, most models developed in cognitive science are not really capable of giving reports of what they are doing because the knowledge they use is only represented implicitly "in the code." Thus, rather than trying to understand why some cognitive processes are implicit (not reportable) it may be more informative to inquire why any cognitive processes are explicit (reportable).

In answering the question of why any knowledge is reportable it is worthwhile to consider what function knowledge reports might have outside of the psychology laboratory. The obvious function of knowledge reports is to inform other members of the species of critical knowledge such as what things are dangerous or how to perform a procedure.[1] Thus, from this perspective we would expect the knowledge which is reportable to be that which is useful to communicate to others. There are a number of criteria that information must satisfy to be reportable. First, it must be relatively reliable: There is little point to reporting the basis for a vague hunch. Second, it needs to be compactly reportable: If the basis for an action is a lifetime of experience no one wants to hear that lifetime recounted. Third, it has to be the kind of knowledge that is potentially capable of being independently verified: The opportunities for deception would be too great otherwise. Fourth, it has to be something that is nonobvious: There is no sense in communicating what every creature knows as part of its genetic endowment.

These criteria often seem to separate out the reportable from the nonreportable pieces of knowledge. Consider, for instance people's tendencies to repeat strategies that have worked as described by Reder and Schunn and by Siegler, Adolph, and Lemaire. Although we have sayings in our society that embody this wisdom ("Stick with what brought you here"), in fact people are often unaware that this is what they are doing and such advice is seldom given in instruction. The tendency to repeat a successful strategy is at best statistically valid, is based on a complex history of situations where that strategy worked and did not work, there is little chance

---

[1]This is not to suggest that language does not have other important functions. The issue here is what the function is of reports of internal processes.

for someone else to objectively verify this experience, and it is the knowledge that is built into all sorts of organisms (see Anderson, 1995, for a review). Therefore, it is the kind of metaknowledge that need not be reportable. On the other hand, consider the advice given to students preparing for a calculus test—check the reasonableness of your integral answers by geometric approximations. This is compact knowledge that can be easily validated and that students have no prior basis for knowing. It is just the kind of knowledge that would be valuable to report to others.

In conclusion, it should come as no surprise to us that much of what we know is implicit and not reportable. It is of more interest that some of this knowledge is reportable. Although reportability may serve other functions, one function for which it is valuable is education. This is one of the critical roles of declarative knowledge that separates it from other types of knowledge. It serves to explain why this is the type of knowledge that Ericsson and Simon identify as occupying verbal reports.

COMMENTS ON KIHLSTROM, SHAMES, AND DORFMAN

Kihlstrom, Shames, and Dorfman succeed admirably in their effort to place intuitions into an information-processing framework—in their words, to move them from California to Pittsburgh. As Reder (Reder & Gordon, in press; Reder & Schunn, this volume; Schunn, Reder, Nhouyvanisvong, Richards, & Stroffino, in press) has done, they relate feelings of knowing and feelings of warmth to activation levels of the declarative knowledge structures. These activation levels are things that are not directly reportable but can nonetheless influence behavior. In the case of recognition one can use the activation levels of a declarative representation of the word as evidence about whether the word has been studied or not. This is contrasted with retrieving an explicit declarative memory recording that the word has been studied. Activation levels are one of the things that are not reportable—nor should they be given the criteria for reportable knowledge that I listed before—they are based on a complex history of experience, they are only statistically related to correct behavior, and (as documented by Anderson & Schooler, 1991) to the extent they are valid their validity is ubiquitous and seems built into most species.

Although Kihlstrom et al. write in terms of activation effects like those in ACT–R they do not write in terms of productions rules. If one were to map their description of recognition judgments into production rule terms, the most direct mapping would probably have their subjects responding according to productions like the following two:

High-Criterion
IF I am asked whether I saw X
  and I am using a high criterion
  and I explicitly remember seeing X
THEN say yes.

Low-Criterion
IF I am asked whether I saw X
  and I am using a low criterion
  and X is active
THEN say yes.

Unfortunately, the second *Low-Criterion* production cannot be implemented in the ACT–R system because activation levels are just the sorts of things that cannot be tested for explicit report. Thus, "X is active" is not the sort of test that can appear in an ACT–R production rule. Activation levels control access to declarative knowledge which can be tested. As a related aside, one can wonder in what sense the subjects in the Kihlstrom et al. experiments were responding implicitly if they can report seeing the words when a low threshold is used.

Implicit knowledge can be made explicit in ACT–R by having the system attend to some detectable behavior that is correlated with the implicit information—for instance, the speed with which a word can be read. Thus, a workable production in ACT–R would be:

Implicit-Low-Threshold:
IF I am asked whether I saw X
  and I am using a low criterion
  and I read X quickly
THEN say yes.

The test "I read X quickly" would match to a self-observation encoded as a declarative structure.[2] This analysis is very much like Jacoby's perceptual fluency theory (Jacoby & Dallas, 1981) with the further claim that perceptual fluency is mediated by activation levels. One might ask where the value added is of postulating activation levels over just perceptual fluency. The answer is that it integrates the role of associative priming as well past exposure in such judgments. For instance, the data reported from Shames shows higher feeling of warmth judgments for interassociated items. Similarly, Reder (Reder & Gordon, in press) has shown that feeling of knowing judgments can be associatively primed.

---

[2]Not that I am offering a theory of self-perception (any more than I am offering a theory of word perception).

Although I am generally in agreement with the Kihlstrom et al. chapter, I have to take issue with the stage assumption in their Fig. 1.1 from Wallas and the "implicit" assumption in their chapter that the implicit processes precede the explicit. There is no evidence for this temporal ordering and, indeed, I suspect if they looked at their latency judgments in the recognition memory task, they would find longer latencies for the implicit low-confidence judgments. What determines what is reportable and what is not is not what comes first or later. Rather, it is the content of these memories. The implicit processes are not the mysterious underpinnings of cognition. They are just parts of cognition that happen not to be reportable.

An elaboration of this difference is to repeat Reder and Schunn's point about subthreshhold versus superthreshhold activation. Kihlstrom et al. paint a model of activation rising over time with lower activations being below the threshold of reportability and higher levels rising above threshold. In the ACT framework it is not level of activation that defines whether something is implicit or not. The activation levels themselves are not reportable; the structures that are activated are reportable.

COMMENTS ON REDER AND SCHUNN

Reder has been stressing for 20 years (Reder, 1976) that subjects are very flexible in choosing the strategies they deploy. It is only recently (Anderson, 1993) that I have elaborated on ACT's conflict resolution to deal with such issues. Perhaps not surprisingly, I find myself (and ACT–R) in basic agreement with the general position of Reder and Schunn on implicit strategy selection. Processes underlying strategy selection are often not reportable because there is no value in reportability and, as Reder and Schunn suggest, it is an extra computational burden to make that knowledge reportable. As they note, Lovett and Anderson (in press) have developed an extensive application of the ACT–R theory to strategy selection in problem solving. The knowledge used by ACT–R for strategy selection is implicit information acquired by Bayesian statistical learning methods about the relative success of alternative production rules.

The heart of their chapter is concerned with the SAC model of activation-based processes used to select between strategies for solving problems by retrieval or computation. There is a good deal in common between the SAC theory presented in Reder and Schunn and the ACT–R theory. However, there are two differences in how the theories conceive of the role of activation and it is worth noting these. One concerns the issue of spread of activation. In the Schunn et al. paper activation can spread many links, whereas in ACT–R, activation only spreads from source nodes in the environment one link to other nodes in memory. In the former ACT*

(Anderson, 1983), activation did spread through chains of links, but the current ACT–R has single-link spread like the SAM theory (Gillund & Shiffrin, 1984; Raaijmakers & Shiffrin, 1981). However, because each node can index each other, this system can mimic the effects of multilink spread. ACT–R adopts the single-link model because strengths of associations are supposed to reflect the probability that one node will be assessed if another one is present. Activations are supposed to be Bayesian estimates of the probability that a node will be used and multilink spread is unnecessary to calculate these probabilities and in fact would lead to incoherent estimates. I think it is a fair summary of the literature on this (McNamara, 1994; Ratcliff & McKoon, 1994) that it is very difficult to empirically distinguish between theories that postulate multilink versus single-link spread. Thus this is unlikely to be an important difference between ACT–R and SAC.

The other difference between ACT–R and SAC seems more consequential. This is the fact that SAC (as Kihlstrom et al.) proposes subjects are responding to levels of activation, whereas ACT–R claims this is not possible. In ACT–R we would model judgments of feeling of knowing in the Reder and Schunn paradigm by production rules like:

Recognize-Components
IF the goal is to find the product of n1 and n2
   and one can remember seeing n1 and n2 together in a problem
THEN set as a subgoal to choose the retrieval method.

This is a production which uses the fact that a pair of numbers like 23 and 31 have been studied together to infer that one should be able to retrieve their product. This production can operate relatively rapidly and so serves as a basis for making the feeling of knowing judgment required by subjects in the experiment. It will also lead to the illusory feeling of knowing judgments they report associated with operator reversal or after seeing a problem many times with inadequate time to answer it.

More generally, ACT–R does not hold that there is an obligatory strategy-selection process before choosing to retrieve. Every production including the one just mentioned needs to retrieve some information from memory before applying. The difference concerns what information is retrieved and how accessible it is. In this case it is information about the co-occurrence of two terms, whereas in the other cases it might be retrieval of the answer. In ACT–R at each cycle all successful productions and their retrieved products are in the conflict set and strategy selection involves a choice among these productions. As described in Lovett and Anderson, it is each production's past history of experience and aptness to the current situation that determine which production is selected in conflict resolution and what happens next. In ACT–R feeling of knowing is not an obligatory stage before one begins to retrieve. Rather, it is an optional matter of using some incidental information (such as the co-occurrence of terms) that can be retrieved early to decide whether to continue to try to retrieve the answer or to try to compute the answer.

ACT–R adopts this stance because levels of activation are not the sorts of things that can be directly tested by production rules. Rather, they are the sorts of things that control access to the information that can be tested. This goes back to the Ericsson and Simon use of working memory to define reportable knowledge. The SAC theory does not have this constraint and is quite explicitly devoted to the proposition that activation levels carry information which can be directly accessible. Although this is a clear difference, it is not so clear how to empirically discriminate the two positions.

COMMENTS ON SIEGLER, ADOLPH, AND LEMAIRE

The Siegler, Adolph, and Lemaire chapter was also concerned with how past history is used to distinguish between strategies. They provide an impressive array of data which is consistent with the general view that strategy selection is implicit and automatic. As in the case of the Reder and Schunn chapter, I would question whether one gathers information in a separate stage that precedes the stage of strategy execution. In this regard, there is an opportunity to compare theories quite directly because we (Lebiere & Anderson, in preparation) have developed an ACT–R model of the development of strategies in arithmetic that has been applied to data from Siegler (1988). So, for instance, the following two productions choose between retrieval and computation in addition:

Retrieve
IF the goal is to find the sum of n1 and n2
   and I can retrieve the sum n1 + n2 = n3
THEN return n3 as the answer.

Compute
IF the goal is to find the sum of n1 and n2
THEN create a subgoal to count up from n1 n2 times.

The decision of which strategy to follow is made by whether the *Retrieve* production can retrieve a sum before the *Compute* production fires, because the *Retrieve* production is more highly valued in conflict resolution. Thus, it is the accessibility of the addition fact that determines the choice among procedures. This is very much like the ASCM model described but does not require a separate assessment of whether it is appropriate to retrieve. If one can retrieve in time, one does.

One of the interesting features of the ASCM model is how it integrates information about the situations in which a strategy works. It stores information about the success of each strategy in the presence of each feature and each feature combination. It is interesting to wonder how different its predictions would be from an exemplar model (Nosofsky, 1986), which would just store what strategies worked in what situations. Such a model would select a strategy for the current situation by taking a weighted average of the strategies in other situations according to their similarity to the current situation.

The ACT–R model does not accumulate statistics about strategy success in each situation or feature combination. Strategies are represented by production rules and production rules can capture certain feature combinations; thus, one can have a rules like:

Calculate-Large
IF the goal is to multiply n1 by n2
    and n1 and n2 are large
THEN use a calculator.

Decompose-Tens
IF the goal is to multiply n1 by n2
    and n2 is n3 * 10
THEN multiply n1 by n3 and add a zero to the product.

However, there are only production rules for certain feature combinations. There are not separate rules that respond to each possible feature combination. Indeed, it is uncertain how any system can even know what all the features are that are to be monitored.

In ACT–R, the decision about what features to attend to (and embed in a rule) is quite deliberate even while the monitoring of the success of the rule is implicit. A number of experimental lines have pointed us in this direction. In the domain of geometry we found that students were quite sensitive to features that were sensibly related to a proof strategy. Thus, subjects were more likely to use angle-side-angle as a proof method when the givens of the proof problem mentioned angles. However, subjects had a hard time in picking up on features that had as strong a statistical relationship but had no sensible relationship (Lewis & Anderson, 1985). For instance, it might be the case that all proof problems that had 3-dimensional diagrams used angle-side-angle but subjects had a hard time picking up on this. The only subjects who did were those who explicitly mentioned the relationship in their protocols. They noticed it after an extensive stage of explicit hypothesis testing trying to figure out what was going on in the experiment.

Certain directions of relationship are easier to pick up on than others. For instance, Lovett and Anderson (in press) found that subjects could respond to problems where hill-climbing metrics predicted the right operator. That is, subjects would tend to select operators that moved them to a state that was more similar to the solution state. More recently, in unpublished research Lovett has done experiments where the better operator was the one that seemed to move away from the solution. Subjects exposed to this condition learned to ignore hill-climbing distance but never learned to prefer the operator that went in the opposite direction. It seems that, as the ACT perspective would predict, subjects are only prepared to learn the feature-operator correlations that make sense to them. In the case of the Siegler, Adolph, and Lemaire chapter, I wonder what would happen if subjects were exposed to conditions where the bigger numbers were easier to retrieve than compute or were steeper slopes where easier to walk down. In such science-fiction worlds, would subjects learn the reverse predictability of the critical features or are they only sensitive to certain feature-operator correlations?

COMMENTS ON GRAF AND BIRT

Graf and Birt's nice review brings up a number of issues relevant to the role of reportability in cognition. First, their review of the role of rehearsal notes the classic age progression with younger children apparently not engaging in rehearsal. However, in fact what these studies show is that younger children do not report rehearsal. Although children undoubtedly do learn more effective ways to memorize material with age, it is extremely unlikely that young children do not engage in rehearsal, given the comparative literature that shows that creatures such as rabbits (e.g., Wagner, Rudy, & Whitlow, 1973) and pigeons (e.g., Maki & Heqvik, 1980) engage in rehearsal. Rather, it seems more likely that these younger children like the other creatures simply have not learned to report the rehearsal that they are doing. The comparative literature also reinforces the point that reportability is not a requirement for metacognition.

Graf and Birt review what is probably my favorite result from the human memory literature: that intention to learn is not critical to learning. Rather, what is critical is how the subjects process the material. They might also have mentioned how, despite Freud, intention to forget is irrelevant if one controls processing over the retention interval. Having run a number of incidental learning experiments in my life, I know the groans one gets from subjects who are told that they will now have to recall material that they were processing with no intention of remembering. I also know their astonishment at how well they actually do (if they were in the right processing condition). This clearly shows the dissociation between reportability and cognitive performance. As Anderson and Schooler (1991) argued and as the ACT–R theory implements, the business of memory is to make most available that information which is most likely to be needed statistically. It shares this goal with the memories of all organisms and performs an admirable Bayesian job of achieving that goal. This is all done implicitly in the associative strengths and activation levels quite out of the view of our ability to report.

Graf and Birt also review the implicit learning experiments concerned with sequence learning. These are the results that I have found most difficult to reconcile with the ACT–R position (articulated in the comments on Siegler, Adolph, and Lemaire)—that one must be conscious of (i.e., represent in declarative memory in a reportable form) the features that get built into production rules. The obvious way to model these tasks in ACT–R had seemed to be in terms of production rules that predict the next key. One could imagine modeling these results in terms of production rules like:

Predict-Key
IF the goal is to hit a key
  and sequence X has occurred
THEN prepare to hit key C.

However, subjects in some conditions fail to ever report the sequential structures, but still take advantage of sequential redundancy. Thus, it is not clear how such a rule could be learned. Various researchers (e.g., Cleeremans & McClelland, 1991; Nissen & Bullemer, 1987) have commented that these results are quite problematic for rule-like models of human cognition such as the ACT theory.

However, we have recently realized that our problem with this literature was that in a sense we were trying too hard to account for it. Rather than having predictive rules like those just presented, one can simply have a more obvious and simpler model which solely consists of rules for doing the task:

Hit-Key
IF the goal is to hit the next key
  and a signal appears in location X
  and location X is associated with key C
THEN hit key C.

This production does not try to predict on the basis of the sequential information. However, that information will be encoded in declarative memory for what has transpired in the experiment. As Servan-Schreiber and Anderson (1991) showed in accounting for the Reber (1967) grammar-learning task, subjects naturally commit to memory subsequences that they encounter in the form of chunks (a rather unsurprising result given the serial memory literature). Thus, location X in the *Hit-Key* production would appear in a number of declarative chunks, encoding the various subsequences in which it had occurred. The sequence chunks that repeated more often would be stronger and provide more priming activation to X and hence speed up the matching of the last production presented. The subject need not be aware of these statistical relationships, but the memory system is and uses them to prime the relevant knowledge. Thus, this is just another case of implicit memory being carried by strengths of association and activation levels.

CONCLUSIONS

These chapters illustrate the extent to which cognitive choices are sensitive to things that we have no ability to report. They present theoretical perspectives in which such implicit metacognition is very natural, which is quite different than what has been the standard assumption in the field. Basically, humans are highly sensitive to the statistical structure of their environment, which enables them to predict profitable courses of action. The last 20 years of research on animal learning has demonstrated similar statistical sensitivities (see Anderson, 1995, for a review). Given that non-verbal creatures have such abilities, we should hardly be surprised to find these abilities implicit in humans. What is more surprising is that there are cases of metacognition which are not implicit but for which there is conscious awareness. Indeed, as noted with respect to the Lewis and Anderson study of geometry discussed earlier, there are cases where subjects display sensitivity only when they can describe the relevant aspects of the environment. In the introduction I tried to suggest that cases of such "reportable" cognition might reflect situations where the knowledge is critical to education. It is not clear that this hypothesis covers all of the cases (indeed, I am not sure how it extends to the Lewis and Anderson experiment). More attention needs to be given to exactly what cognitive processes we can report and how we can manage to report these. Why is the glass half full?

REFERENCES

Anderson, J. R. (1983). *The architecture of cognition.* Hillsdale, NJ: Lawrence Erlbaum Associates.
Anderson, J. R. (1993). *Rules of the mind.* Hillsdale, NJ: Lawrence Erlbaum Associates.
Anderson, J. R. (1995). *Learning and memory.* New York: Wiley.
Anderson, J. R., & Schooler, L. J. (1991). Reflections of the environment in memory. *Psychological Science, 2,* 396–408.

Cleeremans, A., & McClelland, J. L. (1991). Learning the structure of event sequences. *Journal of Experimental Psychology: General, 120,* 235–253.

Ericsson, K. A., & Simon, H. A. (1984). *Protocol analysis: Verbal reports as data.* Cambridge, MA: MIT Press.

Gillund, G., & Shiffrin, R. M. (1984). A retrieval model for both recognition and recall. *Psychological Review, 91,* 1–67.

Jacoby, L. L., & Dallas, M. (1981). On the relationship between autobiographical memory and perceptual learning. *Journal of Experimental Psychology: General, 3,* 306–340.

Lebiere, C., & Anderson, J. R. (in preparation). *An ACT–R model of cognitive arithmetic.*

Lewis, M. W., & Anderson, J. R. (1985). Discrimination of operator schemata in problem solving: Procedural learning from examples. *Cognitive Psychology, 17,* 26–65.

Lovett, M. C., & Anderson, J. R. (in press). History of success and current context in problem solving: Combined influences on operator selection. *Cognitive Psychology.*

Maki, W. S., & Heqvik, D. K. (1980). Directed forgetting in pigeons. *Animal Learning and Behavior, 8,* 567–574.

McNamara, T. P. (1994). Priming and theories of memory: A reply to Ratcliff and McKoon. *Psychological Review, 101,* 185–187.

Nissen, M. J., & Bullemer, P. (1987). Attentional requirements of learning: Evidence from performance measures. *Cognitive Psychology, 19,* 1–32.

Nosofsky, R. M. (1986). Attention, similarity, and the identification-categorization relationship. *Journal of Experimental Psychology: General, 115,* 39–57.

Raaijamakers, J. G. W., & Shiffrin, R. M. (1981). Search of associative memory. *Psychological Review, 88,* 93–134.

Ratcliff, R., & McKoon, G. (1994). Retrieving information from memory: Spreading-activation theories versus compound-cue theories. *Psychological Review, 101,* 177–184.

Reber, A. S. (1967). Implicit learning of artificial grammars. *Journal of Verbal Learning and Verbal Behavior, 5,* 855–863.

Reder, L. M. (1976). The role of elaborations in the processing of prose (Doctoral dissertation, University of Michigan, 1990). *Dissertation Abstracts International, 37B,* 5405–B.

Reder, L. M., & Gordon, J. S. (in press). Subliminal perception: Nothing special cognitively speaking. In J. Cohen & J. Schooler (Eds.), *Cognitive and neuropsychological approaches to the study of consciousness.* Mahwah, NJ: Lawrence Erlbaum Associates.

Schunn, C. D., Reder, L. M., Nhouyvanisvong, A., Richards, D. R., & Stroffino, P. J. (in press). A spreading activation model of feeling-of-knowing and strategy selection. In L. M. Reder (Ed.), *Implicit memory and metacognition.* Hillsdale, NJ: Lawrence Erlbaum Associates.

Servan-Schreiber, E., & Anderson, J. R. (1991). Learning artificial grammars with competitive chunking. *Journal of Experimental Psychology: Learning, Memory, and Cognition, 16,* 592–608.

Siegler, R. S. (1988). Strategy choice procedures and the development of multiplication skill. *Journal of Experimental Psychology: General, 117,* 258–275.

Wagner, A. R., Rudy, J. W., & Whitlow, J. W. (1973). Rehearsal in animal conditioning. *Journal of Experimental Psychology, 97,* 407–426.

Chapter 6

Metacognitive Aspects of Implicit/Explicit Memory

Louis Narens
University of California, Irvine

Aurora Graf
University of Washington

Thomas O. Nelson
University of Maryland at College Park

A widely held belief in the area of implicit/explicit memory research is that implicit memory is revealed when previous experiences facilitate performance on a task that does not require conscious or intentional or deliberate remembrance of those experiences, whereas explicit memory is revealed when performance on a task requires conscious, intentional, or deliberate remembrance of previous experiences (cf. Schacter, 1987). Thus formulated, a key distinction between implicit and explicit memory tasks hinges on whatever is meant by the conscious, intentional, or deliberate remembrance.

Wilson (1994) wrote, "Researchers in the tradition of metamemory and metacognition (e.g., Flavell, 1979; Nelson & Narens, 1990) were among the first to draw attention to the necessity of understanding the way in which meta-beliefs monitor and control nonconscious processing." Accordingly, it might be fruitful to inquire about the applicability of metacognition to the domain of implicit/explicit memory. For instance, *Do the metacognitive components that we and others have been investigating play some useful role in explaining the distinction between implicit and explicit memory?* We present a case here that they do. Because these components use only a portion of the properties of consciousness and awareness, it is natural to ask, *Are these metacognitive components sufficient for explicating the implicit/explicit distinction?* To the extent that they are not, *What other aspects of consciousness or awareness are needed?* For example, these metacognitive components do not utilize qualia—a concept of considerable importance in the philosophical analysis of consciousness. *Do researchers of implicit/explicit memory consider qualia to play an important role in their theories?* If additional components are needed for explanation of the implicit/explicit distinction, then we believe it is likely that such components would also likely be useful in expanding theories of metacognition. Another question of interest is, *What metacognitive components might be involved in both implicit and explicit memory tasks?* Whatever those metacognitive components are, they seem important to highlight just in case their role varies across implicit and explicit memory tasks.

This chapter begins with a brief overview of the metacognitive components that we and others have been investigating, and we show how the theoretical framework that we developed for organizing them can be expanded to accommodate theoretical concepts that others consider important for implicit/explicit memory, for example, the concept of "meta-awareness" from Dulany (1994). We then utilize metacognitive components derived from the framework to analyze a word-fragment completion task in terms of the implicit/explicit distinction. Next, two new experiments are reported that probe connections between metacognitive judgments and implicit/explicit memory during word-fragment completion. The chapter closes with some observations about how metamemory and implicit/explicit memory may be more fruitfully integrated.

A FRAMEWORK FOR METAMEMORY

Nelson and Narens (1990, 1994) introduced the framework in Fig. 6.1 to organize theoretical ideas inherent in their metamemory research and to integrate empirical findings from the literature that bear on metacognitive aspects of memory. Note that the monitoring processes at the top of the figure and the control processes at the bottom (for elaboration, see Nelson & Narens, 1990, 1994) are neither arcane nor artificial, but are directly analogous to the kinds of judgments and control processes that occur routinely in naturalistic learning situations, such as a student studying for and taking exams.

Figure 6.2 provides a theoretical perspective used by Nelson and Narens (1990, 1994) to integrate monitoring and control processes into systems for active learning. This perspective is based on a distinction between the *metalevel* and the *object level* and the flow of information between these levels that gives rise to *monitoring* and *control.* Nelson and Narens (1990) summarized this informational flow:

> The basic notion underlying control—analogous to speaking into a telephone handset—is that the metalevel *modifies* the object level, but not vice versa. In particular, the information flowing from the metalevel to the object level either changes the state of the object-level process or changes the object-level process itself. This produces some kind of action at the object level, which could be: (a) to initiate an action; (b) to continue an action

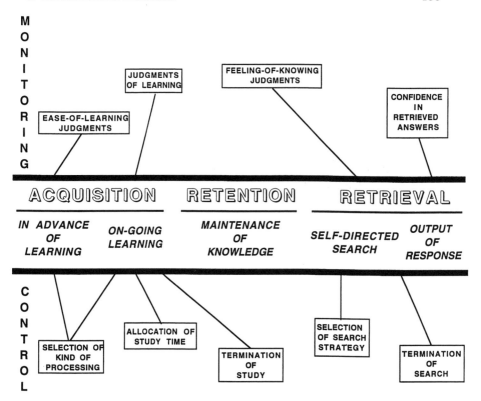

FIG. 6.1. Metacognitive framework. (For elaboration, see Nelson & Narens, 1990, 1994.)

(not necessarily the same as what had been occurring because time has passed and the total progress has changed, e.g., a game player missing an easy shot as the pressure increases after a long series of successful shots); or (c) to terminate an action. However, because control per se does not yield any information from the object level, a monitoring component is needed that is logically (even if not psychologically) independent of the control component. The basic notion underlying monitoring—analogous to listening to the telephone handset—is that the metalevel *is informed by* the object level. (p. 127)

Nelson and Narens (1994) extended this perspective to more than two levels while keeping intact the key distinction between the meta- and object levels. The extended perspective appears to be applicable to some issues in implicit/explicit memory. For example, Dulany (1994) stated, "Implicit memory is no more 'remembering without awareness' than it is 'awareness without remembering'; it is evocative remembering and nonpropositional awareness without deliberative remembering." To better expound this and related ideas, Dulany developed a concept he called *meta-awareness*:

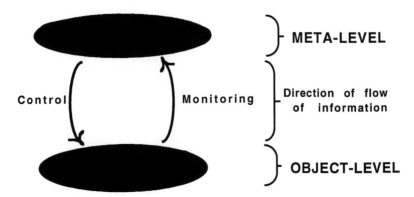

FIG. 6.2. A two-level system with monitoring and control. Adapted from Nelson and Narens (1990). © 1990 by Academic Press. Adapted with permission.

Within a remembering episode, we may be aware of prior modes and contents of awareness [where S_{i1} is conscious state i at time 1]:

$$\text{Aware}_2(\text{Aware}_1[S_{i1}]).$$

By a nonconscious remembering operation, those prior conscious states, like any other natural event, may become objects of symbolic awareness. This amounts to a remembrance theory of second order (reflective) awareness.

In terms of our framework, a perspective similar to Dulany's is obtained by replacing awareness with monitoring and using a chain of three levels (see Fig. 6.3), resulting in a perspective that we call *metamonitoring*. This raises the following interesting question: What, if anything, of *scientific* (as opposed to *philosophical*) importance would be lost if Dulany's analysis is redone using metamonitoring instead of meta-awareness? Also notice that our three-level chain (or an extension of it) is bounded, not infinite (i.e., there is no problem of infinite regress).

Part of our approach to metamemory consists of using monitored object-level and other metalevel information as inputs to a decision rule R whose outputs are control processes. Awareness when attached to a monitoring process M will add nothing to this unless the attached awareness is being monitored by a higher metalevel which has a control process that also has an input into the decision rule R. We can imagine situations where the monitoring of M (i.e., metamonitoring) might be useful in the scientific analysis of memory—as in the situation described earlier by Dulany—and we are very interested in other aspects of awareness and consciousness that might also be involved in metalevel decision rules, but we have not yet found specific examples of the utility of such aspects for metamemory research.

Each of the stages in Fig. 6.1 can be refined (Nelson & Narens, 1990). A refinement of the "termination of study" occurs in Fig. 6.4. A major question

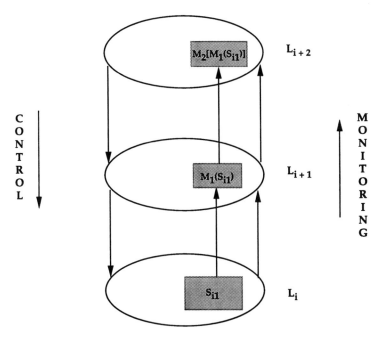

FIG. 6.3. A three-level metacognitive system, analogous to Dulany's (1994) notion of meta-awareness. Note that in representing Dulany's equation, level L_{i+1} is both a metalevel that receives monitored information about level L_i and simultaneously is an object level to L_{i+2}. For instance, L_{i+1} contains the monitored information about episode S_{i1} that occurs at L_i and itself is monitored during an explicit memory task occurring at L_{i+2}.

investigated in this chapter concerns components of this refinement; in particular, the accuracies of JOLs (Judgments of Learning) and FOK (Feeling of Knowing) for monitoring information that eventually is assessed by either an implicit or explicit memory task during word-fragment completion. Two experiments that bear on this and related issues are presented in the following.

WORD-FRAGMENT COMPLETION

Metacognitive Aspects of Retrieval

Metacognitive decisions are required for *explicit retrieval* during word-fragment completion, when the subject is attempting to retrieve a word from a recent study episode (e.g., Roediger, Weldon, Stadler, & Riegler, 1992). Figure 6.5, which for the purposes of this chapter may be considered as one kind of refinement of the "termination of search" stage in Fig. 6.1, portrays theoretical relationships among several of the metacognitive components

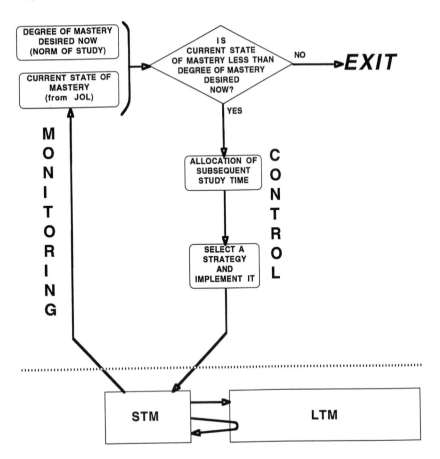

FIG. 6.4. An instantiation of a two-level metacognitive system for acquisition
of information into memory. Adapted from Nelson and Narens (1990).
© 1990 by Academic Press. Adapted with permission.

that can be activated during the retrieval portion of a word-fragment
completion task for implicit/explicit memory. (A related figure providing a
more complete analysis of retrieval of general information from long-term
memory is available in Barnes, Nelson, Dunlosky, Mazzoni, & Narens, 1995.)
In Fig. 6.5, presentation of the word fragment generates a mental image.
This mental image may be an image of the presented word fragment, a word
that completes the fragment, or some other extension of the word fragment.
It is produced implicitly. A metacognitive confidence judgment occurs to
evaluate whether the mental image is a possible answer, and if it is deemed
a possible answer, then another metacognitive confidence judgment is made
about whether it was an answer presented during study, and if it is so deemed,
the possible answer is produced as an output. If the mental image is judged

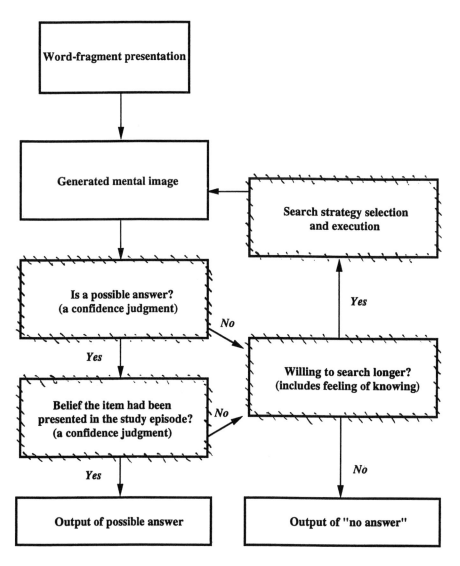

FIG. 6.5. A dynamic generation-recognition model containing metacognitive components (indicated by boxes with hatched borders) that is designed as a partial theoretical analysis of explicit retrieval during word-fragment completion. The primary modification needed for implicit retrieval during word-fragment completion is that the metacognitive belief that the item had been presented in the study episode is not utilized, and the search strategy (and its execution) may produce different cues to initiate the search.

to not be a possible answer, or if the possible answer is judged to not have been presented during prior study, then a metacognitive decision about whether to continue searching for the answer is made. In part, this metacognitive decision is based on the feeling of knowing. If it is negative, then a "no answer" response is produced. If it is positive, then a search strategy is selected and initiated. When initiated, this search generates a new mental image, and another cycle begins (see Fig. 6.5).

In *implicit retrieval* the subject attempts to retrieve a word that completes the fragment, without regard for whether the word occurred during a recent study episode (e.g., Roediger et al., 1992). We propose that the metacognitive decisions for implicit retrieval are qualitatively the same as for explicit retrieval except that (a) the stage of "did the possible answer occur during study" is eliminated, and (b) those subcomponents of the stage of "selecting and executing search strategies" that use aspects of the study episode are eliminated.

The metacognitive component in Fig. 6.5 of deciding whether a possible answer occurred during study is generally acknowledged by researchers of implicit/explicit memory as being an important distinguishing factor between implicit and explicit memory, with its presence indicating explicit memory. Thus in designing implicit memory tests, researchers often go to great lengths to avoid this decision, such as by instructing the subject to output the first completion that comes to mind—a strategy that in essence eliminates the stage of "did the possible answer occur during study." However, there is another component in Fig. 6.5 where a nonimplicit form of memory may be used to advantage. This is the stage of "selecting and executing search strategies." In that stage, the metacognitive subcomponents include strategies that use aspects of the study episode as cues for producing a mental image of the answer or part of the answer. Such subcomponents of nonimplicit memory are rarely discussed in the literature. We believe them to be of importance, because it is plausible that the utilization of the information contained in them may result in different processes/products of generating candidate words during retrieval; for instance, the "generation" component of Jacoby and Hollingshead's (1990) generation-recognition model may occur differently during implicit retrieval than during explicit retrieval.[1]

---

[1] Research by Anderson and Pichert (1978), Bower and Mann (1992), and Gardiner, Craik, and Birtwhistle (1972) show that in other memory situations subjects can at the time of retrieval effectively use retrieved aspects of the study episode to help direct their memory search. Jameson, Narens, Goldfarb, and Nelson (1990) presented research in which subthreshold primes increase recall performance. However, due to the subthreshold nature of the primes, there are no aspects of the priming episode that could help in directed search. Interestingly enough, even though there is an increase in recall performance for primed items, there was no corresponding increase in metacognitive ratings for primed items.

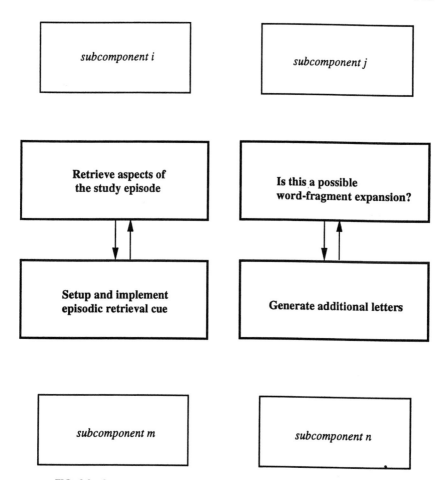

FIG. 6.6. Some potential subcomponents of the "search strategy selection and execution" stage of Fig. 6.5.

Figure 6.5 is our version of a generation-recognition model that stresses multiple cycles of generation. In it, the "generation" aspect comes from two sources: the word-fragment stimulus and the metacognitive component that selects and executes retrieval strategies. The latter component is refined in Fig. 6.6. The stages in Fig. 6.6 represent some metacognitive components that select or execute search strategies. Only four of these are described, and arrows representing flows of information between components other than these four are not included in the figure. The four described components divide into two kinds of metacognitive strategies for generation—a generation strategy that uses aspects of the study episode, and a generation strategy that does not use such aspects.

The issue of whether implicit and explicit retrieval instructions differentially affect the implicit metacognitive components discussed earlier is a sticky one. It appears to us that most researchers of implicit/explicit *assume* that they are not so affected. However, the issue needs empirical investigation. In general, we believe that any complete analysis of implicit/explicit retrieval during word-fragment completion will require empirical investigations of the aforementioned or similar metacognitive components.[2]

EXPERIMENTS

According to Vallone, Griffin, Lin, and Ross (1990):

> In self-prediction . . . people will be prone to make errors to the extent that they have incorrectly inferred details about the objective situations to be faced. . . . They also will be prone to show overconfidence to the extent that they express levels of confidence that make insufficient allowance for the possibility of erroneous inference or misconstrual. (p. 583)

Therefore, one hypothesis about explicit memory is the following: If subjects when making JOLs (in terms of predicting their subsequent retention performance on the recently studied item) are incorrectly inferring the nature of the retention test more for an upcoming implicit-memory test than for an upcoming explicit-memory test, then (a) the accuracy of their JOLs for predicting performance on one item relative to another should be lower in the case of an eventual implicit-memory test than an eventual explicit-memory test, and (b) their JOLs might display more overconfidence in the case of the implicit-memory test than in the case of the explicit-memory test. A similar prediction about the degree of JOL accuracy for one item relative to another (as quantified by the Goodman and Kruskal gamma correlation) can be derived from Patrick, Harbluk, and Lupker (1988), who suggested that metacognitive monitoring such as the feeling of knowing:

> May be based on partial conceptual or elaborative information about the unrecalled items (which is supposed to be the information tapped by explicit tests), instead of perceptual or data driven information (which is supposed to be the information tapped by implicit tests). If so, one would expect that

---

[2]As an example, consider an amnesic patient who displays impaired explicit memory but normal implicit memory. This may be due to either deficiencies in retrieving aspects of the study episode or deficiencies making accurate confidence judgments about whether the retrieved word appeared in the study episode or both.

the gamma correlations in the explicit condition should be higher than in the implicit conditions. (p. 5)

By contrast, another hypothesis, which can be derived from our metacognitive-aspects-of-retrieval model (Fig. 6.5), is that JOLs should be equally accurate for predicting upcoming implicit memory as for predicting upcoming explicit memory, unless the difference between the instructions for implicit versus explicit retrieval affects which of the studied items are retrieved. These and other hypotheses concerning implicit/explicit memory were examined in our two new experiments.

In accord with past research on implicit versus explicit memory, a word-fragment completion task was used in our experiments.[3] A prerequisite for assuming that the instructions at the time of the retention test are adequate for concluding that the investigation was of implicit versus explicit memory is that the earlier encoding of the items by semantic versus graphemic processing should not affect implicit memory but should affect explicit memory (i.e., the retrieval intentionality criterion in Schacter, Bowers, & Booker, 1989). Therefore we also included in our experimental design the independent variable of semantic versus graphemic processing during encoding of the items in the acquisition phase. Our experiments are modeled after the procedure in Roediger et al. (1992), and we thank Roddy Roediger for his helpful advice.

EXPERIMENT 1

Method

Subjects, Design, and Items.   The subjects were 180 University of Washington undergraduates who participated for course credit. The design had one between-subjects variable with three groups (implicit, explicit-withhold, and explicit-guess during the retention test) and one within-subjects variable (half of the items were studied under semantic encoding instructions and the remaining half were studied under graphemic encoding conditions). The 136 items (68 being studied and 68 being nonstudied) were taken verbatim from the words and their corresponding fragments (71% of which had unique solutions in terms of the words they could give rise to) from Roediger et al. (1992, Appendix C). Items were randomly assigned anew for

---

[3]We used word-fragment instead of word-stem completion, because our design ideally required unique correct answers, and word-fragment completion yielded more cases with such answer patterns. Having unique correct answers eliminates the possibility that the JOL accuracy for items from an implicit test could be artifactually lowered by the subject producing a word that is a correct completion but did not occur in the study session.

each subject to study versus nonstudy and to semantic versus graphemic encoding.

Procedure. Subjects were run individually on Macintosh LC II computers, with the exception of the filler tasks (described later). The four distinct phases were: (a) semantic (or graphemic) encoding of words intermingled with JOLs, (b) graphemic (or semantic) encoding of words intermingled with JOLs, (c) filler tasks, and (d) fragment-cued recall. The presentation of semantic and graphemic encoding was counterbalanced for order; half of the subjects studied first under semantic encoding conditions and then under graphemic encoding conditions, and vice versa for the remaining subjects. The verbatim instructions for all phases of the experiment appear in the Appendix at the end of this chapter.

Semantic Encoding. Subjects saw each of 34 words singly at a 7-second rate and were instructed to think of the corresponding referent as each word appeared and to enter a pleasantness rating on a scale from 0 (*extremely unpleasant*) to 7 (*extremely pleasant*). Subjects were told to study each word so that they would be able to remember it later, but were not informed of the upcoming memory test.

Graphemic Encoding. Subjects saw each of 34 words singly at a 7-second rate and were instructed to count the total number of ascenders (e.g., b, d, f, h, k, l, and t) and descenders (e.g., g, j, p, q, and y) in each word and to enter an answer between 0 (no ascenders and no descenders) and 7. Subjects were told to study each word so that they would be able to remember it later, but were not informed of the upcoming memory test.

JOLs. Immediately after the offset of each study word, subjects made a JOL on the following scale: "How confident are you that you will be able to remember the word you just saw? (0 = definitely will recall, 20 = 20% sure, 40 ..., 60 ..., 80 ..., 100 = definitely will recall)." All JOLs were self-paced. Subjects made JOLs alternately with rating the words by making the JOL for a given word immediately after the offset of that word and just before the onset of the next word.

Filler Task. For the 10-minute filler task, the subjects recalled as many U.S. states and capitals as they could for 6 minutes and then tried to solve some box problems for 3 minutes (with one minute for instructions and distribution of materials).

Fragment-Cued Recall. All 136 fragments were included in this phase. Of these fragments, half were portions (identical to those in Roediger et al., 1992) of words that had been studied and the other half were portions of nonstudied words. For each item, the corresponding fragment was displayed on the screen, and subjects were to fill it in with a word that completed the fragment. Subjects had 15 seconds to make a response. In the implicit group, subjects were told that they were going to solve a series of word fragment puzzles. They were instructed to type in the first word they could think of that turned the fragment into a word. In the explicit groups, subjects were told that they were taking a memory test for words seen earlier. They were also told that some of the words they would be tested on had not appeared during study. They were instructed to use the fragments as clues to help them remember the words they had seen during the rating phase. In the explicit-withhold group (modeled after Roediger et al., 1992), subjects were instructed to enter an answer only when certain it had actually appeared at study; if unsure about whether it had appeared at study, subjects were to omit the item. The instructions for subjects in the explicit-guess group (aka "inclusion group" in Jacoby's research) were identical to the explicit-withhold group, except that subjects were encouraged to enter a response even if they could not remember having seen the item at study.

Old/New Recognition and Confidence Judgments. During this phase, subjects saw 136 words (of which 68 were old words that had been studied, and the remaining 68 were new) from the items that completed the fragments from the fragment-cued recall test. The self-paced judgments consisted of a word followed by the prompt, "is this word old or new? ("O" = Old, "N" = New), followed by the prompt, "How sure are you that this word is old/new? (50% = it is equally likely that the word is either old or new, 60 = 60% chance word is old/new, 70 . . . , 80 . . . , 90 . . . , 100 = the word is definitely old/new)" so that the subjects could make confidence judgments about their old/new decisions. Subjects were informed just prior to this phase that half of the words they would judge had appeared during study, whereas the other half of the words had not, and they should therefore expect any given word to be either old or new with a likelihood of 50%.

Results and Discussion

Effect of Group on Baseline Completion (Nonstudied Words). The mean proportion of word-fragment completions on nonstudied items for the implicit, explicit-withhold, and explicit-guess groups was .29 (SEM = .01), .12 (SEM = .01), and .27 (SEM = .01), respectively. The groups were significantly different $F(2, 117) = 53.7$, $p < .01$. Paired comparisons revealed significant differences between the implicit and explicit-withhold groups $t(177) = 9.42$, $p < .01$ and between the explicit-withhold and explicit-guess groups $t(177) = 8.45$, $p < .01$, but not between the implicit and explicit-guess groups, $t(177) = .97$, $p = .33$. This pattern confirms that the instructions were effective, because subjects in the explicit-withhold group should withhold some percentage of the nonstudied items that they mistakenly believed may have been studied.

Effect of Semantic Versus Graphemic Processing. In the implicit group, the mean proportion of correct word-fragment completions was .54 (SEM = .02) for the semantically encoded items and .52 (SEM = .02) for the graphemically encoded items. This difference was not significant by a paired *t*-test $t(59) = 1.24$, $p = .22$. The mean word-fragment-completion performance in the explicit-withhold group was .54 (SEM = .02) for the semantically encoded items and .48 (SEM = .02) for the graphemically encoded items, respectively, which yielded a significant difference, $t(59) = 3.82$, $p < .01$. The mean word-fragment-completion performance for the explicit-guess group was .55 (SEM = .02) for the semantically encoded items and .50 (SEM = .02) for the graphemically encoded items, which yielded a significant difference, $t(59) = 2.74$, $p < .01$. Thus the retrieval intentionality criterion's prerequisite of a nonsignificant effect on implicit memory and a significant effect on explicit memory was satisfied.

Relative Accuracy of Item-by-Item JOLs. The mean levels of JOL accuracy for predicting subsequent memory performance on one item relative to another item (in terms of the Goodman–Kruskal gamma correlation; see Nelson, 1984, for rationale) for the implicit, explicit-withhold, and explicit-guess groups were .16 (SEM = .03), .23 (SEM = .03), and .17 (SEM = .03). These three means were not significantly different by a one-way ANOVA, $F(2, 176) = 1.40$, $p = .25$.

Absolute Accuracy of Item-by-Item JOLs. In contrast to the aspect of relative (i.e., one item relative to another) accuracy, we also analyzed absolute accuracy (i.e., cardinal aspect, aka calibration of overall predicted recall). Figure 6.7 shows the calibration for each group in terms of the mean percentage of correct word-fragment performance as a function of the predicted likelihood of being correct. Perfect predictive accuracy would yield a curve that is atop the main diagonal, and overconfidence is indicated by a curve that is below the main diagonal. As can be seen in both panels, there was no difference between the three groups in terms of calibration being systematically better for one group than another group, and there was no greater overconfidence in the implicit-memory group than in the two explicit-memory groups.

Old/New Recognition of Studied Versus Nonstudied Items. People's accuracy at judging whether the items had been studied versus nonstudied is shown for each of the three groups in Fig. 6.8. Notice that although people's recognition was substantial for discriminating studied items from nonstudied

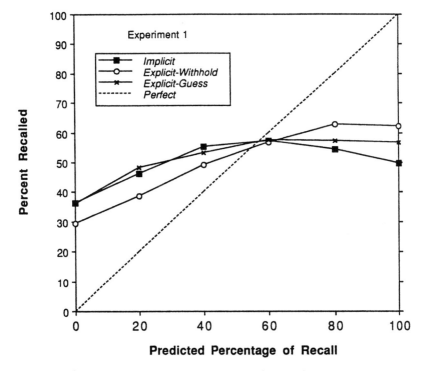

FIG. 6.7. Calibration curves for Experiment 1 showing the mean percent recalled as a function of the predicted percentage recall (from people's JOLs) for the implicit, explicit-withhold, and explicit-guess groups. The main diagonal is a reference line for perfect calibration.

items, their recognition was far from perfect. The probability of saying "studied" to items that had been studied (aka hit rate) was less than 1.0, but even more striking in terms of imperfect recognition, the probability of saying "studied" to items that had not been studied (aka false alarm rate) was substantially above zero. For instance, the explicit-withhold group believed that approximately 20% of the nonstudied items had been in the study episode. This indicates that the corresponding metacognitive component (see Fig. 6.5) contains a degree of inaccuracy for which theories of implicit/explicit memory somehow have to account.

Output of Items by the Explicit-Withhold Group During Word-Fragment Completion. If people in the explicit-withhold group do withhold all of the nonstudied items, then the probability of their completing a word fragment with a nonstudied word would be zero, regardless of whether they believe the item was studied or nonstudied. By contrast, if the decision to withhold is instead based entirely on the person's belief that the item was nonstudied (as suggested in Fig. 6.5), then the probability of outputting an item be-

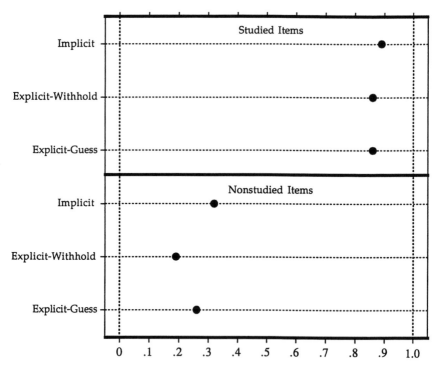

FIG. 6.8. A dot chart for Experiment 1 showing the mean probability that subjects said a given word had been studied (i.e., the mean probability that subjects believed they had seen the item during the study episode) for items that had been studied versus nonstudied by each group.

lieved to be nonstudied should be zero regardless of whether the item had/had not been in the study episode. The mean probability that people in the explicit-withhold group completed a word fragment is shown in Table 6.1 as a joint function of the state of the item during the acquisition episode (i.e., studied versus nonstudied) and of the person's belief that the item had been studied versus nonstudied (as assessed by the old/new recognition test described in the previous paragraph). None of the joint probabilities is exactly zero, and this disconfirms the simple decision rules shown earlier. However, as is also obvious in Table 6.1, the likelihood of an item being output (rather than withheld) depends not so much on whether the item had/had not been studied but rather is dominated by *the person's belief* about whether the item had/had not been studied; the need for postulating such a metacognitive component is particularly obvious from a comparison of the two cells on the main diagonal in Table 6.1. This is analogous to people's feeling of knowing being based less on the frequency of their previous recalls than on people's beliefs about the frequency of their previous recalls (see Nelson & Narens, 1990, Table 2).

TABLE 6.1
Probability of Outputting an Item in the Explicit-Withhold
Group as a Joint Function of State of the Item (Studied/Nonstudied)
and Belief About State of the Item (Experiment 1)

Belief About State of the Item	State of Item During Acquisition Episode	
	Studied	Nonstudied
"Studied"	.62	.46
"Nonstudied"	.15	.09

Note: SEM was less than or equal to .03 for every cell.

The likelihood of outputting (versus withholding) items was also examined as a function of people's confidence about their beliefs of whether the items had been studied/nonstudied. For every pair of items in which one item was believed to have been studied (hereafter, "studied") and the other item was believed to have been nonstudied (hereafter, "nonstudied") and in which one of the two items was output whereas the other item had not been output, we computed the probability that the item that was judged to be the "studied" item was also the item that was output. The mean probability, designated P(output more likely for Item J than Item K | belief of being in study episode is greater for Item J than Item K), is shown in Fig. 6.9 as a function of people's confidence in those beliefs. (Note: Only those pairs wherein the degree of confidence was equal for the two items—i.e., confidence that Item J had been studied and confidence that Item K had not been studied—are included in the analysis.) Several findings are noteworthy. First, the implementation in the explicit-withhold group of a metacognitive rule for outputting all "studied" items and withholding all nonstudied items is not all-or-none (see the earlier discussion of Table 6.1), but rather now can be seen to depend greatly on people's degree of confidence in their beliefs that the items were/were not in the study episode. The likelihood of outputting the "studied" item rather than the "nonstudied" item increased as people's confidence in those beliefs also increased; put another way, the likelihood of outputting "nonstudied" items increased as people's confidence in their beliefs about study/nonstudy decreased toward 50%. Second, relative to the two other groups (whose curves are included in Fig. 6.9 for purposes of comparison), the explicit-withhold group made greater utilization of their confidence, such that the curve is steeper for the explicit-withhold group than for either of the other two groups. Third, when people's confidence in their beliefs about particular items was 100%, the explicit-withhold group's performance was quite close to what would be expected if they were using the simple rule of always outputting the items they believed were more likely to have been studied. Thus the evidence confirms the notion that meta-

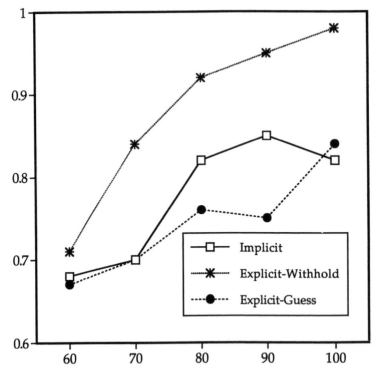

FIG. 6.9. Mean P(output more likely for Item J than Item K │ belief of being in study episode is greater for Item J than Item K) as a function of people's confidence in their beliefs about whether the items had been studied/nonstudied for each group in Experiment 1. See text for elaboration.

cognitive confidence is a component that is useful in the theoretical framework depicted in Fig. 6.5.

EXPERIMENT 2

A recent innovation in metamemory that produces large effects on metacognitive monitoring accuracy is to delay the JOL for at least 30 seconds after study of the item (Nelson & Dunlosky, 1991). Although the psychological mechanisms are not yet known for this delayed-JOL effect (in terms of the advantage in JOL accuracy for delayed JOLs over immediate JOLs), we wanted to see if the delayed-JOL effect might interact with the test conditions of implicit versus explicit memory. However, delayed JOLs require a cue so that the person will know which prior item is being judged, and if the cue is the entire item (i.e., stimulus and response), then the delayed-JOL effect is reduced or eliminated (Dunlosky & Nelson, 1992). Therefore, we used the word fragment itself as the cue for the JOLs. As in Experiment 1, the instructions at the time of the retention test were manipulated so that the retention test was either implicit or explicit memory.

Method

The method was identical to that for Experiment 1 except for the following changes:

1. Delayed JOLs were included, and the kind of JOL (Immediate or Delayed) was blocked as a within-subjects variable. Half of the subjects made immediate JOLs on half of the items prior to making delayed JOLs on the remaining items, and vice versa for the other subjects. Thus 17 items were randomly allocated anew for each subject into each of the following four categories: (a) semantic study with immediate JOLs, (b) graphemic study with immediate JOLs, (c) semantic study with delayed JOLs, and (d) graphemic study with delayed JOLs.

When making immediate JOLs, subjects studied words in the first two aforementioned categories. Following the presentation of each item, subjects made an immediate JOL (i.e., JOLs were intermingled with study, and a JOL was made for each item). After the subjects studied and made JOLs for those items, they studied and made delayed JOLs for the remaining items. When making delayed JOLs, subjects studied words in the third and fourth categories, followed by a delayed JOL on each of those items. Delayed JOLs were made such that there were always at least five intervening items (either words being studied or other JOLs) between the study of an item and its delayed JOL.

The inclusion of the kind of JOL as a blocked variable necessitated a more complex counterbalancing scheme. As in Experiment 1, semantic versus graphemic encoding during study was blocked. The two variables (kind of JOL and kind of encoding) were simultaneously counterbalanced for order. A given subject studied and made JOLs in one of the following eight sets (with each row corresponding to one ordering of conditions), where "S" indicates words semantically encoded, "G" indicates words graphemically encoded, an "(I)" indicates immediate JOLs, and a "(D)" indicates delayed JOLs:

(I) S,G (D) G,S
(I) G,S (D) S,G
(I) S,G (D) S,G
(I) G,S (D) G,S
(D) S,G (I) G,S
(D) G,S (I) S,G

(D) S,G (I) S,G
(D) G,S (I) G,S

Thus, a subject in the first set of conditions (i.e., the first of these eight rows) would study words under semantic instructions and make immediate JOLs, and then study words under graphemic instructions and make immediate JOLs; then the person would study words under graphemic instructions, make delayed JOLs on those words, study words under semantic instructions, and make delayed JOLs on those words. Each of these eight sets constituted a separate subgroup of subjects, and this was crossed with the between-subjects independent variable (kind of retention test). Thus, the counterbalancing scheme required a total of 8 sets * 3 kinds of test = 24 subgroups. Three subjects were run in each subgroup, for a total of 24 * 3 = 72 subjects. Subjects were assigned to subgroups by a block randomization design in which the $i + 1$th subject in a given group was not run until the ith replication was complete (i.e., each run of 24 subjects constituted one replication).

2. The JOLs were made differently in Experiment 2 than in Experiment 1. Experiment 2 used the fragment cue as the cue for the JOL (whereas in Experiment 1 the cue for the JOL was the offset of the just-studied word). For each JOL, the subject was presented with the fragment corresponding to the word seen at study, along with the query, "How likely are you to recall the word you saw at study so as to complete this fragment into that word (0 = definitely will recall, 20 = 20% sure, 40 . . . , 60 . . . , 80 . . . , 100 = definitely will recall)."

Results and Discussion

Effect of Group on Baseline Completion. The mean proportion of word-fragment completions for nonstudied words was .31 (SEM = .02), .14 (SEM = .02), and .31 (SEM = .02) for the implicit, explicit-withhold, and explicit-guess groups, respectively. These three means are significantly different; $F(2, 69) = 18.31$, $p < .01$. Paired comparisons showed that the implicit and explicit-guess groups did not significantly differ, $t(69) = 0$, but the implicit group differed significantly from the explicit-withhold group, $t(69) = 5.24$, $p < .01$, but the explicit-guess group differed significantly from the explicit-withhold group, $t(69) = 5.24$, $p < .01$. Thus, participants in the implicit and explicit-guess groups had higher baseline completion than participants in the explicit-withhold group, thereby confirming that the instructions were effective, as in Experiment 1.

Effect of Semantic Versus Graphemic Processing. In the implicit group, the mean probability of correct word-fragment-completion performance was .66 (SEM = .03) for the semantically encoded items and .63 (SEM = .02) for the graphemically encoded items. This difference was not significant by a paired t test, $t(23) = .90$, $p = .38$. The mean word-fragment-completion performance in the explicit-withhold group was .61 (SEM = .04) for the semantically encoded items and .51 (SEM = .04) for the graphemically encoded items, which was a significant difference, $t(23) = 2.76$, $p < .05$. The mean word-fragment-completion performance for the explicit-guess group was .64 (SEM = .02) for the semantically encoded items and .61 (SEM = .03) for the graphemically encoded items, which was not significant $t(23) = .97$, $p = .34$. These three pairwise comparisons yielded only partial confirmation of the retrieval intentionality criterion. The presence of the word-fragment cues for the JOLs may have partially attenuated the different effects of the encoding instructions on the various kinds of retention tests.

Relative Accuracy of Item-by-Item JOLs.   The mean JOL accuracy (in terms of mean gamma) for the implicit, explicit-withhold, and explicit-guess groups were .62 (SEM = .04), .63 (SEM = .04) and .52 (SEM = .04). These three means were not significantly different by a one-way ANOVA $F(2, 67) = 2.27$, $p = .11$. Notice that the mean gammas were nearly identical for the implicit and explicit-withhold groups, even though other differences between those two groups satisfied the retrieval intentionality criterion.

A more fine-grained breakdown of JOL accuracy (in terms of mean gamma) for kind of JOL by kind of encoding is shown in Table 6.2. Four one-way ANOVAs were performed to determine the effect of group on each of the following dependent variables: (a) accuracy for immediate JOLs after semantic encoding, (b) accuracy for delayed JOLs after semantic encoding, (c) accuracy for immediate JOLs after graphemic encoding, and (d) accuracy for delayed JOLs after graphemic encoding. For the delayed JOLs on semantically encoded items, the effect of groups was significant, $F(2, 64) = 4.08$, $p < .05$. Pairwise comparisons showed that the only significant pairwise comparison was between the explicit-withhold group and the explicit-guess group, $t(64) = 2.84$, $p < .01$. The paired comparison between the implicit and explicit-withhold groups was not significant, $t(64) = 1.73$, $p > .08$, and the pairwise comparison between the implicit and explicit-guess groups was not significant, $t(64) = 1.19$, $p = .24$. Because the aforementioned pattern of significance for delayed JOLs on semantically encoded items would be impossible for population means and therefore probably represents a power problem in (at least) one of the comparisons, it will not be interpreted further but rather is left as a topic for future research. For the immediate JOLs on semantically encoded items, for the immediate JOLs on graphemically encoded items, and for the delayed JOLs on graphemically encoded items, the effect of group was not significant, $F < 1$. Thus, as in Experiment 1, there was no systematic disadvantage in JOL accuracy for memory predictions that were corroborated by implicit-memory tests as compared with explicit-memory tests.

TABLE 6.2
Mean JOL Accuracy as a Function of Kind of Encoding
(Semantic Vs. Graphemic) and Kind of JOL (Immediate Vs. Delayed)
Between JOLs and Word-Fragment Completion in Experiment 2

	Condition			
	Semantic		Graphemic	
	Immediate JOLs	Delayed JOLs	Immediate JOLs	Delayed JOLs
Group				
Implicit	.27 (.12)	.76 (.05)	.37 (.12)	.76 (.09)
Explicit-Withhold	.29 (.10)	.90 (.03)	.32 (.12)	.81 (.04)
Explicit-Guess	.34 (.07)	.68 (.06)	.37 (.09)	.75 (.04)

Note. SEM is in parentheses.

Absolute Accuracy of Item-by-Item JOLs. The calibration curves comparing absolute accuracy for three groups are shown in Fig. 6.10 (immediate JOLs) and Fig. 6.11 (delayed JOLs). As in Experiment 1, there was no systematic difference between the three groups in the absolute accuracy of their predictions (i.e., closeness to the main diagonal of perfect prediction), and there was no evidence of greater overconfidence in the implicit-memory group than in the explicit-memory groups.

Old/New Recognition of Studied Versus Nonstudied Items. People's accuracy at judging whether the items had been studied versus nonstudied is shown in Fig. 6.12 for each of the three groups. As in Experiment 1, although people's recognition was substantial for discriminating studied items from nonstudied items, their recognition was imperfect—for instance, the probability of saying "studied" to items that had not been studied (aka false alarm rate) was substantially above zero. This represents additional confirmation that the metacognitive confidence judgments postulated in Fig. 6.5 contain some inaccuracy, which should be taken into account by theories of implicit/explicit memory.

Output of Items by the Explicit-Withhold Group During Word-Fragment Completion. The mean probability that people in the explicit-withhold group completed a word fragment is shown in Table 6.3 as a joint function of the state of the item during the acquisition episode (i.e., studied versus nonstudied) and of the person's belief that the item had been studied versus nonstudied (as assessed by the old/new recognition test described in the previous paragraph). As in Experiment 1 (Table 6.1), the likelihood of an item being output depends not so much on whether the item had/had not been studied but rather is dominated by *the person's belief*

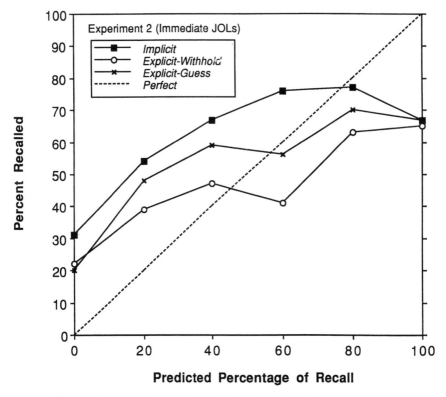

FIG. 6.10. Calibration curves for Experiment 2 showing the mean percent recalled as a function of the predicted percentage recall (from people's immediate JOLs) for the implicit, explicit-withhold, and explicit-guess groups.

about whether the item had/had not been studied. Note that these findings emerged in post hoc analyses that were conducted after the data were collected in both experiments; future research may want include an additional group in which the person's beliefs are assessed at the time of (and in place of) the word-fragment completion in the present groups.

The mean P(output more likely for Item J than Item K | belief of being in study episode is greater for Item J than Item K) is shown in Fig. 6.13 as a function of people's confidence in those beliefs. As in Experiment 1 (Fig. 6.9), the implementation of the explicit-withhold people's metacognitive rule for outputting all "studied" items and withholding all "nonstudied" items is not all-or-none, but instead increased as people's confidence in those beliefs increased. Also, the explicit-withhold group made greater utilization of their confidence than did the two other groups, although the difference between the groups was not as great as in Experiment 1 (e.g., one inversion occurs in Fig. 6.13). Finally, as in Experiment 1, when

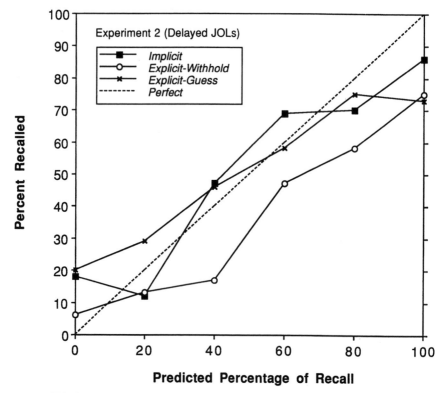

FIG. 6.11. Calibration curves for Experiment 2 showing the mean percent recalled as a function of the predicted percentage recall (from people's delayed JOLs) for the implicit, explicit-withhold, and explicit-guess groups.

people's confidence in their beliefs about particular items was 100%, the explicit-withhold group's performance was almost perfectly compatible with a simple rule of always outputting the items they believed were more likely to have been studied. Thus the evidence from both experiments confirms the important role of metacognitive confidence that was postulated in our theoretical framework (Fig. 6.5).

Related Research Involving the Feeling of Knowing

Patrick et al. (1988) reported that feeling-of-knowing accuracy at predicting subsequent word-stem completion for previously nonrecalled words was equally accurate for word-stem completion following implicit retrieval instructions versus explicit retrieval instructions. This finding is also in accord with the idea that metacognitive monitoring is tapping information in memory whose retrieval may not differ substantially after implicit-memory versus explicit-memory instructions.

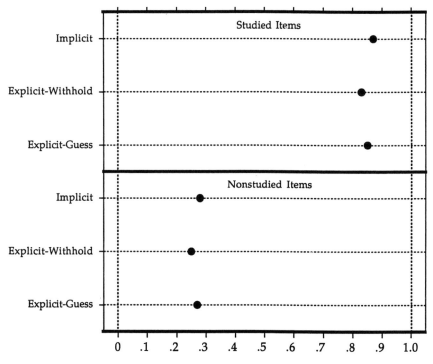

FIG. 6.12. A dot chart for Experiment 2 showing the mean probability that subjects said a given word had been studied (i.e., the mean probability that subjects believed they had seen the item during the study episode) for items that had been studied versus nonstudied by each group.

TABLE 6.3
Probability of Outputting an Item in the Explicit-Withhold Group
as a Joint Function of State of the Item (Studied/Nonstudied)
and Belief About State of the Item (Experiment 2)

Belief About State of the Item	State of Item During Acquisition Episode	
	Studied	Nonstudied
"Studied"	.73	**.55**
"Nonstudied"	**.17**	.11

Note. SEM was less than or equal to .06 for every cell.

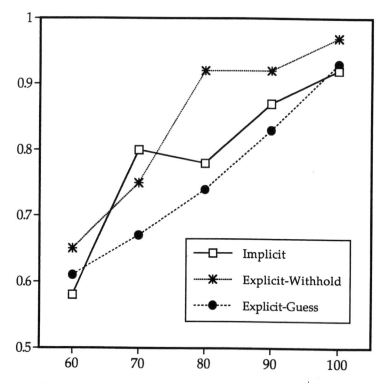

FIG. 6.13. Mean P(output more likely for Item J than Item K | belief of being in study episode is greater for Item J than Item K) as a function of people's confidence in their beliefs about whether the items had been studied/non-studied for each group in Experiment 2. See text for elaboration.

A Methodological Consideration

Researchers of implicit/explicit memory need to deal with the possibility that in the explicit-withhold condition used by us and others (e.g., Roediger et al., 1992; also see Jacoby & Hollingshead, 1990), the withholding of responses arises not from simply one factor (e.g., "conscious awareness") but rather from several factors. In terms of our retrieval model, the following three factors involved in the decision about whether or not to output a retrieved response seem particularly relevant:

1. The subject's tacit assumptions about what is most important. For instance, in terms of payoffs, what is the cost of outputting a nonstudied word, and what is the cost of withholding a studied word? Or alternatively, what is the reward for withholding a nonstudied word and what is the reward for outputting a studied word? These payoffs can be systematically manipulated as is common in yes/no psychophysical experiments, where

the probability of withholding a retrieved word could then be computed. In contrast, most implicit/explicit memory paradigms have *assumed* the conditions of explicit guess (wherein penalty = 0) or explicit withhold. In the explicit-guess condition, the probability of withholding a retrieved word is assumed to be 0. We see no problem with this assumption. However, in the explicit-withhold condition, the probability of withholding, w, is sometimes assumed to be 1. Perhaps instead it should be assumed to be somewhere along almost the full range of the probability scale; namely, $0 < w \leq 1$.

2. The accuracy of recognizing that a retrieved word had previously appeared in the study episode (i.e., old words).

3. The accuracy of recognizing that a retrieved word had not previously appeared in the study episode (i.e., new words).

Notice that the second and third factors here need not be the same; for example, in our two experiments, the subjects were more accurate at recognizing that the studied words had been studied (with probability = .95) and less accurate at recognizing that the nonstudied words had not been studied (with probability = .70). This distinction is analogous to the distinction between the feeling of knowing and the feeling of not knowing in Nelson and Narens (1990).

Also notice that this formulation bears some similarities to the *general* model of signal detection (see Nelson, 1987) wherein there are (*i*) two distributions (corresponding here to a distribution of nonstudied words and a distribution of studied words) that vary in terms of the familiarity/probability of the word as having been in the study episode and (*ii*) the placement of the criterion for outputting a word as having been in the study episode (i.e., the placement of the criterion for the output decision in terms of the word being old). Accordingly, and analogous to the usual signal-detection view, failures to output studied items in the explicit-withhold condition can occur either because the distributions of studied and nonstudied words are not sufficiently separated (e.g., the average familiarity is too similar for the two distributions) or because although the distributions are widely separated the subject chooses to place his or her decision criterion for outputting too high (e.g., so as to withhold items that had not been studied).

Similar to the situation in psychophysics, researchers of implicit/explicit memory need to develop models of withholding the output of presumably nonstudied items (ideally without making arbitrary, untested assumptions about the form of the underlying distributions). We anticipate that several metacognitive components (e.g., placement of the decision criterion for outputting a response as shown in Fig. 6.5, which in turn may be based on a metacognitive evaluation of the payoffs that correspond to withholding studied versus nonstudied items) will play an important role in such models.

CONCLUSIONS

Both metacognitive and implicit/explicit theorists use higher level cognitive processes in the theoretical foundations of their respective subareas. In our own metacognitive theorizing, we have tried to avoid the temptation of using phenomenologically and philosophically rich concepts such as consciousness, awareness, intentionality, and reflexivity. Instead, we have tried to limit ourselves to using only what seem (at least to us) to be the relevant aspects of those richer concepts that are embodied in metacognitive monitoring and control. For example, where some theorists have invoked consciousness or awareness, perhaps instead (meta-) monitoring may suffice; where some theorists have invoked reflexivity, perhaps instead the idea that the metalevel contains an imperfect model of part of the object level may suffice, and so on. Such a limited reductionist approach to higher level cognitive processes may be advantageous for several reasons, not the least of which is that it can be applied to machines as well as to people, thereby potentially extending the reach of psychological theories, hopefully without sacrificing any aspect of consciousness that is scientifically necessary to account for the available data. The extension of scientifically sound psychological principles to machines seems to us to be a potential strength, not a weakness.

We described a partial theoretical task analysis of the word-fragment-completion task, wherein metacognitive components from earlier theoretical formulations played a major role. In our theoretical analysis, the primary difference between implicit and explicit memory performance during word-fragment completion is attributed entirely to two distinct kinds of metacognitive components, one involving metacognitive monitoring (aka recognition of the source of the retrieved item) and its effect on the metacognitive decision to output an answer, and the other involving the metacognitive choice of cues (and metacognitive strategies using aspects of the study episode) to influence the generation of retrieved candidates for an answer in the word-fragment-completion task. We conducted two new experiments that combined standard implicit/explicit memory instructions with standard assessments of metacognitive monitoring and control. Those experiments yielded several findings that can be accounted for by theoretical mechanisms already available in recent theories of metacognitive monitoring and control but that might otherwise be puzzling for a nonmetacognitive theory of implicit/explicit memory. For instance, the output/withholding of answers in an explicit-withhold condition is only partially related to whether the items had/had not been included in the study episode; instead, it is more highly related to whether the person metacognitively believes that the items had/had not been studied, albeit still an imperfect relation. However, the relation between the output/withholding of answers and the person's metacognitive belief about whether the items had/had not been studied will become nearly perfect when the person's metacognitive confidence in that belief increases toward subjective certainty. We suggest that the aforementioned metacognitive components (or their equivalents) are necessary to account for those findings. It appears to us that performance in an implicit/explicit memory task is analogous to what chemists conceptualize as a compound (as opposed to a mixture). If this is so, there may be strong bonds between metacognitive and memory aspects of performance that would be of interest both to metacognitive and implicit/explicit memory researchers. We consider our analysis to be a first step in this direction.

ACKNOWLEDGMENTS

This research was supported by NIMH grant R01–MH32205, a career development award (K05–MH1075) from the NIMH, and an Alexander von Humboldt senior scientist award to the third author. Portions of the research were conducted while the third author was at the University of Washington. Send correspondence to Thomas O. Nelson, Psychology Department, University of Maryland, College Park, MD 20742–4411.

REFERENCES

Anderson, R. C., & Pichert, J. W. (1978). Recall of previous unrecallable information following a shift in perspective. *Journal of Verbal Learning and Verbal Behavior, 17*, 1–12.

Barnes, A. E., Nelson, T. O., Dunlosky, J., Mazzoni, G., & Narens, L. (1995). *An integrative system of metamemory components involved in retrieval.* Unpublished manuscript.

Bower, G. H., & Mann, T. (1992). Improving recall by recoding interfering material at the time of retrieval. *Journal of Experimental Psychology: Learning, Memory, and Cognition, 18*, 1310–1320.

Dulany, D. E. (1994). *Consciousness in the explicit (deliberative) and implicit (evocative).* Unpublished manuscript.

Dunlosky, J., & Nelson, T. O. (1992). Importance of the kind of cue for judgments of learning (JOL) and the delayed-JOL effect. *Memory & Cognition, 20*, 374–380.

Flavell, J. H. (1979). Metacognition and cognitive monitoring: A new area of cognitive-developmental inquiry. *American Psychologist, 34*, 906–911.

Gardiner, J. M., Craik, F. I. M., & Birtwhistle, J. (1972). Retrieval cues from proactive inhibition. *Journal of Verbal Learning and Verbal Behavior, 11*, 778–783.

Jacoby, L. L., & Hollingshead, A. (1990). Toward a generate recognize model of performance on direct and indirect tests of memory. *Journal of Memory and Language, 29*, 433–454.

Jameson, K. A., Narens, L., Goldfarb, K., & Nelson, T. O. (1990). The influence of subthreshold priming on metamemory and recall. *Acta Psychologica, 73*, 55–68.

Nelson, T. O. (1984). A comparison of current measures of feeling-of-knowing accuracy. *Psychological Bulletin, 95*, 109–133.

Nelson, T. O. (1987). The Goodman–Kruskal gamma coefficient as an alternative to signal-detection theory's measures of absolute-judgment accuracy. In E. Roskam & R. Suck (Eds.), *Progress in mathematical psychology* (Vol. 1, pp. 299–306). Nijmegen, The Netherlands: Elsevier North-Holland.

Nelson, T. O., & Dunlosky, J. (1991). The delayed-JOL effect: When delaying your judgments of learning can improve the accuracy of your metacognitive monitoring. *Psychological Science, 2,* 267–270.

Nelson, T. O., & Narens, L. (1990). Metamemory: A theoretical framework and some new findings. In G. H. Bower (Ed.), *The psychology of learning and motivation* (Vol. 26, pp. 125–173). San Diego: Academic Press.

Nelson, T. O., & Narens, L. (1994). Why investigate metacognition? In J. Metcalfe & A. Shimamura (Eds.), *Metacognition: Knowing about knowing* (pp. 1–26). Cambridge, MA: Bradford.

Patrick, A. S., Harbluk, J. L., & Lupker, S. J. (1988). *Analyzing the fate of unrecalled items.* Paper presented at the Twenty-Ninth Annual Meeting of the Psychonomic Society.

Roediger, H. L., Weldon, M. S., Stadler, M. L., & Riegler, G. L. (1992). Direct comparison of two implicit memory tests: Word fragment and word stem completion. *Journal of Experimental Psychology: Learning, Memory, and Cognition, 18,* 1251–1296.

Schacter, D. L. (1987). Implicit memory: History and current status. *Journal of Experimental Psychology: Learning, Memory, and Cognition, 13,* 501–518.

Schacter, D. L., Bowers, J., & Booker, J. (1989). Intention, awareness and implicit memory: The retrieval intentionality criterion. In S. Lewandowsky, J. C. Dunn, & K. Kirsner (Eds.), *Implicit memory: Theoretical issues* (pp. 47–65). Hillsdale, NJ: Lawrence Erlbaum Associates.

Vallone, R. P., Griffin, D. W., Lin, S., & Ross, L. (1990). Overconfident prediction of future actions and outcomes by self and others. *Journal of Personality and Social Psychology, 58,* 582–592.

Wilson, T. D. (1994). *The psychology of meta-psychology.* Unpublished manuscript.

APPENDIX:
INSTRUCTIONS FOR EXPERIMENTS 1 AND 2

In this experiment, we are interested in collecting norms about the characteristics of words for future psycholinguistic research. You will be making ratings that will contribute to these norms in the various word rating tasks that follow.

Semantic Instructions: You are going to rate a series of words for pleasantness. As each word appears on the screen, think about the real world object it represents, and rate it for pleasantness on a scale of 0 (extremely unpleasant) to 7 (extremely pleasant). For example, if you see the word "platypus", you should think of a platypus and then decide whether a platypus is pleasant or not. If a platypus is extremely pleasant, you should assign a rating of 7. If you think a platypus is extremely unpleasant, you should assign a rating of 0. As you rate the words, you should study them carefully. For each word that appears, you will have 7 seconds to study it and make a rating. The word will always stay on the screen for 7 seconds, whether you type in an answer early or not. If you don't make a rating within 7 seconds, the word will disappear.

Graphemic Instructions: You are going to see a series of words for which you are going to count the number of ascending and descending letters. Ascending letters are letters that have lines or "parts" protruding upward from the letter (e.g., b,d,f,h,k,l,and t). Descending letters are letters that have lines or "parts" that protrude downward from the letter (e.g., g,j,p,q, and y). The word "platypus" has two ascenders (1 and t) and three descenders (two p's and a y). This word therefore contains a total of five ascenders and descenders, and would therefore receive a rating of 5. The word "college" has 2 ascenders (two l's) and one descender (the g). It would therefore receive a rating of 3. The letters c, o, and e are neither ascenders nor descenders and therefore don't count toward the rating. You should always enter a rating between 0 and 7, since there will always be between 0 and 7 ascenders and descenders for any given word. As you rate the words, you should study them carefully. For each word that appears, you will have 7 seconds to study it and make a rating. The word will always stay on the screen for 7 seconds, whether you type in an answer early or not. If you don't type in an answer within 7 seconds, the word will disappear. As before, you will also be asked to make memory judgments about the words that you study. You should follow the same procedure here as before. Note: _After_ the subject finishes here, she is instructed to go across the hall to see the experimenter for further instructions.

JOLs: You will also be asked to make memory judgments about the words that you study. For example, if you study and make a rating for the word "platypus", you will be asked to make a judgment about whether you will be able to remember that the word "platypus" was on the list you are studying and rating. You will make these judgments on a percentage scale (0 = definitely will not recall, 20 = 20% sure, 40...,60...,80...,100 = definitely will recall). If you think you definitely will be able to the word "platypus", you should assign a rating of 100. If you think you definitely will not be able to remember the word "platypus", you should assign a rating of 0. There's no need to rush in making your judgments; you can take as much time as you need here. Type in your judgment, and then press the return key to continue. If you have any questions, please ask the experimenter now. Note: Prompt on screen will say: "How confident are you that you will be able to remember the word you just saw? (0 = definitely will not recall, 20 = 20% sure, 40...,60...,80...,100 = definitely will recall).

Implicit Test: You are going to see a series of word fragment puzzles. When you see the fragment, type in the first word you think of that turns the fragment into a word (e.g., if you saw "-ezza----", then you would be correct if you typed in the word "mezzanine"). It is important that you type in the FIRST WORD THAT COMES TO MIND. A given word that first comes to mind may or may not come from the list of words you studied earlier; just ignore that fact, because we don't care about whether or not it was on the list. All we care about is that you should BE SURE to enter the very first word you think of that completes the fragment. Don't think about the words you just studied; instead, think only about what word will complete the fragment and AS SOON AS YOU THINK OF an answer that will complete the fragment, type it into the computer. Thus your job is to type into the computer the first word you think of that will turn the fragment into a word. You will have 15 seconds to figure out each puzzle; after that time the fragment will disappear.

Explicit-Withhold Test: You are going to take a memory test for words seen earlier. The word fragments you will see on the screen are clues to help you remember the words you saw at study. Many of the fragments you will see do not refer to previously studied words; you should leave these fragments blank. DO NOT GUESS at a word that completes the fragment unless you are SURE that the word was on the list you recently studied. Enter a guess ONLY if you are certain it was on the list you just finished studying. For example, if you see the fragment "-ezza----", you should type in the word "mezzanine" if and ONLY IF you remember having seen the word during study. It is important that you enter a response ONLY when you are sure it was on the list you studied; if you are not sure, DON'T TYPE ANYTHING IN. You will have 15 seconds to enter each answer, after that time the fragment will disappear.

Inclusion (Explicit-Guess) Test: You are going to take a memory test for words seen earlier. The word fragments you will see on the screen are clues to help you remember the words you saw at study. Many of the fragments you will see do not refer to previously studied words; but even though you didn't see the item you should still try to complete the fragment whenever you can. Thinking back to the study list will often help you to complete a given fragment, but still feel free to take a guess at every item, whether it was on the study list or not. You should always try to guess; the computer will not penalize you for incorrect guesses, so if you have any guess at all, please type it in response to the fragment as long as it turns the fragment into a word. For example, if you see the fragment "-ezza----", you should type in the word "mezzanine" regardless of whether or not you remember having studied the word in the list you saw earlier. You will have 15 seconds to enter each answer, after that time the fragment will disappear.

Confidence Judgments: Half of the words you will see you have previously studied; the other half of the words will be entirely new. Note therefore that for any given word that you see, there is a 50% chance that the word is old, and a 50% chance that the word is new. For each word that you see, you should first determine whether the word is old or new. A word is considered old if you saw it during study, and new if you did not see it during study. Following this judgment, you will make a confidence rating on a percent scale to indicate how sure you are that the word is old or new. Note that a 50% rating would indicate that you think it is equally likely that the word is old or new, and a 100% rating would indicate that you are absolutely sure the word is old(new). You will make these judgments on the following scale: (50 = it is equally likely that the word is either old or new, 60 = 60% chance word is old/new, 70...,80...,90...,100 = the word is definitely old/new).

The instructions for Exp. 2 were the same except for the following changes.

1) Delayed judgments of learning were included in experiment 2. Thus, type of judgment (Immediate or Delayed) was added as a within-subjects independent variable. The two types of judgments were presented in blocks.

2) The JOLs in experiment 2 were made differently. Experiment 2 used a fragment cue in the prompt to the subject. For each JOL, the subject was presented with a word fragment corresponding to a word seen at study together with the following query: "How likely are you to recall the word you saw at study so as to complete this fragment into that word (0 = definitely will not recall, 20 = 20% sure, 40...,60...,80...,100 = definitely will recall)."

JOL instructions for immediate blocks: You will also be asked to make memory judgments about the words that you study. For this section of the experiment, you will make a memory judgment on each word IMMEDI-ATELY after studying that word. For example, if you study and make a rating for the word "platypus", you will immediately be asked to make a judgment about whether you will be able to recall the word you saw at study so as to complete the word fragment "pl-t-pu-". You will make these judgments on a percentage scale (0 = definitely will not recall; 20 = 20% sure, 40...,60...,80...,100 = definitely will recall). If you think you definitely will be able to complete the word fragment "pl-t-pu-" to make the word "platypus", you should assign a rating of 100. If you think you definitely will not be able to complete the word fragment "pl-t-pu-" to make the word "platypus", you should assign a rating of 0. There's no need to rush in making your judgments; you can take as much time as you need here. Type in your judgment, and then press the return key to continue. If you have any questions, please ask the experimenter now.

JOL instructions for delayed blocks: You will also be asked to make memory judgments about the words that you study. For this section of the experiment, you will make memory judgments AFTER you have studied all of the words. For example, if you study and make a rating for the word "platypus", you will later be asked to make a judgment about whether you will be able to recall the word you saw at study so as to complete the word fragment "pl-t-pu-". You will make these judgments on a percentage scale (0 = definitely will not recall, 20 = 20% sure, 40...,60...,80...,100 = definitely will recall). If you think you definitely will be able to complete the word fragment "pl-t-pu-" to make the word "platypus", you should assign a rating of 100. If you think you definitely will not be able to complete the word fragment "pl-t-pu-" to make the word "platypus", you should assign a rating of 0. There's no need to rush in making your judgments; you can take as much time as you need here. Type in your judgment, and then press the return key to continue. If you have any questions, please ask the experimenter now.

Chapter 7

In the Mind but Not on the Tongue: Feeling of Knowing in an Anomic Patient

Margaret Funnell
Dartmouth College

Janet Metcalfe
Columbia University

Kyrana Tsapkini
Dartmouth College

Much psychological data converge on the idea that feeling-of-knowing judgments are based on subjects' quick assessment of the familiarity or the fluency of the retrieval cue. Consider a situation in which the subject cannot immediately retrieve the answer to a question or retrieve a word that completes a sentence. If the cue is highly familiar, the subject is likely to give a high feeling-of-knowing judgment to that cue. This high feeling of knowing is not based on retrieval of the answer, but rather on the familiarity of the cue. This judgment may be accurate or inaccurate. The cue may be familiar for a variety of reasons—because it deals with a topic with which the subject is an aficionado, because it is a familiar topic to most people, or because the cue may have been made artificially familiar (by a previewing of some part of that cue, say). The heuristic of giving a high feeling-of-knowing rating if the cue is highly familiar and a low rating if the cue is unfamiliar, while not guaranteeing accuracy, will often have favorable predictive consequences for later recognition performance. In general, if one is an expert in a field, one will be able to distinguish the correct answer from the nonsense. The novice is much less likely to be able to do so. People generally have better success in those domains that they know well. Thus, if unable to immediately retrieve the name of the monetary unit of Nicaragua, the frequent traveler to Central America would and should probably give a higher feeling-of-knowing rating than the stay-at-home. The former would also have a better chance than the latter of

171

choosing the correct response from the alternatives: CORDOBA, PESO, BOLIVAR, PESETA, ESQUDO, INTI, COLON, BOLIVIANO, CRUZEIRO.

A number of findings in the literature suggest that feeling-of-knowing judgments may be attributable to a cue-based familiarity monitor. In the standard recall, judge, recognize (RJR) paradigm, subjects first attempt to recall the target and if they cannot do so, they are asked to judge the probability of recognizing the answer in a multiple-choice format. Subjects therefore only make feeling-of-knowing judgments about questions to which they *cannot remember* the answers. By definition of the task, subjects have exhibited evidence that they cannot retrieve the explicit target information. It is thus plausible to suppose that the judgments are made on the basis of information other than the explicit target information; that is, on the basis of a familiarity monitor.

There are two possible rejoinders to this argument. The first is that there is partial subliminal activation of the retrieved item, not enough to allow recall, but enough to drive feeling-of-knowing judgments. We find this idea to be unlikely (cf. Narens, Jameson, & Lee, 1994) because we understand the feeling-of-knowing judgment to be an *explicit* task and to rely on *explicit* knowledge. Indeed the judgment of what and how much you know about what you know or will know is a classic, almost definitional, explicit task. Explicit tasks do not appear to be open to subliminal information, although implicit performance may be altered by subliminal information. Because feeling-of-knowing judgments are explicit, it is unlikely that subliminal activation could affect these judgments.

The second rejoinder is that perhaps some subjects, some of the time, actually retrieve the target information, but for one reason or another they are unable to say it. The overt and public output may be different from a subject's internal phenomenological state. If a person has retrieved a replete internal representation but cannot convert that retrieved representation into an utterance that satisfies the demands of a recall test—that is, verbal output—the explicit retrieved information may nevertheless be available to conscious inspection and usable as the basis for metacognitive judgments. We explore this possibility in the main section of this chapter and suggest that, at least for some patients, it is a plausible scenario.

EXPERIMENTAL EVIDENCE FOR
THE CUE-FAMILIARITY HYPOTHESIS

Experimental evidence points to the likelihood that feeling-of-knowing judgments in normal subjects are based primarily on assessment of cue familiarity. Studies have focused on such things as the relationship between error types and feeling-of-knowing ratings, the latency of these judgments, the effect of priming cues and targets, and on explicit "don't know" information. This type of evidence converges on the conclusion that feeling-of-knowing judgments are not based on retrieval of the target but rather on familiarity of the cue.

Examination of error types indicates that the differences in feeling of knowing among different error types do not follow the pattern one might expect if subjects were basing their judgments on the retrieval of partial target information. Presumably, if a subject were basing feeling-of-knowing judgments on what is retrieved but the experimenter informed the subject that what had just been retrieved was wrong, such questions should be assigned a low feeling-of-knowing rating. Krinsky and Nelson (1985), however, found that the ratings given to errors of commission were in fact higher than those given to omission errors. It seems that the cues that provoked the errors of commission were familiar enough to retrieve *something* from memory, whereas the cues for omission errors were so unfamiliar that they produced no response (cf. Koriat, 1993).

Another type of evidence in favor of the cue familiarity hypothesis is the latencies of feeling-of-knowing judgments as compared to retrieval latencies. Reder (1987, 1988) argued that if feeling-of-knowing judgments are based on explicitly retrieved information, then one might expect that the latencies to make these judgments would be at least as slow or slower than retrieval latencies. In contrast to this prediction, however, Reder and her colleagues found that judgment latencies were actually faster than retrieval latencies. The fast latencies of normal feeling-of-knowing judgments point to a cue-based rather than a retrieval-based source for the judgments. Reder has been especially interested in the functional import of the preretrieval judgments. She has hypothesized that these rapid judgments are used by the subjects to determine what strategy to adopt in solving a problem. A quick familiarity assessment is of key importance in this strategy selection. For example, if a cue is found to be highly familiar, a subject may decide to retrieve the episode that gives the answer for a problem rather than deciding to work through the problem.

Further evidence for cue-based feeling-of-knowing judgments comes from studies that manipulate the salience of either the cue or the target. Reder (1987, 1988) altered only the cue familiarity—leaving target information unaffected—by embedding parts of the cues in a list of words that subjects made judgments about before the feeling-of-knowing task. Such priming of the cues spuriously increased subjects' feelings of knowing without changing the retrievability of the answers. Schwartz and Metcalfe (1992) followed up these findings in four experiments that simultaneously manipulated cue familiarity, via priming, and target retrievability, via a generation/read manipulation. Cue familiarity but not target retrievability affected the feeling-of-knowing judgments. Similarly, Glenberg, Sanocki, Epstein, and Morris (1987) found a positive correlation between the subjects' domain knowledge, or the "familiarity" of the cues, and their confidence ratings, even in the absence of any accuracy of detailed predictions. Finally, Metcalfe, Schwartz, and Joaquim (1993) used an interference theory paradigm to independently vary the number of repetitions of the cue and the retrievability of the target. They found that the feeling-of-knowing judgments followed the number of repetitions of the cue (i.e., cue familiarity) rather than the memorability of the target (i.e., target retrievability).

Jameson, Narens, Goldfarb, and Nelson (1990) altered the retrievability of targets without affecting the feeling-of-knowing judgments. Cue familiarity and target retrievability are often confounded in the world, with more familiar cues being linked to more retrievable targets. Jameson et al. presented subjects with some answers to general information questions at a duration that was at or close to the threshold of consciousness. This priming resulted in an increase in recall but had no discernible effect on feeling-of-knowing judgments.

A final issue concerns "don't know" information. Specifically, the question is whether subjects explicitly know that they do not know something or whether they conclude this when a search of memory does not result in retrieval of the target information. Kolers and Palef (1976) asserted that people know what they do not know. Empirically, "don't know" judgments can be made very quickly. Kolers and Palef argued these short latencies indicate that people do not make these judgments by trying to retrieve what they do know. If subjects had to perform an exhaustive search of memory in order to conclude that they do not know something, this would require a long time interval. Instead of such a strategy, people seem to have immediate knowledge that they know nothing whatsoever about a given topic. Furthermore, explicit "don't know" information results in impairment on "don't know" judgments rather than an enhancement of such judgments. Glucksberg and McCloskey (1981) gave subjects statements indicating that certain information was not known. An example of such a statement is, "It is not known whether Madonna plays a harp." If subjects were basing their judgments on what they retrieved, they should have been better and quicker at making "don't know" judgments as a result of this information. If, however, judgments were made on the basis of the cue-familiarity monitor, the presentation of the explicit "it is unknown whether" statement would not result in more rapid or more accurate performance. In fact, because the statement is similar to the question used to cue memory ("Does Madonna play the harp?"), the statement would make the question seem more familiar, and hence would hurt performance. The empirical finding that the explicit "don't know" information slowed people down in making their judgments is consistent with the cue-familiarity hypothesis.

MEMORY AND METAMEMORY: DISSOCIABLE FUNCTIONS

The cue familiarity hypothesis depends on the notion that metamemory is dissociable from memory. Schacter (1991) has reviewed a number of studies indicating that monitoring of one's memory is dissociable from the goodness of memory per se. If metamemory is entirely dependent on memory retrieval, then this dissociation between metamemory judgments and memory performance should not have been found.

McGlynn and Schacter (1989) suggested that monitoring, including monitoring of one's own capabilities, is a frontal lobe function. In contrast, pure amnesic syndromes generally result from damage to the temporal lobes, and in particular to the hippocampal formation. Depending on the nature of the brain damage, there can be differential effects on memory and metamemory. These researchers point out that some patients, such as B.Z. (described in McGlynn, Schacter, & Glisky, 1989), may have impaired memory coupled with impaired monitoring. B.Z. is an interesting case because he appears to judge himself as having his pretrauma abilities, and claims to still have these superior abilities, even though his immediate test scores show severe memory deficits. In contrast, other memory impaired patients such as H.D. (also described by McGlynn et al.) have significant memory deficits but are well aware of these deficiencies.

Shimamura and Squire (1986) showed a similar dissociation among different kinds of amnesics. Most amnesics, although showing profound memory deficits, also showed normal metacognitions. Korsakoff patients, however, were not only memory impaired but also had impaired metamemory judgments. Interestingly, in keeping with the hypothesis that the monitoring and judgment might be frontally controlled, the Korsakoff patients are thought by some researchers to have frontal lobe damage, whereas the other memory impaired patients had no frontal damage. To complete the story, Janowsky, Shimamura, and Squire (1989) presented data showing that a metacognitive impairment may be found in frontal patients who exhibit no memory impairment.

FEELING OF KNOWING IN A MEMORY MODEL

CHARM is a computational neural model of human episodic memory (Metcalfe, 1990, 1991, 1993a, 1993b; Metcalfe Eich, 1982, 1985; Metcalfe, Cottrell, & Mencl, 1993). An overview of the model is presented in Fig. 7.1. In this model, events are perceived up to the level of a preepisodic semantic memory "lexicon," which provides the semantic level of representation. These events are represented as vectors. They are associated with one

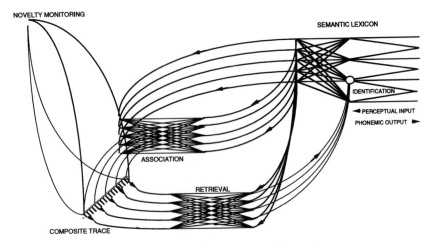

FIG. 7.1. CHARM model showing novelty monitor.

another, episodically, by the operation of convolution. This operation completely intermeshes every element of one event with every element of the other event (or in the case of an autoassociation, with itself), resulting in a thoroughly interactive association. Successive associations are stored by being added into the same single composite memory trace, which is itself a vector. The composite memory trace causes interactions among the various items and associations, and is responsible for many of the important, and confirmed, psychological predictions of the model. These predictions include interference effects as shown in the Osgood surface (Metcalfe Eich, 1982), gradual rather than catastrophic learning (Metcalfe Eich, 1982), positive and negative effects of elaboration (Metcalfe Eich, 1985), the effects of misleading information in the eyewitness testimony paradigm (Metcalfe, 1990), and other context effects (Metcalfe Eich, 1985).

A particular mathematical property of this composite memory trace is that each time a new association is entered into it, the variability of the trace (i.e., the absolute values of elements of the trace) tends to increase. Without some kind of control, there are no bounds on this increase. If the trace is considered to be a real system—say a neural system—then this boundless increase in the values is impossible. To keep this from happening, a novelty monitor and feedback control system is needed. It can be shown that the variability of the trace increases more, on average, the more similar the incoming association is to the information that is already stored in the trace; that is, the more familiar is the cue. Because the monitor gives high values for high matches between the incoming event and the trace, and low or zero values for mismatches between the incoming event and the trace, it could be considered to be a quick prestorage familiarity (or at the other end of the dimension—novelty) monitor, and it is this aspect of the monitor that is of interest for feeling-of-knowing judgments. It is assumed that people use the value produced by this novelty monitor as the basis of their feeling-of-knowing ratings. In this model, the monitoring/control system is conceptually, functionally, and anatomically separable from the underlying basic memory system.

The feeling of novelty or familiarity is basically a feeling that a fact, object, person, word, situation, scenario, or mental event is old or new, familiar or not. The feeling perceived as a result of this memory monitoring process, therefore, is literally a *feeling* of knowing or not knowing—"knowing" when the monitor indicates familiarity; "knowing not" when it indicates novelty. The monitor itself does not say what aspects of the event are old or new, why an event is old, where or when it was experienced, under what circumstances it became known, how frequently an event was experienced, with what it was associated, how recently, or whether it might not have been precisely that event that is causing a feeling of familiarity, but rather, perhaps just some other event that was fairly similar. The value yielded up by the monitor is simply a scalar. It is not representational—just a strength value or an unanalyzable feeling. In the model, however, this value is computed on information in the explicit-memory system. Thus, monitoring this familiarity value is part of the explicit, rather than implicit, memory system.

Figure 7.1 shows the locus of the monitor in the model. Breakdown in this monitor is thought to correspond to frontal lobe impairments, although this is not the only function of the frontal lobes. Retrieval itself could be impaired or not. If it is not impaired, the situation would be one in which feeling-of-knowing judgments are distorted, but memory is not impaired, as in Janowsky et al.'s (1989) study. If both the basic memory system and the novelty monitoring system are impaired, the situation would be similar to that demonstrated by Korsakoff patients in that both memory and metamemory are impaired, as in Shimamura, Janowsky, and Squire's (1991) study. If only the memory system but not the monitoring system is impaired, the results would be like those shown for patient H.D. and many other amnesics (McGlynn et al., 1989)—metacognition is spared and memory is impaired.

FEELING OF KNOWING WHEN THE TARGET INFORMATION IS RETRIEVED BUT CANNOT BE ARTICULATED

Burke, MacKay, Worthley, and Wade (1991) recently presented a linguistically-based model of the *tip-of-the-tongue (TOT) phenomenon* (i.e., the feeling that recall is imminent) in aging patients that is quite different from (although we think compatible with) the Metcalfe (1993a, 1993b) model. In the linguistic model (MacKay, 1982), there is a semantic level of representation that is distinct from the phonological level, and the connections between the semantic and phonological levels may fail. A person might have excellent knowledge at the semantic level and be able to retrieve a semantic representation of the target, but because of a breakdown at the articulatory/phonological level, he or she may be unable to express the response. In such a case, the person would be in a tip-of-the-tongue state and would be expected to have a high feeling of knowing.

A recall test would suggest that the person in this situation "doesn't know" the answer. This conclusion, however, would be incorrect if "knowing" refers to appropriate activation of a node at the semantic level. A recognition test would allow circumvention of the articulatory requirements hard hit by the missing connections—showing that the person did actually know the target at the semantic level. If the person were able to directly monitor the knowledge base at the semantic level for the items that could not be articulated, he or she would be able to produce accurate feeling-of-knowing ratings.

We suggest that the feeling-of-knowing ratings might be higher for a patient suffering from a semantic–phonemic disconnection than are the ratings of normal subjects, who do not have this disconnection. The reason the ratings would be much higher would be because there would be many more "unrecalled" items contributing to the set of items on which the judgments would be based. For the normal subject, only those items which do not sufficiently activate a semantic representation would be included. For the patients, however, all or nearly all items would be included—both those that do not activate the semantic representations, *and also those that do*. This kind of patient, therefore, would have many feeling-of-knowing responses that are based on *retrieved* information rather than on cue familiarity. As long as there is no impairment of the judgment process itself, we might expect the patient to tell us that he knows these items, because, in fact, his or her semantic representations are intact and activated, and he or she does know the items. Burke et al. (1991) argued that the model applies especially well to older patients, in whom the connections between the semantic and phonemic levels may be particularly fragile. We now present data from an anomic patient, H.W., who appears to illustrate a classic case of such a disconnection.

THE EXPERIMENT

We hypothesized that H.W. may exhibit a clear semantic–phonemic dissociation and would thus base his feeling-of-knowing judgments on semantic accessibility, whereas normal college students would base their judgments on cue familiarity. Therefore, the purpose of the experiment was to contrast H.W.'s performance with that of normal subjects.

The Patient

H.W. was born on February 24, 1927. After serving in the army in World War II, he attended college and then started his own company. After several years, he sold this company and attended Harvard Business School where he earned an MBA. He went on to set up his own multimillion dollar business in industrial gasses. He continues to be involved in running this business along with two of his three sons. On the 13th of December, 1987, he suffered a stroke that resulted in massive left hemisphere infarction, particularly in the parietal occipital lobe. The frontal lobes, often thought to be responsible for metamemory judgments, were spared.

Administration of the Boston Diagnostic Aphasia Examination in May 1991 (Baynes & Iven, 1991) indicated that he is in the 81st percentile in auditory comprehension, the 76th percentile in his understanding of written language (but his only errors were in comprehension of oral spelling), and the 38th percentile in oral expression. His oral expression subtest scores indicate that he is impaired in all areas of verbal output including repetition of words and phrases, oral reading of words and sentences, responsive naming, visual confrontation naming, and generating members of a given category. Further evidence for his impaired word retrieval is seen in his performance on the Boston Naming Test in which he named only 1 out of 60 items (the word "house").

In contrast to his verbal language impairments, his intellectual abilities remain intact. Raven's Coloured Progressive Matrices (RCPM) were administered annually between 1989 and 1992. This is a test of visuospatial reasoning and does not require language skills. The test items consist of visual pattern matching and analogy problems (Lezak, 1995). H.W.'s performance on the RCPM places him between the 91st and 95th percentiles of an age matched group. The Wechsler Adult Intelligence Scale–Revised was administered in 1991 and his untimed performance IQ was 121 (timed score was 92). A verbal IQ score could not be obtained due to his severe word retrieval deficits. H.W. is acutely aware of his deficits and is able to provide revealing introspections about his thought processes and about his progress since his stroke.

Despite the language difficulties suggested by H.W.'s test scores, he provides an inspiring picture of compensation for what would be considered by most physicians and clinicians to be a devastating brain injury. H.W. can converse intelligently about such complex topics as his own background, the progress of cognitive neuroscience as a discipline, or Stephen Hawking's *A Brief History of Time*. His conversations, although at a high intellectual and conceptual level, often have the disturbing quality of a game of charades, because he is rarely able to express precise concepts and must describe them using the very limited productive vocabulary he has available. He uses circumlocution remarkably effectively and is adept at prompting his listener to produce specific words he is unable to say. His utterances are punctuated by pointing, pantomiming, and, often, by drawing the first letter of the word he is trying to say. Usually, the first letter is correct. An example of his spontaneous speech follows. This excerpt is in response to a question about where he grew up:

M.F.: And where was that?

H.W.: It was, uh … Leave out of here and where's the next legally place down from here (gestures down).

M.F.: Down? Massachusetts.

H.W.: Next one (gestures down again).

M.F.: Connecticut.

H.W.: Yes. And that's where I was. And at that time, the closest people to me were this far away (holds up five fingers).

M.F.: Five miles?

H.W.: Yes, okay, and, and everybody worked outside but I also, I went to school at a regular school. And when you were in school, you didn't go to school by people brought you to school, you went there by going this way (uses his arms to pantomime walking).

M.F.: By walking.

H.W.: And to go all the way from there to where you where you went to school was actually, was, uh, uh (counts in a whisper) twelve.

M.F.: Twelve miles?

H.W.: Yes, and in those years you went there by going this way (pantomimes walking). When it was warm, I, I found an old one of these (uses his arms to pantomime bicycling).

M.F.: Bicycle.

H.W.: And I, I fixed it so it would work and I would used that when it was warm and when it got cold you just, you do this (pantomimes walking).

Procedure

To test our hypothesis, we used the classic recall–judgment–recognition (RJR) paradigm. The patient and 16 normal college students were shown sentences with the target word omitted and asked to recall the target. If they were unable to retrieve the target, they were asked to make a feeling-of-knowing judgment on a scale of 1 to 10 with 10 being highly confident. They were then given a nine-alternative recognition test and asked to pick the correct alternative. The lures in the recognition test were plausible and related to the target. Previous testing (Baynes & Funnell, 1996) indicated that H.W. is better able to retrieve adjectives than verbs and that his retrieval of nouns is more impaired than for either of the other two word classes. This pattern is observed in spontaneous speech as well as in structured tasks such as oral reading and repetition. We therefore expected that his recall performance would be the worst for nouns and that his feeling-of-knowing judgments would be based on target information for this word class but perhaps on cue familiarity for adjectives and verbs because his word retrieval is better for these word classes. In this way, he might serve as his own control. Although this expectation proved to be unfounded, this was the reason we constructed our materials to explicitly target three different word classes—adjectives, nouns, and verbs.

The materials consisted of 150 sentences each with the target word omitted. The sentences were divided into 3 groups according to word class (50 adjectives, 50 nouns, and 50 verbs). An example of each type of sentence follows (adjective, noun, and verb, respectively): "When something is chronologically out of place, it is _____."; "People who explore caves are called _____."; "Some kinds of snakes _____ every spring, shedding their old skins and leaving them behind." Each student was tested on all three sets of stimuli during one testing session. H.W. was tested on one word class per session to prevent fatigue from affecting his performance. He was later tested again on this task 6 months after initial testing. The stimulus items were the same, but the order of presentation was rerandomized. The procedure for testing H.W. was identical to that used for the students except that the stimuli were also read to him as they appeared on the computer screen to ensure comprehension of the items.

The dependent measures of interest were: probability recalled on the first test, the mean rating of the feeling-of-knowing judgment (and the distributions of those judgments), probability of correct recognition on the final recognition test, and the (gamma) correlation relating the judgments to the final recognition performance. We also attempted to measure latencies for the feeling-of-knowing judgments for H.W. after the data were collected. We thought that the timing measurements would be informative because of Reder's (1987, 1988) theory about rapid preretrieval judgments. This theory suggests that cue-based feeling-of-knowing judgments might be quick, whereas target-based judgments, which require a slow process of retrieval to occur, might be much slower. This distinction might be useful in differentiating between the loci of the judgments in different subject and patient groups.

EXPERIMENTAL RESULTS

Recall

The pattern of responses for H.W. was very different than that of normal subjects. H.W. was able to recall only 1 of 300 words in our test. During the first testing period, he attained a score of 1 item correct for 150 sentences

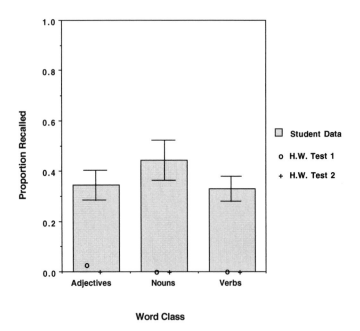

Initial Recall of Target Words

FIG. 7.2. Initial recall of target words. The bars on the student data columns represent the 99% confidence interval of their responses.

(an adjective, "fastest"). He was then retested several months later on the same materials. Despite having had the exact test (although in a different order) before, there was no improvement in the recall score. This time he got none of the answers. By way of contrast, college students were correct on roughly a third of the answers as is shown in Fig. 7.2. T-tests (with a Bonferroni correction) were done to compare H.W.'s test 1 and test 2 performance to that of the students in the three word classes. H.W.'s performance was significantly worse than that of the students ($p < .0001$ for all contrasts). This profound impairment typifies H.W.'s deficit.

Judgments

H.W.'s feeling-of-knowing judgments were also very different from those of the students. His mean confidence rating was much higher than was that of the students. We were concerned, however, that an item selection effect might have artificially inflated H.W.'s feeling-of-knowing ratings. In the RJR paradigm used in this experiment, feeling-of-knowing judgments and recognition responses are made only for unrecalled items. However, because H.W. was so much worse than the students at recall, he made feeling-of-knowing judgments and recognition responses for virtually all of the items—items that the students easily recalled as well as the ones that they were unable to recall. Presumably, H.W.'s feeling-of-knowing judgments would be higher for the easier items, and because these items are included in his data but not in the students' data, his mean feeling-of-knowing rating could be higher for this reason. This item selection effect has the potential to distort the results of the feeling-of-knowing analysis as well as the recognition analysis.

To circumvent this interpretive problem, we tried to equate the difficulty of the questions for H.W. with those of the students. Within each word class, we rank ordered all of the questions in terms of their probability of recall by the students. We then selected those questions that were the least likely to be recalled by the students and were therefore the questions on which the students made feeling-of-knowing and recognition judgments. As an example, the mean recall for the students in the adjective set was 34% correct. Based on the ranking ordering of this stimuli set, we selected those items that were in or above the 34th percentile in ranked difficulty. We then reanalyzed H.W.'s data based only on these items. This conditionalized analysis is designed to more closely equate the difficulty of the set of questions on which the students made their feeling-of-knowing judgments with those on which H.W. made his judgments.

The 99% confidence interval for the students is shown in Fig. 7.3, and H.W.'s conditionalized confidence is well outside the bounds. He was much more confident that he would be able to recognize the answers than were the students even when only the most difficult questions were used in the analysis (all t-tests were significant with a Bonferroni correction). The distributions of his responses as compared to those of students are shown in Fig. 7.4. As can be seen from the figure, whereas students distributed their judgments over the entire scale, H.W. nearly always showed the highest possible confidence on every response. Only occasionally were any responses given less than the maximum rating.

Recognition

H.W.'s recognition scores were indistinguishable from those of normal subjects. These good recognition scores indicate that he does have semantic information about the answers, but, as his clinical diagnosis indicates, he is unable to orally express the words. We were concerned, however, that the same item selection effect that had the potential to inflate his feeling-of-knowing judgments would also bias H.W.'s recognition performance. We therefore analyzed his recognition data in two ways. First, we included all of the questions he had missed on the initial test. This method nominally corresponds to the procedure we used for the students. His recognition

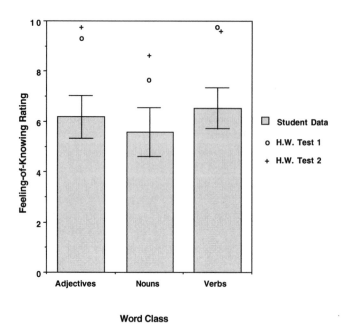

FIG. 7.3. Mean confidence of predictions. The bars on the student data columns represent the 99% confidence interval of their responses. H.W.'s data is conditionalized (see text).

was the same as normal. We then conditionalized H.W.'s recognition data as was described in the preceding section to more closely equate the difficulty of the set of questions on the recognition test. Once again, H.W.'s recognition performance was the same as that of the students (see Fig. 7.5). This was confirmed by t-tests, none of which were significant. His high recognition performance is therefore not attributable to the questions that tend to be easy. Recognition was also high even when the questions were the difficult pool on which the students made their judgments.

Predictive Accuracy of the Feeling-of-Knowing Judgments

Because nearly all of H.W.'s feeling-of-knowing judgments were the same, and on the ceiling, it was not possible to get a large number of highly reliable gamma correlations from him. We designed the experiment so that we could attain a maximum of seven gamma correlations for each of the three word classes. There were 50 items in each word class set and we used seven questions to make up each gamma. Because H.W. recalled only one word during the two testing sessions, we obtained 49 data points for

Frequency Distributions for Adjectives

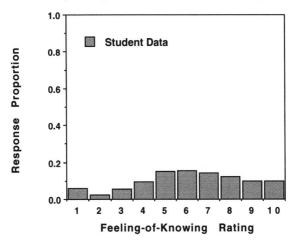

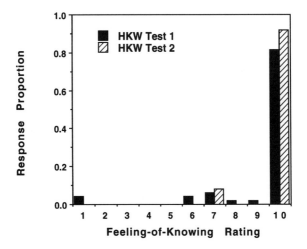

FIG. 7.4. *(Continued)*

each of the word classes in both testing sessions. This should have yielded 7 gamma correlations for each of the word classes with a total of 21 gammas per test, or 42 gammas total for the two testing sessions. As previously noted, however, H.W. gave significantly higher feeling-of-knowing ratings than did the students. During initial testing, he gave a feeling-of-knowing rating of "10" to 77.6% of the items. This rose to 86.6% during the retest. In order to compute gamma correlations, some variability in the judgment data is required. As a result, most of the gamma correlations were composed of fewer than seven observations and some could not be computed at all.

Frequency Distributions for Nouns

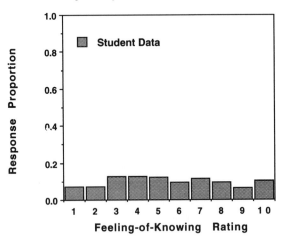

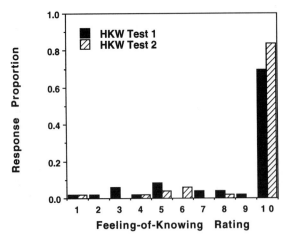

FIG. 7.4. *(Continued)*

Schwartz and Metcalfe (1994) outlined the problem of restricted range in interpretation of feeling-of-knowing data (see also Reder, 1987, for a related problem). This is clearly an issue in this experiment because H.W.'s feeling-of-knowing judgments tended to be on the ceiling, which has the potential to obscure a real correlation. Using the conditionalized data as previously described, we were able to obtain at least two gammas for each condition/session. We also collapsed all attainable gammas for H.W. within each of the two tests in order to stabilize the data. The gamma correlations from the initial test are more reliable than those from the retest because

Frequency Distributions for Verbs

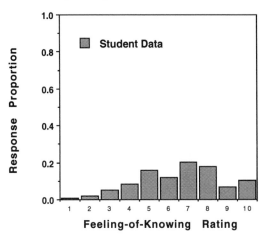

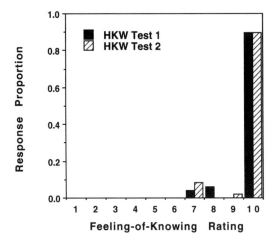

FIG. 7.4. Frequency distributions of feeling of knowing responses for the students and H.W. presented for adjectives, nouns, and verbs (pp. 185–187).

more observations were included in each calculation. The student data were more reliable and the 99% confidence intervals are presented in Fig. 7.6, along with H.W.'s gammas.

There is no reason to suppose that H.W.'s predictive accuracy, when that accuracy can be computed, is any different from that of students. H.W.'s gammas vary around the values shown by normal students. Because

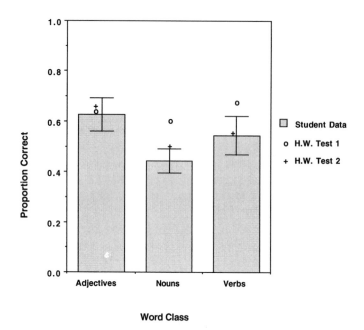

FIG. 7.5. Final recognition performance. The bars on the student data columns represent the 99% confidence interval of their responses. H.W.'s data is conditionalized (see text).

of the measurement difficulties outlined above, however, we cannot make any firm conclusions about the accuracy of his judgments. Further testing will be necessary before any definitive conclusions on this issue can be drawn.

Timing

Because of Reder's theory, we wanted to investigate the timing of H.W.'s feeling-of-knowing responses. As predicted from this theory, the student responses were rapid, with students very rarely taking more than half a second on a judgment. H.W., in contrast, would labor over the decision, and there was nearly always a long pause while he tried to remember the word and then come up with some way to express it. Despite the subjective impression that the timing was very different for H.W. than for normal subjects, we were unable to provide a reliable numerical estimate. Each of H.W.'s testing sessions was audiotaped and we attempted to make measurements of response latency using these tapes. Because of the variability of the

Accuracy of Feeling-of-Knowing Judgments

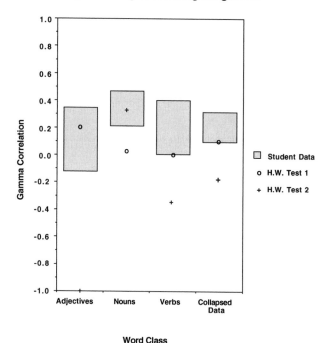

FIG. 7.6. Accuracy of feeling of knowing judgments. The student data columns represent the 99% confidence interval of their responses. H.W.'s data is conditionalized (see text).

way in which he responded, however, these measurements were highly unreliable. For example, during the recall section, he would often spend considerable time thinking about each item. For some items, he would comment to the experimenter that he was sure he would get it later, but that it was another one of those words that he knew but could not say. Later, when the time would come to make the judgment, he would frequently simply recall his assessment from the initial viewing. Before the experimenter had even read the question aloud he would say "10." On other items when asked for his feeling-of-knowing judgment, he would try again to recall the target word, and the experimenter would then need to redirect him to simply provide a feeling-of-knowing judgment. Other sources of response variability included changing his mind about judgments after giving an initial rating and occasional difficulty outputting the specific number he was trying to say. In the latter instances, he would count up to the number he was trying to say. Due to his response variability, we were unable to obtain meaningful response latencies. In order to illustrate H.W.'s response style, an excerpt of a testing session is included below.

M.F.: The division of a cell into two new cells so that each of the resulting cells has only a half set of chromosomes, is called . . . what. Now on a basis of 1 to 10, how confident do you think you are that you will be able to pick it out of a bunch of choices. If you're sure you'll get it—

H.W.: Well, if you're going to give me different ones of that, I should be able to make that with no problem.

M.F.: Okay, on a basis of 1 to 10, what do you think?

H.W.: I would assume . . . I won't be able to necessarily say it.

M.F.: No, you don't have to say it. All you're going to have to do is, I'm going to give you a bunch of choices and you're going to have to pick it.

H.W.: Ten.

M.F.: You think 10. Okay. What is the game where the terms gutter and alley are used. One to 10, how likely do you think you are to recognize it?

H.W.: I should be able to do it a hundred, uh, uh, I should be a 10.

M.F.: Ten. Okay.

H.W.: Because I know it completely.

M.F.: Okay, good. The furry animal that attacks cobra snakes is the what. On the basis of 1 to 10.

H.W.: The problem is I can't remember in my own head. It's not that I can't say it. I know what it is and I can't know how to say the name. I don't know what the name is of what they are.

M.F.: Okay, so probably not a 10. What do you think?

H.W.: I, I, again, I would say at the most 50%.

M.F.: Okay, so five.

H.W.: Yeah, that's about right.

M.F.: Okay, what is the automobile instrument that measures mileage. One to 10.

H.W.: Oh, I should come out with that one if you're going to do it that way. Again (counts in a whisper) 10.

M.F.: Ten. Okay.

CONCLUSIONS

Experimental evidence indicates that normal subjects usually make feeling-of-knowing judgments based on cue familiarity. In some populations, however, it appears that feeling-of-knowing judgments are based on target retrievability. Burke et al. (1991) hypothesized that this is true for elderly patients due to a breakdown between the semantic and phonological levels. Based on our experimental findings, we conclude that this may also be the case for certain brain-damaged patients. H.W., a production anomic, appears to base his feeling-of-knowing judgments on target retrievability because of a semantic–phonemic disconnection due to the nature of his brain lesion. The output deficit results in tip-of-the-tongue states because the lexical items are activated at the semantic level, but there is no way for him to express them due to the disconnection between the semantic and phonological levels.

The pattern of deficits demonstrated by H.W. can be related to the CHARM model. We hypothesize that the novelty monitor in the model is able to "see" the lexicon (which corresponds to the Burke et al., 1991, semantic level). The connection between the lexicon and the phonological output would be impaired in patient H.W. The novelty monitor is thought to represent the monitoring functions of the frontal lobes and H.W.'s frontal lobes are intact. Because H.W. retrieves the correct lexical item and his monitoring functions are intact, he is able to make metamemory judgments based on accurate semantic retrieval. Hence, his feeling-of-knowing judgments are high. This pattern suggests a different locus of impairment than that shown by Korsakoff amnesics whose metamemory judgments are impaired.

Another way of viewing H.W.'s deficit is in terms of the distinction between implicit and explicit memory. Explicit memory results from conscious recollection whereas implicit memory is demonstrated by facilitation of performance without conscious recollection (Schacter, 1987). Moscovitch (1994) argued that consciousness is an inherent property of memories mediated by the hippocampal system. Implicit memory tasks rely on perceptual modules that function outside conscious awareness. When we are consciously aware of something, however, the hippocampal component attaches conscious awareness to the event so that consciousness becomes an inherent property of the memory. This type of a model relates to our findings with H.W. We suggest that H.W.'s explicit memory and his explicit representations are unimpaired. He is able to access the target explicitly but is simply unable to output what he has retrieved.

Because he has explicit access to the target, he can consciously devise strategies for conveying the target in either direct or indirect ways. The following is an example of his use of strategies when asked to repeat the word "blue":

H.W.:   Okay, the first one is going to be—again, I cannot say it.

M.F.:   Okay.

H.W.:   I cannot say it. Well, wait a minute, wait a minute. All right. The first one is this, this, this (draws the letter "B" in the air). Okay, but let me try the whole thing. Let me do colors. What, what color did you say you wanted?

M.F.:   Blue.

H.W.:   Okay. Green, red, blue—blue! That's it!

It is clear that H.W.'s explicit memory is intact although his ability to output what he has retrieved is impaired. When he knows a word but cannot directly output it, he is adept at accessing it in different ways and, failing that, he is also adept at conveying his knowledge using indirect methods such as gesturing, pantomiming, and circumlocuting. Because H.W. so eloquently demonstrates that he knows what he knows, we suggest that his metacognitive abilities are not only intact but are what allow him to compensate so effectively for his verbal output deficits.

ACKNOWLEDGMENTS

We gratefully acknowledge the support of NIMH grant MH48066-05 to the second author. We thank H.W. for his participation in our experiment, Elizabeth Wolf for her assistance in developing the test stimuli, George Wolford for his statistical advice, and Kathleen Baynes for her insights into H.W.'s language deficits.

REFERENCES

Baynes, K., & Iven, C. (1991, October). *Access to the phonological lexicon.* Paper presented at the Academy of Aphasia, Rome, Italy.

Baynes, K., & Funnell, M. (1996). *Access to the phonological lexicon in an aphasic patient.* Unpublished manuscript.

Burke, D. M., MacKay, D. G., Worthley, J. S., & Wade, E. (1991). On the tip of the tongue: What causes word finding failures in young and older adults? *Journal of Memory and Language, 30,* 542–579.

Glenberg, A. M., Sanocki, T., Epstein, W., & Morris, C. (1987). Enhancing calibration of comprehension. *Journal of Experimental Psychology: General, 116,* 119–136.

Glucksberg, S., & McCloskey, M. (1981). Decisions about ignorance: Knowing that you don't know. *Journal of Experimental Psychology: Human Learning and Memory, 7,* 311–325.

Jameson, K. A., Narens, L., Goldfarb, K., & Nelson, T. O. (1990). The influence of near-threshold priming on metamemory and recall. *Acta Psychologica, 73,* 55–68.

Janowsky, J. S., Shimamura, A. P., & Squire, L. R. (1989). Memory and metamemory: Comparisons between frontal lobe lesions and amnesic patients. *Psychobiology, 17,* 3–11.

Kolers, P. A., & Palef, S. R. (1976). Knowing not. *Memory and Cognition, 4,* 553–558.

Koriat, A. (1993). How do we know that we know? The accessibility model of the feeling of knowing. *Memory and Cognition, 4,* 244–248.

Krinsky, R., & Nelson, T. O. (1985). The feeling of knowing for different types of retrieval failure. *Psychological Review, 100,* 609–639.

Lezak, M. D. (1995). *Neuropsychological assessment* (3rd ed.). New York: Oxford University Press.

MacKay, D. G. (1982). The problems of flexibility, fluency and speed-accuracy trade-off in skilled behavior. *Psychological Review, 89*, 483–506.

McGlynn, S. M., & Schacter, D. L. (1989). Unawareness of deficits in neuropsychological syndromes. *Journal of Clinical and Experimental Neuropsychology, 11*, 143–205.

McGlynn, S. M., Schacter, D. L., & Glisky, E. L. (1989). Unawareness of deficits in organic amnesic syndrome. *Journal of Clinical and Experimental Neuropsychology, 11* [abstract], 50.

Metcalfe, J. (1990). Composite holographic associative recall model (CHARM) and blended memories in eyewitness testimony. *Journal of Experimental Psychology: General, 119*, 145–160.

Metcalfe, J. (1991). Recognition failure and the composite memory trace in CHARM. *Psychological Review, 98*, 529–553.

Metcalfe, J. (1993a). Novelty monitoring, metacognition and control in a composite holographic associative recall model: Implications for Korsakoff amnesia. *Psychological Review, 100*, 3–22.

Metcalfe, J. (1993b). Monitoring and gain control in an episodic memory model: Relation to P300 event-related potentials. In A. Collins, M. Conway, S. Gathercole, & P. Morris (Eds.), *Theories of memory* (pp. 327–354). Hillsdale, NJ: Lawrence Erlbaum Associates.

Metcalfe, J., Cottrell, G. W., & Mencl, W. E. (1993). Cognitive binding: A computational-modeling analysis of a distinction between implicit and explicit memory. *Journal of Cognitive Neuroscience, 4*, 289–298.

Metcalfe, J., Schwartz, B. L., & Joaquim, S. G. (1993). The cue familiarity heuristic in metacognition. *Journal of Experimental Psychology: Learning, Memory, and Cognition, 19*, 851–861.

Metcalfe Eich, J. (1982). A composite holographic associative recall model. *Psychological Review, 89*, 627–661.

Metcalfe Eich, J. (1985). Levels of processing, encoding specificity, elaboration, and CHARM. *Psychological Review, 92*, 1–38.

Moscovitch, M. (1994). Models of consciousness and memory. In M. S. Gazzaniga (Ed.), *The cognitive neurosciences* (pp. 1341–1356). Cambridge, MA: MIT Press.

Narens, L., Jameson, K. A., & Lee, V. A. (1994). Subthreshold priming and memory monitoring. In J. Metcalfe & A. P. Shimamura (Eds.), *Metacognition: Knowing about knowing* (pp. 71–92). Cambridge, MA: MIT Press.

Reder, L. M. (1987). Strategy selection in question answering. *Cognitive Psychology, 19*, 90–138.

Reder, L. M. (1988). Strategic control of retrieval strategies. In G. Bower (Ed.), *The psychology of learning and motivation* (Vol. 22, pp. 227–259). San Diego, CA: Academic Press.

Schacter, D. L. (1987). Implicit memory: History and current status. *Journal of Experimental Psychology: Learning, Memory, and Cognition, 13*(3), 501–518.

Schacter, D. L. (1991). Unawareness of deficit and unawareness of knowledge in patients with memory disorders. In G. P. Prigatano & D. L. Schacter (Eds.), *Unawareness of deficit after brain injury: Clinical and theoretical issues* (pp. 127–151). New York: Oxford University Press.

Schwartz, B. L., & Metcalfe, J. (1992). Cue familiarity but not target retrievability enhances feeling-of-knowing judgments. *Journal of Experimental Psychology: Learning, Memory, and Cognition, 18*, 1074–1083.

Schwartz, B. L., & Metcalfe, J. (1994). Methodological problems and pitfalls in the study of human metacognition. In J. Metcalfe & A. P. Shimamura (Eds.), *Metacognition: Knowing about knowing* (pp. 93–114). Cambridge, MA: MIT Press.

Shimamura, A. P., Janowsky, J. S., & Squire, L. R. (1991). What is the role of frontal lobe damage in amnesic disorders? In H. S. Levin, H. M. Eisenberg, & A. L. Benton (Eds.), *Frontal lobe function and dysfunction* (pp. 173–195). New York: Oxford University Press.

Shimamura, A. P., & Squire, L. R. (1986). Memory and metamemory: A study of the feeling-of-knowing phenomenon in amnesic patients. *Journal of Experimental Psychology: Learning, Memory, and Cognition, 12*, 452–460.

Chapter 8

Manufacturing False Memories Using Bits of Reality

Elizabeth F. Loftus
James A. Coan
Jacqueline E. Pickrell
University of Washington

The controversy over the recovery of repressed memories provides a contemporary place where the concepts of metacognition and implicit memory both come into play. The idea that adult problems stem from the harboring of deeply repressed memories gained widespread attention when it became the cornerstone of Freud's (1916–1917) theory of mental functioning. Freud used a rather charming spatial metaphor to convey his view of repression and of the relationship between the unconscious, which he compared to a large hall, and consciousness, which was more like a smaller reception room:

> On the threshold between the two there stands a . . . door-keeper, who examines the various mental excitations, censors them, and denies them admittance to the reception room when he disapproves of them. . . . When (the mental excitations) have pressed forward to the threshold and been turned back by the door-keeper . . . we call them then repressed. . . . The door-keeper is what we have learnt to know as resistance in our attempts in analytic treatment to loosen the repressions. (pp. 306–307)

Freud was clear in his views of the goals of psychoanalysis; namely, to undo repression and get the patient to remember the forgotten traumatic events of childhood. Freud appeared to accept without questioning the therapeutic benefits of digging for hidden treasures in the depths of his patient's mind (Arlow, 1995).

The repression theory, as it is used today, goes beyond Freud's imagination. Well articulated by Steele (1994), it is the theory:

> That we forget events because they are too horrible to contemplate; that we cannot remember these forgotten events by any normal process of casting our minds back but can reliably retrieve them by special techniques; that these forgotten events banished from consciousness, strive to enter it in disguised forms; that forgotten events have the power to cause apparently unrelated problems in our lives, which can be cured by excavating and reliving the forgotten events. (p. 41)

In terms of metacognition, the repression theory expresses a number of widely held beliefs about the way human memory allegedly works. These include the belief that some events are so horrible to contemplate that they are automatically banished into the unconscious, and even an endless stream of traumas can be banished in this way. Briere (1989) has been explicit about the claim that these memories are removed from awareness:

> Repression . . . refers to an unconscious dissociation or splitting off of memories from awareness, in order to avoid the painful affects which would otherwise accompany such recollections. . . . As it applies to sexual abuse trauma . . . repression refers to some survivors' ability to banish from memory the most painful aspects of early childhood victimization. (p. 49)

Terr (1994) has claimed that multiple traumas are the most likely candidates for such banishment: "Multiple traumas and particularly long-standing childhood traumas are the types of memory most likely to be repressed" (p. 4).

The repression theory also includes the belief that the excavation of these recalcitrant memories can be done in some reliable way, and that such excavation leads to a cure of the patient. Kritsberg (1993), for example, emphasized his view that "complete repression" exists, but body, emotions, and cognitive mind "remember" and moreover that "release of repressed memories is crucial to healing" (p. 85).

The repression theory also expresses a number of beliefs akin to some notions of implicit memory. In this theory the banished events are not available to consciousness, yet express themselves in the form of symptoms and problems such as low self-esteem or body memories (Van der Kolk, 1994). These theoretical ideas might be harmless except for the fact that many psychotherapists engage in practices and assume they are true, practices which may be risky if not dangerous (Poole, Lindsay, Memon, & Bull, 1995).

Even psychotherapists who adhere to the theory of repression have acknowledged the mistakes made by some of their colleagues. In her book

Trauma and Recovery, Herman (1992) made this point: Whereas an earlier generation of therapists might have been discounting or minimizing their patients' traumatic experiences, the recent rediscovery of psychological trauma has led to errors of the opposite kind. Some contemporary therapists have been known to tell patients, merely on the basis of a suggestive history or "symptom profile," that they definitely had a traumatic experience. Even if there is no memory, but merely some vague symptoms, certain therapists will inform a patient after a single session that they were very likely the victim of a Satanic cult. Once "diagnosed," the therapist urges the patient to pursue the recalcitrant memories. Although some therapists recommend against persistent, intrusive probing to uncover early traumatic memories, others unfortunately engage in these therapeutic strategies.

In addition to intrusive probing, the worrisome activities include attempts at excavating the "repressed" memories through age regression, guided visualization, trance writing, dream work, body work, hypnosis, and sodium amytal. What dangers are inherent in these activities that arise from an abiding faith in the constellation of beliefs about memory that underlie the repression theory? Numerous commentators have worried that risky or dangerous therapeutic interventions are leading patients to construct false memories about their past (Lindsay & Read, 1994; Loftus, 1993; Ofshe & Watters, 1994; Pendergrast, 1995; Poole et al., 1995).

The hypothesis that false memories could be manufactured by suggestive therapy in particular, or suggestion in general, invites an inquiry into what is generally known about false memories. Since the mid-1970s at least, investigations have been done into the creation of false memories through exposure to misinformation. Now, nearly two decades later, we have hundreds of studies to support a high degree of memory distortion. People have recalled nonexistent broken glass and tape recorders, a clean-shaven man as having a mustache, straight hair as curly, and even something as large and conspicuous as a barn in a bucolic scene that contained no buildings at all (Belli, 1989; Chandler, 1991; Loftus, 1979; Loftus & Ketcham, 1991). This growing body of research shows that new, postevent information often becomes incorporated into memory, supplementing and altering a person's recollection. The new information invades us, like a Trojan horse, precisely because we do not detect its influence. Understanding how we can become tricked by revised data about our past is central to understanding the hypothesis that suggestions in popular writings or therapy sessions can affect our autobiographical recall.

One frequently heard comment about the research on memory distortion is that the changes induced by misinformation are about trivial details (Darton, 1991). There is no evidence, the argument goes, that you can tinker with memories of real traumatic events or that you can inject whole events into the human mind for things that never happened. Although a century of anecdotes—both literary and real—reflect the not-uncommon human experience of entirely false memories, now these anecdotes have been bolstered by recent experimental evidence.

On the literary front, the subject of false memories brings to mind a piece of literature from Mark Twain (1916). In his short story "The Man That Corrupted Hadleyburg," a character named Mr. Richards stands to be rewarded a large sum of money if he can manage to remember a good deed that he may or may not have done for a man named Mr. Goodson. Richards desperately needs the money, but he cannot recall ever having talked to Goodson, and cannot bring himself to lie. Further, lying would be useless, as Goodson's spokesman had not informed anyone of what the good deed actually was. The first person to come forward with the good deed information earns the money. Richards mulls this over and develops an abiding faith that he, being the righteous soul that he is, must have been the one to have done the good deed—if only he could remember it.

Richards resolves to remember at any cost, and, after concentrating for several hours, refusing to sleep until the recalcitrant memory appears, a memory does appear. Richards remembers rescuing Goodson's reputation with some timely information that saves him from marrying an allegedly tainted woman. Twain eloquently described Richards' thoughts: "It was all clear and simple now, and the more he went over it, the more luminous and certain it grew, and at last, when he nestled to sleep satisfied and happy, he remembered the whole thing, just as if it had been yesterday" (p. 108).

Although Twain's story is fictional, it is a valuable springboard for asking questions that are central to this chapter. Is Richards' memory authentic? Was he induced to develop a memory by the promise that a certain Good Samaritan would be rewarded? What role if any was played by the potential that a memory would hold as a solution to his poverty? If the memory is false, what is the mechanism by which it was created? Can such false memories be distinguished from those that are authentic?

Whole memories can be implanted into a person's real-life autobiography, as is best shown by foremost developmental psychologist Jean Piaget's (1972) classic childhood memory of an attempted kidnapping. The false memories were with him for at least a decade:

> One of my first memories would date, if it were true, from my second year. I can still see, most clearly, the following scene, in which I believed until I was about fifteen. I was sitting in my pram, which my nurse was pushing in the Champs Elysees, when a man tried to kidnap me. I was held in by the strap fastened round me while my nurse bravely tried to stand between me and the thief. She received various scratches, and I can still see vaguely those on her face. . . . When I was about fifteen, my parent received a letter from my former nurse . . . she wanted to confess her past faults, and in particular

to return the watch she had been given as a reward. . . . She had made up the whole story . . . I, therefore, must have heard, as a child, the account of this story, which my parents believed, and projected into the past in the form of a visual memory. (p. 48)

Although widely disseminated and impressive at first glance, Piaget's false memory is still but a single anecdote and subject to other interpretations. Was this really a memory, or an interesting story? Could it be that the assault actually happened and the nurse, for some inexplicable reason, lied later? Given these alternative interpretations for Piaget's report, it would be nice to find stronger evidence that a false memory for a complete event was genuinely implanted.

FALSE CASES OF FALSE MEMORY FOR BEING LOST

Could we experimentally implant memories for nonexistent events of a mildly traumatic nature? Could it be done in a way that balances the need to protect subjects and the scientific interest in examining the process of memory development? We have now developed a paradigm for instilling a specific childhood memory for being lost at the age of 5. We chose "getting lost" because it is clearly a great fear of both parents and children.

Could subjects be made to believe that they were lost on a particular occasion when they were about 5 years of age? Consider the following five cases, presented in some detail here to show what examples led to the design of a formal study (see Loftus & Ketcham, 1994, for details on the development of these ideas).

Jenny (Age 8)

Jenny was convinced by her father that she had been lost when she was 5. Jenny's father pulled Jenny aside during a birthday party. He began the memory injection with a simple question: "Hey, Jenny, do you remember the time that you got lost at the Bellevue Mall?" At first, Jenny resisted the suggestion, and a funny expression came across her face. Her father pressed on with more details: "You were about 5 years old." Jenny still resisted: "How do you expect me to remember that far back?" But the father provided more details: "Don't you remember that I told you that we would meet at the Tug Boat (a landmark inside the Bellevue Mall). And you got lost and I couldn't find you." He embellished the experience with known facts about the mall and whenever he sensed resistance, he reminded her that "was a real scary time." Soon Jenny began to "remember," and to provide some novel details. She even remembered how she felt at the time.

When her father recalled "I was so scared," she replied, "Not as scared as I was."

Brittany (Age 8)

Eight-year-old Brittany was convinced by her mother that she too had been lost when she was about 5. Her mother reminded her that she and her best friend had gotten lost in a condominium complex, Selby Ranch, where the best friend lived. This is the "story" Brittany was told by her mother as if it were the truth: "A kind old lady who lived in the complex found Brittany and took her into her condo and gave her a cookie. The lady had a beautiful daughter who was a model in San Francisco and the daughter gave Brittany a bouquet of balloons."

Eighteen days later, a friend of the family interviewed Brittany under the pretense of getting information for a school newspaper article on childhood memories. The friend asked about some genuine memories, and then asked about the implanted one. Brittany failed to remember anything about one of the actual events, her sixth birthday party at Aunt Sue's farm. She was pressed:

Q: Don't you remember it?

A: I don't. It was in our house at Houston.

Q: Don't you remember what you did?

A: No.

Q: Do you remember who was there?

A: No . . . well, I know Samantha was there. No she wasn't. She wasn't born yet.

When the interviewer asked Brittany about the false memory, she had quite a bit to say:

Q: Do you remember where you were?

A: Selby Ranch . . . I can't remember like how it looked. But I think it was there. There was like hay. It was around Halloween, so there were pumpkins around.

Q: Who was with you?

A: Um . . . Christina, Camille . . . and, me and my mum were visiting my grandparents.

Q: What were you doing?

A: Well, we were playing, and, but then Christina left. I think she had to make a phone call or something. And then me and Camille went off playing in the woods. And . . . um . . . I really can't remember this, but I think this happened when we went to this girl's house. Her daughter was a model. And then we made cookies at her house. And then my mum finally found us. But everyone like my grandparents called my mum but Christina called them.

Brittany embellished further: The lady whose house they went to not only gave them one cookie but baked a batch of cookies with them. Her home became a "small cottage outside the gates of Selby Ranch." (Note: the houses in the area are predominantly 4000 sq. ft contemporary California style ranches.) When Brittany's mother found her, she allegedly said, "Thank goodness I found you, I was looking all over for you."

Chris (Age 14)

Chris was convinced by his older brother that he had been lost in a shopping mall when he was 5 years old. In the first phase, Chris was asked to write about some of his childhood memories. Three of the events actually happened, and the fourth did not. A short paragraph introduced the event to be remembered, and Chris wrote about the events each day for 5 days. He was instructed to write "I don't remember" if he could not recall an event on any particular day.

Chris's brother introduced the false memory thus:

It was 1981 or 1982. I remember that Chris was 5. We had gone shopping at the University City shopping mall in Spokane. After some panic, we found Chris being led down the mall by a tall, oldish man (I think he was wearing a flannel shirt). Chris was crying and holding the man's hand. The man explained that he had found Chris walking around crying his eyes out just a few moments before and was trying to help him find his parents.

Here is precisely what Chris wrote each day:

Day 1: "I remember a little bit about that man. I remember thinking, 'Wow! he's really cool!' "

Day 2: "That day I was so scared that I would never see my family agin. I knew that I was in trouble." (sic)

Day 3: "I remember mom telling me never to do that agin."

Day 4: "I also remember that old man's flannel shirt."

Day 5: "I sort of remember the stores."

In summarizing his memory, Chris produced not exactly a summary, but a new fact. He remembered a conversation with the man who found him: "I remember the man asking me if I was lost."

It would be natural to wonder whether perhaps Chris was simply trying to please or help his brother and was producing "memories" for extraneous motivations. Evidence against this possibility comes from Chris's responses to one of the true memories. Recall that Chris was told to write "I can't remember" if he could not recall a particular event. For one of the true memories, he did precisely this.

Here, he describes that true memory:

> It was sometime in 1981 or 1982. Dad was gone and winter was coming. We had very little money and no oil. When I tried to chop all that wood that we had delivered, I did a very bad job of it (I was only 12). Dick O'Brien, the old man next door, saw what I was doing and came over to help. He wound up chopping almost all the wood, even though it must have been very hard for him. I think he wore a black coat and a cap.

Here are his daily responses—verbatim:

Day 1: "I can't remember."
Day 2: "I still can't remember."
Day 3: "I still can't remember."
Day 4: "I still can't remember."
Day 5: "I still can't remember."

When asked to summarize, he simply said: "I'm sorry I can't remember this incident."

It would be natural to wonder whether perhaps Chris had really gotten lost that day. Maybe it happened, but his brother forgot. To shed further light on this possibility, we obtained data from Chris's mother, who was allegedly a participant that day in the mall. Chris's mother confirmed no memory for the created event. She tried hard to remember, but simply could not, as her first 2 days of attempted recollection reveal:

Day 1: "I have thought about this day, but I am having trouble rembering the details." (sic)
Day 2: "I have tried and tried to rember this day. I see us looking under clothes racks for Christopher's feet, but I can't honestly say that this was that time."

After five days of trying, she summarized: "For some reason I feel guilty about this, that I can't remember."

A couple of weeks later, Chris was reinterviewed. He was first asked to describe each of the four events, and to rate each one according to how clear it was, on a scale from 1 (*not clear at all*) to 11 (*very very clear*). For the three true memories, Chris gave ratings of 1, 10, and 5. For the false shopping mall memory, he gave a rating of 8. Thus his false memory was amongst the clearest.

When he described the false getting-lost memory, he greatly expanded on it:

> I was with you guys for a second and I think I went over the look at the toy store, the Kay-Bee toy and uh, we got lost and I was looking around and I thought, "Uh-oh. I'm in trouble now." You know. And then I . . . I thought I was never going to see my family again. I was really scared, you know. And then this old man, I think he was wearing a blue flannel, came up to me. . . . He was kind of old. He was kind of bald on top. . . . He had like a ring of gray hair . . . and he had glasses.

Thus, in two short weeks, Chris now could even remember the balding head and the glasses worn by the man who rescued him. He characterized his memory and reasonably clear and vivid.

Then, Chris was debriefed. When told that his "getting lost" memory was made up, he clung to it: "Really???? I thought I remembered being lost . . . and looking around for you guys. I do remember that. And then crying. and mom coming up and saying, 'Where were you. Don't you. . . . Don't you ever do that again.' "

Chris's debriefing was designed with an appreciation of the sensitivity of the situation. He was told that misremembering things is very common in life, and that his behavior was perfectly normal. His was given a chance to express his feelings and reactions to the study. He was made to feel that the experience was a valuable one for him to participate in. He was interviewed on numerous subsequent occasions to assess long-term reactions to the experience. On one occasion he visited the University, met with the research team, and joined in a discussion of the meaning of the experience for him.

Chris was 14 years old when he constructed the false getting-lost memory. Could the same thing be done with people who were now adults?

John (Age 22)

John, a 22-year-old man, was convinced by his aunt that he had been lost at a large sporting goods store (REI) at the age of 5 or 6. This is the story John was told by his aunt as if it were the truth:

> Fairly soon after we moved to our house in Madronna (so you must have been 5 or 6), Dan and I took you and Lisa with us to REI. Somehow we lost you. We had just started searching for you when we spotted you being led along by an older man. He was very nice and explained that he had

found you at the foot of that long included ramp, crying and looking around. It apparently took us a while to notice that we had lost you.

A day after the attempted memory injection, John had no memory: "After first reading this, I have no memory of the event at all. I don't even remember ever talking about it. I of course have other memories of being in REI." Two days afterward, however, his memory was starting to develop: "I have a vague memory of being at the top of the ramp, crying. I don't remember what happened next. This came to me suddenly as I was trying to remember the event."

Bill (Age 42)

Bill, a 42-year-old man, was convinced by his sister that he had been lost. To instill the memory, she gave him this description:

> I remember when you were about 5 or 6 and you got lost at Sears. Mother had taken us there to get some shoes. I guess while I was trying some on, you wandered off. After mother realized you were gone, she told me to stay where I was and I had just started to look for you when we saw you being led along by an elderly man. You were crying and holding his hand. He explained that he had found you by the candy counter looking confused and crying a little.

A day after getting the description from his sister, Bill tried to remember the specific location: "I think I remember (or can imagine?) getting lost—I remember what Sears looked like in Santa Monica—or was it at J.C. Penney's? I felt panicky—where were Mom and Linda; I felt scared." The next day, Bill remembered more: "I remember going up or down the stairway at Sears. I remember the elevator bell at Sears. Now I remember—it was Sears and not J.C. Penney's."

These five individuals, ages 8 to 42, were, with little difficulty, led to develop a false memory, or at least a partial one, for something that never happened. The memories pertained to a specific episode of being lost. Are their memories real to them? If the willingness to expand on the memory and to provide details that were not initially suggested is any indication, then the answer is yes. Jenny remembered being scared. Brittany embellished the memory with pumpkins and batches of cookies. Chris embellished his memory with conversations and flannel shirts. Bill added elevator bells.

These examples are still only anecdotes, but they take us somewhat beyond the Piagetian anecdote that has survived in the psychological literature for over 30 years. The examples tell us that implantation of an entire childhood memory is not a particularly difficult thing to do, and reveal a means by which it can be done. Of course, many questions remain. How often can false memories of this type be implanted in people? Who is particularly susceptible to memory implantation and conversely who is resistant? Under what conditions might people be resistant to such memory implantation, and are there ways to protect people from these mental invasions? Some of these questions have been explored in subsequent research utilizing a procedure that grew out of these initial observations.

CREATING MEMORIES OF BEING LOST

Loftus and Pickrell (1995) reported the results of a study involving 24 individuals who were asked to recall events that were supplied by a close relative. As with the case example, Chris, three of the events were true, and one was a research-crafted false event about getting lost in a shopping mall, department store, or other public place. The subjects, who ranged in age from 18 to 53, thought they were taking part in a study of childhood memories. In phase 1, they completed a booklet containing four short stories about events from their childhood provided by a parent, sibling, or other older relative. Three events actually happened, and the fourth, always in the third position, was false. The events were described in a single paragraph.

The false event was constructed from information provided by the relative who gave us details about a plausible shopping trip. The relative was asked to provide the following kinds of information: (a) where the family would have shopped when the subject was about 5 years old; (b) which members of the family usually went along on shopping trips; (c) what kinds of stores might have attracted the subject's interest; and (d) verification that the subject had not been lost in a mall around the age of 5. The false event was then crafted from this information. The false events always included the following elements about the subject: (a) lost for an extended period of time, (b) crying, (c) lost in a mall or large department store at about the age of 5, (d) found and aided by an elderly woman, (e) reunited with the family.

Here is a paragraph created for a 20-year-old Vietnamese American woman who grew up in the State of Washington:

> You, your mom, Tien and Tuan, all went to the Bremerton K-Mart. You must have been 5 years old at the time. Your Mom gave each of you some money to get a blueberry ICEE. You ran ahead to get into the line first, and somehow lost your way in the store. Tien found you crying to an elderly Chinese woman. You three then went together to get an ICEE.

Subjects completed the booklets by reading what their relative had told us about each event, and then writing what they remembered about each event. If they did not remember the event, they were told to write, "I do not remember this."

When the booklets were returned, subjects were called and scheduled for two interviews. These occurred approximately 1 to 2 weeks apart. We told the subjects we were interested in examining how much detail they could remember, and how their memories compared with those of their relative. The event paragraphs were not read to them verbatim, but rather bits of them were provided as retrieval cues. When the subject had recalled as much as possible, they were asked to rate the clarity of their memory for the event on a scale of 1 to 10, with 1 being not clear at all and 10 being extremely clear. Next, subjects rated their confidence on a scale of 1 to 5 that given more time to think about the event they would be able to remember more details (1 = *not confident* and 5 = *extremely confident that they would be able to remember more*).

In all, 72 true events were presented to subjects, and they remembered something about 49 (or 68%) of these. This figure did not change from the initial report through the two follow-up interviews. That nearly 70% of the true events were consistently remembered can be seen in Fig. 8.1.

The rate of "remembering" the false event was lower. Seven of 24 subjects "remembered" the false event—either fully or partially—in the initial booklet, but in the follow-up interviews only 6 subjects (25%) remembered the event. These data also appear in Fig. 8.1.

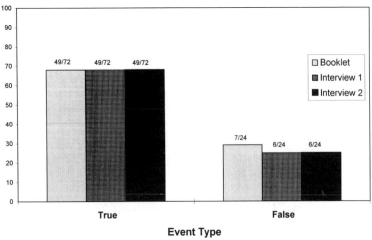

FIG. 8.1. Data from Loftus and Pickrell (1995): Percentage of true and false events that were remembered. Adapted with permission.

There were some differences between the true memories and the false ones. For example, subjects used more words when describing their true memories, whether these memories were fully or only partially recalled. Also, the clarity ratings for the false memories tended to be lower than for true memories produced by those same subjects. Interestingly, there was a tendency for the clarity ratings of the false memories to rise from the first interview to the second. Subjects also rated how confident they were that they would be able to recall additional details at a later time. In general, the confidence ratings were low, but lower for the false event than the true ones.

Our results show that people can be led to believe that entire events happened to them after explicit suggestions to that effect. We make no claims about the percentage of people who might be able to be misled in this way, only that these cases provide an existence proof for the phenomenon of false memory formation. To show how richly detailed these false memories can be, and how fervently subjects can cling to them, we present a detailed case that emerged in an unusual way.

The Case of Becca

Becca's case arose after the *McNeil/Lehrer News Hour* approached us about filming the creation of a false memory. To their disappointment, our main experiment had been completed and no subjects were currently being run. We agreed, however, to conduct a demonstration of the study with two individuals, both women supplied by the news program. These women gave their informed consent, but additionally agreed that their materials could be used in a demonstration for a television news story. Due either to the good luck of *McNeil/Lehrer* or the superbly persuasive skills of the implanting research associate, both women adopted a false memory of being lost. We describe in detail the evolving recollections of one of those women—a 20-year-old college student who was an occasional baby-sitter for the producer of the program.

Becca was told that her mother had provided several events that occurred when Becca was between the ages of 4 and 6. She tried to recall these events three times, with the interviews separated by 10 or 11 days.

The True Events. One of the true events involved taking a trip from California to Washington in a Volkswagen at Christmas time. Becca was never able to clearly recall this event. Her clarity rating went from "1, maybe even half" to a "3," although she maintained that she did not remember much. Another true event involved a summer car trip, sitting on her mother's lap, commenting on the moon. Becca remembered this event, although there were changes in her recollection across the interviews. Her clarity rating went from "6" to "5." Another involved a birthday party attended by Becca and her mother in Old Mill Park. Becca remembered this event, and added new information (her cousins were probably there). Those who were "probably" there in the first interview were recalled as having clearly been there by the third interview. Both clarity ratings were "5."

The False "Lost-in-the-Mall" Event. This experience was supposed to have occurred at the Tacoma Mall where Becca had gone with both her mother and father. She was supposedly last seen playing on the escalators, not far from a pet store. Becca began trying to remember by first placing herself in the situation, repeating "I was lost," and stating that she had "a vague memory of being lost." Becca provided details of what she "probably" would have done and felt. Most interesting were changes in her recollection of the pet store, the older woman, whether she was crying, and the messages that blared over the PA system during this alleged encounter.

During Becca's first attempt to recall getting lost at the Tacoma Mall, she remembers the pet store: "I do remember like there was one mall that did like have a pet store and stuff and I used to like always want to go in there. I would always be wanting to look at the dogs or whatever." Although she does not appear to remember being involved with the pet store on the day she was supposedly lost in the mall, by the second recall attempt Becca brings up the pet store on her own in response to a question about what stores she might have passed when she was lost: "Well, it must have been something . . . that I was obviously interested in. . . . So you had previously mentioned there was a pet store there, so I was probably playing with puppies or something." By the third recall attempt, Becca seems to be remembering: "I remember being somewhere and looking at the dogs." Toward the end of this last recollection, Becca is asked if there is anything else she can remember about the event: "No. Just the basic interior of the mall. And like what the puppy store looked like and stuff like that."

The PA system enters into Becca's recollection during her first attempt at recall when she is considering what her parents might have done in this situation: "Well, they probably would have gone back to where they originally thought that I would have gone and then more than likely they probably would have gone to like the security or whatever and had me paged." In response to a probe—"Do you ever remember hearing your name on the PA system?"—Becca does, saying: "Yeah, I do remember that." This "could have been" the time when she was lost. By the second recollection, Becca volunteers a memory of the PA system: "I kind of remember my name going over the PA system." And by the third recollection, there is a major change in the PA system element of her memory: "And then the next memory I have after that is um going to the security station and then hearing them call my mother and father's name over the loud-speaker." Thus, Becca reversed this aspect of her memory. Initially Becca leaned toward remembering her own name over the PA system, by the final interview she recalls hearing her parents' names over the loudspeaker.

Becca's recollection of the older woman also changed across interviews. Initially, Becca does not remember any older woman. By the end of the first interview, she accepts the possibility that the elderly woman could have come up to her: "Yeah, she could have come up to me or um actually I think more than likely I probably would have tried to look for them myself first. And then gone up to someone maybe after that." At this point, the older woman appears to be more of a possibility than a memory. During the second interview, Becca still does not really remember the older woman: "I don't really remember um the old lady." And later still, "I don't remember the old woman. . . . Ah, although, I guess I kind of remember somebody asking my name." Although she remains consistent that she does not remember the older woman, she leaves the possibility open with the memory of someone asking her name. However, by the third interview Becca's recollections now include a woman: "And then someone asking me if I was lost. And I'm not sure if that was the perfume woman or just some nice woman who um just happened, you know to look at me or whatever." And later in that same interview, when pressed for details about the woman who came up to her, she replies: "I don't, I, I almost remember her like wearing a long skirt or sweater but, um, I'm not quite sure of that . . . I'm sure that there was a dress or something. But I don't specifically remember what she looked like." And when pressed further: "I don't remember her taking my hand, but I do remember her um, asking me if I was lost, and um and then asking my name and then saying something about taking me to security." So, it appears that Becca, who was unable to remember specifically an older woman in the first two interviews, now is able to recall details about what the woman was wearing and some conversation with her.

As for memories of crying, Becca described her feelings initially: "I'm sure that I was like very frightened and stuff. Um, but I can't see myself like screaming or crying or anything like that." When the interviewer expressed some doubt in the question: "Not—not crying at all?" Becca reconsidered her recollection: "I don't—well, let me think. No, I can't see myself like crying until like after I found them and then being like really freaked out and then like crying and stuff." Later in the interview there is more discussion of being upset, but the language reveals an expression of what would have happened as opposed to what did happen:

> Oh yeah, I would have been panicked. I would have been really freaked out, but . . . like I said I don't think that I um just like my personality—just remembering as I was as a child. I don't see myself like um as I said freaking out and crying and screaming or anything like that.

She seems to be thinking merely about how she might have reacted. During the second interview her recollections of crying have a bit of the same quality:

> I'm sure that after, I didn't cry during, looking for them I don't think. . . . I don't remember crying but I'm sure I cried afterwards, I'm positive if I didn't do it before I'm sure I did it after when I first saw them.

During the third interview, she maintains her position that any crying "probably" happened only after she had seen her parents again after being lost: "I probably started crying as soon as I saw them. But um, I don't think I was crying before" and later she recalls that any crying "was probably after I had already seen her and my dad walking up."

Over the course of the three recollections, Becca provides a tremendous amount of detail about the event. She remembers her feelings of panic, her thought processes during her ordeal, and her parents' reactions. "Actually, my dad had that look on his face like . . ." was one of her strongest visualizations. Becca's clarity ratings were consistently "5," about the same ratings that she gave for the best recalled of her true experiences.

Comments on Becca.   Becca provides a nice example of the evolution of a false memory. What begins as a collection of details that "would have happened" or "probably happened" later turns into a collection of things that did happen. This kind of change occurred also with portions of the true experiences as she tried repeatedly to recall them. Becca is a very articulate woman and was able to express some of the thought processes she engaged in as she tried to reconstruct her memories. She considered what might have happened, how she and others might have reacted, how she would have felt, and she used her knowledge of herself as a child to reconstruct plausible details of events she was trying to remember.

One last relevant bit of data was gathered from Becca during her debriefing and afterward. During debriefing, the purpose of the demonstration was explained, and Becca was asked to guess which memories were true and which were false. She reported that she was pretty sure that the birthday party and getting lost in the mall actually happened. She guessed that the trip from California to Washington at Christmas time might have been false.

When Becca was told that her memory of getting lost was false, she expressed surprise: "I never was lost? I had to have been lost." When the interviewer insisted that she had not been lost, Becca replied: "I'm going to ask my mother 'cause I'm sure I was." Becca was so convinced that after the demonstration, she contacted her mother, who insisted that nothing like this had ever happened. Still seeking confirmation, Becca contacted her father, who had long been divorced from the mother and was now living out of state. Becca's father insisted this event had never happened. On receiving independent disconfirmation from her parents, Becca accepted that the memory had been "implanted" and was not real.

A Comment on Being Lost. A predictable comment about the false memories of getting lost is that people may have actually been lost in their lives, however briefly, and they may be confusing this actual experience with the false memory description. However, our subjects were not asked about any experience of being lost. They were asked to remember being lost around the age of 5—in a particular location with particular people present, being frightened, and ultimately being rescued by an elderly person. This is not to say that the actual experience of being lost briefly or of hearing about someone else being lost is not important.

The development of the false memory of being lost may evolve first as the mere suggestion of being lost leaves a memory trace in the brain. Even if the information is originally tagged as a suggestion rather than an historic fact, that suggestion can become linked to other knowledge about being lost (stories of others). As time passes and the tag which indicates that being lost in the mall was merely a suggestion, it slowly deteriorates. The memory of a real event—visiting a mall—becomes confounded with the suggestion that you were once lost in a mall. Finally, when asked whether you were ever lost in a mall, your brain activates images of malls and those of being lost. The resulting memory can even be embellished with snippets from actual events, such as people once seen in a mall. Now you "remember" being lost in a mall as a child. By this mechanism, the memory errors occur because grains of experienced events or imagined events are integrated with inferences and other elaborations that go beyond direct experience.

MORE FALSE MEMORIES

Could false memories be created about events that were more unusual than getting lost? Using a similar procedure, Hyman and his colleagues (Hyman, Husband, & Billings, 1995) successfully implanted in the minds of adult subjects, some rather unusual childhood memories. In one study, college students were asked to recall actual events that had been reported by their parents, and one experimenter-crafted false event. The false event was an overnight hospitalization for a high fever with a possible ear infection, or else a birthday party with pizza and a clown. Parents confirmed that neither of these events had happened, yet subjects were told that they had experienced one of the false events at about the age of 5.

Subjects tried to recall childhood experiences that they thought had been supplied by their parents, under the belief that the experimenters were interested in how people remember shared experiences differently.

All events, both true ones and the false one, were first cued with an event title (family vacation, overnight hospitalization) and an age. If subjects could not recall the event they received brief additional cues, such as location or other people involved. After the first interview subjects were encouraged to continue thinking about the events, but not to discuss them, and to return for a second interview 1 to 7 days after the first.

To facilitate comparisons across the various studies, Hyman's data are plotted in Fig. 8.2, using a graph structure common for most of the figures in this chapter. In all, 74 true events were presented to subjects, and they remembered something about 62 (84%) of these in the first interview and 65 (88%) in the second interview. As for the creation of false memories, no subject recalled the false event during the first interview, but 4 of 20 subjects (20%) did by the time of the second interview. One subject "remembered" that the doctor was a male, but the nurse was female—and also a friend from church.

In a second study, Hyman et al. (1995) tried to implant three new false events that were rather unusual, such as attending a wedding reception and accidentally spilling a punch bowl on the parents of the bride or having to evacuate a grocery store when the overhead sprinkler systems erroneously activated. In this study, the experimental demands were intensified somewhat by, for example, pressures for more complete recall.

The results of this study are shown in Fig. 8.3. In all 205 true events were presented to subjects, and they remembered something about 182 (or 89%) of these in the first interview. Somewhat higher percentages were

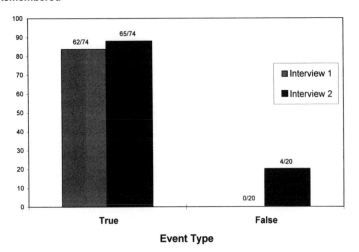

FIG. 8.2. Data from Hyman et al. (in press) Experiment 1. Adapted with permission.

**Percentage
Remembered**

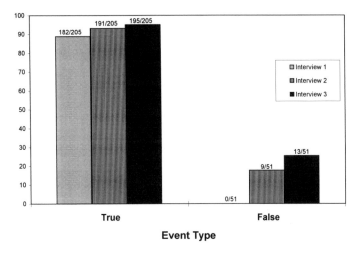

FIG. 8.3. Data from Hyman et al. (1995) Experiment 2. Adapted with permission.

remembered during the second (93%) and third (95%) interviews. As for the false events, again no subject recalled these during the first interview, but 13 (or 25%) did so by the third interview. For example, one subject had no recall of the wedding "accident," stating, "I have no clue. I have never heard that one before." By the second interview, the subject said, "It was an outdoor wedding and I think we were running around and knocked something over like the punch bowl or something and um made a big mess and of course got yelled at for it."

In a third study (Hyman & Billings, 1996), the punchbowl false event was used again, in a study designed to explore individual differences in susceptibility to the creation of false memories. Subjects were given two to five true events that had been supplied by their parent, and the false event, which was again in the third position. They tried to recall these events on two occasions separated by a day. The main results are shown in Fig. 8.4.

In all, 218 true events were presented to subjects and they remembered something about 74% in the first interview and 85% in the second interview. False memories—either full or partial—were expressed by less than 1% of the subjects during the first interview, but by 27% during the second interview. During the second interview, one subject remembered extensive details about the unfortunate man who had punch spilled on him:

A heavy-set man, not like fat but like tall and big [with] kind [of a] big beer belly, and I picture him having a dark suit on, like grayish dark and like

Percentage
Remembered

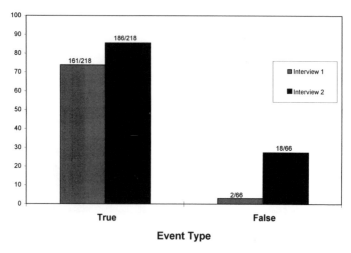

FIG. 8.4. Data from Hyman and Billings (1996). Adapted with permission.

having grayish dark hair and balding on top, and uh I picture him with a wide square face and I just picture him getting up and being kind of irritated or mad.

There were two individual differences measures that correlated strongly with the creation of false memories. The first is the Dissociative Experiences Scale (DES). The DES measures the tendency to have dissociative experiences or normal integration of awareness, thought, and memory. Also correlated was the Creative Imagination Scale (CIS), which is a measure of hypnotizability, and also can be construed as a self-report measure of the vividness of mental imagery.

A variation of this procedure has also been used with children whose ages ranged from 3 to 6 (Ceci, Huffman, Smith, & Loftus, 1994). They were interviewed individually about real (parent-supplied) and fictitious (experimenter-contrived) events, and had to say whether each event happened to them or not. One "false" event concerned getting one's hand caught in a mousetrap and having to go to the hospital to get it removed; another concerned going on a hot air balloon ride with their classmates. The children were interviewed many times. Some of the results, replotted in a format to demonstrate similarities and differences with prior studies, are shown in Figs. 8.5 and 8.6. The data for the younger children, shown in Fig. 8.5, reveal that the children remembered the true events approximately 90% of the time and this figure remained relatively flat between the first and seventh session. As for the false memories, the young children

**Percentage
Remembered**

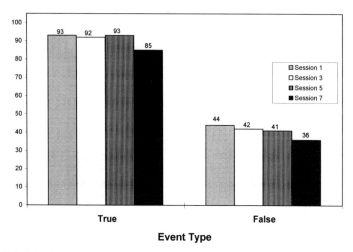

FIG. 8.5. Data from Ceci, Huffman, et al. (1994)—3–4-year-old children. Adapted with permission.

**Percentage
Remembered**

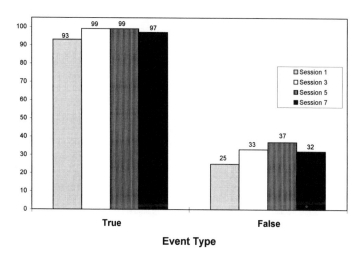

FIG. 8.6. Data from Ceci, Huffman, et al. (1994)—5–6-year-old children. Adapted with permission.

assented to them 44% of the time during the first session, and 36% of the time during the seventh session. The pattern for the older children was similar in many ways, as seen in Fig. 8.6. The true events were remembered at a higher rate (approximately 95% of the time), remaining flat across sessions. The false event was remembered at a somewhat lower rate (25% in the first session, 32% in the seventh session), also remaining relatively flat across sessions.

Although repeated interviews did not significantly increase the false beliefs, in a similar study involving more interviews about different fictitious items (i.e., falling off a tricycle and getting stitches in the leg), the rate at which children bought into the false memory was greater with more interviews (Ceci, Loftus, Leichtman, & Bruck, 1994). In this study, children aged 3–6 were interviewed about experiences in their past after being told that their mothers had reported the events had actually occurred. Over the course of up to 12 sessions, these children were instructed to make a picture of the event in their head and to think about it for a minute. Over time, children increasingly assented to the fictional events, as can be seen in Fig. 8.7. False assent rates are shown separately for the negative event (falling off a tricycle) and a positive event (going on a hot air balloon ride), and separately for the younger and older children. Notice that the younger children assented more than the older ones, and the false assent rate was higher for the positive than negative event. Also, children increased their

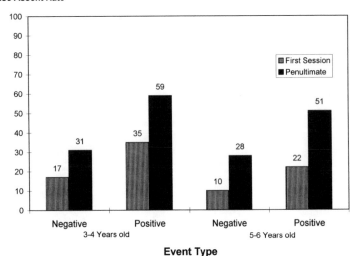

FIG. 8.7. Data from Ceci, Loftus, et al. (1994)—Increasing false assent rates for positive and negative events in younger and older children. Adapted with permission.

false assent rates between the first and penultimate session. (The last session data were omitted due to procedural differences occurring during this session, but the same conclusion would be reached using data from this session.)

Thus, the Ceci, Loftus, et al. data reveal that children tended to increasingly make false assents as they participated in more and more sessions. Hyman's adult subjects also did so (Hyman et al., 1995). In other studies, the rate of assent has not increased after the first session. At this point we are uncertain as to when the rate of buying into the false memory will increase over successive interviews and when it will not.

Taken together, these results show that people will falsely recall childhood experiences in response to misleading information and the social demands inherent in repeated interviews. The process of false recall appears to depend, in part, on accessing some relevant background information. Hyman and his colleagues hypothesized that some form of schematic reconstruction may account for the creation of false memories. What people appear to do, at the time they encounter the false details, is to call up schematic knowledge that is closely related to the false event. Next they think about the new information in conjunction with the schema, possibly storing the new information with that schema. Now, when they later try to remember the false event, they recall the false information and the underlying schema. The underlying schema is helpful for supporting the false event—it adds actual background information and provides the skeletal or generic scenes.

THE ROLE OF IMAGINATION

One critical element in the creation of false memories may be the part played by inducing subjects to imagine events that they do not remember happening to them. The literature contains a number of instances in which people have confused the memory of actually doing something with the memory of only imagining doing it (e.g., Anderson, 1984; Johnson, Hashtroudi, & Lindsay, 1993). However, these results usually pertain to recently experienced events of little importance, such as tracing or imagining tracing the outline of a line drawing. A recent study has shown that the simple act of imagining a childhood event increases a person's subjective confidence that the event happened to them in the past—a phenomenon called *Imagination Inflation* (Garry, Manning, Loftus, & Sherman, 1996). In this study, subjects were asked about a long list of possible childhood events (e.g., broke a window with your hand) and they told us the likelihood that these events had happened to them as a child. Two weeks later, subjects were instructed to imagine that some of these events had actually happened to them. Then, finally, they responded for a second time about the likelihood of that long list of possible childhood events.

Consider one of the critical items:

Imagine that it is after school and you are playing in the house. You hear a strange noise outside, so you run to the window to see what made the noise. As you are running, your feet catch on something and you trip and fall.

While imagining themselves in this position, subjects answer some questions such as: "What did you trip on?" They further imagine: "As you're falling you reach out to catch yourself and your hand goes through the window. As the window breaks you get cut and there's some blood." While imagining themselves in this predicament, they answer further questions, such as: "What are you likely to do next?" "How did you feel?"

Garry et al. (1995) confined their analysis to items that subjects explicitly said were unlikely to have happened in the first place. The reason for this is straightforward. When subjects imagine something that actually did happen to them, the imagining task is actually a remembering task (Sarbin, 1995). Taking only subjects who said it was unlikely that they had broken a window with their hand, a 1-minute act of counterfactual imagination led to positive changes in a significant minority of subjects. After engaging in this act of imagination, 24% of subjects increased their subjective confidence that something like this actually happened to them. For those who had not imagined the event, only 12% showed a corresponding increase. The other seven critical items used in this study similarly showed increased subjective confidence after imagination.

These findings show that even a single act of imagining a known counterfactual event can increase the subjective likelihood that the event happened in the past. Interestingly, simply asking about the event twice also led to an increase in subjective confidence, although not as large an increase as the act of imagination produced. Other research in cognitive psychology has shown that repeating a question can increase the sense of familiarity that a subject feels the second time the question appears (Reder & Ritter, 1992). Even simply repeating some of the parts of a question can lead to these familiarity enhancing consequences. Analogously, the mere repetition of the item in the Garry et al. (1995) research might similarly produce an enhanced sense of familiarity—familiarity that is then misattributed to a possible childhood experience. This process is then exacerbated when imagination activities are introduced into the picture.

We and others have expressed concerns that imaginations may be one of the steps down the royal road to creating false memories. If so, therapists may need to think twice about the wisdom of using or recommending imagination strategies for the express purpose of eliciting allegedly buried abuse memories. Maltz (1991), for example, explicitly recommended this risky procedure: "Spend time imagining that you were sexually abused, without worrying about accuracy, proving anything, or having your ideas make sense. As you give rein to your imagination, let your intuitions guide your thoughts" (p. 50). In a recent study of licensed clinical psychologists, a surprising 11% admitted that they had tried to help clients remember childhood sexual abuse by encouraging them to "let the imagination run wild," and 22% said that they had done this by encouraging subjects to "give free rein to the imagination" (Poole et al., 1995). The findings of Garry et al. suggest the wisdom of the larger percentages who indicated that these techniques were inappropriate for use with suspected abuse victims. Specifically, 44% said that it was not appropriate to encourage clients to "let the imagination run wild" and 24% said it was not appropriate to encourage clients to "give free rein to the imagination."

FINAL REMARKS

Nearly two decades of research on the misinformation effect has revealed that people can be led to remember events differently than they really were. When distortions of memory are induced in people, they can be quite confident about their false memories and express them in substantial detail. Newer work shows that you can go further with people—you can lead them to believe that entirely false events happened to them when they were children. The precise mechanisms by which such false memories are constructed out of elements of historical truth are still unknown, although engaging people in acts of counterfactual imagination may play some role. In his classic book *The Go-Between*, Hartley (1953) made an apt remark about the past: "The past is a foreign country. . . . they do things differently there." Today we might add to Hartley's metaphor: "The past is one of many foreign countries . . . depending on how you want things to have been done there."

REFERENCES

Anderson, R. E. (1984). Did I do it or did I only imagine doing it? *Journal of Experimental Psychology: General, 113*, 594–613.

Arlow, J. A. (1995). Stilted listening: Psychoanalysis as discourse. *Psychoanalytic Quarterly, 64*, 215–233.

Belli, R. F. (1989). Influences of misleading postevent information: Misinformation interference and acceptance. *Journal of Experimental Psychology: General, 118*, 72–85.

Briere, J. N. (1989). *Therapy for adults molested as children*. New York: Springer.

Ceci, S. J., Loftus, E. F., Leichtman, M. D., & Bruck, M. (1994). The possible role of source misattributions in the creation of false beliefs among preschoolers. *International Journal of Clinical and Experimental Hypnosis, 42*, 304–320.

Ceci, S. J., Huffman, M. L. C., Smith, E., & Loftus, E. F. (1994). Repeatedly thinking about a non-event: Source misattributions among preschoolers. *Consciousness and Cognition, 3*, 388–407.

Chandler, C. C. (1991). How memory for an event is influenced by related events: Interference in modified recognition tests. *Journal of Experimental Psychology: Learning, Memory, and Cognition, 17*, 115–125.

Darton, N. (1991, Oct. 7). The pain of the last taboo. *Newsweek*, pp. 70–72.

Freud, S. (1916–1917). *A general introduction to psychoanalysis* [Lecture 19–*Resistance and repression*]. New York: Washington Square Press.

Garry, M., Manning, C., Loftus, E. F., & Sherman, S. J. (1996). Imagination inflation. *Psychonomic Bulletin and Review, 3*, 208–214.

Hartley, L. P. (1953). *The go-between.* London: Hamish Hamilton.

Herman, J. L. (1992). *Trauma and recovery.* New York: Basic Books.

Hyman, I. E., & Billings, F. J. (1996). *Individual differences and the creation of false childhood memories.* Unpublished manuscript.

Hyman, I. E., Husband, T. H., & Billings, F. J. (1995). False memories of childhood experiences. *Applied Cognitive Psychology, 9*, 181–197.

Johnson, M. K., Hashtroudi, S., & Lindsay, D. S. (1993). Source monitoring. *Psychological Bulletin, 114*, 3–28.

Kritsberg, W. (1993). *The invisible wound: A new approach to healing childhood sexual trauma.* New York: Bantam.

Lindsay, D. S., & Read, J. D. (1994). Psychotherapy and memories of childhood sexual abuse: A cognitive perspective. *Applied Cognitive Psychology, 8*, 281–338.

Loftus, E. F. (1979). *Eyewitness testimony.* Cambridge, MA: Harvard University Press.

Loftus, E. F. (1993). The reality of repressed memories. *American Psychologist, 48*, 518–537.

Loftus, E. F., & Ketcham, K. (1991). *Witness for the defense; The accused, the eyewitness, and the expert who puts memory on trial.* New York: St. Martin's Press.

Loftus, E. F., & Ketcham, K. (1994). *The myth of repressed memory.* New York: St. Martin's Press.

Loftus, E. F., & Pickrell, J. (1995). The formation of false memories. *Psychiatric Annals, 25*, 720–725.

Maltz, W. (1991). *The sexual healing journey: A guide for survivors of sexual abuse.* New York: HarperCollins.

Ofshe, R., & Watters, E. (1994). *Making monsters: False memories, psychotherapy, and sexual hysteria.* New York: Scribner's.

Pendergrast, M. (1995). *Victims of memory: Incest accusations and shattered lives.* Hinesburg, VT: Upper Access Books.

Piaget, J. (1972). Problemes de psychologie genetique (English translation, 1973, The child and reality: Problems of genetic psychology). New York: Grossman.

Poole, D. A., Lindsay, D. S., Memon, A., & Bull, R. (1995). Psychotherapy and the recovery of memories of childhood sexual abuse: U.S. and British practitioners' opinions, practices, and experiences. *Journal of Consulting and Clinical Psychology, 63*, 426–437.

Reder, L. M., & Ritter, F. E. (1992). What determines initial feeling of knowing? Familiarity with the question terms, not with the answer. *Journal of Experimental Psychology: Learning, Memory, and Cognition, 18*, 435–451.

Sarbin, T. R. (1995). On the belief that one body may be host to two or more personalities. *International Journal of Clinical and Experimental Hypnosis, 43*, 163–183.

Steele, D. R. (1994, March). Partial Recall. *Liberty*, 37–47.

Terr, L. C. (1994). Unchained memories: Are they real? *The Menninger Letter, 2*, 4–5.

Twain, M. (1916). *The mysterious stranger and other stories.* New York: Harper & Brothers.

Van der Kolk, B. A. (1994, January/February). The body keeps the score: Memory and the evolving psychobiology of posttraumatic stress. *Harvard Review of Psychiatry*, pp. 253–265.

Chapter 9

On Carving Nature
With Our Words

Robyn M. Dawes
Carnegie Mellon University

A word does not a concept make. Some words do, of course, denote meaningful concepts—and even in the absence of denotative specificity, words can communicate important concepts to those who share a common social (here social/scientific) "ground." My own view is that the social sciences, even psychology, tend to be so awash in a sea (often riptide) of words that the assumption—explicit or implicit—that certain words convey scientific concepts shoulders a burden of proof. For example, just because we label phenomena "implicit memory" or "repression" or "forgetting" does not imply a unity to be assumed rather than proved. In this critique, I point out distinctions that the authors of the three chapters I am discussing do not make—and question some they do make.

THE NARENS, GRAF, AND NELSON CHAPTER

The distinction made between implicit versus explicit memory in Chapter 6 of this volume is—in my view—a questionable one. I am not arguing that some general distinction between these two types of memories is not important, but that the way in which the current authors define implicit versus explicit memory creates a distinction that may not in fact exist. Their distinction is based on one made by Schacter (1987) in terms of *task requirements.* The basic idea is that memory can be said to be implicit when a previous experience facilitates performance on a task without requiring conscious *or* intentional *or* deliberate recall of that experience. Such implicit memory is to be differentiated from explicit memory, which is revealed when a task does require conscious recollection of previous experience. If explicit memory is the negation of implicit memory (so that all memory is either implicit or explicit), then to be consistent, the authors would have to postulate explicit memory whenever a task requires recall that is conscious *and* intentional *and* deliberate (given that the negation of a disjunction is a conjunction of negations). The problem, however, is that the distinction does not work. We usually differentiate between implicit versus explicit memory in terms of what subjects are *actually recalling*, not in terms of task "requirements." The core problem is that it is not clear whether something that is recalled and consequently facilitates task performance can be claimed to be "required" by the task.

A brief history of the distinction—as it is made here—might reveal the problem. In Graf and Schacter (1985), we read: "Implicit memory is revealed when performance on a task is *facilitated* in the absence of conscious recollection; explicit memory is revealed when performance in a task *requires* conscious recollection of previous experience" (italics added; p. 501). A distinction between what is facilitated versus what is required (as opposed to facilitated versus not or required versus not) also appears on page 501 in Schacter (1987; the identical page number is a coincidence.) In this later article, however, we also read on the same page that implicit memory occurs when "information that was encoded during a particular episode is subsequently expressed without conscious or deliberate recollection." This latter statement involves a definition that appears reasonable to many of us (although not precise), because we would wish to distinguish between implicit versus explicit memory on the basis of what a subject is actually doing—that is, recalling on a conscious or deliberate basis or not—rather than on what a task "requires" or on what "facilitates" performance on it.

Moving from what people actually do (which may be unobservable) to what "facilitates" task performance to what a task "requires" appears to be a progression from a "subjective" distinction to a precise one. The appearance is misleading. The problem with this distinction is well illustrated in the actual results. The instructions in the "*explicit*-guess" condition are minimally different from those in the "*implicit*-test" condition. In the "implicit-test" condition the subject is told to type in the "first word you think of that turns the fragment into a word," whereas in the "explicit-guess" condition the subject should feel free "to take a guess at every item, whether it was on the study list or not." The only difference I can understand between these two conditions is that—were I in both—I may in the "explicit-guess" condition have a set of letters that comes to mind to complete the word one way (the "first word"), but I then realize that it could be completed another way—and I believe that the second way it could be completed was probably more likely than the first way to be the word I had seen. Consequently, I "guess" the second way. But such Byzantine reasoning is unlikely to occur, given that 70% of the words can be completed in only one way.

It is not surprising, then, that there are virtually no differences between the implicit group and the "explicit-guess" group—either in terms of accuracy, predictability from judgments of learning, or anything else that I can find. Only if we to make the distinction between explicit versus implicit memory in terms of task *requirements* would we expect such a difference. From the subject's perspective, however, the conditions are virtually identical.

(I might also mention that there is a finding across both studies that I believe to be not as important as the authors do. It is that the belief about the state of an item—"studied" or "nonstudied"—is a more important determinant of the "probability of outputting" the item then whether the item was actually studied or not. If we simply hypothesize that the ability to fill in the blank letters is used as a *cue* in the judgment of whether an item was studied or unstudied, this result is not surprising. The hypothesis is supported by the fact that in both studies the judgment of whether or not the item was studied follows the task of filling in the missing letters.)

THE FUNNELL, METCALFE, AND TSAPKINI CHAPTER

Having read Chapter 7 of this volume and watched the video of Mr. H.W., I agree completely that he has explicit knowledge of the targets and therefore his judgments are based on well-elaborated representational information that is available to self-reflective conscious inspection. Because so many *other* judgments of feeling of knowing that predict recognition for *other* people are based on *other* factors, it is not surprising that the relationship between his judgments and subsequent recognition is different from the relationship for others.

A feeling of knowledge based on the "tip-of-the-tongue state" is probably a quite different feeling—and due to different factors—then one based on an understanding about one's own general knowledge. Consider, "Who is the Elephant Man?" The feeling of knowing from people who cannot recall his name might be based either on the tip-of-the-tongue phenomenon, *or* based on knowing one has seen the play or movie, *or* based on knowing one's general educational level—which implies that one has or has not been exposed to the answer—or based on a proven ability to recognize distracters (e.g., Newt Gingrich), and so on. I suspect that just as the inference is quite different when based on these three factors (although sometimes the inference may be based on more than one of these factors), the relationship between feeling of knowing and subsequent recognition should be different. To return, for example, to Nelson's original studies, there is a very strong relationship between feeling of knowing judgments on the part of the individual and the *base rates* of accurate recall on the part of groups of which the individual is a member. Both predict subsequent recognition (Nelson, Leonesio, Landwehr, & Narens, 1986)—the latter a little better than the former. But that is wholly different from the problem faced by Mr. H.W.

Another difference that I think is important is that although the authors of this study talk about memory and metamemory, there is clearly a distinction between being able to say a word out of context at the suggestion of an examiner versus using it in an appropriate context. The very fact that Mr. H.W. attempts to generate a requested word by using sentences in which he believes it appears testifies to this distinction. I do not see that distinction in the model that the investigation of Mr. H.W. presumably supports.

Anxiety may be a critical variable in this difference. Again, it does not occur in the model, and I am concerned that the description of what is going on fails to make the important distinctions between his ordinary performance and his performance when challenged.

THE LOFTUS, COAN, AND PICKRELL CHAPTER

Chapter 8 of this volume begins with a reference to "the controversy over the recovery of repressed memories" and subsequently extends earlier work of Loftus and colleagues on influencing people to remember events that did not occur. The research is, in my view, extraordinarily important—mainly because of a distinction that can be drawn between memory from materials that are presented *to* subjects, who might even have some reason to believe that their recall of it will be tested later—versus autobiographical memory. The latter involves us, and our actions, and what happens to us. At the time that the actions and events occur, we are focusing our attention on them; we are certainly not attempting to code them in a way that will facilitate recall later, and we have no reason to believe that when we do try to recall them, success or failure in doing so in any way reflects favorably or unfavorably on our cognitive abilities.

Moreover, at least for some of us, autobiographical material is coded primarily in visual form. The type of recall studied by Bartlett involved verbal materials presented *to* subjects, whereas the "controversy of the recovery of repressed memories" involves the autobiographical recall of a visual nature. What Loftus and colleagues have done is to extend the earlier work of Loftus—which went from verbal to visual but nevertheless involved materials presented *to* subjects—to autobiographical memory. I believe that is an important advance, because the areas in which most of us are most interested (not just the "recovered repressed memory" area) involves asking people to recall what it is that happened to them.

Here, I would like to suggest that there are some additional distinctions involving autobiographical memory that might inform future work. These distinctions are related to the recovered repressed memory phenomena, but transcend it.

The first concerns the distinction between recall of plausible experience versus recall of implausible experience. As Pearson, Ross, and Dawes (1991) pointed out, many of the systematic distortions of retrospective memory about one's own life are compatible with socially accepted explanations of stability and change in the life course. Memory researchers may, thus, wish to examine the role of plausibility in reconstructing (historically accurate or historically inaccurate) memories. Being lost in a shopping mall is a very plausible experience to most people who are young enough that they wandered around shopping malls as young children. But what about eating babies in satanic cult rituals? One of the objections to the work of Loftus is that although she is able to manipulate people to believe in plausible experiences that didn't occur, such experiences as eating babies while being continually sexually abused in satanic rituals (perhaps on spacecrafts) are so implausible that "the subjects couldn't have made them up." Certainly, the argument runs, "no one would want to believe anything so horrible if it weren't true"—unlike being lost in a shopping mall (although at least one critic of the work of Loftus seems to believe that she permanently traumatized her subjects by making them believe they were actually lost for a few hours). Could subjects (ethically) be led to believe that they had had a totally implausible experience?

That question raises the possibility that prior belief may be an extraordinarily important variable in constructing false memories. Moreover, what is plausible to some people may not be plausible to others. (One of my least favorite arguments was with a close friend in psychology who maintained that there must be something to reports of satanic ritual abuse because "the stories are so similar"; this person never owned a television set, or—to the best of my knowledge—ever even watched a TV program; consequently she was unable to have the sort of experience that I have had of flipping through so-called "religious" channels late at night and observing depiction of satanic rituals.) This plausibility question leads to subsidiary ones that I believe might be quite important; for example, the role of fictional presentation in the development of prior belief (hence "plausibility") that may be critical in determining whether a false memory can be encouraged.

Social consensus may as well be critical. For example, Fiore (1989) claims that a *symptom* of having been abducted by aliens is interest in UFOs and stories of alien abduction. When the patient comes with this symptom, the therapist can then help cure the client by discovering the details of the client's actual abduction. The technique is (counter)hypnosis; the theory is that the aliens have hypnotized people to forget their abduction, but that because every single experience no matter how trivial (or in this case nontrivial) is stored somewhere in the brain exactly as it occurred, such hypnosis can never be completely successful; the therapist uses her or his own hypnotic influence to unlock these memories. (Exactly why hypnosis leads to tweaking the neural connections that are there but have previously been blocked by hypnosis from leading to conscious awareness is not explained.) Of course, a simpler explanation of the role of the prior interest in UFOs is that such interest makes the abduction experience a plausible one; especially when predisposed people join groups of others similarly inclined, the prior probability that they have had this experience is enhanced—and enhanced most of all by a believing therapist.

The one other distinction that Loftus and colleagues might consider is that between events that result from personal initiation or internal feelings versus events that happened "to" people who experience them more-or-less passively. The reason that I suggest this distinction is that Loftus does mention Freudian theory, and athough there is some evidence that Freud occasionally postulated repression of experiences in which people were essentially passive victims, the bulk of his argument about repression concerns the repression of our own instincts, desires, and unacceptable impulses (Freud, 1915/1959, 1918/1959). Thus, according to Freud, it is "the return of the repressed" (p. 93) when defense mechanisms fail that leads to neurotic symptoms, and the problem posed to the psychoanalyst is of how to help the person deal with this material in an unusual way through psychotherapy and hence sublimation—rather than in the usual way through repression, denial, and so on (which have ceased "working"). The point is that these impulses and desires are believed to be ongoing factors in the individual's psyche, whereas a particular experience would not be— and hence from a strictly Freudian perspective, could not have the effects of the "repressed memories" prior to recovery that the advocates of "recovered repressed memory" therapy claim. I do not want to argue all the intricacies of the Spaceship Psychoanalytic Theory (Dawes, 1995), but do wish to point out that this theory does lead to an active versus passive distinction for life events that may inform future research.

REFERENCES

Dawes, R. M. (1995 November/December). Spaceship psychoanalytic theory. *FMS Foundation Newsletter*, p. 7. [Comments inspired by Crews, F., et al. (1995). *The memory wars: Freud's legacy in dispute. New York Review*, New York, NY.]

Fiore, E. (1989). *Encounters: A psychologist reveals case studies of abduction by extraterrestrials*. New York: Bantam Doubleday Dell.

Freud, S. (1959). From a history of infantile neurosis. In A. Strachey & J. Strachey (Eds.), *Collected papers: Volume 3* (pp. 473–585). New York: Basic Books. (Original work published 1918)

Freud, S. (1959). Repression. In A. Strachey & J. Strachey (Eds.), *Collected Papers: Volume 4* (pp. 84–98). New York: Basic Books. (Original work published 1915)

Graf, P., & Schacter, D. L. (1985). Implicit and explicit memory for new associations in normal and amnesiac subjects. *Journal of Experimental Psychology: Learning, Memory, and Cognition, 11,* 501–518.

Nelson, T. O., Leonesio, R. J., Landwehr, R. S., & Narens, L. (1986). A comparison of three predictors of an individual's memory performance: The individual's feeling of knowing versus the normative feeling of knowing versus base-rate item difficulty. *Journal of Experimental Psychology: Learning, Memory, and Cognition, 12,* 279–287.

Pearson, R. W., Ross, M., & Dawes, R. M. (1991). Personal recall and the limits of retrospective questions in surveys. In J. M. Tanur (Ed.), *Questions about questions: Inquiries into the cognitive bases of surveys* (pp. 65–94). New York: Russell Sage Foundation.

Schacter, D. L. (1987). Implicit memory: History and current status. *Journal of Experimental Psychology: Learning, Memory, and Cognition, 13,* 501–518.

Chapter 10

Implicit Memory, Explicit Memory, and False Recollection: A Cognitive Neuroscience Perspective

Kenneth A. Norman
Daniel L. Schacter
Harvard University

Over the past decade, research exploring the relation between implicit and explicit forms of memory has generated an impressive array of new findings, theoretical perspectives, and procedures for investigating the effects of past experience on subsequent behavior (for reviews, see Graf & Masson, 1993; Richardson-Klavehn & Bjork, 1988; Roediger & McDermott, 1993; Schacter, 1987a; Schacter, Chiu, & Ochsner, 1993). Studies of implicit memory have also exposed gaps in our understanding of conscious, explicit recollection. One such gap involves the distinction between retrieving stored information, on the one hand, and the subjective experience of remembering, on the other. Logically, retrieval and remembering are not the same thing; the subjective experience of remembering, at its core, involves taking retrieved information and interpreting it as depicting or pertaining to some past experience. For years, however, the question of how retrieved information becomes a conscious memory was ignored by memory researchers, in large part because on tests of explicit memory (i.e., recall and recognition), retrieval and remembering are coextensive: By explicitly asking subjects to think back to the study phase, the experimenter is forging the link between present and past that, outside of the lab, subjects have to discover on their own (cf. Schacter & Tulving, 1982; Tulving, 1989).

Research on implicit memory has helped to revive interest in the relationship between memory and remembering, by demonstrating (in studies of college students, amnesic patients, elderly adults, young children, and even anesthetized patients) that the effects of prior exposure to stimuli can be expressed implicitly, as changes in test performance, without any subjective sense of remembering the study episode. The most extensively studied form of implicit memory is the phenomenon of direct or repetition priming, where exposure to a word or object influences subsequent processing of the item (cf. Roediger, 1990; Schacter, 1994; Tulving & Schacter, 1990). For example, if people are asked to complete three-letter stems (e.g., GAR___) with the first word that comes to mind, their completions will be reliably biased by previously studied words. The priming effect operates normally even in amnesic patients, who have great difficulty explicitly remembering previously studied words (e.g., Graf, Squire, & Mandler, 1984; Warrington & Weiskrantz, 1974).

The existence and robustness of implicit memory phenomena force us to confront the question: If memory can sometimes be expressed without remembering, what factors determine when remembering will occur? To answer this question, we need to understand in greater detail the metacognitive processes that are responsible for interpreting present information processing in terms of the effects of past experience.

Our chapter examines implicit memory and metacognition from the perspective of contemporary cognitive neuroscience. Cognitive neuroscience analyses attempt to shed light on the neurocognitive bases of memory and other fundamental capacities by drawing on evidence from patients with brain lesions, modern functional neuroimaging techniques, and research on nonhuman animals (for more on the logic of cognitive neuroscience, see Kosslyn & Koenig, 1992; Schacter, 1992). We apply the cognitive neuroscience perspective to the understanding of implicit memory, explicit memory, and the problem of how metacognitive processes analyze retrieved information and forge links with the past. We begin by discussing the "raw material" of memory: changes in brain activity brought about as a result of prior exposure to various kinds of stimuli. Specifically, we focus on some recent studies using the neuroimaging technique of positron emission tomography (PET) that provide insights into the brain bases of implicit and explicit memory.

Next, we focus on the role of the frontal lobes in metacognitive processes that are relevant to the subjective experience of remembering past events. We first review evidence showing that damage to the frontal lobes leads to specific impairments in linking retrieved information to the past. Frontal lobe patients frequently show a disproportionate impairment in source memory—linking facts to the circumstances in which the facts were acquired (e.g., Janowsky, Shimamura, & Squire, 1989). We then focus on the inaccurate or false recollections that are observed in some patients with frontal lobe damage. Sometimes frontal patients confabulate memories of events that never actually happened (Moscovitch, 1989, 1995), and sometimes they show a pathological tendency toward false recognition (Curran, Schacter, Norman, & Galluccio, in press; Delbecq-Derouesne, Beauvois, & Shallice, 1990; Parkin, Bindschaedler, Harsent, & Metzler, 1995; Schacter, Curran, Galluccio, Milberg, & Bates, in press). We consider studies of such patients and delineate their theoretical implications. We believe that careful consideration of false recollections in patients with frontal lesions can be revealing theoretically, and perhaps provide insights into the brain mechanisms of memory distortions in normal, non-brain-damaged subjects (cf. Ceci, 1995; Loftus, Feldman, & Dashiell, 1995; McClelland, 1995; Schacter, 1995).

Finally, we offer some suggestions and speculations regarding the kind of theoretical approach that can help to illuminate the range of memory deficits associated with frontal lobe damage. We consider the possibility that a variety of memory deficits that are associated with frontal lobe damage, from poor recall of source information to confabulation to false recognition, can be viewed in terms of an inability to generate (in a top-down fashion) representations of context, where we use "context" to mean "the circumstances surrounding the target event." In so doing, we deliberately blur the line between processes involved in retrieval and processes involved in monitoring retrieved information.

NEURAL CORRELATES OF IMPLICIT MEMORY: PRIMING AND THE BRAIN

In this section, we consider evidence regarding the brain bases of priming (for recent reviews of priming, see Roediger & McDermott, 1993; Schacter, 1994). Many investigators have found it useful to draw a distinction between perceptual and conceptual forms of priming (cf. Blaxton, 1989). Perceptual priming occurs on so-called data-driven implicit memory tests, such as perceptual identification and word completion. It is modality specific and little influenced by depth of encoding (Roediger, 1990; Schacter, 1990; but see Brown & Mitchell, 1994). Conceptual priming occurs on semantic or conceptually driven implicit tests, such as category instance production. It is modality nonspecific and sensitive to depth of encoding (e.g., Blaxton, 1989; Hamman, 1990).

A variety of theoretical proposals have been put forward to account for perceptual priming, conceptual priming, and the relation between them (cf. Keane, Gabrieli, Fennema, Growdon, & Corkin, 1991; Masson & Macleod, 1992; Moscovitch, 1994a; Roediger, 1990; Schacter, 1994; Squire, 1994; Tulving & Schacter, 1990). Perceptual priming has been studied and discussed more extensively than conceptual priming, so we focus on it here. In a series of articles, Schacter and colleagues (1990, 1994; Tulving & Schacter, 1990) have argued that priming on completion, identification, and similar tasks is influenced heavily by a perceptual representation system

(PRS). The PRS has been characterized as a collection of domain-specific subsystems that represent information about the form and structure, but not the meaning and associative properties, of words and objects. Based on independent neuropsychological observations, it has been proposed that a visual word form subsystem (Warrington & Shallice, 1980), auditory word form subsystem (Ellis & Young, 1988), and structural description subsystem (Riddoch & Humphreys, 1987) contribute to visual word priming (Schacter, Rapscak, Rubens, Tharan, & Laguna, 1990), auditory word priming (Schacter & Church, 1992), and visual object priming (Schacter, Cooper, & Delaney, 1990), respectively. At the level of brain systems, Schacter (1990, 1994) argued that the PRS subsystems, and the priming effects that they support, are subserved by various regions in posterior cortex that are spared in amnesic patients. Explicit remembering of past events, by this account, depends on the hippocampus and other medial temporal lobe/diencephalic structures that are typically compromised in amnesic patients (cf. Johnson & Chalfonte, 1994; Moscovitch, 1994b; and Squire, 1994, for roughly similar perspectives).

Functional neuroimaging studies provide a potentially powerful way of testing these ideas. For example, several investigators (cf. Keane et al., 1991; Schacter, 1990) have speculated that visual priming on data-driven implicit memory tests involves regions of extrastriate occipital cortex that have been implicated in visual word processing (Petersen, Fox, Snyder, & Raichle, 1990). An early PET study by Squire et al. (1992) provides relevant data. In PET experiments, measurements of regional cerebral blood flow are related to task performance in different conditions. The general idea is that brain regions that are relatively more involved in performing a particular task will exhibit increased levels of blood flow compared to regions that are relatively less involved or uninvolved. Comparisons are made by subtracting estimates of blood flow in one experimental condition from estimates of blood flow in another condition. Ideally, the two conditions are closely matched except for a critical difference that is introduced by the experimenter (for a review of PET studies of memory, see Buckner & Tulving, 1995).

In the experiment by Squire et al. (1992), subjects studied a list of familiar words prior to the initiation of PET scanning. Several minutes later, they were asked to complete three-letter word stems with the first word that comes to mind. Subjects were scanned in one condition where some of the stems could be completed with studied words (the priming condition), and they were also scanned in another condition where none of the stems could be completed with studied words (the baseline condition). Squire et al. compared estimates of blood flow in the baseline condition with estimates of blood flow in the priming condition. They found that priming is associated with decreased blood flow in regions of extrastriate occipital cortex (bilaterally, with a larger decrease on the right than on the left). The finding of a priming-related blood flow decrease suggests that priming enhances the efficiency of generating a completion for a studied item—that is, in the primed condition, less perceptual processing of the stem is required in order to trigger a completion. More importantly, the finding of a priming-related blood flow decrease in extrastriate occipital cortex provides support for the PRS account of visual word priming.

Importantly, however, a further result from the Squire et al. (1992) study is inconsistent with the PRS view: There was a significant blood flow increase in the hippocampus during priming in comparison to baseline. Given prior findings of normal stem completion priming in amnesic patients (who suffer from damage to the hippocampal system), such a result is surprising. However, careful examination of Squire et al.'s behavioral data suggests a likely explanation. In the Squire et al. experiment, subjects studied a short list of target words twice with a semantic encoding task, and were tested only a few minutes later. It is quite possible under these conditions that priming was "contaminated" by explicit memory—that is, subjects either intentionally or unintentionally remembered that the target completions had appeared previously on the study list (cf. Jacoby, 1991; Schacter, Bowers, & Booker, 1989). Consistent with this suggestion, subjects completed 72% of stems with target words in the priming condition, compared to a baseline completion rate close to 10%. This is an unusually large priming effect—virtually indistinguishable from the 76% target completion rate that was observed in a separate "memory" condition in which subjects were given three-letter stems and instructed to remember target words from the study list. The hippocampus showed significant blood flow increases during this latter condition, implying that some aspect of explicit memory contributed to the hippocampal activation that Squire et al. observed in the priming condition (for further discussion, see Curran & Schacter, in press; Schacter, 1994).

These suggestions have been tested in a recent PET study by Schacter et al. (1996). If hippocampal activation during priming is attributable to explicit contamination, then it should be possible to eliminate the hippocampal activation by eliminating the explicit contamination. To accomplish this objective, Schacter et al. gave subjects a single study-list exposure to target items and had them perform a perceptual orienting task (counting the number of t-junctions in a word). Behavioral results indicated that this manipulation was successful in eliminating explicit contamination. Analysis of the PET data revealed two key findings: (a) priming was associated with significant blood flow decreases in extrastriate occipital cortex; and (b) there was no hint of hippocampal activation in connection with priming.

These results strongly imply that Squire et al.'s earlier finding of hippocampal activation in association with priming is attributable to the intentional or unintentional influence of explicit remembering during the priming condition of their experiment. Note, however, that a number of PET studies have failed to activate the hippocampus during explicit retrieval (for review, see Buckner & Tulving, 1995). Accordingly, the fact that Schacter et al. (1996) did not detect hippocampal activation in association with priming could reflect a Type II error: The hippocampus may be difficult to reliably activate in PET studies.

To address this possibility, Schacter et al. (1996) carried out an experiment in which subjects were tested with the same three-letter stems used in the priming study, together with explicit memory instructions (i.e., to think back to the study list). Prior to the test, subjects studied some words in a condition designed to promote high levels of explicit recall (semantic encoding task, four study-list exposures) and other words in a condition that was designed to promote low levels of explicit recall (perceptual encoding task, one study-list exposure). These encoding conditions were not scanned. Separate blocks of test cues were then given for words that had been studied in the high and low recall conditions, respectively. Results revealed strong evidence of hippocampal activation when subjects were given stems that could be completed with words from the high recall condition. There was no evidence of hippocampal activation when subjects were given stems that could be completed with words from the low recall condition. Indeed, when estimates of blood flow in the low explicit memory conditions were subtracted from the high explicit memory conditions, there was a significant blood flow increase in the right hippocampus, but no significant increases in any other brain region.

When considered together with the absence of evidence for hippocampal activation in Schacter et al.'s priming experiment, these results provide strong evidence that the hippocampus is specifically associated with explicit remembering of a word. Conversely, it is also now clear that priming is associated with blood flow changes in extrastriate occipital cortex—not in the hippocampus. The overall pattern of results fits nicely with the PRS view sketched earlier. Further supportive evidence is provided by a recent experiment from Gabrieli, Fleischman, Keane, Reminger, and Morrell (1995), who found that visual priming was eliminated in a patient with damage to occipital cortex.

The foregoing studies support the claim that priming reflects modulation of activity in the brain structures involved in carrying out the particular task employed during the test phase. Further relevant observations come from a recent PET study of visual object priming (Schacter, Reiman, et al., 1995). In this study, subjects studied a series of line drawings depicting possible or impossible three-dimensional objects. Later, subjects were presented with separate blocks of new (nonstudied) possible objects, new impossible objects, studied possible objects, and studied impossible objects.

Each object was flashed for about 50 msec, and subjects were asked to decide whether the line drawing depicts a possible object or an impossible object.

Previous studies using this object decision task have revealed that subjects show priming for possible objects but not for impossible objects. Schacter, Cooper, and Delaney (1990) argued that object decision priming occurs because subjects form, at the time of study, a representation of the global, three-dimensional structure of an object—what has been termed a structural description (e.g., Riddoch & Humphreys, 1987). This structural description is tapped when subjects make object decisions at test. According to this view, priming occurs for possible but not for impossible objects because global structural descriptions can be formed for the former but not the latter type of object (for an alternative account, see Ratcliff & McKoon, 1995; cf. Schacter & Cooper, 1995). Several lines of evidence from brain-damaged patients and single-cell recordings in monkeys suggest that regions of inferior temporal cortex play an important role in representing the global shape of visual objects (e.g., Plaut & Farah, 1990). Based on this evidence, Schacter, Cooper, and Delaney (1990) suggested that structural descriptions are computed by a specialized system that involves the inferior temporal region.

In the PET study, Schacter, Reiman, et al. found increased blood flow in inferior temporal regions and the nearby fusiform gyrus when subjects made object decisions about either old or new possible objects, compared to a no-decision baseline in which subjects passively viewed the objects. More specifically, the right inferior temporal region was preferentially activated when subjects made object decisions about new possible objects (compared to baseline); both left and right inferior temporal regions were activated when subjects made object decisions about previously studied possible objects (compared to baseline). Left inferior temporal regions were preferentially activated when subjects made object decisions about studied possible objects as compared to nonstudied possible objects. Importantly, no significant blood flow increases were found in left or right inferior temporal regions when subjects made object decisions about either studied or nonstudied impossible objects.

This pattern of results is consistent with the suggestion made by Schacter and Cooper (1993) that inferior temporal regions play a role in the representation and priming of structurally possible novel objects. The data are also consistent with the idea that it is difficult to form a representation of the global structure of an impossible object—hence the inferior temporal region is not engaged when subjects make possible/impossible decisions about impossible objects.

Also, on a yes/no recognition test for previously studied objects and nonstudied objects, Schacter, Reiman, et al. found blood flow increases in the vicinity of the hippocampus in association with explicit memory for previously studied possible objects. By contrast, there were no comparable hippocampal blood flow increases in association with explicit memory for previously studied impossible objects. Insofar as possible objects were re-membered more accurately than were impossible objects, these PET find-ings are consistent with the results of the previously mentioned high recall versus low recall PET study of familiar words: They suggest that hippocam-pal activations during retrieval in PET studies are related to the overall level of memory performance, or some aspect of subjects' recollective experience during retrieval.

The PET data that we have considered are generally supportive of the PRS account of perceptual priming. The evidence concerning blood flow correlates of stem completion and object decision performance is also consistent with the idea that priming on a specific task is supported by representations in the cortical regions that are involved in carrying out that task. Explicit recollection, by contrast, is often associated with the hippocampal activation. Thus, at the level of brain systems, implicit memory may occur when representations in posterior cortical regions affect task performance without the involvement of the hippocampus.

RELATING IMPLICIT AND EXPLICIT MEMORY

Our discussion of the neural correlates of implicit memory raises a key question: How are the various modifications in neural activity that underlie priming related to the conscious experience of remembering a past event? We believe, along with others (e.g., Moscovitch, 1994b), that two brain regions play a key role in the process of explicit recollection. The medial temporal region, consisting of the hippocampus and surrounding struc-tures, is responsible for binding together all of the distinct, distributed traces corresponding to a particular episode into a coherent trace, and also for reactivating them together at some later point in time (McClelland, McNaughton, & O'Reilly, 1995; Squire, 1992). Frontal lobe structures, on the other hand, are responsible for generating retrieval cues aimed at activating stored episodic traces. They also play a role in linking retrieved information back to the episodic context in which it was acquired. We consider medial temporal and frontal contributions to retrieval in turn.

As noted earlier, the idea that medial temporal structures are involved in forming and retrieving episodic traces comes from studies of amnesic patients with medial temporal damage. These patients perform extremely poorly on explicit memory tests, yet nevertheless exhibit various implicit memory effects, such as priming (for a review of medial temporal amnesia, see Squire, 1994). When the medial temporal system is damaged, specific brain regions can still be modified by experience, but the modifications associated with a particular experience are not bound together (McClelland et al., 1995; see also Cohen & O'Reilly, 1996). Because of this, patients with medial temporal damage are unable to reactivate (in a coherent fashion) distributed patterns of neural activity corresponding to past episodes; this accounts for the explicit memory impairment manifested by these patients. However, on tasks which do not require retrieval of coherent episodic traces (e.g., identifying a word that was presented earlier in the experiment), individual (unbound) modifications can facilitate performance; priming still occurs.

Recently, detailed models have been proposed that specify how the hippocampus binds together episodic traces (McClelland et al., 1995; Treves & Rolls, 1994). These models argue that, initially, the distributed neocortical representations which make up an episodic memory trace are all associated with a single hippocampal "index," thereby allowing for coherent reactivation of the trace by way of this shared index. At this point, the different neocortical components of the trace are not associated with each other. Each time the new trace is triggered, however, direct connections between its components are strengthened. Eventually, the hippocampal index ceases to play a critical role in maintaining the coherent trace; therefore, the medial temporal region plays a temporary or time-limited role in storing episodic memories (Squire, 1992).

We have argued that medial temporal structures must be intact in order for subjects to bind up distributed cortical representations as an episodic memory, and that medial temporal structures play a necessary role in retrieval of recently acquired episodic traces. Evidence for this idea is provided by the PET studies we reviewed earlier indicating that the hippocampus is especially active in conditions that yield high levels of explicit recollection compared to ones that yield low levels of recollection. Our claim is that reactivation of episodic traces (mediated initially by medial temporal structures) is necessary but not sufficient in order for a subjective experience of remembering to occur; after the trace is activated, it is still necessary to attribute the retrieved information to a specific past episode. This is the point at which metacognitive processes become relevant to remembering. From a cognitive neuroscience perspective, we want to know which brain structures are involved in, or responsible for, this interpretive activity.

PET studies provide some useful hints concerning this point. A large number of PET studies (e.g., Buckner et al., 1995; Shallice et al., 1994; Squire et al., 1992; Tulving, Kapur, Markowitsch, et al., 1994) have found that regions of prefrontal cortex (most prominently, right dorsolateral prefrontal cortex) "light up" when subjects are asked to consciously recollect studied information. The Schacter et al. (1996) study of stem-cued recall provides pertinent data concerning the nature of the frontal involvement in explicit retrieval. Schacter et al. observed extensive activation in dorsolateral prefrontal regions in the "low recall" condition discussed earlier. Here, subjects were "working hard" in an attempt to retrieve studied items, but were not successfully remembering many of them. By contrast, there was no significant frontal activation in the "high recall" condition, where subjects easily remembered most of the study list items. These results suggest that frontal activation may be indexing, among other things, the effort involved in trying to consciously recollect stored information.

PET data, of course, can never demonstrate that an activated area plays a necessary or essential role in a particular task. To determine whether processes carried out by the frontal lobes are essential for interpreting retrieved information, we can examine the effects of frontal lobe damage on memory retrieval; if our story is correct, frontal lobe damage should lead to a selective deficit in "contextualizing" retrieved information (i.e., determining that retrieved information pertains to a specific, previously experienced event, and characterizing the circumstances surrounding this event).

INTERPRETING RETRIEVED INFORMATION: NEUROPSYCHOLOGICAL PERSPECTIVES

In the preceding section, we noted that damage to medial temporal brain structures results in generalized impairments of both explicit recognition and recall. Medial temporal amnesia does not reflect a selective impairment in interpreting retrieved information. It is better characterized as a generalized impairment in forming and retrieving coherent episodic traces. Once retrieved, these traces constitute the input to processes that attempt to link retrieved information back to its source. What kinds of brain damage selectively impair these "linking" processes?

Evidence from neuropsychology indicates that frontal regions play a role in correctly interpreting retrieved information. One striking characteristic of memory impairments associated with damage to the frontal region (where "frontal region" refers to both frontal cortex and surrounding structures, such as the basal forebrain and the basal ganglia) is the sheer number of qualitatively distinct patterns of memory impairment that can result from roughly similar lesions (Shimamura, 1995). Relevant to our present aims, some frontal patients show a disproportionate impairment in remembering source information (the circumstances under which a particular fact was acquired), and in memory for temporal order (e.g., Janowsky et al., 1989; Milner, Corsi, & Leonard, 1991). These problems also show up in elderly subjects, who suffer from frontal lobe deterioration (Craik, Morris, Morris, & Loewen, 1990; Schacter, Kaszniak, Kihlstrom, & Valdiserri, 1991), and young children, whose frontal lobes are not fully developed (Schacter, Kagan, & Leichtman, 1995; for a general review of source monitoring, see Johnson, Hashtroudi, & Lindsay, 1993). Furthermore, some frontal patients manifest a pathological tendency to confabulate (that is, to recall episodes that did not actually transpire); the plausibility and internal consistency of confabulated incidents varies widely between patients (Baddeley & Wilson, 1986; Dalla Barba, 1993a, 1993b; Moscovitch, 1995). Also, some frontal patients make abnormally high numbers of false alarms on yes–no recognition tests (Curran et al., in press; Delbecq-Derouesne et al., 1990; Parkin et al., 1995; Schacter et al., in press).

Source amnesia, confabulation, and false recognition can occur together in the same patient, but sometimes this is not the case. For example, in a case that we describe here later, false recognition occurred without evidence of spontaneous confabulation. One obstacle to mapping out patterns of co-occurrence among these deficits is that case studies often do not assess performance in enough detail to determine the extent to which the aforementioned deficits are present, and the relevant terms and phenomena are not sufficiently clearly defined. For instance, intrusions on recall tests for newly learned information are sometimes treated as indexing a subject's tendency to confabulate (Dalla Barba, 1993b), but the link between intrusions on these tests, and the tendency to report confabulated autobiographical incidents, has not been fully explored.

In most memory-impaired patient groups, recall and recognition performance are equally impaired (Haist, Shimamura, & Squire, 1992). However, recall is frequently more impaired than recognition in patients with frontal lobe damage (Moscovitch, 1989; Parkin & Leng, 1993); frontal-damaged patients who show false recognition represent an exception to this pattern, insofar as these patients show both poor recall (often characterized by numerous intrusions; Delbecq-Derouesne et al., 1990) and poor recognition. Frontal damage can also result in dissociations within the domain of recognition memory: For example, Parkin, Yeomans, and Bindschaedler (1994) described a patient, CB, who showed disproportionately impaired performance on yes/no (single-probe) recognition tests relative to forced-choice recognition tests. An additional point is that the deficits mentioned earlier can be domain-specific: That is, patients sometimes show memory impairments for one class of stimulus materials (say, verbal stimuli) but performance with other materials (e.g., pictorial stimuli) is relatively spared. This point is exemplified by patient ROB (Hanley, Davies, Downes, & Mayes, 1994), who suffered selective damage to her left caudate nucleus as a result of a ruptured anterior communicating artery (ACoA) aneurysm; ROB shows impoverished performance on both free and cued recall tests when verbal stimuli are employed, but shows entirely intact recall of nonverbal stimuli (cf. Milner et al., 1991).

Looking over the aforementioned memory deficits, it is clear that frontal circuits play a key role in explicit recollection of stored episodes. Is this a unitary role carried out by a single process, or should we posit multiple frontal lobe processes that make distinct contributions to memory retrieval? The construct of "frontal lobe damage," as traditionally employed, is quite imprecise. It has been used to refer to lesions in dorsolateral prefrontal cortex, orbitofrontal cortex, ventromedial prefrontal cortex, premotor cortex, various parts of the basal ganglia, and various basal forebrain structures. Given the heterogeneity of these structures, it makes sense that different frontal structures might be engaged in different retrieval-related processes. Also, the wide range of qualitatively distinct patterns of "frontal" memory impairment, documented earlier, would seem to argue in favor of the multiple-process view.

One popular means of fractionating frontal contributions to retrieval has been to posit separate processes involved in retrieving information and in evaluating (monitoring) retrieved information (Delbecq-Derouesne et al., 1990; Hanley et al., 1994; Shallice, 1988). A number of conceptually distinct functions are subsumed under this general notion of monitoring. First, the frontal lobes are held to implement reality monitoring: determining whether retrieved information pertains to a past episode that actually transpired, as opposed to an episode that was only imagined (Johnson, 1991; Johnson & Raye, 1981). Next, the retrieved information needs to be assigned to a specific context, or, if people are engaged in trying to remember a particular episode, it is necessary to verify that what is retrieved actually corresponds to the target episode. According to this framework, impaired recall can be explained in terms of damage to processes involved in dredging up stored information from memory, and phenomena like confabulation can be explained in terms of damaged monitoring processes (which fail to reject retrieved information that does not pertain to the sought-after episode). Because different processes are responsible for retrieving correct information, and rejecting inappropriate information, recall of correct information and recall of incorrect information are free to vary independently, thereby accommodating the fact that not all patients with retrieval impairments confabulate (e.g., patient ROB, studied by Hanley et al., 1994, is severely impaired at recalling verbal material but does not confabulate). Monitoring processes are frequently localized to ventromedial frontal regions, based on the finding that damage to this area appears to be a prerequisite for confabulation (Moscovitch, 1995).

We suggest, however, that models that sharply distinguish between retrieval and monitoring processes fail to take into account various important similarities between retrieving information, on the one hand, and monitoring retrieved information, on the other. Specifically, both processes depend on reinstating (in a top-down fashion) contextual information associated with the target episode.

First, we examine the role that top-down reinstatement of context plays in episodic memory retrieval. Moscovitch (1989, 1995) pointed out that retrieval cues which are typically provided on autobiographical memory tests ("Tell me about your wedding reception") need to be elaborated on (e.g., Where was the reception? Who was there?) before they overlap well enough with the sought-after trace to activate that trace. The same is true of free-recall tests, where subjects have to generate their own contextual cues in order to retrieve studied items. According to Moscovitch (1995), the frontal lobes "[initiate and organize] a search that uses whatever knowledge is available, whether semantic or episodic, to reinstate the appropriate context and locate the cue that allows local, associative processes to operate [i.e., to trigger the sought-after trace]" (p. 234). Moscovitch (1995) also set forth a useful distinction between strategic retrieval processes ("problem solving routines applied to memory" that are implemented by the frontal lobes, and are responsible for reinstating context), and associative retrieval processes (which activate stored traces according to the degree to which the retrieval cue overlaps with the trace in question).

Next, why do we claim that monitoring processes need to reinstate contextual information associated with the sought-after episode? The point of monitoring processes is to assess whether or not retrieved information pertains to the episode that you are trying to remember. This necessarily involves comparing retrieved information to some kind of representation of the sought-after episode, to determine whether the two are compatible. To reject retrieved information as inappropriate, you must notice some incompatibility between the retrieved information and a representation of the to-be-remembered episode (or else the retrieved information has to lack some feature that you take to be characteristic of the sought-after episode). Therefore, to the extent that subjects are unable to reinstate contextual information associated with the sought-after episode, they will be less likely to notice subtle (and even not-so-subtle) reasons why the retrieved information might be inappropriate.

To recap, we are suggesting that strategic retrieval involves reinstating contextual information associated with the sought-after episode, in order to trigger the trace of that episode stored in memory. Monitoring involves using the same representation of context to assess whether or not retrieved information pertains to that episode. From this perspective, strategic retrieval and monitoring reflect two different uses of the same computational machinery. Therefore, it may not be necessary to assign strategic retrieval and monitoring to separate neural circuits.

At this point, it is also useful to consider the role of strategic retrieval processes in recognition memory performance. Numerous researchers have pointed out that both familiarity and conscious recollection can serve as the basis for responding on a recognition task (e.g., Jacoby, 1991; Mandler, 1980). Recently, Jacoby and others have argued that familiarity should be understood as an attribution based on fluent bottom-up processing of the test stimulus (Kelley & Jacoby, 1990); that is, familiarity involves inferring that the stimulus was presented at study, based on the fact that the stimulus is processed fluently at test. The key distinction for our purposes is that familiarity is thought to be triggered automatically, in a bottom-up fashion, and hence is relatively unaffected by more deliberate, "top-down" attempts at fleshing out a representation of the study context. Therefore, familiarity-based recognition should be relatively unaffected by damage to strategic retrieval processes.

The other way that items can be recognized is when, in connection with a particular test item, people retrieve some information that is taken to be diagnostic of the item having been presented during the study phase. This kind of recognition clearly depends on what features are considered to be diagnostic of the item having been presented at study; that is, it depends on a mental representation of what took place during the study phase. For example, say that you study a series of words printed in bright green ink; later, you encounter the word "truck" on a recognition test, and this triggers an image of "truck" printed in green ink. This retrieved image will count as evidence that you studied "truck" to the extent that "I saw green words" is part of your representation of what took place at study. This means of determining whether or not an item is "old" depends heavily on a person's ability to construct in a top-down fashion a representation of the characteristics of the study episode.

Therefore, if processes that generate these representations of the study context are severely damaged, such that subjects are totally unable to construct a representation (at test) of what transpired at study, subjects will be forced to rely on raw (bottom-up) familiarity when making their recognition judgments. This describes the pattern of preserved recognition performance manifested by patient CB, who suffered frontal lobe damage as a result of a ruptured ACoA aneurysm (Parkin et al., 1994). He performs well on forced-choice recognition tests, in which the correct answer can be selected simply by comparing the relative familiarity of the choices. But he is impaired on yes/no (single-probe) recognition tests, where a criterion must be set as to what kinds of recollected information merit an "old" response. In our view, criterion-setting involves both (a) placing a "cutoff" on a one-dimensional familiarity scale (that is, determining how familiar studied items are going to be, relative to nonstudied items), and (b) deciding which dimensions of recollective experience, apart from familiarity, are going to be relevant to the recognition decision (e.g., if all studied items were drawn in bright colors, the subject might decide that memory for color should count as evidence that an item was presented at study). Both of these steps entail some ability to recollect general characteristics of the study phase (What encoding operations were performed on studied items? How were studied items presented? How long was the study-test interval?) and to adjust one's criteria accordingly. For example, remembering how "deep" or "shallow" encoding was, and how long the study-test interval was, are both essential in determining the familiarity cutoff.

The idea we have been exploring, that both monitoring and strategic retrieval depend critically on an ability to reinstate the context associated with a particular episode, is attractive to us because it is relatively parsimonious. However, is it flexible enough to account for the range of distinct patterns of memory impairment that can result from frontal lobe damage? Phrased another way, if frontal-damaged patients all suffer from the same core deficit (inability to retrieve contextual information pertaining to the sought-after episode), why do they manifest such a heterogeneous collection of memory impairments?

Our solution to this dilemma is to posit that context-retrieval processes can break down in multiple, distinct ways. Specifically, we wish to contrast the implications of context-retrieval processes breaking down completely (such that the subject is totally unable to generate a representation of the contextual features that define the sought-after episode), with the implications of a deficit in generating what we refer to as a focused representation of context—a representation that uniquely implicates the sought-after episode; that is, certain kinds of brain damage might degrade the output of context-retrieval processes, without abolishing context representations outright. The notion of "focusing" is crucial to what follows, so we elaborate on it here. We suggest that, in order to maximize the probability of successful retrieval, the retrieval cue should overlap maximally with the trace corresponding to the sought-after episode, and overlap minimally with competing episodic traces. That is, the cue should include a maximal number of features that are characteristic of the sought-after trace, but are not characteristic of competing traces. Representations that include a large number of features that discriminate between the sought-after trace and competing traces (in the manner described earlier) are focused. Conversely, contextual representations that fail to discriminate between the sought-after trace and competing traces are unfocused.

We have already noted what happens to recognition memory when patients completely fail to generate a representation of the study context. Forced-choice recognition will be intact, because assessments of relative familiarity can take place without a representation of what took place at study; yes/no (single-probe) recognition will be impaired, because, in this task, subjects have to set a criterion for saying "old," and (according to our theory) accurate criterion setting depends on the ability to recollect general characteristics of the study phase (when it took place, how items were presented, and so on). But what about patients who have a focusing deficit—that is, patients who generate indistinct (degraded) representations of the study context? Some insight into this question comes from patient BG, a patient with frontal damage who has been studied extensively in recent experiments conducted in our laboratory (Curran et al., in press; Schacter et al., in press).

FOCUSING DEFICITS AND FALSE RECOGNITION: A CASE STUDY

BG is a 67-year-old man who suffered a right frontal infarction in December 1993. In October 1994, an MRI scan was performed, revealing an extensive right frontal lesion, primarily involving motor and premotor cortex. BG shows no signs of amnesia, does not offer spontaneous confabulations, is alert, attentive, and cooperative, and has no difficulty understanding or following task instructions. When testing BG's recognition memory, Schacter et al. (in press) used the "remember/know" technique pioneered by Tulving (1985) and Gardiner (Gardiner & Java, 1993). Whenever BG indicated that an item was "old" (presented at study), he was asked to indicate whether (a) he possessed a specific recollection of encountering the word previously, such as an image or association that he made when studying the word (a "remember" response), or (b) he just "knew" that the item appeared on the list, even though he did not have a specific recollection of having encountered it.

The first experiment that Schacter et al. (in press) conducted with BG involved visual presentation of words at study; for some words, BG rated how much he liked the word, and for other words BG counted the number of t-junctions in the word. At test, words appeared on the computer monitor and BG responded with either a "remember," "know," or "new" judgment. BG's overall hit rate was quite high and did not differ from that of a matched group of eight control subjects. On the other hand, BG's false alarm rate was much higher than, and outside the range of, control subjects' false alarms: BG responded "old" to 50% of new words, in contrast to the 17% false alarm rate of control subjects. Perhaps most strikingly, BG claimed to "remember" 38% of new items, whereas controls provided "remember" responses to only 5% of the new words. By contrast, BG and controls provided a virtually identical number of "know" false alarms.

This general pattern of normal hit rate, accompanied by an abnormally high number of "remember" false alarms, was replicated in multiple experiments using a variety of different stimulus materials (words, nonwords, environmental sounds, and pictures of objects). One important point to note is that BG's pathological false recognition is not attributable to perceptual or associative similarity between targets and lures. Schacter et al. (in press) manipulated both perceptual and associative similarity of distractor items and found that (a) BG made an abnormally high number of false alarms to distractors that are not related to targets, and (b) BG is not especially affected by similarity of distractors to targets. Furthermore, based on the finding that BG false alarmed excessively to nonword letter strings that (presumably) he had never encountered before, we can conclude that BG's false recognition is not a simple matter of confusing preexperimental familiarity with familiarity induced by encountering the stimulus during the study phase. Finally, although BG's performance on single-probe recognition tests is often consistent with a simple bias toward saying "old," this "bias" account falls short when we consider the fact that BG is impaired on some forced-choice recognition tests (he performed poorly on a two-alternative face recognition subtest of the Warrington Recognition Memory Test, although he showed normal performance on a two-alternative word recognition subtest of the Warrington test).

Having established that BG shows a pathological false alarm rate to a wide range of materials, Schacter et al. (in press) set out to devise manipulations that would stop BG from committing excessive numbers of false alarms. It was found that BG's false alarms could be curtailed sharply by presenting pictures of inanimate objects from various categories at study (e.g., furniture, articles of clothing; the encoding task involved asking subjects to name each picture) and, on a subsequent recognition test, using three separate types of nonstudied items: (a) pictures from studied categories, (b) pictures from miscellaneous categories of inanimate objects that were not represented on the study list, (c) pictures of animate objects (i.e., animals). BG claimed to "remember" many of the lure items that were drawn from previously studied categories of inanimate objects. However, he almost never claimed to "remember" lure items that were not members of previously studied categories.

These results suggest an apparent paradox: BG does not false alarm to exemplars from nonstudied categories, yet in experiments using noncategorized stimuli BG false alarms frequently to lure items that have no associative relationship to words that appeared on the study list. To resolve the paradox, Schacter et al. (in press) appealed to a distinction made by Conway and Rubin (1993), between general event knowledge and event-specific knowledge. General events refer to high-level episodes, such as going to the movies, whereas event-specific knowledge refers to particular episodes that are nested within the general event, such as spilling popcorn or being surprised by the end of the film. With respect to a memory experiment, the general event might be represented as "seeing a list of words," or "seeing some pictures of clothing and furniture," whereas event-specific knowledge would refer to memory for specific details pertaining to items that were presented at study; for example, what the items looked like when they appeared on the computer monitor, or thoughts triggered by particular words at study.

Schacter et al. (in press) argued that subjects in recognition experiments normally say that they recollect a particular item when they retrieve event-specific knowledge pertaining to that item's presentation at study. BG, on the other hand, claims to recollect items when they match his general event description of what transpired at study. In terms of the framework we have been developing, BG has a problem generating focused descriptions of what went on at study. Therefore, when BG studies a list of unrelated words, his general event description may be something like "saw a bunch of words," which would explain his false alarms to unrelated lures in experiments with noncategorized stimuli. On the other hand, when BG studies a list of categorized words, his general event description may include category information, such as "saw some pictures of furniture and clothes"; this could explain why BG false alarms to nonstudied exemplars from studied categories, but not to exemplars from nonstudied categories.

To summarize, one way to decide that an item is old is to compare the information that is activated by the item at test to a mental representation of what took place at study (or, more specifically, information activated by the item at test is matched against a set of features that you take to be characteristic of the study phase). For normal subjects, these characteristic features are relatively specific (e.g., "Can I recall exactly what the item looked like when it was presented on the computer monitor at study?"), but for BG, the characteristic features are extremely vague ("Is the item a member of one of the categories I studied?"). That is, BG fails to generate a description of what took place at study that is focused enough to exclude the information triggered by lures; the fact that BG fails to set an appropriate criterion for responding "old" to test items may arise from his inability to generate a focused description of the study context. This "focusing" hypothesis also explains why BG has difficulty with some forced-choice recognition tests (in contrast with other frontal patients; e.g., Parkin's ACoA patient CB, described in Parkin et al., 1994); BG incorrectly chooses lures on these recognition tests because these lures match his unfocused description of what transpired at study. Frontal patients who completely fail to generate a description of the study context are not subject to these "spurious matches," and hence can perform reasonably well on forced-choice recognition tests (based on familiarity alone).

THE PERILS OF POOR FOCUS

In the preceding section, we attempted to explain BG's false recognition deficit in terms of his impaired ability to form focused or "event-specific" representations of what transpired at study. BG's deficits contrast with patients who are completely unable to generate representations of what happened at study; the latter group makes recognition judgments based purely on assessments of familiarity.

The idea that retrieval of contextual descriptions can break down in two separate ways (with one kind of damage leading to degraded, unfocused representations of context, and the other kind leading to an outright failure to generate representations of context) is helpful in thinking about false recognition. Can this distinction also help us understand confabulation? In order to explain confabulatory behavior, we have to explain both what triggers the inappropriate (confabulated) information, and why subjects accept this information as veridical. Consider what happens when a frontal patient completely fails to generate a representation of the sought-after episode. Patients in this group will be severely impaired both at retrieving stored episodic information, and in evaluating retrieved information; as stated earlier, subjects rely on their representation of what took place at study to evaluate the appropriateness of retrieved information. Because these patients are (by hypothesis) unable to reinstate contextual information associated with the sought-after episode, the only time they will retrieve any memories (nonveridical or veridical) is when stored information is associatively triggered by cues in the environment. To account for confabulatory behavior in these patients, we would therefore have to argue that confabulations are built up around information associatively triggered by environmental cues.

Consider, then, what happens when a frontal patient generates unfocused retrieval descriptions; that is, retrieval cues that fail to discriminate between the sought-after trace and other, competing episodic traces. In this situation, it might happen that the retrieval cue overlaps more with a competing trace than with the sought-after trace, in which case the unfocused cue can serve to actually "pull in" inappropriate traces. Furthermore, according to our suggestions, these inappropriate traces may seem appropriate to the patient because monitoring processes will compare the retrieved information against the same unfocused contextual representation that triggered the incorrect information in the first place. Once a trace is retrieved (appropriate or inappropriate), therefore, the subject will tend to treat this retrieved information as veridical.

To recap, we suggest that generative, strategic retrieval can break down in two ways. First, brain damage can lead to a general degradation or "unfocusing" of contextual constraints; this can result in both false recognition and confabulation, in addition to deficits in retrieval of sought-after episodic information. Because false recognition and confabulation are most common following damage to the ventromedial frontal lobes and the basal forebrain area (which often happens following ruptured ACoA aneurysms), we speculate that structures in this region are somehow implicated in "focusing" contextual constraints.

Second, in contrast to the "blurring" or "defocusing" described earlier, certain kinds of brain damage can completely eliminate the ability to apply contextual constraints (possibly, by directly compromising the neural structures which implement these constraints). Crucially, although most of the previous discussion (for the sake of simplicity) treats "the ability to apply contextual constraints" as if it were a single, domain-general faculty, deficits in applying contextual constraints tend to be domain-specific. These deficits manifest themselves behaviorally as impaired recall in the affected domain or domains, coupled with intact forced-choice recognition (studied items can be recognized by comparing the "raw familiarity" of these items to the familiarity of lures). For example, patient ROB (studied by Hanley et al., 1994), who suffered damage to the left caudate nucleus, has a well-defined domain-specific deficit: She is completely unable to recall verbal material, but is unimpaired on tasks that require recall of visuo-spatial material (e.g., the Visual Reproduction subtest of the Wechsler Memory Scale).

Additional pertinent evidence on domain-specific retrieval deficits comes from Milner et al. (1991), who found that patients with right frontal damage are selectively impaired at making relative recency judgments for pictorial stimuli (as compared to verbal stimuli), and patients with left frontal damage are selectively impaired at making relative recency judgments for verbal stimuli (as opposed to pictorial stimuli). Similarly, Schacter et al. (in press) found that patient BG (who has a deep right frontal lesion, affecting both frontal cortex and underlying white matter) has greater recognition difficulties with nonverbal materials (i.e., faces) than with verbal materials (i.e., words); Schacter et al. (in press) also reported some evidence that BG false alarms more to pictures than to words. One way of mapping these effects onto the brain is to postulate that parallel circuits linking dorsolateral prefrontal cortex (hereafter abbreviated as DLPFC) and the basal ganglia (see Alexander, DeLong, & Strick, 1986, for discussion of these circuits) are responsible for implementing contextual constraints in different domains (e.g., visuo-spatial, verbal). Lesions affecting DLPFC or the basal ganglia will therefore lead to domain-specific impairments in top-down construction of representations of context. For instance, the evidence suggesting that BG makes more false alarms more to pictures than to words can be explained in terms of an inability to incorporate distinctive visual information into his representation of what transpired at study.

Another important distinction to make is between deficits that affect the ability to construct representations in top-down fashion, and deficits that involve disruption of the neural networks involved in storing information per se. For example, Dalla Barba (1993a, 1993b) described two confabulating patients, one with intact semantic memory (MB) and another with impaired semantic memory (SD). Dalla Barba (1993a) observed that MB's confabulations all describe events that might possibly have happened:

> MB confabulates when he claims that the day before he had gone to see his wife with his mother or when he claims that he is in Bologna in an

Italian doctor's office ... yet these sentences, even if so obviously confabulatory considered in MB's biographical context, prove to be perfectly appropriate from the point of view of their semantic structure. (p. 14)

On the other hand, SD's confabulations often are semantically anomalous. For instance, SD once claimed that the preceding day "he had won a running race and that he had been awarded with a piece of meat that was put on his right knee" (Dalla Barba, 1993b, p. 573). The question is whether we should try to explain this difference in the content of MB's and SD's confabulations in terms of differences in the ability to retrieve stored information, or in terms of differences in the integrity of stored knowledge. Dalla Barba cited a number of clinical test results, showing that MB's performance on semantic memory tasks is perfectly normal, whereas SD's semantic memory is severely impaired (e.g., SD has problems defining words and detecting semantically anomalous sentences); based on this evidence, Dalla Barba attributed the bizarreness of SD's confabulations to damaged semantic structures. It seems clear that we must be careful not to ascribe a pattern of impaired performance to a retrieval deficit when the deficit can also be explained in terms of disruption of the stored information itself (in this case, semantic memory).

Lastly, another possibility we should consider is that different brain structures are responsible for activating the sought-after episodic trace, and for inhibiting traces that are incompatible with your description of the sought-after episode. Shimamura (1995) argued that frontal lobe structures implement a dynamic filtering or gating mechanism that inhibits extraneous activity in the rest of the brain:

Effective filtering thus increases the availability of relevant sensory and cognitive activity by filtering signals from irrelevant noise ... the manifold behavioral disorders that result from damage to different regions in the prefrontal cortex do not occur because each region is performing different computations or doing something different. Instead, each region is performing the same computation, only the result is different because specific prefrontal regions are connected to different areas in posterior cortex, and thus are filtering different aspects of cognitive function. (p. 810)

This idea is similar in many respects to our "focusing hypothesis": The inhibitory control ("filtering") mechanisms postulated by Shimamura serve to focus activity elsewhere in the brain, and damage to these (hypothesized) mechanisms could result in the focusing deficits described earlier. One potential problem with Shimamura's account is that, in order to inhibit inappropriate representations, some brain circuit needs to specify what the appropriate (sought-after) representation is. It seems more parsimonious to us to claim, until there is compelling evidence to the contrary, that the primary responsibility of frontal cortex is to activate (and maintain the activation of) a description of the sought-after episode, and that inhibition of inappropriate traces is a by-product of this activation process.

CONCLUSIONS AND FUTURE DIRECTIONS

We began by pointing out that memory and remembering can be dissociated: Conscious remembering involves making a connection between the thoughts one is presently having, and the past events that are shaping those thoughts; myriad studies of implicit memory have demonstrated that specific past events can have specific effects on present information processing, even when subjects are completely unaware of the relevance of these past events to the task at hand.

Our focus has been on elucidating the metacognitive processes that allow us to understand what we are experiencing presently in terms of what we experienced in the past: What brain circuits implement these processes? How many distinct processes contribute to our ability to forge links to past episodes, and can we spell out mechanistically what these processes are doing? We considered the claim that different processes are involved in deliberately retrieving stored episodic traces, and in monitoring (evaluating) the appropriateness of retrieved information, and we gave reasons why it might be more useful to think of strategic retrieval and monitoring as two different uses of the same computational machinery. Strategic retrieval and successful monitoring both depend on creating focused representations of contextual information associated with the sought-after episode—that is, representations that discriminate between the sought-after episodic trace, and similar, competing traces.

Based on evidence from PET studies of episodic memory retrieval, we argued that frontal lobe structures are involved in effortful retrieval of stored episodic information. To further specify the nature of the role played by the frontal lobes in explicit retrieval, we reviewed evidence from studies of brain-damaged patients regarding how memory can be impaired by frontal lobe damage. To account for the varied nature of retrieval impairments that can result from damage to frontal structures, we suggested that context-retrieval processes can break down in two distinct ways: First, subjects might completely fail to retrieve the context associated with the sought-after episode, and second, subjects might generate an unfocused representation of the context associated with the sought-after episode. To explain why confabulation and false recognition sometimes occur following frontal damage, but do not reliably accompany other "frontal" memory impairments, we argued that confabulation and false recognition are likely to occur when subjects generate an unfocused representation of the sought-after episode, as in the case of BG.

Lastly, we pointed out that memory deficits following frontal lobe damage are frequently domain-specific. Left frontal lesions tend to selectively impair memory for verbal material, and right frontal lesions tend to selectively impair memory for visuospatial material. Based on the fact that confabulation and false recognition are more common following ventromedial frontal damage than dorsolateral frontal damage, we argued that ventromedial frontal damage (most commonly caused by ruptured aneurysms of the anterior communicating artery) might lead to a global impairment in creating focused representations of the sought-after episode, whereas dorsolateral frontal (and basal ganglia) lesions might selectively impair the ability to incorporate certain kinds of constraints into representations of the sought-after episode (e.g., visuospatial constraints, in the case of patients with right dorsolateral frontal damage).

These ideas comprise the sketchy beginnings of a cognitive neuroscience approach to the mechanisms of metamemory (cf. Shimamura, 1995). To go beyond the admittedly preliminary account given here, we need to flesh out the processes described earlier until they begin to yield testable predictions regarding patterns of preserved and impaired memory functioning that will result from various different kinds of frontal damage. How exactly do we "reinstate the context" of the sought-after episode, and what kind of computational deficit might cause subjects to generate unfocused representations of the sought-after episode? We need to map out specific mechanisms that indicate how frontal lobe structures can influence activity in other parts of the brain, and describe specific ways in which these mechanisms can break down to yield the range of memory and other cognitive deficits that have been observed in frontal-damaged patients.

One promising set of ideas concerns the role of neuromodulators such as dopamine and acetylcholine in creating focused representations. Cohen and Servan-Schreiber (1992) argued that dopamine governs the "signal-to-noise ratio" of activity in frontal neural networks; they set forth a connectionist model in which the effects of dopamine are operationalized in terms of the "gain" of individual units (basically, the extent to which units show a well-defined, "all or none" response threshold, as opposed to responding in a more graded fashion to inputs) within parts of the model meant to correspond to prefrontal cortex. This kind of mechanism might be a good way of concretely instantiating the construct of focus that we have discussed.

We also need to flesh out the empirical database regarding how memory breaks down following different kinds of frontal damage. So far, studies of frontal-damaged patients have, for the most part, been aimed at characterizing in great detail specific patterns of impairment (e.g., false recognition), at the expense of relating the different consequences of frontal damage to each other. To constrain the kinds of models discussed earlier, we need better information on how "frontal" memory impairments (false recognition, confabulation, intrusions in cued recall, domain-specific deficits in recalling studied information, source amnesia) relate to one another, within individual patients. How many underlying dimensions of variation are there (cf. Goldman-Rakic, 1987; Schacter, 1987b; Shimamura, 1995)? Furthermore, how do these different memory impairments relate to other cognitive deficits (poor planning, perseveration) exhibited by frontal patients (Stuss, Eskes, & Foster, 1994)? We also need more sophisticated ways of characterizing what neural circuits are disrupted by frontal damage. For example, ruptured anterior communicating artery aneurysms often disrupt connections between frontal cortex and midbrain structures involved in neuromodulation. In light of our earlier suggestion regarding neuromodulation and "focusing," we need to be able to characterize which neuromodulatory systems (if any) are most likely to have been disrupted by a particular frontal lesion.

These analyses of metamemorial processes and the frontal lobes should interact closely with ongoing research concerning implicit memory. Little is yet known about how frontal lobe lesions interact with implicit memory phenomena, such as priming (for an exception to this rule, see Shimamura, 1992). In the earlier discussion, we have focused on how metacognitive processes interact with (i.e., retrieve and interpret) coherent episodic traces. However, situations frequently arise (even outside of implicit memory experiments!) in which people fail to retrieve a full-blown episodic trace associated with a particular experience, yet they are still influenced in some way by that experience. In these situations, metacognitive processes implemented by the frontal lobes are given the job of interpreting isolated images, thoughts, or feelings (Squire, in press). Jacoby and others (e.g., Kelley & Jacoby, 1990) have offered useful cognitive analyses of how metacognitive processes interpret subtle changes in processing brought on by prior exposure to stimuli. However, there are limits as to how well we can understand the mechanisms of metacognition without looking more directly (by means of functional brain imaging and studies of brain-damaged patients) at how the brain maps our present thoughts and feelings onto specific past episodes. It appears to us that the time is ripe to develop, in greater detail, a cognitive neuroscience perspective on the processes that allow us to take full, conscious possession of the past.

ACKNOWLEDGMENTS

The writing of this chapter was supported by a National Defense Science and Engineering Graduate Fellowship awarded to the first author, National Institute of Neurological Disorders and Stroke Grants PO1 NS27950 and NS26895, and National Institute on Aging Grant RO1 AG08441.

REFERENCES

Alexander, G. E., DeLong, M. R., & Strick, P. L. (1986). Parallel organization of functionally segregated circuits linking basal ganglia and cortex. *Annual Review of Neuroscience, 9,* 357–381.

Baddeley, A., & Wilson, B. (1986). Amnesia, autobiographical memory, and confabulation. In D. C. Rubin (Ed.), *Autobiographical memory* (pp. 225–252). New York: Cambridge University Press.

Blaxton, T. A. (1989). Investigating dissociations among memory measures: Support for a transfer appropriate processing framework. *Journal of Experimental Psychology: Learning, Memory, and Cognition, 15,* 657–668.

Brown, A. S., & Mitchell, D. B. (1994). A reevaluation of semantic versus nonsemantic processing in implicit memory. *Memory & Cognition, 22,* 533–541.

Buckner, R. L., Petersen, S. E., Ojemann, J. G., Miezin, F. M., Squire, L. R., & Raichle, M. E. (1995). Functional anatomical studies of explicit and implicit memory retrieval tasks. *The Journal of Neuroscience, 15*(1), 12–29.

Buckner, R. L., & Tulving, E. (1995). Neuroimaging studies of memory: Theory and recent PET results. In F. Boller & J. Grafman (Eds.), *Handbook of neuropsychology, Vol. 10* (pp. 439–466). Amsterdam: Elsevier.

Ceci, S. J. (1995). False beliefs: Some developmental and clinical considerations. In D. L. Schacter, J. T. Coyle, G. D. Fischbach, M. M. Mesulam, & L. E. Sullivan (Eds.), *Memory distortion: How minds, brains, and societies reconstruct the past* (pp. 91–125). Cambridge, MA: Harvard University Press.

Cohen, J. D., & O'Reilly, R. C. (1996). A preliminary theory of the interactions between prefrontal cortex and hippocampus that contribute to planning and prospective memory. In M. Brandimonte, G. O. Einstein, & M. A. McDaniel (Eds.), *Prospective memory: Theory and applications* (pp. 267–295). Mahwah, NJ: Lawrence Erlbaum Associates.

Cohen, J. D., & Servan-Schreiber, D. (1992). Cortex, context, and dopamine: A connectionist approach to behavior and biology in schizophrenia. *Psychological Review, 99*(1), 45–77.

Conway, M. A., & Rubin, D. C. (1993). The structure of autobiographical memory. In A. F. Collins, S. E. Gathercole, M. A. Conway, & P. E. Morris (Eds.), *Theories of memory* (pp. 103–137). Hillsdale, NJ: Lawrence Erlbaum Associates.

Craik, F. I. M., Morris, L. W., Morris, R. G., & Loewen, E. R. (1990). Relations between source amnesia and frontal lobe functioning in older adults. *Psychology and Aging, 5,* 148–151.

Curran, T., & Schacter, D. L. (in press). Implicit memory and perceptual brain mechanisms. In D. Herrmann, C. McEvoy, C. Hertzog, P. Hertel, & M. K. Johnson (Eds.), *Basic and applied memory. Vol. 1: Theory in context.* Mahwah, NJ: Lawrence Erlbaum Associates.

Curran, T., Schacter, D. L., Norman, K. A., & Galluccio, L. (in press). False recognition after a right frontal lobe infarction: Memory for general and specific information. *Neuropsychologia.*

Dalla Barba, G. (1993a). Confabulation: Knowledge and recollective experience. *Cognitive Neuropsychology, 10*(1), 1–20.

Dalla Barba, G. (1993b). Different patterns of confabulation. *Cortex, 29,* 567–581.

Delbecq-Derouesne, J., Beauvois, M. F., & Shallice, T. (1990). Preserved recall versus impaired recognition. *Brain, 113,* 1045–1074.

Ellis, A. W., & Young, A. W. (1988). *Human cognitive neuropsychology.* Hove, UK: Lawrence Erlbaum Associates.

Gabrieli, J., Fleischman, D., Keane, M., Reminger, S., & Morrell, F. (1995). Double dissociation between memory systems underlying explicit and implicit memory in the human brain. *Psychological Science, 6,* 76–82.

Gardiner, J. M., & Java, R. I. (1993). Recognizing and remembering. In A. F. Collins, S. E. Gathercole, M. A. Conway, & P. E. Morris (Eds.), *Theories of memory* (pp. 163–188). Hillsdale, NJ: Lawrence Erlbaum Associates.

Goldman-Rakic, P. S. (1987). Circuitry of primate prefrontal cortex and regulation of behavior by representational memory. In F. Plum (Ed.), *Handbook of physiology: The nervous system, Vol. 5* (pp. 373–417). Bethesda, MD: American Physiological Society.

Graf, P., & Masson, M. E. J. (Eds.). (1993). *Implicit memory: New directions in cognition, development, and neuropsychology.* Hillsdale, NJ: Lawrence Erlbaum Associates.

Graf, P., Squire, L. R., & Mandler, G. (1984). The information that amnesic patients do not forget. *Journal of Experimental Psychology: Learning, Memory, and Cognition, 10,* 164–178.

Haist, F., Shimamura, A. P., & Squire, L. R. (1992). On the relationship between recall and recognition memory. *Journal of Experimental Psychology: Learning, Memory, and Cognition, 18,* 691–702.

Hamman, S. B. (1990). Level of processing effects in conceptually driven implicit tasks. *Journal of Experimental Psychology: Learning, Memory, and Cognition, 16,* 970–977.

Hanley, J. R., Davies, A. D. M., Downes, J. J., & Mayes, A. R. (1994). Impaired recall of verbal material following rupture and repair of an anterior communicating artery aneurysm. *Cognitive Neuropsychology, 11*(5), 543–578.

Jacoby, L. L. (1991). A process dissociation framework: Separating automatic from intentional uses of memory. *Journal of Memory and Language, 30,* 513–541.

Janowsky, J. S., Shimamura, A. P., & Squire, L. R. (1989). Source memory impairments in patients with frontal lobe damage. *Neuropsychologia, 27,* 1043–1056.

Johnson, M. K. (1991). Reality monitoring: Evidence from confabulation in organic brain disease patients. In G. P. Prigatano & D. L. Schacter (Eds.), *Awareness of deficit after brain injury: Clinical and theoretical issues* (pp. 176–197). New York: Oxford University Press.

Johnson, M. K., & Chalfonte, B. L. (1994). Binding of complex memories: The role of reactivation and the hippocampus. In D. L. Schacter & E. Tulving (Eds.), *Memory systems 1994* (pp. 311–350). Cambridge, MA: MIT Press.

Johnson, M. K., Hashtroudi, S., & Lindsay, D. S. (1993). Source monitoring. *Psychological Bulletin, 114*(1), 3–28.

Johnson, M. K., & Raye, C. L. (1981). Reality monitoring. *Psychological Review, 88*(1), 67–85.

Keane, M. M., Gabrieli, J. D. E., Fennema, A. C., Growdon, J. H., & Corkin, S. (1991). Evidence for a dissociation between perceptual and conceptual priming in Alzheimer's disease. *Behavioral Neuroscience, 105,* 326–342.

Kelley, C. M., & Jacoby, L. R. (1990). The construction of subjective experience: Memory attributions. *Mind and Language, 5*(1), 49–68.

Kosslyn, S. M., & Koenig, O. (1992). *Wet mind: The new cognitive neuroscience.* New York: The Free Press.

Loftus, E., Feldman, J., & Dashiell, R. (1995). The reality of illusory memories. In D. L. Schacter, J. T. Coyle, G. D. Fischbach, M. M. Mesulam, & L. E. Sullivan (Eds.), *Memory distortion: How minds, brains, and societies reconstruct the past* (pp. 47–68). Cambridge, MA: Harvard University Press.

Mandler, G. (1980). Recognizing: The judgment of previous occurrence. *Psychological Review, 87,* 252–271.

Masson, M. E. J., & MacLeod, C. M. (1992). Re-enacting the route to interpretation: Context dependency in encoding and retrieval. *Journal of Experimental Psychology: General, 121,* 145–176.

McClelland, J. L. (1995). Constructive memory and memory distortions: A parallel-distributed processing approach. In D. L. Schacter, J. T. Coyle, G. D. Fischbach, M. M. Mesulam, & L. E. Sullivan (Eds.), *Memory distortion: How minds, brains, and societies reconstruct the past* (pp. 69–90). Cambridge, MA: Harvard University Press.

McClelland, J. L., McNaughton, B. L., & O'Reilly, R. C. (1995). Why there are complementary learning systems in the hippocampus and neocortex: Insights from the successes and failures of connectionist models of learning and memory. *Psychological Review, 102*, 419–437.

Milner, B., Corsi, P., & Leonard, G. (1991). Frontal-lobe contribution to recency judgments. *Neuropsychologia, 29*, 601–618.

Moscovitch, M. (1989). Confabulation and the frontal systems: Strategic versus associative retrieval in neuropsychological theories of memory. In H. L. Roediger & F. I. M. Craik (Eds.), *Varieties of memory and consciousness: Essays in honor of Endel Tulving* (pp. 133–160). Hillsdale, NJ: Lawrence Erlbaum Associates.

Moscovitch, M. (1994a). Memory without conscious recollection: A tutorial review from a neuropsychological perspective. In C. Umlita & M. Moscovitch (Eds.), *Attention and performance XV: Conscious and nonconscious information processing* (pp. 619–660). Cambridge, MA: MIT Press.

Moscovitch, M. (1994b). Memory and working with memory: Evaluation of a component process model and comparisons with other models. In D. L. Schacter & E. Tulving (Eds.), *Memory systems 1994* (pp. 269–310). Cambridge, MA: MIT Press.

Moscovitch, M. (1995). Confabulation. In D. L. Schacter, J. T. Coyle, G. D. Fischbach, M. M. Mesulam, & L. E. Sullivan (Eds.), *Memory distortion: How minds, brains, and societies reconstruct the past* (pp. 226–251). Cambridge, MA: Harvard University Press.

Parkin, A. J., Bindschaedler, C., Harsent, L., & Metzler, C. (1995). *Pathological false alarm rate following damage to left frontal cortex.* Manuscript submitted for publication.

Parkin, A. J., & Leng, N. R. C. (1993). *Neuropsychology of the amnesic syndrome.* Hillsdale, NJ: Lawrence Erlbaum Associates.

Parkin, A. J., Yeomans, J., & Bindschaedler, C. (1994). Further characterization of the executive memory impairment following frontal lobe lesions. *Brain and Cognition, 25*, 23–42.

Petersen, S. E., Fox, P. T., Synder, A. Z., & Raichle, M. E. (1990). Activation of extrastriate and frontal cortical areas by visual words and word-like stimuli. *Science, 249*, 1041–1044.

Plaut, D. C., & Farah, M. J. (1990). Visual object representation: Interpreting neurophysiological data within a computational framework. *Journal of Cognitive Neuroscience, 2*, 320–343.

Ratcliff, R., & McKoon, G. (1995). Bias in the priming of object decisions. *Journal of Experimental Psychology: Learning, Memory, and Cognition, 21*, 754–767.

Richardson-Klavehn, A., & Bjork, R. A. (1988). Measures of memory. *Annual Review of Psychology, 36*, 475–543.

Riddoch, M. J., & Humphreys, G. W. (1987). Visual object processing in optic aphasia: A case of semantic access agnosia. *Cognitive Neuropsychology, 4*, 131–186.

Roediger, H. L., III. (1990). Implicit memory: Retention without remembering. *American Psychologist, 45*, 1043–1046.

Roediger, H. L., III, & McDermott, K. B. (1993). Implicit memory in normal human subjects. In H. Spinnler & F. Boller (Eds.), *Handbook of neuropsychology* (pp. 63–131). Amsterdam: Elsevier.

Schacter, D. L. (1987a). Implicit memory: History and current status. *Journal of Experimental Psychology: Learning, Memory, and Cognition, 13*, 501–518.

Schacter, D. L. (1987b). Memory, amnesia, and frontal lobe dysfunction. *Psychobiology, 15*, 21–36.

Schacter, D. L. (1990). Perceptual representation systems and implicit memory: Toward a resolution of the multiple memory systems debate. *Annals of the New York Academy of Sciences, 608*, 543–571.

Schacter, D. L. (1992). Understanding implicit memory: A cognitive neuroscience perspective. *American Psychologist, 47*(4), 559–569.

Schacter, D. L. (1994). Priming and multiple memory systems: Perceptual mechanisms of implicit memory. In D. L. Schacter & E. Tulving (Eds.), *Memory systems 1994* (pp. 233–268). Cambridge, MA: MIT Press.

Schacter, D. L. (1995). Memory distortion: History and current status. In D. L. Schacter, J. T. Coyle, G. D. Fischbach, M. M. Mesulam, & L. E. Sullivan (Eds.), *Memory distortion: How minds, brains, and societies reconstruct the past* (pp. 1–43). Cambridge, MA: Harvard University Press.

Schacter, D. L., Albert, M., Alpert, N., Rauch, S., & Savage, C. (1996). Conscious recollection and the human hippocampal formation: Evidence from positron emission tomography. *Proceedings of the National Academy of Sciences, 193,* 321–325.

Schacter, D. L., Bowers, J., & Booker, J. (1989). Intention, awareness and implicit memory: The retrieval intentionality criterion. In S. Lewandowsky, J. C. Dunn, & K. Kirsner (Eds.), *Implicit memory: Theoretical issues* (pp. 47–69). Hillsdale, NJ: Lawrence Erlbaum Associates.

Schacter, D. L., Chiu, C. Y. P., & Ochsner, K. N. (1993). Implicit memory: A selective review. *Annual Review of Neuroscience, 16,* 159–182.

Schacter, D. L., & Church, B. (1992). Auditory priming: Implicit and explicit memory for words and voices. *Journal of Experimental Psychology: Learning, Memory, and Cognition, 18,* 915–930.

Schacter, D. L., & Cooper, L. A. (1993). Implicit and explicit memory for novel visual objects: Structure and function. *Journal of Experimental Psychology: Learning, Memory, and Cognition, 19*(5), 1–15.

Schacter, D. L., & Cooper, L. A. (1995). Bias in the priming of object decisions: Logic, assumptions, and data. *Journal of Experimental Psychology, 21,* 768–776.

Schacter, D. L., Cooper, L. A., & Delaney, S. M. (1990). Implicit memory for unfamiliar objects depends on access to structural descriptions. *Journal of Experimental Psychology: General, 119,* 5–24.

Schacter, D. L., Curran, T., Galluccio, L., Milberg, W. P., & Bates, J. (in press). False recognition and the right frontal lobe: A case study. *Neuropsychologia.*

Schacter, D. L., Kagan, J., & Leichtman, M. D. (1995). True and false memories in children and adults: A cognitive neuroscience perspective. *Psychology, Public Policy, and Law, 1,* 411–428.

Schacter, D. L., Kaszniak, A. K., Kihlstrom, J. F., & Valdiserri, M. (1991). On the relationship between source monitoring and aging. *Psychology and Aging, 6,* 559–568.

Schacter, D. L., Rapscak, S. Z., Rubens, A. B., Tharan, M., & Laguna, J. M. (1990). Priming effects in a letter-by-letter reader depend on access to the word form system. *Neuropsychologia, 28,* 1079–1094.

Schacter, D. L., Reiman, E., Uecker, A., Polster, M. R., Yun, L. S., & Cooper, L. A. (1995). Brain regions associated with retrieval of structurally coherent visual information. *Nature.*

Schacter, D. L., & Tulving, E. (1982). Memory, amnesia, and the episodic/semantic distinction. In R. L. Isaacson & N. L. Spear (Eds.), *The expression of knowledge* (pp. 33–61). New York: Plenum.

Shallice, T. (1988). *From neuropsychology to mental structure.* Cambridge, England: Cambridge University Press.

Shallice, T., Fletcher, P., Frith, C. D., Grasby, P., Frackowiak, R. S. J., & Dolan, R. J. (1994). Brain regions associated with acquisition and retrieval of verbal episodic memory. *Nature, 368,* 633–635.

Shimamura, A. P. (1992). Intact implicit memory in patients with frontal lobe lesions. *Neuropsychologia, 30,* 931–937.

Shimamura, A. P. (1995). Memory and frontal lobe function. In M. S. Gazzaniga (Ed.), *The cognitive neurosciences* (pp. 803–813). Cambridge, MA: MIT Press.

Squire, L. R. (1992). Memory and the hippocampus: A synthesis from findings with rats, monkeys, and humans. *Psychological Review, 99,* 195–231.

Squire, L. R. (1994). Declarative and nondeclarative memory: Multiple brain systems supporting learning and memory. In D. L. Schacter & E. Tulving (Eds.), *Memory systems 1994* (pp. 203–231). Cambridge, MA: MIT Press.

Squire, L. R. (1995). Biological foundations of accuracy and inaccuracy in memory. In D. L. Schacter, J. T. Coyle, & G. D. Fischbach (Eds.), *Memory distortion: How minds, brains, and societies reconstruct the past* (pp. 197–225). Cambridge, MA: Harvard University Press.

Squire, L. R., Ojemann, J. G., Miezin, F. M., Petersen, S. E., Videen, T. O., & Raichle, M. E. (1992). Activation of the hippocampus in normal humans: A functional anatomical study of memory. *Proceedings of the National Academy of Sciences, 89*, 1837–1841.

Stuss, D. T., Eskes, G. A., & Foster, J. K. (1994). Experimental neuropsychological studies of frontal lobe functions. In F. Boller & J. Grafman (Eds.), *Handbook of neuropsychology* (pp. 149–185). Amsterdam: Elsevier.

Treves, A., & Rolls, E. T. (1994). A computational analysis of the role of the hippocampus in memory. *Hippocampus, 4*, 374–391.

Tulving, E. (1985). Memory and consciousness. *Canadian Psychologist, 26*, 1–12.

Tulving, E. (1989). Remembering and knowing the past. *American Psychologist, 77*, 361–367.

Tulving, E., Kapur, S., Markowitsch, H. J., Craik, F. I. M., Habib, R., & Houle, S. (1994). Neuroanatomical correlates of retrieval in episodic memory: Auditory sentence recognition. *Proceedings of the National Academy of Sciences, 91*, 2012–2015.

Tulving, E., & Schacter, D. L. (1990). Priming and human memory systems. *Science, 247*, 301–306.

Warrington, E. K., & Shallice, T. (1980). Word-form dyslexia. *Brain, 30*, 99–112.

Warrington, E. K., & Weiskrantz, L. (1974). The effect of prior learning on subsequent retention in amnesic patients. *Neuropsychologia, 12*, 419–428.

Chapter 11

The Role of the Prefrontal Cortex in Controlling and Monitoring Memory Processes

Arthur P. Shimamura
University of California, Berkeley

Neuropsychological analyses of memory function have helped to isolate components of explicit memory, implicit memory, and metacognition. Studies of brain-injured patients suggest that different brain regions contribute to these components of memory in different ways. For example, the medial temporal lobe is critical for the establishment of explicit or declarative memory (see Schacter & Tulving, 1994; Squire, 1992), but this brain region does not appear to be significantly involved in implicit forms of learning and memory (for review, see Schacter, 1987; Shimamura, 1986, 1993; Squire, 1987). This chapter focuses on the prefrontal cortex, a brain region that appears to contribute significantly to metacognition. In particular, this brain region plays a vital role in the control and monitoring of memory processes.

The prefrontal cortex comprises the most anterior 28% of the human neocortex. This brain region is richly connected to many neocortical and subcortical regions (see Fuster, 1989; Goldman-Rakic, 1987). Cognitive disorders following damage to this brain region are multifaceted, impinging on processes associated with attention, short-term memory, retrieval strategies, language, and problem solving (for review, see Levin, Eisenberg, & Benton, 1991; Shimamura, 1994a; Stuss, Eakes, & Foster, 1994). Many of these disorders appear to be related to impairment in *working memory* (Baddeley, 1986; Moscovitch, 1994; Shimamura, 1994a). Because the role of working memory is to direct and control information processing, disruption of this function could likely lead to problems in metacognition.

Thus, the notion that the prefrontal cortex is involved in working memory functions is consistent with the view that metacognitive processes are associated with this brain region.

Early studies of patients with Korsakoff's syndrome provided the first evidence of metacognitive impairment following brain injury. Korsakoff's syndrome is generally associated with explicit memory disorders in which deficits in new learning ability and memory for remote events are part of the syndrome (Albert, Butters, & Levin, 1979; Butters, 1984; Squire, Haist, & Shimamura, 1989). Korsakoff's syndrome develops following years of chronic alcohol abuse and nutritional deficiency. Both pathological and neuroimaging studies of Korsakoff's syndrome have identified brain damage along the diencephalic midline, typically involving the dorsomedial thalamic nuclei, the mammillary nuclei, and other adjacent nuclei (Mayes, Meudell, Mann, & Pickering, 1988; Mair, Warrington, & Weiskrantz, 1979; Shimamura, Jernigan, & Squire, 1988; Squire, Amaral, & Press, 1990; Victor, Adams, & Collins, 1989). Neocortical damage, particularly in the frontal lobes, is also apparent in both pathological and neuroimaging studies of these patients (Shimamura et al., 1988; Victor et al., 1989).

Metacognitive deficits in patients with Korsakoff's syndrome can be observed in patients' knowledge of mnemonic strategies. For example, Hirst (1982) reported that patients with Korsakoff's syndrome had limited knowledge of strategies that could improve memory. In addition, the use and control of mnemonic strategies were impaired in these patients compared to control subjects. Similarly, Squire and Zouzounis (1988) showed that patients with Korsakoff's syndrome were unreliable in making self-rating judgments about their own memory abilities. That is, these patients had problems monitoring their own memories. Interestingly, other amnesic disorders, such as those caused by medial temporal lobe lesions (e.g., anoxia), do not produce disorders of metacognition. That is, although patients with medial temporal lobe lesions exhibit severely impaired learning and memory, they express knowledge about mnemonic strategies and are able to make valid self-ratings about their own memory disability.

Other neurological disorders can cause impairment in self-knowledge of memory abilities. Sunderland, Harris, and Baddeley (1983) gave memory tests and a self-rating questionnaire to patients who had experienced severe traumatic head injury. Ratings did not reliably predict memory test performance in patients who had been tested 2 to 8 years after incurring head injury. Assessments of these patients' disorders by relatives (e.g., parent, spouse), however, were reliably correlated with the patients' objective memory scores. These findings suggest that patients had poor metacognitive knowledge about their own memory impairment. A similar finding was observed in patients with Alzheimer's disease (McGlynn & Kaszniak, 1991). In that study, patients tended to underestimate their own memory impairment, whereas relatives of the patients were more accurate in rating the patient's abilities.

Findings from studies of memory-impaired patients suggest that poor metacognition in the form of impaired use of mnemonic strategies and lack of awareness about their own memory problems can accompany disorders of explicit memory. Indeed, brain damage due to Korsakoff's syndrome, head injury, or Alzheimer's disease produce a spectrum of cognitive and memory disorders as a result of rather widespread neuropathology. In all of these cases, damage to the prefrontal cortex can contribute to cognitive disorders. Interestingly, in patients with circumscribed medial temporal lobe lesions, memory impairment can occur without problems in metacognition (Hirst, 1982; Squire & Zouzounis, 1988). Thus, metacognitive impairment does not appear to be an obligatory deficit associated with explicit memory impairment. In this chapter, a review of more recent findings is presented in which patients with circumscribed frontal lobe lesions exhibit metacognitive impairment without severe impairment in explicit memory, such as that observed in patients with amnesic disorders.

The patients described in this chapter all have lesions in the dorsolateral prefrontal cortex (see Fig. 11.1). These patients perform in the normal range on standardized tests of intelligence and tests of long-term memory (see Janowsky, Shimamura, Kritchevsky, & Squire, 1989; Shimamura, Gershberg, Jurica, Mangels, & Knight, 1992). In addition, these patients can be selected to have no or minimal language disorders, which can produce secondary problems on verbal memory tests. Patients with frontal lobe lesions, however, commonly exhibit problems on tests of short-term memory (e.g., digit span) and problem solving (e.g., Wisconsin Card Sorting Test).

As a way to characterize metacognitive disorders associated with lesions of the prefrontal cortex, we adopt a framework for the analysis of metacognitive function developed by Nelson and Narens (1990). In this framework, "metalevel" processes act to monitor and control a variety of domain-specific "object-level" processes. This framework offers a useful context within which to describe prefrontal functions, because findings from patients with frontal lobe lesions suggest that both the ability to *monitor* and to *control* information processing are severely disrupted in these patients (Shimamura, 1994b).

CONTROLLING MEMORY

Mnemonic Strategies

Disorders in the ability to initiate and guide memory strategies suggest a problem in the metacognitive control of information processing. Only a few neuropsychological studies have addressed this issue. Shallice and Evans (1978) observed deficits in the ability to retrieve factual information that require inferential reasoning. Subjects were asked to derive reasonable

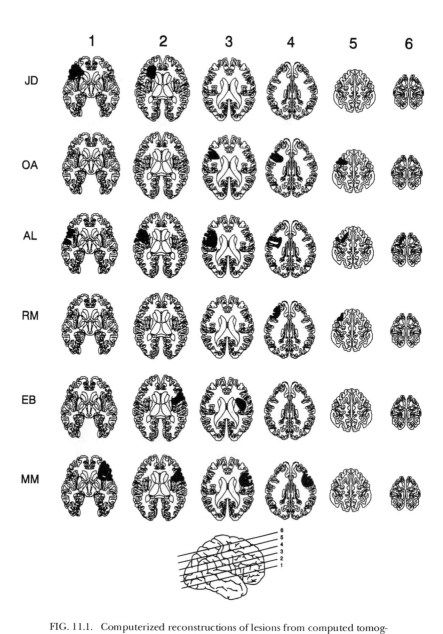

FIG. 11.1. Computerized reconstructions of lesions from computed tomography (CT) in 6 patients with unilateral frontal lobe lesions (average lesion volume = 30.9 cc). Four patients had left frontal lesions and two patients had right frontal lesions. Black areas represent lesion cites and numbers correspond to level at which CT scan was taken (1 = most inferior, 6 = most superior).

answers to questions such as, "How tall is the average English woman?" or "How long is the average man's necktie?" Patients with frontal lobe lesions tended to produce grossly inaccurate estimates. Similarly, Smith and Milner (1984) found that patients with frontal lobe lesions have difficulty making estimates of the price of everyday objects (Smith & Milner, 1984). Making inferences require extensive search strategies because it is generally the case that retrieval of information is not automatic. That is, performance depends on directed or controlled access to knowledge.

Other reports suggest that patients with frontal lobe lesions exhibit impaired ability to control or utilize mnemonic strategies important for learning. In three studies patients with frontal lobe lesions exhibit reduced subjective organization on tests of free recall for unrelated words (Eslinger & Grattan, 1994; Gershberg & Shimamura, 1996; Stuss et al., 1994). That is, the recall performance by the patients indicate that they were less likely to associate study words in an organized fashion. Similarly, patients with frontal lobe lesions were less likely to show semantic clustering on learning trials involving categorized word lists (Gershberg & Shimamura, 1995). In all of these studies, patients with frontal lobe lesions also exhibited significantly impaired free-recall performance. Impairment in free recall is often observed in these patients (see Janowsky et al., 1989) and suggests a particular problem in memory organization and retrieval. Indeed, problems in subjective organization and semantic clustering may be the cause of impaired free-recall performance in patients with frontal lobe lesions.

Some evidence suggests that cueing or instructions to use mnemonic strategies can reduce the free-recall impairment observed in patients with frontal lobe lesions. Just prior to learning, Hirst and Volpe (1988) informed subjects that a word list would consist of categorized words. This knowledge improved recall performance by patients with frontal lobe lesions to the level of performance by control subjects. Gershberg and Shimamura (1995) provided category cues as a way for subjects to organize information. On three separate study-test sessions, patients with frontal lobe lesions and control subjects were provided category cues either at the time of study, at the time of test, or both at the time of study and test. Patients with frontal lobe lesions benefited from category cues presented at either study or test, suggesting organizational problems at both encoding and retrieval phases. However, even when category cues were available at both study and test, performance by frontal patients did not reach the level of performance by control subjects.

Memory Retrieval

Findings of impaired use of organizational strategies during learning suggest that patients with frontal lobe lesions have difficulty in the control or organization of information processing at the time of encoding. Other findings, such as the benefit of cues at the time of testing, suggest that these patients also have difficulty controlling information processing during retrieval. In studies of new learning, it is difficult to disambiguate impairments that occur at the time of encoding from those that occur at the time of retrieval. Tests of remote memory (e.g., past public events, past famous faces), however, can assess the specific impairment associated with retrieval deficits, because memory can be tested for information learned well before the onset of brain damage.

The role of the prefrontal cortex in memory for remote information has not been tested extensively. Some studies have suggested that the remote memory impairment (i.e., retrograde amnesia) that is observed in patients with Korsakoff's syndrome is related to frontal lobe atrophy (Kopelman, 1989; Shimamura & Squire, 1986a). In particular, Kopelman found that remote memory performance of patients with Korsakoff's syndrome was correlated with performance on tasks sensitive to frontal lobe pathology (e.g., verbal fluency, card sorting, cognitive estimation). However, computerized tomography (CT) measures of frontal lobe atrophy in patients with Korsakoff's syndrome was not significantly correlated with performance on tests of remote memory.

Della Sala, Laiacona, Spinnler, and Trivelli (1993) assessed memory for remote autobiographical information in patients with prefrontal lesions. Subjects were asked to recollect memories from various time periods (e.g., "Can you remember anything in particular that happened to you or to a member of your family before you reached the age of 15?"). The four patients with bilateral frontal lobe lesions exhibited impairment on this test of autobiographical memory. However, only 2 of 12 patients with unilateral frontal lobe lesions exhibited impairment on this test. Across all 16 patients, performance on the autobiographical test was correlated with performance on tests of executive working memory (e.g., verbal fluency, sorting, digit cancellation). The authors suggest that the frontal lobes are important in mediating search strategies which facilitate retrieval of autobiographical memory.

In a recent study, patients with unilateral prefrontal lesions were given tests of memory for public events and famous faces (Mangels, Gershberg, Shimamura, & Knight, 1996). The tests were ones previously used to assess retrograde amnesia in patients with severe memory disorders (Albert et al., 1979; Cohen & Squire, 1981; Squire et al., 1989). For the public events test, measures of free recall and recognition memory were obtained for events that spanned from the 1940s to the 1990s (e.g., "Who shot John Lennon?" [Chapman]). For the famous faces test, subjects were asked to recall or recognize the names of famous faces (e.g., Michael Dukakis, Meryl Streep). On both tests of remote memory, patients with frontal lobe lesions exhibited significant impairment on free recall measures but recognition memory performance was much less impaired (see Fig. 11.2).

Famous Faces

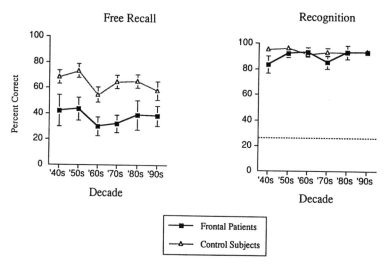

FIG. 11.2. Recall impairment for remote memory in patients with frontal lobe lesions. Subjects were presented photographs of famous faces who became famous at various decades during the past 55 years. Four-choice recognition performance was not significantly impaired in patients with frontal lobe lesions (dotted line indicates chance performance).

Findings of impaired remote memory extend the array of memory deficits observed in patients with prefrontal lesions. They suggest an impairment in retrieval processes, because in many instances the information tested was learned many years prior to brain injury. The disproportionate impairment of free recall compared to recognition memory observed on these tests of remote memory is similar to that observed on tests of new learning. Performance on recall tests depends significantly on the implementation of search and retrieval strategies. Thus, a recall deficit for retrieval of remote memory is consistent with problems in metacognitive control processes.

MONITORING MEMORY

Memory monitoring involves the access and evaluation of information stored in object-level representations. Some but not all aspects of memory monitoring are impaired following frontal lobe lesions. Deficits occur when monitoring involves the access of object-level information embedded within a semantic context, such as monitoring one's feeling of knowing. They also occur when monitoring involves access to information embedded within a temporal–spatial context, such as source monitoring. The following sections provide examples of memory monitoring impairment associated with frontal lobe lesions.

Feeling of Knowing

Feeling of knowing refers to the sense of familiarity for information that cannot be completely recalled. In the typical feeling-of-knowing experiment, subjects are asked to rate their feeling of knowing for information (e.g., general information knowledge, recently learned paired associates), and the feeling-of-knowing accuracy is assessed by obtaining recognition memory performance for unrecalled information. The accuracy of feeling-of-knowing ratings can be assessed by correlating recognition performance with the ratings. In one neuropsychological analysis of feeling-of-knowing accuracy (Shimamura & Squire, 1986b), patients with Korsakoff's syndrome, other amnesic patients (e.g., patients with medial temporal lobe lesions), and control subjects were presented a series of general information questions (e.g., "Where is Angels Falls located?"). If subjects could not recall the answer to a question (e.g., Venezuela), they were asked to rate their feeling of knowing on a 7-point scale. Subjects were also asked to rank order the questions from the one judged to have the highest feeling of knowing (i.e., most likely to be recognized) to the one judged to have the lowest feeling of knowing (i.e., pure guess). Patients with Korsakoff's syndrome, but not other amnesic patients, exhibited impaired feeling of knowing. This finding corroborates the finding reported by Hirst (1982) in which patients with Korsakoff's syndrome exhibited poor knowledge about mnemonic strategies.

Janowsky et al. (1989a) assessed feeling-of-knowing judgments in patients with lesions restricted to the frontal lobes. The patients performed well on a feeling-of-knowing test involving general information questions, yet they were impaired on a test of feeling-of-knowing involving recently learned information. However, these patients exhibited poor feeling-of-knowing accuracy on the sentence recall test compared to control subjects. Subjects were asked to learn sentences (e.g., Mary's garden was full of marigolds). After a 1- to 3-day retention interval, subjects were given a cued recall test for the last word in each sentence (e.g., Mary's garden was full of _____). Feeling-of-knowing ratings were made for nonrecalled sentences, and feeling-of-knowing accuracy was assessed by correlating the ratings to performance on a subsequent recognition memory test. Although recall and recognition memory performance were similar between groups, the patients with frontal lesions exhibited poor feeling-of-knowing accuracy.

These findings indicate feeling-of-knowing impairment when retrieval of information is less accessible. On tests of general information, the items were heterogeneous in terms of memory strength, and patients with frontal lobe lesions were able to make accurate feeling-of-knowing judgments. Also, both patients with frontal lobe lesions and patients with Korsakoff's syndrome can make reliable confidence ratings (i.e., assessing the accuracy of recognition judgments; Shimamura & Squire, 1988). In sum, these findings suggest that certain monitoring abilities may be affected in patients with frontal lobe damage. They point to the necessity of evaluating these patient groups on other memory monitoring abilities, such as ease of learning or judgments of learning.

Source Monitoring

Source monitoring refers to the ability to remember the time, place, and person that presented some information. Findings of source monitoring impairment suggest a distinction between memory for facts and memory for source information (Hirst, 1982; Mayes et al., 1985; Tulving, 1983). In one study, Janowsky et al. (1989a) assessed source memory in patients with prefrontal lesions, age-matched control subjects, and younger control subjects. Subjects learned a set of 20 general-information facts that could not be previously recalled (e.g., *The name of the dog on the Cracker Jack box is Bingo*). After a 6–8-day retention interval, fact recall was tested for the 20 learned facts (e.g., *What is the name of the dog on the Cracker Jack box?*) and for 20 new facts. When subjects correctly answered a fact question, they were asked to recollect the source of the information ("Can you tell me where you learned the answer?"; "When was the most recent time you heard that information?").

Disproportionate source memory impairment was observed in patients with frontal lobe lesions. That is, the patients could remember the answers to general-information questions, but they forgot where they learned the answers. For answers that were provided during the previous learning session, patients often indicated that the answers were learned from a different source, such as on TV or in the newspaper. Source memory impairment also occurred as a result normal aging, as indicated by the finding that older control subjects (mean age = 63.9 years) made more source errors than younger control subjects (mean age = 49.4 years; Janowsky et al., 1989a—see also McIntyre & Craik, 1987). Neuronal cell loss associated with normal aging does occur prominently in the frontal lobes (see Haug et al., 1983), which suggests that source memory impairment in normal aging may also be related to subtle frontal lobe dysfunction.

Remembering source information requires the association of temporal information to factual knowledge (When did I learn that information?). Thus, a critical feature of source monitoring is memory for the temporal order of events. Milner (1971) was the first to report that patients with frontal lobe lesions exhibit an impairment in memory for temporal order. She reported a study of recency judgments in which subjects are shown a series of stimuli (e.g., words, pictures) and are asked to judge which one of two stimuli was presented more recently (see Milner, Corsi, & Leonard, 1991). In another test of temporal order memory (Shimamura, Janowsky, & Squire, 1990), subjects were presented a list of 15 words one at a time and then asked to reconstruct the list order from a random display of the words. In this list reconstruction test, memory for temporal order was assessed by correlating a subject's judged order with the actual presentation order of the list of words. Patients with prefrontal lesions exhibited impaired memory for temporal order on this test.

There is evidence that semantic associations can interfere with memory for temporal order. In one study (Mangels & Shimamura, 1993), college undergraduates were given incidental learning of a list of unrelated words with no categorical relatedness or a list of related words with four exemplars from each of five categories. Compared to the unrelated list, item recall was enhanced by semantic associations among words as indicated by better recall performance in the related condition. However, memory for temporal order using the list reconstruction test was better for the unrelated word list compared to the related word lists (see Fig. 11.3). Patients with frontal lobe lesions also appear to be particularly affected on temporal order tests when related word lists are used (Mangels & Shimamura, 1993). These findings suggest that memory for temporal order may be particularly disrupted by interference from extraneous associations and that patients with frontal lobe lesions may be more susceptible to such interference.

METACOGNITION AND IMPLICIT MEMORY

Controlling and monitoring information processing has been viewed as a conscious process. As presented in this chapter, these metacognitive functions are related to working memory and executive control. As such, metacognitive process may be less involved in automatic functions, such as implicit memory. One interpretation is that implicit memory operates at the object level. Squire (1987) suggested that there may be many domains of implicit or nondeclarative memory, with each domain being subserved by different neural systems. A cognitive architecture in which there are many object-level processors working in parallel to analyze different aspects of stimulus information is consistent with neuropsychological evidence. Explicit memory, which requires the medial temporal region, may refer to the binding of information across these diverse domains.

One aspect of implicit memory is the phenomenon of priming. Priming effects appear to be preserved in amnesic patients (for review, see Shimamura, 1986, 1993). For example, Graf, Squire, and Mandler (1984) devel-

Incidental Learning

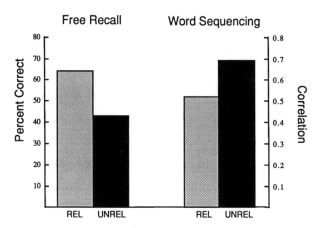

FIG. 11.3. College students were given tests of free recall or memory for temporal order (word sequencing test) following incidental learning of a list of related words (REL) or a list of unrelated words (UNREL). Although semantic relatedness facilitated word recall performance, it significantly disrupted memory for temporal order.

oped a word-stem-completion test in which subjects were asked to say the first word that comes to mind when presented three-letter word stems (e.g., MOT). Amnesic patients used recently presented words in this implicit memory test as often as control subjects. Shimamura, Salmon, Squire, and Butters (1987) replicated these findings and also showed that patients with Alzheimer's disease exhibit reduced priming on the word-stem-completion test. This impairment in patients with Alzheimer's disease suggests that priming may be mediated by posterior cortical regions, as these regions are severely affected in Alzheimer's disease. This view has been recently confirmed in a study of patients with temporal–occipital lesions following infarction of the posterior cerebral artery (Nielson-Bohlman, Ciranni, Shimamura, & Knight, 1995). These patients exhibited significantly reduced priming effects on the word-stem-completion test.

If metacognitive processes involve the prefrontal cortex and implicit memory processes (i.e., object-level processes) involve posterior cortical regions, then damage to the prefrontal cortex should not disrupt implicit memory. In fact, priming effects are not affected by frontal lobe lesions. Shimamura et al. (1992) showed that patients with frontal lobe lesions perform as well as control subjects on the word-stem-completion test (see Fig. 11.4). Also, patients with frontal lobe lesions exhibit normal priming effects on implicit tests of conceptual information. In two experiments, patients with frontal lobe lesions performed as well as control subjects when

Lexical Priming in Neurological Patients

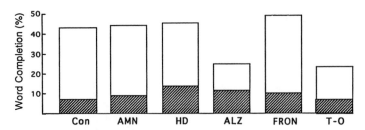

FIG. 11.4. Implicit memory performance in five groups of neurological patients. Following incidental learning of words (e.g., MOTEL), subjects were given three-letter word stems (e.g., MOT) and asked to complete the stems with the first word that came to mind. Amnesic patients (AMN), patients with Huntington's disease (HD), and patients with frontal lobe lesions performed as well as control subjects (CON). However, patients with Alzheimer's disease and patients with temporal–occipital lesions exhibited reduced priming on this implicit memory task (shaded area refers to baseline guessing rates).

subjects were asked to provide semantic associates (Gershberg, in press). For example, subjects were given words such as APPLE and BANANA and later asked to free associate to the category name FRUITS.

It is possible that certain aspects of implicit memory are impaired following lesions of the prefrontal cortex. For example, although patients with dorsolateral prefrontal lesions do not exhibit impaired priming effects on either word or conceptual priming tests (Gershberg, in press; Shimamura et al., 1992), Keane et al. (1993) reported a conceptual priming impairment in a patient with ventromedial frontal involvement following repair of the anterior communicating artery. Such patients often incur memory impairment similar to that observed in Korsakoff's syndrome. In addition, this area may be important for implicit semantic retrieval. Thus, some prefrontal regions may be associated with aspects of implicit memory. Another domain of implicit memory that has not been well studied in patients with frontal lobe lesions is the phenomenon of skill learning. To the extent that the prefrontal cortex is involved in the integration and coordination of motor programs, this brain region may be critical for the establishment of new skills.

THEORETICAL INTERPRETATIONS

Many of the cognitive disorders observed in patients with frontal lobe lesions suggest an impairment in working memory. Baddeley (1986) suggested that these patients exhibit a "dysexecutive" syndrome in which the supervision of information processing is disrupted. Other working memory interpretations have focused on filtering or controlling interference. For example, Moscovitch (1992, 1994) suggested that the frontal lobes are involved in strategic retrieval processes that draw heavily on attentional resources. In one study (Moscovitch, 1994), performance decrements by normal subjects under dual-task interference conditions simulated patterns of memory deficits observed in patients with frontal lobe lesions. Shimamura (1994a) suggested a filtering impairment in which a variety of attention, memory, and problem-solving disorders can be attributed to problems in filtering extraneous or irrelevant information. For example, patients with frontal lobe lesions can perform well on initial tests of paired-associate learning involving related words (e.g., LION–HUNTER), but they exhibit heightened interference on subsequent tests in which the cues are associated with other words (e.g., LION–CIRCUS; Shimamura, Jurica, Mangels, Gershberg, & Knight, 1995). Others have suggested that the prefrontal cortex may be involved in inhibitory control or interference gating (Cohen & Servan-Schreiber, 1992; Dempster, 1992; Diamond, 1990).

Metcalfe (1993) suggested another view of metamemory disorders associated with frontal lobe lesions. By this view, the frontal lobe is used to monitor or discriminate familiar information from novel information. Metcalfe (1993) offered a useful augmentation of the CHARM model, in which a familiarity check is computed between new information and what is already stored in memory. Without this operation, the computational model mimics various aspects of frontal lobe dysfunction (e.g., failure to release from proactive interference). Interestingly, novelty detection in this model can be used directly to assess feelings of familiarity. Thus, this model provides a direct link between FOK deficits and frontal lobe pathology.

In summary, neuropsychological findings suggest that the frontal lobes are involved in the online supervision or control of information processing. The notion of working memory captures many aspects of this control mechanism. It is likely that impairment in this mechanism would affect metacognition. Indeed, the findings presented here suggest that both the control and monitoring of information processing appear to be related to frontal lobe function.

ACKNOWLEDGMENTS

Preparation of this chapter was supported by NIMH Grant MN48757 and NINDS Grant NS 17778.

REFERENCES

Albert, M. S., Butters, N., & Levin, J. (1979). Temporal gradients in the retrograde amnesia of patients with alcoholic Korsakoff's disease. *Archives of Neurology, 36,* 211–216.
Baddeley, A. (1986). *Working memory.* Oxford, UK: Oxford University Press.

Butters, N. (1984). Alcoholic Korsakoff's syndrome: An update. *Seminars in Neurology, 4,* 226–244.

Cohen, J. D., & Servan-Schreiber, D. (1992). Context, cortex, and dopamine—A connectionist approach to behavior and biology in schizophrenia. *Psychological Review, 99,* 57–77.

Cohen, N. J., & Squire, L. R. (1981). Retrograde amnesia and remote memory impairment. *Neuropsychologia, 19,* 337–356.

Della Sala, S., Laiacona, M., Spinnler, H., & Trivelli, C. (1993). Autobiographical recollection and frontal damage. *Neuropsychologia, 31,* 823–839.

Dempster, F. N. (1992). The rise and fall of the inhibitory mechanism: Toward a unified theory of cognitive development and aging. *Developmental Review, 12,* 45–75.

Diamond, A. (1990). Developmental time course in human infants and infant monkeys, and the neural bases of inhibitory control in reaching. *Annals of the New York Academy of Sciences,* 608.

Eslinger, P. J., & Grattan, L. M. (1994). Altered serial position learning after frontal lobe lesion. *Neuropsychologia, 32,* 729–739.

Fuster, J. M. (1989). *The prefrontal cortex* (2nd ed.). New York: Raven Press.

Gershberg, F. B. (in press). Implicit and explicit conceptual memory following frontal lobe damage. *Journal of Cognitive Neuroscience.*

Gershberg, F. B., & Shimamura, A. P. (1995). The role of the frontal lobes in the use of organizational strategies in free recall. *Neuropsychologia, 13,* 1305–1333.

Goldman-Rakic, P. S. (1987). Circuitry of primate prefrontal cortex and regulation of behavior by representational memory. In F. Plum (Ed.), *Handbook of physiology: The nervous system* (Vol. 5, pp. 373–417). Bethesda, MD: American Physiological Society.

Graf, P., Squire, L. R., & Mandler, G. (1984). The information that amnesic patients do not forget. *Journal of Experimental Psychology: Learning, Memory, and Cognition, 10,* 164–178.

Haug, H., Barmwater, U., Eggers, R., Fischer, D., Kuhl, S., & Sass, N. L. (1983). Anatomical changes in aging brain: Morphometric analysis of the human prosencephalon. In J. Cervos-Navarro & H. I. Sarkander (Eds.), *Brain aging: Neuropathology and neuropharmocology* (pp. 1–12). New York: Raven Press.

Hirst, W. (1982). The amnesic syndrome: Descriptions and explanations. *Psychological Bulletin, 91,* 435–460.

Hirst, W., & Volpe, B. T. (1988). Memory strategies and brain damage. *Brain and Cognition, 8,* 379–408.

Janowsky, J. S., Shimamura, A. P., Kritchevsky, M., & Squire, L. R. (1989). Cognitive impairment following frontal lobe damage and its relevance to human amnesia. *Behavioral Neuroscience, 103,* 548–560.

Janowsky, J. S., Shimamura, A. P., & Squire, L. R. (1989a). Memory and metamemory: Comparisons between patients with frontal lobe lesions and amnesic patients. *Psychobiology, 17,* 3–11.

Janowsky, J. S., Shimamura, A. P., & Squire, L. R. (1989b). Source memory impairment in patients with frontal lobe damage. *Neuropsychologia, 27,* 1043–1056.

Keane, M. M., Gabrieli, J. D. E., Monti, L. A., Cantor, J. M., & Noland, J. S. (1993). Amnesic patients show normal priming and a normal depth-of-processing effect in a conceptually driven implicit memory task. *Society for Neuroscience Abstracts, 19,* 1079.

Kopelman, M. D. (1989). Remote and autobiographical memory, temporal context memory and frontal atrophy in Korsakoff and Alzheimer patients. *Neuropsychologia, 27,* 437–460.

Levin, H. S., Eisenberg, H. M., & Benton, A. L. (1991). *Frontal lobe function and dysfunction.* New York: Oxford University Press.

Mair, W. G. P., Warrington, E. K., & Weiskrantz, L. (1979). Memory disorder in Korsakoff's psychosis: A neuropathological and neuropsychological investigation of two cases. *Brain, 102,* 749–783.

Mangels, J. A., Gershberg, F. B., Shimamura, A. P., & Knight, R. T. (1996). Impaired retrieval from remote memory in patients with frontal lobe lesions. *Neuropsychology, 10*, 32–41.

Mangels, J. A., & Shimamura, A. P. (1993). Effects of semantic distinctiveness on temporal order in frontal patients. *Abstracts of Society for Neurosciences, 19*, 1002.

Mayes, A. R., Meudell, P. R., Mann, D., & Pickering, A. (1988). Location of lesions in Korsakoff's syndrome: Neuropsychological and neuropathological data on two patients. *Cortex, 24*, 367–388.

Mayes, A. R., Meudell, P. R., & Pickering, A. (1985). Is organic amnesia caused by a selective deficit in remembering contextual information? *Cortex, 21*, 167–202.

McGlynn, S. M., & Kaszniak, A. W. (1991). When metacognition fails: Impaired awareness of deficit in Alzheimer's disease. *Journal of Cognitive Neuroscience, 3*, 183–198.

McIntyre, J. S., & Craik, F. I. M. (1987). Age differences in memory for item and source information. *Canadian Journal of Psychology, 42*, 175–192.

Metcalfe, J. (1993). Novelty monitoring, metacognition, and control in a composite holographic associative recall model: Implications for Korsakoff amnesia. *Psychological Review, 100*, 3–22.

Milner, B. (1971). Interhemispheric differences in the localization of psychological processes in man. *British Medical Bulletin, 127*, 272–277.

Milner, B., Corsi, P., & Leonard, G. (1991). Frontal-lobe contribution to recency judgements. *Neuropsychology, 29*, 601–618.

Moscovitch, M. (1992). A neuropsychological model of memory and consciousness. In L. R. Squire & N. Butters (Eds.), *Neuropsychology of memory* (2nd ed., pp. 5–22). New York: Guilford.

Moscovitch, M. (1994). Cognitive resources and dual-task interference effects at retrieval in normal people: The role of the frontal lobes and medial temporal cortex. *Neuropsychology, 8*, 524–534.

Nelson, T. O., & Narens, L. (1990). Metamemory: A theoretical framework and new findings. *The Psychology of Learning and Motivation, 26*, 125–141.

Nielson-Bohlman, L., Ciranni, M., Shimamura, A. P., & Knight, R. T. (1995). *Impaired implicit memory in patients with temporal–occipital lesions.* Manuscript submitted for publication.

Schacter, D. L. (1987). Implicit memory: History and current status. *Journal of Experimental Psychology: Learning, Memory, and Cognition, 13*, 501–518.

Schacter, D. L., & Tulving, E. (Eds.). (1994). *Memory systems 1994.* Cambridge, MA: MIT Press.

Shallice, T., & Evans, M. E. (1978). The involvement of the frontal lobes in cognitive estimation. *Cortex, 14*, 294–303.

Shimamura, A. P. (1986). Priming in amnesia: Evidence for a dissociable memory function. *Quarterly Journal of Experimental Psychology, 38*, 619–644.

Shimamura, A. P. (1993). Neuropsychological analyses of implicit memory: Recent progress and theoretical interpretations. In P. Graf & M. E. Masson (Eds.), *Implicit memory: New directions in cognition, development, and neuropsychology* (pp. 265–285). Hillsdale, NJ: Lawrence Erlbaum Associates.

Shimamura, A. P. (1994a). Memory and frontal lobe function. In M. S. Gazzaniga (Ed.), *The cognitive neurosciences* (pp. 803–813). Cambridge, MA: MIT Press.

Shimamura, A. P. (1994b). The neuropsychology of metacognition. In J. Metcalfe & A. P. Shimamura (Eds.), *Metacognition: Knowing about knowing* (pp. 253–276). Cambridge, MA: MIT Press.

Shimamura, A. P., Gershberg, F. B., Jurica, P. J., Mangels, J. A., & Knight, R. T. (1992). Intact implicit memory in patients with frontal lobe lesions. *Neuropsychologia, 30*, 931–937.

Shimamura, A. P., Janowsky, J. S., & Squire, L. R. (1990). Memory for the temporal order of events in patients with frontal lobe lesions and amnesic patients. *Neuropsychologia, 28*, 803–813.

Shimamura, A. P., Jurica, P. J., Mangels, J. A., Gershberg, F. B., & Knight, R. T. (1995). Susceptibility to memory interference effects following frontal lobe damage: Findings from tests of paired-associate learning. *Journal of Cognitive Neuroscience, 7*, 144–152.

Shimamura, A. P., Jernigan, T. L., & Squire, L. R. (1988). Korsakoff's Syndrome: Radiological (CT) findings and neuropsychological correlates. *Journal of Neuroscience, 8*, 4400–4410.

Shimamura, A. P., & Squire, L. R. (1986a). Korsakoff syndrome: A study of the relation between anterograde amnesia and remote memory impairment. *Behavioral Neuroscience, 100*, 165–170.

Shimamura, A. P., & Squire, L. R. (1986b). Memory and metamemory: A study of the feeling-of-knowing phenomenon in amnesic patients. *Journal of Experimental Psychology: Learning, Memory, and Cognition, 12*, 452–460.

Shimamura, A. P., & Squire, L. R. (1988). Long-term memory in amnesia: Cued recall, recognition memory, and confidence ratings. *Journal of Experimental Psychology: Learning, Memory, and Cognition, 14*, 763–770.

Smith, M. L., & Milner, B. (1984). Differential effects of frontal-lobe lesions on cognitive estimation and spatial memory. *Neuropsychologia, 22*, 697–705.

Squire, L. R. (1987). *Memory and brain.* New York: Oxford University Press.

Squire, L. R. (1992). Memory and the hippocampus: A synthesis from findings with rats, monkeys, and humans. *Psychological Review, 99*, 195–231.

Squire, L. R., Amaral, D. G., & Press, G. A. (1990). Magnetic resonance measurements of hippocampal formation and mammillary nuclei distinguishes medial temporal lobe and diencephalic amnesia. *Journal of Neuroscience, 10*, 3106–3117.

Squire, L. R., Haist, F., & Shimamura, A. P. (1989). The neurology of memory: Quantitative assessment of retrograde amnesia in two groups of amnesic patients. *Journal of Neuroscience, 9*, 828–839.

Squire, L. R., & Zouzounis, J. A. (1988). Self-ratings of memory dysfunction: Different findings in depression and amnesia. *Journal of Clinical and Experimental Neuropsychology, 10*, 727–738.

Chapter 12

Neural Mechanisms for the Control and Monitoring of Memory: A Parallel Distributed Processing Perspective

James L. McClelland
Carnegie Mellon University and the
Center for the Neural Basis of Cognition

The chapters by Shimamura (11), Norman and Schacter (10) and Funnell, Metcalfe, and Tsapkini (7) in this volume exhibit a striking integration of neuroscientific and psychological approaches to metacognition. It seems evident that the boundaries that once existed between these approaches are in the process of vanishing completely. Behavioral, functional imaging, and neuropsychological investigations are providing converging constraints. These constraints are leading to the emergence of theories of (a) the mechanisms of control of information processing; (b) the mechanisms of explicit and implicit memory; and (c) the interplay of these mechanisms in the monitoring and control of memory.

Several modeling frameworks have been developed in which theories relevant to these matters can be cast. Metcalfe's CHARM model (Metcalfe, 1990, 1993; Metcalfe, Cottrell, & Mencl, 1993) and Anderson's ACT framework (Anderson, 1983, 1993; Kimberg & Farah, 1993) have both been used productively in efforts to understand aspects of control, memory, and metacognition–cognition. Other theories have been developed within the context of the Parallel Distributed Processing (PDP) framework (Rumelhart, McClelland, & the PDP Research Group, 1986; McClelland, Rumelhart, & the PDP Research Group, 1986), as this has continued to evolve in research at Carnegie Mellon. This framework provides the prospect of an eventual bridge between the neural and cognitive levels of description, because the constructs used in these models—the units and connections—have a relatively direct mapping to the elements found in the brain—the neurons and synapses. For practical reasons, actual models generally simulate very large populations of neurons with small or moderate numbers of simulated units, but there is an explicit effort to understand the relationship between these two levels of modeling and to incorporate known aspects of the physiology into the modeling effort. Thus, aspects of the physiology can influence model details in ways that are relatively direct and explicit compared to the other approaches.

In this commentary, I consider the relationship between the concepts introduced in these theories and the ideas and findings reported in the three chapters that are the subjects of this commentary. First I review existing models relevant to the aforementioned points a–c, with primary focus on the theories that have been developed within the PDP framework. Then I consider how they might address, or be extended to address, the phenomena introduced in the chapters by Shimamura, by Norman and Schacter, and by Funnell et al. I also relate the interpretations offered by the PDP models to those offered in these three chapters.

CONTROL OF PROCESSING

A recent series of papers develop a PDP model of the mechanisms through which cognitive processes can be controlled. The essential idea was first presented in Cohen, Dunbar, and McClelland (1990) and has since been elaborated and extended in several other publications (Cohen & Huston, 1994; Cohen & Servan-Schreiber, 1992; Cohen, Servan-Schreiber, & McClelland, 1992). The initial version of the model from Cohen et al. (1990) illustrates the basic theoretical proposal (see Fig. 12.1). The idea is that information processing takes place in processing pathways consisting of interconnected modules, subject to control by activity in another module which we might call the "task" module.

The connection weights among the units in the pathways come through practice to encode stimulus–response relationships, so that the presentation of an appropriate stimulus at the input end of one of these pathways tends to lead to the activation of a corresponding response at the output end. The model was applied to the specific case of the Stroop tasks, in which words are printed in colored ink, and the task is to either name the color of the ink or read the word. To model these tasks, two pathways are introduced—one for processing the color of the ink, and one for processing the identity of the word; these converge on the same response outputs, so that both pathways can contribute to the determination of a response. Connections in these pathways are set by a learning rule; more training on word reading than color naming translates into stronger connections in the word reading pathway than the color-naming pathway, making the

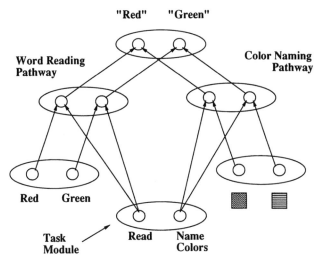

FIG. 12.1. (a) A sketch of the PDP model of control of processing in the Stroop task proposed by Cohen et al. (1990). Colored inputs corresponding to Red and Green are indicated with diagonal and horizontal stripes, respectively. © 1990 by the American Psychological Association. Adapted with permission.

former stronger than the latter. The processing is cascaded (McClelland, 1979), so that activations build up gradually over time; responses are emitted when the activation of one of the output units reaches a fixed threshold. Stronger pathways tend to lead to faster responses, and the speedup produced by practice tends to follow a power law.

In the absence of influence from the task module, each pathway may be capable of producing a correct output when an appropriate stimulus is presented to it, and when color and word are pitted against each other (e.g., the word RED is shown in green ink), the stronger word reading path will dominate. The task module contains units that serve to modulate processing in the two pathways, so that the intrinsically weaker pathway can dominate performance on conflict trials when the task is color naming. In the model as implemented, there are individual units for representing each task; for example, when the task is color naming, the color task unit is activated. This task unit has connections that allow it to prime the units in the intermediate layer of the color-naming pathway while at the same time inhibiting the intermediate layer of the word reading pathway; this facilitates processing in the color-naming pathway and suppresses processing in the word-reading pathway so that the color pathway can determine which response unit will reach threshold first. The strong-word pathway still exerts some influence, thereby accounting for the fact that there are interference and facilitation effects of word identity, when the task is color naming. When the task is word reading, the combined effect of task-based priming and the relatively greater intrinsic strength of the word-reading pathway are such that the effect of the color-naming pathway is overwhelmed, thereby accounting for the fact that words influence color naming but colors do not influence word reading.

The aforementioned approach places control of processing in the "task units"; these units do not actually carry out the task, but they influence units elsewhere that do. Deficits in the activation of these units would, therefore, be expected to lead to deficits in the control of processing. This idea is the basis for the model of schizophrenic deficits in the control of processing offered by Cohen and Servan-Schreiber (1992). They proposed that the task modules necessary for control of behavior are located in the prefrontal cortex, and that a schizophrenia produces a deficit in dopamine systems that project to the prefrontal cortex, giving rise to a reduction of responsivity of prefrontal neurons involved in maintaining task representations, and a corresponding reduction in control of behavior. They were able to use this model to account for several aspects of schizophrenic deficits in information processing tasks, including a reduction in the ability to inhibit prepotent responses to stimuli and override them with alternative responses consistent with task instructions, as in the Stroop task. Cohen and Servan-Schreiber also generalized the notion of the task representation considerably, to accommodate the fact that schizophrenic deficits appear to apply not just to the control of behavior by the general form of the task, but also to the influence on responding of contextual information. For example, in one experiment, schizophrenics were impaired in the use of context to select a relatively infrequent meaning of an ambiguous word (e.g., PEN, as fenced enclosure rather than writing implement). They argued that the frontal lobes play a crucial role in maintaining representations of context—whether generalized task context or specific local context—in a form that allows it to influence information processing, and their simulations encompassed deficits in use of both task context and local language context.

As originally formulated, the model of Cohen and Servan-Schreiber (1992) does not provide any account of more complex tasks that depend on frontal functions, such as motor sequencing or the Wisconsin Card sort task. These tasks have, however, been addressed in other models of frontal functioning. Indeed, Kimberg and Farah (1993) simulated both of these tasks using a production system model based on Anderson's ACT–R framework (Anderson, 1993). Production system models are useful in such cases, because the implementation of sequential processes in connectionist models can be cumbersome, and the graded strengths and activations provided by contemporary production system models allows them to capture what for present purposes may be the crucial characteristics of these sequential processes as they would arise in a connectionist system. In any case, Kimberg and Farah (1993) simulated performance of normals and frontal patients in the motor sequencing and Wisconsin Card Sort tasks (as well as a memory task to be considered here later). To simulate the effects of frontal lesions, they assumed that frontal damage weakens associations among elements in working memory. In many ways the model is quite similar to the model of Cohen and Servan-Schreiber, and it seems very likely that a version of this model could be developed even more in keeping with the assumptions of Cohen and Servan-Schreiber, if it was reformulated so that effects of damage weakened the activations of elements in working memory, rather than the associations between these elements. In the following I proceed as if this point were established, with the proviso that it does need checking through simulations.[1]

MEMORY

To apply the ideas embodied in the models discussed earlier to the domain of memory, we need a brain-systems model of the organization of memory function. Such a model has recently been formulated in the connectionist framework by McClelland, McNaughton, and O'Reilly (1995). A sketch of the overall structure of the model is shown in Fig. 12.2. This model shares with the models already discussed the idea that information processing takes place through the propagation of activation via processing pathways. Processing originates with peripheral sensory pathways that transduce inputs to higher level perceptual areas that are interconnected with other higher level areas, including higher level movement or response-planning areas that can propagate activation to muscles to produce overt responses, via peripheral motor pathways. The pathways of the Stroop model just described are like the pathways envisioned for this system, and the assumption that the skill of color-word reading is mediated by the strengths of connections in the word reading pathway still applies: This skill is thought of as reflecting the gradual accumulation of small changes to connections within the processing pathways that take place on every learning trial. In this model, implicit learning phenomena reflect these small changes (as well as other possible aftereffects, such as slight changes in the thresholds for activations of neurons in these pathways that have recently been activated). The small changes, however, that mediate implicit learning are not

---

[1]It seems likely that the specific assumptions Kimberg and Farah (1993) made about the nature of the information in working memory and the contents of the actual productions used to carry out task performance would have to be adjusted before the reformulated model could be successful.

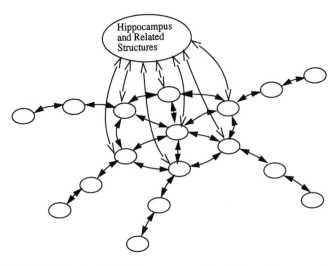

FIG. 12.2. A sketch of the brain systems model of information processing and memory proposed by McClelland et al. (1995). See text for further discussion. From McClelland (1994). Reprinted with permission of the publisher.

thought to be sufficient to support the rapid formation of new explicit memories. The reason for this is that explicit memories require the formation of associative links between arbitrary elements, and the formation of such associations requires much larger changes to the strengths of connection weights than those that are sufficient to produce implicit learning. McClelland et al. (1995) argued that it is crucial to the successful development of cortical processing systems that they learn slowly; if the large connection-weight changes necessary to form associative links between arbitrary materials were made quickly, they would lead to catastrophic interference with the structured knowledge and skills that are gradually built up in the cortex through the gradual accumulation of small changes (see McClelland et al., 1995, for further discussion).

In any case, McClelland et al. (1995) have argued that the hippocampus and related structures in the medial temporal lobes collectively called "the hippocampal system" provide a second learning system optimized to allow the rapid formation of associations between arbitrary elements. Such associations are assumed to underlie episodic and semantic memories in the form in which they are initially acquired. Loss of the hippocampal system therefore prevents the formation of new semantic and episodic memories and removes the substrate of recently formed semantic and episodic memories, thereby accounting for the anterograde and retrograde amnesia for such material found in patients with extensive lesions to these structures. Through repetition, however, both episodic and semantic memories can become integrated directly into the connections among units in the cortical processing pathways. This integration process accounts for the fact that retrograde amnesia for both semantic and episodic material is temporally limited in scope after extensive damage to the hippocampal system.

Before turning to the role of the frontal lobes in memory, it will be useful to characterize in a bit more detail the processes McClelland et al. (1995) assume take place during the storage and later retrieval of a new episodic memory, and to relate these to aspects of the memory models developed in other frameworks. Experiencing an episode, in the McClelland et al. model, produces a pattern of activity that is widely distributed over the higher level areas of the cortical processing system, including all (attended) aspects of the experience and any elaborations and associations to this experience that arise at the time. For example, an individual might hear the words "locomotive–dishtowel" paired together during an experimental session, and might form an elaborated representation involving a dishtowel wrapped around a (toy) locomotive, perhaps held in the hands of a small boy drying the locomotive after dropping it in a sink by accident. Pathways from these cortical areas into the hippocampal system produce a reduced description of the entire pattern. The elements of this reduced description are then bound together by associative synaptic modification within the hippocampal system. Later, an opportunity arises for recall of the learned episode whenever a part of the experience becomes reactivated in the neocortex. For example, an experimenter might remind the individual of an earlier session in which a series of word pairs were presented, and then ask the subject to recall the second member of each word pair, after presentation of the first. The subject might then use the reminder of the earlier session as a retrieval cue to recall the general context of the session, and might hold this in mind as the probe words are presented. When "locomotive" is presented, the context together with the probe would be used together to probe the memory system. A neocortical representation containing these two would be projected to the hippocampal system, where it would produce a reduced description that would serve as a probe of the associative memory. The associative synaptic modifications that took place during storage would then lead to the completion of the rest of the pattern. Return connections from the hippocampal system to the neocortex would then provide the basis for the reinstatement of a pale replica of the entire neocortical pattern that had been present during study, which (in successful cases) would provide enough of a reinstatement of the locomotive–dishtowel representation to allow for the readout of an appropriate overt response.

Perhaps it is worth considering briefly the relation of this model to other models, such as Metcalfe's CHARM and Anderson's ACT. All of the models view retrieval as dependent on associative connections and all provide mechanisms in which the memory probe plays a crucial role (see also Humphreys, Bain, & Pike, 1989). CHARM adds a notion of familiarity monitoring not explicitly used in McClelland et al. (1995), but that is consistent with many physiological findings. Most of the physiological work suggests that the actual computation of familiarity is carried out in the medial temporal lobes; this does not necessarily contradict Metcalfe's suggestion that a deficit in monitoring familiarity in frontal lobes could account for some frontal deficits, because the results of the computation might well be propagated to the PFC, for use in the control of processing.

CONTROL OF MEMORY: MAINTENANCE OF CONTEXT

Given all of the previous discussion, we are now in a position to consider what role the frontal lobes might play in various memory tasks. The natural suggestion is that they provide the mechanisms responsible for the control of memory; specifically, those neural structures responsible for the formation and maintenance of contextual representations that are normally part of the input to the hippocampal memory system during learning and during test. Such representations can be thought of as being among the contents of the active or working memory of the subject.

This general hypothesis, which I will call the *maintenance of context* hypothesis, needs further elaboration before it will serve as even a useful starting place for the development of a model of the role of the frontal lobes in memory retrieval. In the following section I review the relevant data and suggest some directions that might be followed toward the formulation of these elaborations.

MEMORY DEFICITS RESULTING FROM FRONTAL LESIONS

We can now consider the pattern of deficits seen in frontal patients in light of the hypothesis just stated. Simulations will ultimately be necessary to substantiate the claims I make in this section, but in most cases the claims can be supported by pointing to relevant characteristics of existing simulation models that illustrate the ideas in other contexts.

As an initial phenomenon to be explained, we can note that frontal patients generally show disproportionate deficits in recall relative to recognition; that the recall deficit is most pronounced in free recall; and that the deficit is substantially reduced if recall cues to individual memory traces are provided. Shimamura (Chapter 11, this volume) provides extensive discussion of these points. He suggests that the deficit may lie in the ability to formulate and maintain internal representations of retrieval cues sufficient to focus the retrieval process on the desired memory target.

These proposals are, of course, virtually equivalent to the maintenance of context hypothesis. Once the hypothesis is formulated within an explicit computational framework, its implications for processing can be directly assessed. Although such a model for memory retrieval remains to be developed, some of these implications can perhaps be anticipated, based on observations of the effects of degradation of context representations in the model of Cohen and Servan-Schreiber (1992). Their simulations illustrated that degradation of context representations tended to produce two complementary effects: first, degradation reduced the ability to produce *less* typical or frequent responses; second, it led to an increase in the tendency to intrude *more* typical or frequent responses. Cohen and Servan-Schreiber used this finding to argue that both types of findings could reflect a single underlying deficit. In this light it is interesting to note that frontal patients often intrude strong preexisting associates, overriding newly acquired, context-specific associations in memory experiments. By extension of the proposal of Cohen and Servan-Schreiber, we might suggest that both poorer overall recall, and the intrusion of preexisting associates results from the failure to form an adequate representation of the context that restricts recall to the desired target.

However, there are two very different ways of thinking about the reasons why frontal patients might have difficulty forming and maintaining appropriate representations of context. One way would be to assume that there is damage directly to the module or modules containing the units that actually represent the characteristics of the context. Such damage would be expected to degrade the context representation, leading it to serve as a relatively poor retrieval cue. Alternatively, one could assume that other modules that support the formation and maintenance of the context representation are affected.

It seems likely that something more like the latter is involved, at least for some patients. One reason for this is the observation that if information about the context is supplied as part of the memory probe, some frontal patients can show very mild deficits. Problems arise when the patient must generate and maintain the context, at least in some frontal patients (perhaps those with lesions in the dorsolateral prefrontal cortex).

It is possible, however, that other portions of the frontal lobes are directly responsible for the representation of certain types of content; specifically, content related to personal history and episodic structure. The analysis of patient DRB by Damasio, Eslinger, Damasio, Van Hoesen, and Cornell (1985) raises this possibility. This patient had extensive damage to the basal forebrain, cingulate gyrus, and inferolateral temporal cortex, as well as the medial temporal lobes, and exhibited very slight residual memory of his own personal history; he confabulated wildly about his own recent episodic experiences. The picture is quite different from that presented by pure medial temporal lobe patients, in which remote memory about personal history and early episodic information is retained. Whereas Damasio et al. suggested that inferolateral temporal cortex may play a crucial role in the loss of episodic memory, recent cases reported by Hodges, Graham, and Patterson (1995) suggested that lesions restricted to these areas produce a profound deficit of the semantic content of episodes but leave the memory for the event itself intact (the patient confuses similar objects within events but clearly remembers particular events subject to such confusions). Thus, the possibility remains that a portion of the frontal lobes, such as the basal forebrain, may play a crucial role in the representation of self-in-context. If so, disorders in this area would lead to gross disturbances in the ability to probe memory episodically, thus accounting for disturbances of some aspects of context memory in some frontal patients.

These last comments dovetail with Norman and Schacter's ideas about differential effects of different types of frontal lesions. They suggest that some types of frontal lesions may lead to a degradation of representations of context, either by eliminating some aspects of the context representation, or by making the activation of such information very diffuse. This latter possibility is certainly consistent with the notion that some portion of the frontal lobes might actually provide the representation of self in relation to context. The possibility that severe degradation of these representations might be the basis for memory confabulation deserves careful exploration.

Obviously the ideas just presented are highly speculative. There is an obvious need to elaborate a neuropsychological model of the retrieval process and to specify how the aspects of the model relate to various regions of the brain in order to address these and other aspects of the data.

These ideas are also quite incomplete. The monitoring of memory is clearly an important function, and there seems to be general consensus that frontal damage disturbs these monitoring functions, but I have hardly touched on this matter in these comments. One possible way of relating the maintenance of context hypothesis to failures of memory monitoring might be to suggest that, at least in some cases, it may not be the monitoring per se that is at fault, but the ability to maintain representations that reflect the results of monitoring, so that they can be used to guide future behavior. This idea is consistent with the observation of preservation errors in tasks like the Wisconsin Card Sort, where the patient is given clear feedback and is clearly aware of the feedback at some level, but is unable to use it to guide his behavior.

Obviously, then, we remain a long way from a full characterization of the neural basis of the control and monitoring of memory. We can expect rapid growth in our empirical understanding of the role played by various parts of the frontal lobes, and other brain areas, in memory and the control of memory through the continued use of neuropsychological and functional imaging approaches. Additional computational modeling work should help clarify and integrate the results of these empirical investigations.

REFERENCES

Anderson, J. R. (1983). *The architecture of cognition.* Cambridge, MA: Harvard University Press.

Anderson, J. R. (1993). *Rules of the mind.* Hillsdale, NJ: Lawrence Erlbaum Associates.

Cohen, J. D., Dunbar, K., & McClelland, J. L. (1990). On the control of automatic processes: A parallel distributed processing model of the stroop effect. *Psychological Review, 97,* 332–361.

Cohen, J. D., & Huston, T. A. (1994). Progress in the use of interactive models for understanding attention and performance. In C. Umilta & M. Moscovitch (Eds.), *Attention & performance xv: Conscious and nonconscious information processing* (pp. 453–476). Cambridge, MA: MIT Press.

Cohen, J. D., & Servan-Schreiber, D. (1992). Context, cortex, and dopamine: A connectionist approach to behavior and biology in schizophrenia. *Psychological Review, 99,* 45–77.

Cohen, J. D., Servan-Schreiber, D., & McClelland, J. L. (1992). A parallel distributed processing approach to automaticity. *American Journal of Psychology, 105,* 239–269.

Damasio, A. R., Eslinger, P. J., Damasio, H., Van Hoesen, G. W., & Cornell, S. (1985). Multimodal amnesic syndrome following bilateral temporal and basal forebrain damage. *Archives of Neurology, 42,* 252–259.

Hodges, J. R., Graham, N., & Patterson, K. (1995). Charting the progression in semantic dementia: Implications for the organisation of semantic memory. *Memory, 3,* 463–495.

Humphreys, M. S., Bain, J. D., & Pike, R. (1989). Different ways to cue a coherent memory system: A theory for episodic, semantic, and procedural tasks. *Psychological Review, 96,* 208–233.

Kimberg, D. Y., & Farah, M. J. (1993). A unified account of cognitive impairments following frontal lobe damage: The role of working memory in complex, organized behavior. *Journal of Experimental Psychology: General, 122,* 411–428.

McClelland, J. L. (1979). On the time relations of mental processes: An examination of systems of processes in cascade. *Psychological Review, 86,* 287–330.

McClelland, J. L. (1994). The organization of memory: A parallel distributed processing perspective. *Rev. Neurol.* (Paris), *150,* 570–579.

McClelland, J. L., McNaughton, B. L., & O'Reilly, R. C. (1995). Why there are complementary learning systems in the hippocampus and neocortex: Insights from the successes and failures of connectionist models of learning and memory. *Psychological Review, 102,* 419–457.

McClelland, J. L., Rumelhart, D. E., & the PDP Research Group (1986). *Parallel distributed processing: Explorations in the microstructure of cognition. Volume 2: Psychological and biological models.* Cambridge, MA: MIT Press.

Metcalfe, J. (1990). Composite holographic associative recall model (CHARM) and blended memories in eyewitness testimony. *Journal of Experimental Psychology: General, 119,* 145–160.

Metcalfe, J. (1993). Novelty monitoring, metacognition and control in a composite holographic associative recall model: Implications for Korsakoff amnesia. *Psychological Review, 100,* 3–22.

Metcalfe, J., Cottrell, G. W., & Mencl, W. E. (1993). Cognitive binding: A computational-modeling analysis of a distinction between implicit and explicit memory. *Journal of Cognitive Neuroscience, 4,* 289–298.

Rumelhart, D. E., & McClelland, J. L., & the PDP Research Group (1986). *Parallel distributed processing: Explorations in the microstructure of cognition. Volume 1: Foundations.* Cambridge, MA: MIT Press.

Chapter 13

Memory Attributions: Remembering, Knowing, and Feeling of Knowing

Colleen M. Kelley
Macalester College

Larry L. Jacoby
MacMaster University

Over the last several years, much of our research has been aimed at un-covering the bases for the subjective experience of memory and devising methods to separately measure those bases. We have been particularly interested in the effects of implicit memory or automatic influences of memory on judgments. How does that work relate to questions about metacognition? After agreeing to write this chapter, we went through a long period thinking the answer was "it doesn't." As the deadline for the chapter drew near, we became more creative (desperate?) in our analysis, and have now arrived at the position that metacognition and implicit memory are so similar as to not be separate topics. Questions concerning awareness are central for both metacognition and for implicit memory.

We first describe our analysis of the fluency heuristic: the notion that one basis for the feeling of familiarity is the ease of perceiving events or retrieving ideas. We describe experiments that manipulated fluency to create illusions of memory, and other experiments that manipulated flu-ency via providing past experiences to create illusions of perception, fame, knowing, and believing. The misinterpretation of effects of past experience shapes current subjective experience, which can influence people's pre-dictions for others as well as for themselves. Some of those experiments could be described either as investigations of implicit memory or as inves-tigations of metacognition.

Next, we argue that the problems that arise when one attempts to separate different bases for judgments are relevant to questions about metamemory. In particular, we suggest that there is an important relation between theories that propose that familiarity serves as an alternative to recollection as a basis for recognition memory, and theories about the feeling-of-knowing and the tip-of-the-tongue phenomenon. The subjective experience of recollection carries with it a specification of the source of a memory and so affords people control over whether they will be influenced by a particular prior experience. In contrast, the subjective experience of familiarity does not specify its source and so affords less control. For metacognition as well as for recognition memory, it is important to separate such nonanalytic bases for judgments that can be affected by irrelevant factors from more analytic bases for judgments that allow people to selectively control the factors that enter into their judgments.

FLUENCY AS A BASIS FOR JUDGMENTS

One important basis for the subjective experience of memory is the ease with which to-be-recognized items are perceived and the ease with which to-be-recalled items are generated (Jacoby & Dallas, 1981; Jacoby, Kelley, & Dywan, 1989). Because prior experiences commonly bias perception and cognition, the fluency of perception and thinking is generally a valid indicator that one has seen something before. For example, perceptual identification of briefly presented words is enhanced if the words have been studied previously (Jacoby & Dallas, 1981).

If ease of perceptual processing is a cue that can serve as the basis for the feeling of remembering, then it should be possible to subtly manipulate ease of perceptual processing and create illusions of remembering. To create memory illusions, Jacoby and Whitehouse (1989) varied the ease with which words on a recognition memory test were perceived. Subjects studied a list of words and then took a recognition test. For some recognition test words, a brief preview of the word occurred immediately beforehand. For both old and new words on the recognition memory test, the preview of the test item increased the probability of judging an item "old," presumably by facilitating perceptual processing of the test word (for similar results, see Rajaram, 1993; Whittlesea, Jacoby, & Girard, 1990).

An important contrast in the Jacoby and Whitehouse (1989) study is between a condition under which participants were aware of the preview word versus a condition under which participants were unaware of the preview word. When the preview word was presented for a longer duration and could be clearly seen, there was no effect on the subjective experience of "oldness" of the recognition test words. Presumably, participants correctly interpreted the familiarity of the recognition test word as stemming from the preview. In fact, participants had a tendency to overcorrect for the influence of the preview word on the familiarity of the recognition test word, and were slightly less likely to call a recognition test item "old" when it was preceded by a matching preview word in the aware condition. The contrast between the aware and unaware conditions in Jacoby and Whitehouse fits with the notion that the subjective experience of memory is an attribution or inference.

Fluency reflecting conceptually driven processing can also be misattributed and give rise to an illusion of memory. Whittlesea (1993) created illusions of memory by presenting the recognition test word at the end of a sentence that strongly predicted the word, such as "The stormy seas tossed the BOAT." Again, hiding the source of fluency was important for creating the memory illusion. Lindsay and Kelley (1996) found that ease of generating an item during cued recall contributes to the subjective experience of remembering. Subjects could escape the false memory effect if they were informed of the manipulation that led some words to be easily generated.

Although fluency of perception and ease of recalling is a generally valid indicator of past experience, it does not perfectly specify its source, which is why we can create illusions of memory. Because of this lack of specificity, people can also misinterpret the fluency resulting from past experience as actually being due to other factors. For example, fluent perceptual processing contributes to the subjective experience of duration and intensity of a stimulus, so fluency due to prior experience can lead people to think a visually presented word is exposed for a longer duration (Witherspoon & Allan, 1985) or that auditorally presented sentences are exposed against lower background noise (Jacoby, Allan, Collins, & Larwill, 1988). Affective judgments such as pleasantness are also partially based on the ease of processing of stimuli. Jacoby et al. (1989) suggested that the "mere exposure effect" in studies of aesthetic preferences is a case of the misattribution of the fluency due to prior experience. In accord with this, Bornstein and D'Agostino (1994) found that the mere exposure effect was largest under conditions where participants were unlikely to realize that past experience was actually the source of perceptual fluency occurring during the pleasantness judgments (see also Seamon et al., 1995).

FLUENCY AND METACOGNITIVE JUDGMENTS

Fluency is also an important constituent of more cognitive judgments such as knowing and believing. In the "false fame" paradigm, reading a list of nonfamous names increases the nonspecific familiarity of those names. Consequently, when participants are later asked to judge whether the names are famous or nonfamous they are apt to misinterpret that familiarity as fame (Jacoby, Woloshyn, & Kelley, 1989). Misattribution of the familiarity as fame was particularly likely when participants could not remember having studied the name in the first phase. In some experiments, we placed the fame effect in opposition to recognition of the source of familiarity (the study list) by correctly informing participants that all names studied in the first list were nonfamous. This "method of opposition" ensured that any increase in false fame resulting from study of the names in the first phase was due to familiarity in the absence of recollection, and so let us identify familiarity as a separate process. In fact, manipulations such as dividing attention during the study phase vastly reduced participants' ability to recollect having studied an item on the list, but did not affect familiarity as measured by the fame judgments.

Another judgment that depends partially on familiarity is truth. Repeated exposure to statements about obscure topics (e.g., the length of the right arm of the Statue of Liberty) increased the rated truth of those statements (Begg, Armour, & Kerr, 1985; Hasher, Goldstein, & Toppino, 1977). Such "illusions of truth" depend on the misattribution of the familiarity of facts due to prior exposure to those facts being true (Begg, Anas, & Farinacci, 1992).

The metacognitive judgment of confidence in the answers to general knowledge questions also depends partially on fluency, in particular, the fluent generation of an answer to the question. To illustrate, what was Buffalo Bill's last name? If an answer comes quickly to mind, how do you know it was correct? Kelley and Lindsay (1993) found negative correlations between the latency to think of an answer and confidence in that answer (see also Nelson & Narens, 1990). They then manipulated the speed with which participants thought of answers by having them read a list of answers prior to attempting to answer the questions. Prior exposure to correct answers (e.g., Cody) increased the speed and frequency with which correct answers were given on the general knowledge test and increased participants' confidence in those answers. Even stronger evidence for the claim that the speed with which an answer comes to mind is a basis for confidence was gained by changing what answers came to mind. Illusions of knowing occurred when participants studied closely related but incorrect answers (e.g., Hickock). Those studied incorrect answers were more likely to be confidently given as answers to the general knowledge questions. Kelley and Lindsay (1993) argued that those effects of prior study could occur without conscious memory for the list of words. In fact, when memory of the answers was placed in opposition to correctness by informing participants that all studied answers were incorrect, prior study nonetheless influenced what answers were produced when memory was rendered poor by dividing subject's attention during study or during test.

PREDICTING FOR OTHERS

We have also explored the misattribution of fluency due to past experience when people are attempting to make judgments for others. Some researchers have extended the domain of metacognition to predictions for others, notably Jameson, Nelson, Leonesio, and Narens' (1993) studies of the feeling of another's knowing. The aim of those studies was to explore the cues to the feeling of knowing that were not privileged access to an internal monitor, but rather observable and socially shared. They found that an observer who watched a target person attempt to recall the answers to general knowledge questions predicted the target's performance on a later recognition test better than a judge who knew nothing more than the identity of the question. Observers used information about the speed of the target's response and the content of the recall attempt as a basis for their predictions. Brennan and Williams (1995) found that people who listened in on speakers' attempts to answer general knowledge questions based their FOAK ratings on intonation and response latency: Rising intonation and longer latencies led to lower FOAK ratings for answers; longer latencies led to higher FOAK ratings for nonanswers. Listeners are capable of using such cues to model the speakers' states of knowledge and so communicate more effectively.

The ability to make accurate predictions of judgments for others is central for clear communication and smooth social interactions. We began our research by proposing that in a variety of domains, judgments for others are actually based on one's own subjective experience. Subjective experience is often an accurate and efficient basis for judgment. Because people have nearly identical sensory and perceptual systems, they can accurately judge how others will experience the loudness or brightness of stimuli. Those judgments are experienced as objective judgments of the stimuli rather than an inductive leap from one's own experience. Only when people try to predict for others who are different in an important way does it become apparent that the judgment is not objective, as when older people caution their children that it is too dim in a room to read and they should turn on a light before they "ruin their eyes."

More cognitive experiences also appear to faithfully mirror the objective characteristics of materials. However, subjective experience can be spoiled as a basis for judging for others because of the effect of specific past experiences. A commonplace example concerns the readability of a paper that one has written. We send a paper off to a journal convinced that it is beautifully written, only to get it back a few months later to find that the writing has deteriorated during the delay. We have mistaken our knowledge and fluent reading of the paper for that which is on the page. Happily, editors are likely to suffer the same cognitive illusion, so they can feel great satisfaction that their recommended revision helps the paper, when what they are actually experiencing is the effect of past experience on their current reading of the paper.

We have investigated effects of this sort within the task of judging the difficulty of anagrams for others. In one of those experiments (Jacoby & Kelley, 1987), participants judged the difficulty of anagrams for others under three conditions. Anagrams were either new at the time of test, or the solution to the anagram had been read in an earlier phase of the experiment, or, in a third condition, the solution word was presented with the anagram that was to be solved, such as scarf fscar. The third condition prevented participants from having any subjective experience of the anagram's difficulty, and forced them to rely on a theory or collection of rules such as "low frequency words would be harder to solve." Participants judged how difficult anagrams would be for others to solve using a 7-point scale.

The Anagram With Solution condition served as a benchmark of theory-based judgments. In contrast, when participants had the opportunity to solve the anagrams, they used their own subjective experience as a basis for judging the difficulty of anagrams for others, as shown by the high average correlations between speed of solving the anagram and its rated difficulty (Table 13.1). Subjects were able to rapidly judge anagram difficulty when they could base it on subjective experience, relative to the theory-based judgments made in the Anagram With Solution condition. Having earlier read the solution to an anagram resulted in the anagram being judged as easier for others to solve even though it was stressed that others would not study the earlier presented list of words which contained the solution to the anagram. The correlation between RT to solve the anagram and rated difficulty was as high for old anagrams as for new anagrams, even though the participants' subjective experience of anagram difficulty was spoiled as a basis for judging for others.

TABLE 13.1
Effects of Prior Reading of Anagram
Solution on Judged Difficulty for Others

| | Item type | | |
Variable	New Anagrams	Old Anagrams	Anagrams With Solution
% solved	.65	.82	—
RT (ms)	10726	7115	—
Rating	3.7	3.0	3.20
Average r RT × rating	.84	.80	—
RT to rate	3017	2596	3489

Note. Rt to solve and RT to rate are in msec. Difficulty was rated on a 7-point scale from *Very Easy* to *Very Difficult.*

Were participants better at judging the difficulty of anagrams for others when they avoided using spoiled subjective experience? To answer that question, we looked at the correlation between rated difficulty and the criterion variable of time for others to solve the anagrams, when the solutions to the anagrams had not been presented, in an item analysis collapsed across subjects. Those results showed that judgments based on spoiled subjective experience captured the ranking of anagram difficulty as well as did judgments based on the experience of solving new anagrams. In contrast, depriving people of the chance to try solving the anagrams hurt people's ability to predict the performance of others.

Are our anagram studies investigations of metacognition or are they investigations of implicit memory? The answer is "both." Predicting for others is a metacognitive task, and judging the difficulty of anagrams for others in this paradigm clearly qualifies as an implicit test. A final experiment examined the importance of awareness of earlier reading a solution word for judging anagram difficulty (Kelley & Jacoby, 1996, Experiment 2).

In that experiment, participants first studied a list of words that included solutions to anagrams that would be presented in the test phase. There were three test conditions. A first test condition was the same as in the earlier experiment, in that participants were asked to solve anagrams and judge the difficulty for others. Some anagrams were new, and some were old in that the solution words had been studied in the first phase. For a second test condition, participants were informed that some of the anagrams could be solved using a word that was earlier studied, and were required to recognize whether their solution word was old or new. We thought that directing participants toward prior presentation of the solution words might eliminate its effect on judgments of difficulty. A third condition was the same as the second condition except we explained that earlier reading of a solution word would make the anagram seem easy to solve. We stressed that participants should not be misled by this apparent ease when making their judgments for others. Ratings were made by moving a game paddle to a point on a 255-point scale.

Results showed that the test of recognition memory did not eliminate the effects of prior presentation on judgments of difficulty (Table 13.2). Although recognition memory for solution words was high, participants relied on spoiled subjective experience when judging the difficulty of anagrams for others. However, they did avoid doing this when they were both warned that their subjective experience was spoiled and were forced to make recognition judgments.

Others have also shown that subjective experience is a better predictor of behavior than is a poor theory; in particular, Wilson and colleagues' work on affective versus reasoned judgments. For example, Wilson and Schooler (1991) showed that rating of jams correlated better with the ratings made by experts if people did not have to justify their ratings. They argued that

TABLE 13.2
Judgments of Anagram Difficulty by Condition

| | Condition and Item Type | | | | | |
| | Uninformed | | Recognition | | Informed Plus Recognition | |
	Old	New	Old	New	Old	New
Difficulty ratings	74.6	97.1	76.4	96.0	96.4	101.5

Note. Difficulty was rated on a 255-point scale, from *Very Easy* to *Very Difficult.* Reprinted from Kelley and Jacoby Experiment Two (1996) with permission.

forcing participants to justify their ratings turned an affective response into a cognitive decision, and in this case the cognitive judgments may have been based on a bad theory. In some domains, unanalyzed affect may capture more dimensions and weight them more appropriately than cognitive analysis.

We think people's use of subjective experience as a basis for social prediction is widespread. For example, the social psychological literature on the "false consensus" effect may stem from people using subjective experience as a basis for predicting for others. In the typical false consensus paradigm (Ross, Green, & House, 1977), people note their preference between two options, or their attitude about a topic, and then attempt to judge how many people would make the same choice or hold the same attitude. People tend to think that their preference or attitude is more common than the alternative. The false consensus effect may be analogous to our experiments on judging anagram difficulty, in that subjective experience is misinterpreted as a direct reflection of objective characteristics of the situation, unaffected by one's own prior experience and abilities.

In another case of metacognitive monitoring of others, Goranson (1985) demonstrated how teachers may be particularly prone to errors in their estimation of their students' future performance. Goranson asked a group of college instructors to fill out a quiz they were about to administer "as the average student in your class will do." Although the instructors accurately captured the ordering of difficulty of items on the quiz, they greatly overestimated how well the students would do. The instructors presumably used their own subjective experience of item difficulty as a basis for judging for the students, even though their understanding was not a good basis for prediction. This is the same pattern of results that we have found in our anagram experiments.

Similarly, Nickerson, Baddeley, and Freeman (1987) and Fussell and Krauss (1992) found that people use their own knowledge as a basis for judging what other people will know. However, we suspected that people would not take into account the effects of recent experience on the accessibility of knowledge. To test this, we had participants read a list of terms, including the answers to a set of general knowledge questions. In a second phase, participants first attempted to answer general knowledge questions and then rated the number of college students out of 100 who would know the correct answer. As in the Kelley and Lindsay (1993) study outlined earlier, prior study of the correct answers led participants to answer more questions correctly, and decreased the latency of their response. Presumably, this increase in accessibility of the answers led to the subjective experience that the "old" questions were easier than the new questions. In fact, participants estimated that more people would know the answers to questions for which the participants had read the correct answer in the first phase. As in the anagram paradigm, subjective experience of difficulty is a nonanalytic basis for predicting for others, which gives no signal as to what proportion of the accessibility of the answer is due to the answer being easy, and what proportion is due to recent reading of the answer.

ANALYTIC VERSUS NONANALYTIC BASES FOR JUDGMENTS

An important contrast in the work we have reviewed is between nonanalytical bases for judgments such as the fluency heuristic and more analytic bases for judgments such as a theory or collection of rules. Nonanalytic judgments reflect the contribution of a variety of factors operating en masse to produce a certain experience, such as the familiarity of a name or the difficulty of an anagram. In contrast, analytic judgments allow people to specify the factors that enter into a judgment. We think the distinction between nonanalytic and analytic bases for judgments applies in a wide variety of domains, including recognition memory, categorization, predictions for others, attitudes, and metacognition (see Jacoby & Brooks, 1984; Jacoby & Kelley, 1987).

How can one separate bases for judgments? In the anagram experiments, we studied people's use of a theory rather than subjective experience as a basis for judging difficulty by depriving participants of any subjective experience of anagram difficulty. This was accomplished by presenting the solution word with the anagram. In the false fame studies, we arranged it such that participants could counteract the effect of prior study of the names on later familiarity by recollecting that the name had been studied in the first phase, and then following the rule that "all studied names were not famous." This "method of opposition" allowed us to argue that all remaining effects of prior study of the words on later fame judgments was due to familiarity in the absence of conscious recollection of the names. The method of placing two bases for judgments such as familiarity and recollection in opposition to one another provides a demonstration of the existence of familiarity as a separate process. However, if familiarity and recollection are independent processes, the method of opposition leads us to underestimate the familiarity gained from prior study of a name, because recollection and familiarity can co-occur. Under the opposition conditions, whenever recollection and familiarity co-occur, familiarity cannot affect fame judgments because it is opposed by recollection.

We have also used deadlines to separate slower analytic judgments from nonanalytic judgments. We tested first-year undergraduates at Macalester College on their attitudes toward homosexuals. Subjects were required to answer yes/no questions such as "I would feel comfortable if a member of my sex were attracted to me" after either a short deadline or with a long time to respond. First-year undergraduates appeared homophobic when forced to respond rapidly, but not when they were able to answer the questions at their own pace. The two bases for judgment may be a "gut-level" reaction versus a more reasoned and perhaps socially desirable response. Interestingly, for fourth-year undergraduates, the difference between short-deadline and long-deadline responses was no longer present. By their fourth year, students had acquired new attitudes that were expressed automatically, or were so practiced in expressing the socially desirable response that they could do so automatically.

Dovidio and Fazio (1991) used a deadline procedure to assess attitudes and found that short-deadline responses better predicted subsequent behavior than did responses made after a long deadline. That behavior is better predicted by attitudes that are automatically accessed may reflect the fact that we live in a state of mindlessness (Langer, 1989) with little reflection and analysis to guide behavior. Or perhaps our pervasive use of nonanalytic judgments when behaving indicates that we live in the "divided attention" condition.

METACOGNITION AND BASES
FOR RECOGNITION MEMORY

One important focus of research in metacognition is the basis for judgments. Feeling-of-knowing judgments can be based on the familiarity of the retrieval cues, as shown by the fact that prior study of cues alone can increase FOK (Metcalfe, Schwartz, & Joaquim, 1993; Reder & Ritter, 1992; Schwartz & Metcalfe, 1992). The extent to which FOK based on cue familiarity is an accurate basis for predicting later recognition of the target depends on whether the cue and target have a shared history of presentation. It might also depend on the extent to which the identity of the cue and of the target are submerged in a larger unit.

An alternative theory of the basis for the FOK is Koriat's (1993, 1994) accessibility hypothesis. Koriat found that FOK can be based on access to partial information such that the more partial information one retrieves, the stronger the FOK. The extent to which FOK based on partial information is an accurate basis for predicting later recognition of the target stems from a fundamental property of memory—items that are committed to memory are more likely to give rise to access to correct (rather than incorrect) partial information. Thus, understanding the relation between feeling-of-knowing judgments and the information one is trying to remember (as assessed by recognition or recall) involves understanding the bases for the feeling of knowing and the relation among those bases, and the relation of each basis to later target recognition or recall.

We think these two components of FOK, cue familiarity and access to partial information, as well as final access to the target information, map onto a distinction found in recognition memory. Many two-process models of recognition memory distinguish between the ability to recollect details of a prior event versus simply having a feeling of familiarity. Here we attempt to integrate theorizing across domains by exploring the relation between theories that propose two bases for recognition memory and research on the feeling of knowing. We argue that the process underlying "Know" responses when the "Remember/Know" procedure is used to reveal two bases for recognition memory is also involved in the "feeling of knowing." Then we suggest that the advantage to be gained by relating metacognition to theories of recognition memory is that criteria for establishing the existence of and relation between different processes has recently been extensively explored in theories of memory.

First, consider examples that describe familiarity in the absence of recollection as a basis for recognition memory. Examples of this sort have been described by Wundt, James, and even Aristotle, showing that the phenomenological difference between bases for recognition is a compelling one. Brewer (1992) reviewed early philosophers who described the subjective experience of recollection and argued that it is a "natural kind." Perhaps the best known example of familiarity without recollection is George Mandler's example of meeting a person on a bus who seems familiar, but that familiarity was not accompanied by recollection of when and where the person had been encountered. Mandler later recollected that the person was his butcher. The familiarity-without-recollection state holds a striking similarity to the feeling of knowing. If a person in that state were asked whether he would be able to recognize the familiar person's occupation from a list of alternatives, he would almost certainly say yes, and would probably be successful in doing so. Also, Mandler's description of the subjective experience of familiarity without recollection sounds strikingly similar to the tip-of-the-tongue phenomenon.

Tulving (1985) developed an experimental paradigm to study familiarity without recollection, which has been used extensively by Gardiner and his colleagues (Gardiner & Java, 1993). For that "Remember/Know" procedure, participants are given a test of recognition memory, and for items that they call "old" are asked to indicate whether they "remember" the prior presentation of the item or only "know" that the item was on the list. For an item to qualify as "remembered," participants are told that they must remember details of the prior presentation of the item such as what they thought about when the item was presented or the context in which the item occurred. "Know" was defined with an example similar to the butcher on the bus.

A first experiment tested the possibility that the feeling of knowing revealed by use of the Remember/Know procedure is the same as the feeling of knowing investigated in studies of metacognition. In particular, the question was whether "Know" responses predict performance on a subsequent test of memory just as do feeling-of-knowing responses.

In the first phase of the experiment, participants were presented related and unrelated pairs of words that they were told to study and remember for a later test of memory (Fig. 13.1). The unrelated pairs in that list were

Phase 1:   Study related and unrelated word pairs.

    half   whole
    blue   treat
    alert   green

Phase 2:   Recognition memory test of single words as "remembered," know," or "new."

    whole
    treat
    green
    table

Phase 3:   Pair-recognition memory test.

                    half
        whole
                    down

                    alert
        green
                    blue

FIG. 13.1. Outline of procedure for knowing and feeling-of-knowing experiment.

formed by re-pairing words from related pairs. In the second phase of the experiment, a list of words presented for a test of recognition memory included one word from each pair intermixed with new words. For each word on that recognition-memory test, participants were to say "remember," "know," or "new," depending on their memory for the word. In the third and final phase of the experiment, participants were given a test of pair recognition. For that test, words tested in Phase 2 were presented with two alternative words, one of which had been presented with the tested word during study. For each pair of alternatives, one word was related to the test word whereas the other word was unrelated to the test word. Both of the alternatives had been presented during study. Subjects were to select the alternative that had been paired with the test word during study.

Our interest was in the extent to which Remember/Know judgments in Phase 2 predicted pair recognition performance in Phase 3. A finding that pair recognition was better for words called "know" when tested alone than for words called "new" would correspond to results reported for feeling-of-knowing judgments in studies of metacognition, because the subjective experience of memory for the cue in Phase 2 would predict recognition of the target in Phase 3.

Results (Table 13.3) showed that pair recognition was most accurate for words called "remember," next most accurate for words called "know," and poorest for words called "new" in Phase 2. These results were found both for words studied in related pairs and for those studied in unrelated pairs. However, pair recognition was higher for words studied in related pairs because participants showed a bias toward selecting the alternative that was semantically related to the test word.

The results of this experiment, therefore, show that "knowing" revealed by Remember/Know judgments predicts subsequent performance just as do feeling-of-knowing judgments. Furthermore, "remembering" predicts an even higher level of subsequent recognition of the target than does "knowing." This makes sense, because one important basis for the feeling of "remembering" the cue word is retrieval of the target word, although

TABLE 13.3
Probability of Correct Pair Recognition in Phase 3
as a Function of Memory Judgment in Phase 2

	Study Pair	
	Related	Unrelated
Judgment in Phase 2		
Remember	.94	.79
Know	.82	.65
New	.72	.59

the retrieval of any other context would also lead to a response of "remembering." However, to better understand those results, we need to understand the relationship between remembering and knowing.

Gardiner and his colleagues have emphasized the finding of dissociations between "remember" and "know" responses produced by manipulated variables. For example, they find that directions to forget reduces the probability of a "remember" response but does not change the probability of a "know" response. The dissociations between "remember" and "know" responses are likened to dissociations between performance on direct and indirect tests of memory. The finding for directed forgetting, for example, is treated much the same as would be a finding that directions to forget reduced performance on a direct test of memory but left performance on an indirect test unchanged. Knowing is identified with familiarity that reflects automatic influences of memory or implicit memory.

The next experiment that we describe is one that shows a dissociation between "remember" and "know" responses produced by the manipulation of the number of study presentations of an item. Words were presented one, two, or three times during study, and participants made remember/know judgments. Number of presentations influenced "remembering" but left the probability of a "know" judgment invariant (Table 13.4). If familiarity is identified with the probability of a "know" response, the conclusion is that familiarity is uninfluenced by the number of prior presentations of an item. That conclusion ought to be a difficult one to accept, and we return to it later.

The major reason for interest in introspective reports is that awareness serves as a basis for control of behavior. That this is the case is illustrated by Weiskrantz (1986) in his discussion of blindsight patients, who can make some accurate forced-choice decisions about visual events in the absence of the subjective experience of seeing. However, their visual abilities do not afford them meaningful control: Even if it could be shown that blindsight patients did well on an indirect test of seeing, one would not want to let them drive. We have done a number of experiments to show the relationship between the subjective report of recollection in the form of a "remember"

TABLE 13.4
The Relationship Between Remembering
and Knowing: Effects of Study Repetition

	Number of Study Presentations			
	1	*2*	*3*	*New*
Memory judgment				
Remember	.40	.51	.59	.01
Know	.35	.37	.35	.11

Study Two Lists of Words.

> List 1:   Read words one, two, or three presentations
>
> List 2:   Heard words.

**Exclusion Test: If word was heard, respond "Old."
                     If word was read, respond "New."**

> Group 1:   Short response deadline
>
> Group 2:   Long response deadline

FIG. 13.2. Outline of procedure for the experiment placing familiarity and recollection in opposition, with short versus long response deadline.

judgment, and the use of recollection as a basis for control of behavior, including the decision to withhold or produce a memory response. I (Jacoby) described some of those experiments during the CMU conference devoted to consciousness (Jacoby, Yonelinas, & Jennings, in press).

A next experiment was done to examine the effects of number of presentations on control of subsequent use of memory. Subjects read a list of words in which words were presented one, two, or three times, and then heard a second list of words (Fig. 13.2). An exclusion test condition was used to examine the effects of recollection on the control of behavior. For that test condition, participants were told to call an item old only if it was one that they heard in the experiment. They were warned that the test list would include words that they had read, and if they recollected earlier reading a word they could be certain that it was not one that they had heard. Consequently, participants should call an earlier-read word old only if it was familiar but they failed to recollect its earlier presentation. These requirements would seem to be roughly the same as the requirements for making a "know" response to a word.

The experiment was designed to show the existence of two memory processes by manipulating response deadline. Results showed that for a short deadline condition, increasing the number of presentations increased the probability of a read word being mistakenly accepted as heard, whereas the opposite was found when a long deadline was used (Table 13.5). That is, results from the short deadline showed that increasing the number of presentations increased familiarity. With a long deadline, the increase in familiarity was opposed by an increase in recollection that also resulted from increasing the number of study presentations. Reliance on recollection requires more time for responding than does a judgment based on familiarity.

We have done a large number of experiments of this sort. Dividing attention during study also reduces later recollection, but leaves familiarity

TABLE 13.5
The Advantage of Opposition of Familiarity and Recollection:
Effect of Short Versus Long Deadline to Respond on
Familiarity, as Assessed by Failure to Exclude Read Words

| | Number of Study Presentations | | | |
	1	2	3	New
Deadline				
Short	.38	.43	.47	.36
Long	.32	.29	.23	.14

intact just as does use of a short deadline. Also, words that are called "remember" on an earlier test are more likely to be correctly excluded on a later test than are words that are called "know." The opposition strategy used for these experiments is the same as for our "fame" experiments that we mentioned earlier.

Placing processes in opposition is sufficient to show the existence of two processes but does not allow one to measure their contribution to performance on a task. Performance on the exclusion task reflects the contribution of recollection as well as that of familiarity. To separate processes, one must make an assumption about their relationship.

Conclusions drawn from Remember/Know experiments differ with different assumptions about the relationship between processes. The major options are exclusivity, independence, or redundancy (see Jones, 1987). The way one calculates familiarity depends on the assumption one makes, and most research using the Remember/Know procedure has implicitly adopted an exclusivity assumption by identifying familiarity with the proportion of "know" responses, calculated as a straight proportion of the number of old items. This calculation presumes that the two processes cannot operate simultaneously. However, although the subjective experience of "remembering" probably overshadows the familiarity that is the basis for "knowing," it seems unlikely that the two processes cannot co-occur. Returning to the results of the experiment on the effects of study repetitions on "remember" versus "know," it is the exclusivity assumption that leads to the conclusion that familiarity, reflected by the probability of a "know" response, is invariant across number of repetitions. Under an independence assumption we reach a different conclusion: Both familiarity and recollection increased with number of presentations. For the independence assumption, one divides the probability of a "know" response by (1 – Remember) so as to take into account the opportunity for making such a response in the absence of "remembering."

A study of how the processes underlying "Remember" versus "Know" are affected by aging serves to further contrast the independence versus exclusivity assumptions. Experiments analyzed under the exclusivity assumption lead to the peculiar conclusion that aging produces a decrement in the process that gives rise to "remembering," but enhances the process that gives rise to "knowing" (Parkin & Walker, 1992). In contrast, experiments analyzed under the independence assumption find a decrement in "remembering" but no effect of aging on "knowing" (Jennings & Jacoby, 1993). Similarly, experiments analyzed under the exclusivity assumption find that presenting shapes in a different size rather than the same size at study and test paradoxically increased the familiarity of old shapes (Rajaram & Roediger, in press), whereas under the independence assumption changing the size decreased familiarity (Yonelinas & Jacoby, in press). It seems far more plausible that study/test similarity increases familiarity rather than decreases it. There is a great deal of converging evidence for the independence assumption (Jacoby, Yonelinas, & Jennings, in press).

The aforementioned results cast doubt on the claim that an event cannot be both remembered and familiar—the exclusivity assumption. How do those results relate to metacognitive judgments? It is standard to request FOK judgments only for questions that cannot be correctly answered. Thus, the relation between FOK judgments and correct responses is the same as that between Know and Remember judgments. Analyzing FOK without reference to the probability of correct responding relies on an exclusivity assumption of the form that correct responding cannot co-occur with the familiarity that underlies FOK. This assumption is unattractive because familiarity is also likely to accompany correct responses. Investigations of metamemory have generally not focused on the bases for making correct responses (for an exception, see Koriat, 1993, 1994). Such differences might be important, as an example, for explaining why prior presentation of the answer to a question increases the probability of correct responding but does not influence FOK (Schwartz & Metcalfe, 1992). That pattern of results is similar to the finding, described earlier, that repetition increases "remembering" but does not influence the probability of a "Know" response. Closer examination of the Remember/Know results suggested that the lack of a change in "knowing" with repetition was because the increase in familiarity underlying "know" responses was masked by an increase in recollection. Similarly, an increase in familiarity underlying FOK produced by prior presentation of the answer to a question might be masked by an increase in correct responding.

In studies of the TOT, the effect of variables such as number of study presentations (Smith, 1994) or the presence of a phonological or semantic cue word (Meyer & Bock, 1992) is also complicated by the effect of those variables on correct responding. If the number of study presentations increases the likelihood of a correct response, how can one interpret a decrease in the likelihood of a TOT experience? Obviously, when one can provide the name of an item, one is precluded from having a TOT experience. If in reality the TOT is based on cue familiarity or partial information, however, one would be incorrect in concluding that number of study presentations does not increase the basis for the TOT. Clearly, the assumptions one makes about the basis for the TOT and the basis for correct responding is critical for interpreting experiments.

SUMMARY AND CONCLUSIONS

Our general strategy has been to place processes in opposition as in the exclusion test paradigm to reveal the existence of separate processes and to produce illusions of memory. For example, one might use a manipulation of unconscious perception to produce false familiarity (Jacoby & Whitehouse, 1989). This approach differs from the strategy of examining how well feeling of knowing predicts subsequent behavior. However, the two approaches are clearly related. If one can produce false knowing, one knows the prediction gained from feeling of knowing is not a reading of a monitor in direct contact with the contents of memory, but is probably an inference or interpretation of certain evidence.

Are metacognition and implicit memory totally unrelated, or are the two topics so closely related that they must be treated within the same theoretical framework? Much of the excitement surrounding the dissociations that are taken as evidence for implicit memory stems from the possibility that we are pervasively and unconsciously influenced by past experiences. In contrast, metamemory research focuses on conscious experience. However, the importance of subjective experience is revealed by its absence as well as its presence. We have shown that subjective experience serves as a basis for judgments in a variety of domains, and along with others, speculate that subjective experience arises from a nonanalytic and unconscious inference or attribution.

We have generally avoided references to *implicit memory* and instead have preferred the term *automaticity*. One reason for this preference is that implicit memory implies a level of unity in its referents that we think is missing, whereas automaticity acknowledges that effects are task and situation specific. Here, again, there is a parallel to *metacognition*. That term also implies a unity of referents, perhaps linked by the operation of a servo-mechanism or monitor. For example, some have claimed that Korsakoff patients suffer a deficient monitor. We might instead focus on the basis for the Korsakoff patients' correct responses in the first phase of a feeling-of-knowing test to understand what remains to serve as a basis for their feeling-of-knowing judgments on items for which they make an error of commission or omission. Our assumption that subjective experience relies on an inference or attribution regarding various kinds of influences points to no single entity underlying subjective experience. Our strategy has been to unpack the different bases for judgments such as recognition memory and to attempt to understand the heuristics that give rise to various judgments. Errors that result from relying on an availability heuristic or accessibility heuristic are useful for revealing the basis for judgments, but do not reflect a deficient monitor.

REFERENCES

Begg, I., Anas, A., & Farinacci, S. (1992). Dissociation of processes in belief: Source recollection, familiarity and the illusion of truth. *Journal of Experimental Psychology: General, 121*, 446–458.

Begg, I., Armour, V., & Kerr, T. (1985). On believing what we remember. *Canadian Journal of Behavioral Science, 17*, 199–214.

Blaxton, T. A. (1989). Investigating dissociations among memory measures: Support for a transfer appropriate processing framework. *Journal of Experimental Psychology: Learning, Memory, and Cognition, 15*, 657–668.

Bornstein, R. F., & D'Agostino, P. R. (1994). The attribution and discounting of perceptual fluency: Preliminary tests of a perceptual fluency/attributional model of the mere exposure effect. *Social Cognition, 12*, 123–128.

Brennan, S. E., & Williams, M. (1995). The feeling of another's knowing: Prosody and filled pauses as cues to listeners about the metacognitive states of speakers. *Journal of Memory and Language, 34*, 383–398.

Brewer, W. F. (1992). Phenomenal experience in laboratory and autobiographical memory. In M. A. Conway, D. C. Rubin, H. Spinnler, & W. Wagenaar (Eds.), *Theoretical perspective on autobiographical memory*. The Netherlands: Kluwer.

Dovidio, J. F., & Fazio, R. H. (1991). New technologies for the direct and indirect assessment of attitudes. In J. Tanure (Ed.), *Questions about questions: Inquiries into the cognitive bases of surveys*. New York: Russell Sage Foundation.

Fussell, S. R., & Krauss, R. M. (1992). Coordination of knowledge in communication: Effects of speakers assumptions about what others know. *Journal of Personality and Social Psychology, 62*, 378–391.

Gardiner, J. M., & Java, R. I. (1993). Recognizing and remembering. In A. Collins, M. A. Conway, S. E. Gathercole, & P. E. Morris (Eds.), *Theories of memory* (pp. 163–188). Hillsdale, NJ: Lawrence Erlbaum Associates.

Goranson, R. E. (1985). *Studies of communication effectiveness*. Unpublished manuscript.

Hasher, L., Goldstein, D., & Toppino, T. (1977). Frequency and the conference of referential validity. *Journal of Verbal Learning and Verbal Behavior, 16*, 107–112.

Jacoby, L. L., Allan, L. G., Collins, J. C., & Larwill, L. K. (1988). Memory influences subjective experience: Noise judgments. *Journal of Experimental Psychology: Learning, Memory, and Cognition, 14*, 240–247.

Jacoby, L. L., & Brooks, L. R. (1984). Nonanalytic cognition: Memory, perception, and concept learning. In G. H. Bower (Ed.), *The psychology of learning and motivation: Advances in research and theory* (Vol. 18, pp. 1–47). New York: Academic Press.

Jacoby, L. L., & Dallas, M. (1981). On the relationship between autobiographical memory and perceptual learning. *Journal of Experimental Psychology: General, 3*, 306–340.

Jacoby, L. L., & Kelley, C. M. (1987). Unconscious influences of memory for a prior event. *Personality and Social Psychology Bulletin, 13*, 314–336.

Jacoby, L. L., Kelley, C. M., & Dywan, J. (1989). Memory attributions. In H. L. Roediger, III, & F. I. M. Craik (Eds.), *Varieties of memory and consciousness: Essays in honour of Endel Tulving* (pp. 391–422). Hillsdale, NJ: Lawrence Erlbaum Associates.

Jacoby, L. L., & Whitehouse, K. (1989). An illusion of memory: False recognition influenced by unconscious perception. *Journal of Experimental Psychology: General, 118*, 126–135.

Jacoby, L. L., Woloshyn, V., & Kelley, C. M. (1989). Becoming famous without being recognized: Unconscious influences of memory produced by dividing attention. *Journal of Experimental Psychology: General, 118*, 115–125.

Jacoby, L. L., Yonelinas, A. P., & Jennings, J. M. (in press). The relation between conscious and unconscious (automatic) influences: A declaration of independence. In J. Cohen & J. W. Schooler (Eds.), *Scientific approaches to the question of consciousness*. Mahwah, NJ: Lawrence Erlbaum Associates.

Jameson, A., Nelson, T. O., Leonesio, R. J., & Narens, L. (1993). The feeling of another person's knowing. *Journal of Memory and Language, 32*, 320–335.

Jennings, J. M., & Jacoby, L. L. (1993). Automatic versus intentional uses of memory: Aging, attention and control. *Psychology and Aging, 8*, 283–293.

Jones, G. V. (1987). Independence and exclusivity among psychological processes: Implications for the structure of recall. *Psychological Review, 94*, 229–235.

Kelley, C. M., & Jacoby, L. L. (1996). Adult egocentrism: Subjective experience versus analytic bases for judgment. *Journal of Memory and Language, 35*, 157–175.

Kelley, C. M., & Lindsay, D. S. (1993). Remembering mistaken for knowing: Ease of retrieval as a basis for confidence in answers to general knowledge questions. *Journal of Memory and Language, 32*, 1–24.

Koriat, A. (1993). How do we know that we know? The accessibility model of the feeling of knowing. *Psychological Review, 100*, 609–639.

Koriat, A. (1994). Memory's knowledge of its own knowledge: The accessibility account of the feeling of knowing. In J. Metcalfe & A. P. Shimamura (Eds.), *Metacognition: Knowing about knowing* (pp. 115–135). Cambridge, MA: Bradford.

Langer, E. J. (1989). *Mindfulness*. Reading, MA: Addison–Wesley.

Lindsay, D. S., & Kelley, C. M. (1996). Creating illusions of familiarity in a cued recall remember/know paradigm. *Journal of Memory and Language, 35*, 197–211.

Metcalfe, J., Schwartz, B. L., & Joaquim, S. G. (1993). The cue-familiarity heuristic in metacognition. *Journal of Experimental Psychology: Learning, Memory, and Cognition, 19*, 851–861.

Meyer, A. S., & Bock, K. (1992). The tip-of-the-tongue phenomenon: Blocking or partial activation? *Memory & Cognition, 20*, 715–726.

Nelson, T. O., & Narens, L. (1990). Metamemory: A theoretical framework and new findings. In G. Bower (Ed.), *The psychology of learning and motivation* (Vol. 26, pp. 125–173). New York: Academic Press.

Nickerson, R. S., Baddeley, A., & Freeman, B. (1987). Are people's estimates of what other people know influenced by what they themselves know? *Acta Psychologica, 64*, 245–259.

Parkin, A. J., & Walker, B. (1992). Recollective experience, normal aging, and frontal dysfunction. *Psychology and Aging, 7*, 290–298.

Rajaram, S. (1993). Remembering and knowing: Two means of access to the personal past. *Memory & Cognition, 21*, 89–102.

Rajaram, S., & Roediger, H. L., III (in press). In J. Cohen & J. W. Schooler (Eds.), *Scientific approaches to the question of consciousness*. Mahwah, NJ: Lawrence Erlbaum Associates.

Reder, L. M., & Ritter, F. E. (1992). What determines initial feeling of knowing? Familiarity with question terms, not with the answer. *Journal of Experimental Psychology: Learning, Memory, and Cognition, 18*, 435–451.

Ross, L., Green, D., & House, P. (1977). The "false consensus" effect: An egocentric bias in social perception and attribution processes. *Journal of Experimental Social Psychology, 13,* 279–301.

Schwartz, B. L., & Metcalfe, J. (1992). Cue familiarity but not target retrievability enhances feeling-of-knowing judgments. *Journal of Experimental Psychology: Learning, Memory, and Cognition, 18,* 1074–1083.

Seamon, J. G., Williams, P. C., Crowley, M. J., Kim, I. J., Langer, S. A., Orne, P. J., & Wishengrad, D. L. (1995). The mere exposure effect is based on implicit memory: Effects of stimulus type, encoding conditions, and number of exposures on recognition and affect judgments. *Journal of Experimental Psychology: Learning, Memory, and Cognition, 21,* 711–721.

Smith, S. M. (1994). Frustrated feelings of imminent recall: On the tip of the tongue. In J. Metcalfe & A. P. Shimamura (Eds.), *Metacognition: Knowing about knowing* (pp. 27–45). Cambridge, MA: Bradford.

Tulving, E. (1985). Memory and consciousness. *Canadian Psychologist, 26,* 1–12.

Weiskrantz, L. (1986). *Blindsight: A case study and implications.* Oxford, England: Oxford University Press.

Whittlesea, B. W. A. (1993). Illusions of familiarity. *Journal of Experimental Psychology: Learning, Memory, and Cognition, 19,* 1235–1253.

Whittlesea, B. W. A., Jacoby, L. L., & Girard, K. A. (1990). Illusions of immediate memory: Evidence of an attributional basis for feelings of familiarity and perceptual quality. *Journal of Memory and Language, 29,* 716–732.

Wilson, T. D., & Schooler, J. W. (1991). Thinking too much: Introspection can reduce the quality of preferences and decisions. *Journal of Personality and Social Psychology, 60,* 181–192.

Witherspoon, D., & Allan, L. G. (1985). The effects of prior presentation on temporal judgments in a perceptual identification task. *Memory & Cognition, 13,* 101–111.

Yonelinas, A. P., & Jacoby, L. L. (in press). The relation between remembering and knowing as bases for recognition: Effects of size congruency. *Journal of Memory and Language.*

Chapter 14

Retrieval Fluency as a Metacognitive Index

Aaron S. Benjamin
Robert A. Bjork
University of California, Los Angeles

How readily information "comes to mind" is one index humans use to assess the accuracy of that information and, more generally, the adequacy of their own state of knowledge in a given domain. Such *retrieval fluency* provides, in fact, a useful heuristic: In general, information that is better learned, more recent, and more strongly associated to the cues guiding recall (or any combination of the three) will tend to be more readily retrievable. Fluent retrieval can, however, reflect factors unrelated to accuracy or degree of prior learning. In that sense, making appropriate use of retrieval fluency (or the lack thereof) as a metacognitive index becomes a problem of inference.

There are both practical and theoretical reasons why it is important to understand the metacognitive assumptions that underlie such inferential processes. On the practical side, understanding these processes can enable us to better construct regimens of training and practice that educate the learner's *subjective experience* as well as objective performance. As Jacoby, Bjork, and Kelley (1994) have emphasized recently, the reading an individual takes of his or her level of comprehension and competence can be as important as his or her actual comprehension or competence. The kinds of tasks for which we volunteer, whether we seek additional instruction, and whether we see ourselves "fit" for a difficult task, all rest on our reading of our state of knowledge or efficiency. To the degree that such readings may be in error, we can become a liability or hazard to ourselves and others, particularly in real-world settings such as air-traffic control and police work, where mistakes can be devastating.

From a theoretical standpoint, understanding the metacognitive assumptions that underlie the interpretation of subjective indices, such as retrieval fluency, has the potential to reveal how our mental model of ourselves as learners and rememberers succeeds and fails in capturing the complexity of our own memory. Because such an interpretation guides the selection and execution of control processes relevant to learning and remembering, understanding this mental model may provide insight into traditional failures in self-paced learning and memory use.

In the next several sections we summarize how fluency—perceptual fluency as well as retrieval fluency—influences (and sometimes misleads) a variety of metacognitive judgments. The latter half of the chapter presents a series of assumptions that appear to underlie the occasional misreliance on retrieval fluency as a predictive index. We demonstrate that subjects utilize retrieval fluency in their metamnemonic assessments, not only in circumstances in which retrieval fluency is an unreliable index, but also in circumstances where it provides for *completely backwards predictions*. That is, the reliance on retrieval fluency can apparently supercede other metamnemonic strategies to the point that subjects predict high future retention for items which they are unlikely to retain, and low future retention for items which they indeed are likely to retain.

USING ONE INDEX TO PREDICT ANOTHER

In general, we face an inferential problem when making judgments about the objective nature of a perception or a memory. In some sense, this problem may be dubbed the "New Look" at metacognition: We realize that our perceptions and memories are heavily influenced not just by the objective event or knowledge, but also by the host of previous experiences we bring to bear on that mental event. Judgments thus become inferences of how we think the world might be or how extensive we think our knowledge might be, given subjective data concerning the ease with which we perceive a stimulus or retrieve a memory. This task is accomplished by utilizing subjective indices—such as ease of perception or ease of retrieval— to predict the objective nature of events or memories.

Perceptual Fluency

The arguments we present in this chapter have been motivated in part by recent advances in the understanding of misattributions in memory (e.g., Jacoby & Kelley, 1987) and metamemory (e.g., Reder & Ritter, 1992; Schwartz & Metcalfe, 1992). This body of work has demonstrated that perceptual fluency—the sense of familiarity that a stimulus evokes, or ease with which a stimulus can be *perceived*—affects subjects' metacognitive judgments of their current level of knowledge and their future performance. In that sense, it may be said that perceptual fluency serves as a metamnemonic heuristic. Before we turn to an analysis of retrieval fluency as a heuristic, it is useful to summarize the influence of perceptual fluency on metacognitive judgments, because those influences illustrate inferential processes analogous to those we argue apply to retrieval fluency.

Misattributing Perceptual Fluency to Stimulus Characteristics. Jacoby and his colleagues (e.g., Jacoby, Allan, Collins, & Larwill, 1988) have documented a number of ways that the ease with which a subject perceives a stimulus affects metacognitive judgments. Although it is fairly useful to assume that the clarity with which a stimulus that is perceived reflects an underlying property thereof, such as accuracy or clarity, such may not always be the case. The oversimplicity of such a heuristic is clearly evidenced in the following demonstrations.

In an experiment by Jacoby et al. (1988), subjects were presented a series of trials on each of which a spoken sentence was played against a background of white noise. Some of the sentences (the *primed* sentences) had been exposed earlier in an ostensibly unrelated exercise and others had not. Subjects were asked to evaluate the level of background noise during each sentence presentation. Given the prior exposure, we can assume that subjects heard the primed sentences more clearly than the unprimed sentences. They attributed that subjective difference, however, not to its actual cause, but rather to a difference in the level of background noise—they rated the background noise as lower for the previously heard sentences than for the novel ones.

In another experiment, Witherspoon and Allan (1985) had subjects perform a perceptual identification task in which words were presented at very rapid rates and subjects were asked to identify the words if they could. The subjects were also asked to estimate the exposure duration for each word. Consistent with noise-judgment findings, subjects rated previously exposed words as having had a longer exposure duration than did non-primed words. Again, the subjects misattribute an influence of prior priming to a stimulus characteristic—in this case, prolonged exposure time.

Such demonstrations illustrate the inferential nature of introspections. Attributions concerning the nature of one's performance are made to some degree "on the fly," and are easily misled in contrived experimental situations. However, these misattributions are even more dangerous when subjects make judgments concerning their own state of learning. Some evidence suggests that just such a reliance on perceptual fluency may underly errors in metacognition.

Misattributing Perceptual Fluency to One's State of Learning. Recent work (e.g., Reder & Ritter, 1992; Schwartz & Metcalfe, 1992) has demonstrated clearly that *feeling-of-knowing* (FOK) judgments are influenced by perceptual fluency. This phenomenon has been termed the *cue-familiarity effect.* Consider the following example from Reder (1987).

In Reder's "game-show" paradigm, subjects make rapid judgments as to whether or not they think they will be able to answer a given question. Such judgments can be made more quickly than actually producing the answer, yet are often of considerable accuracy. Reder found that priming words (like *golf* and *par*) that were to appear in questions such as "What is the term in golf for one under par?" led to increased subjective estimates of knowing the answer, despite the fact that such prior exposure did not alter actual rates of producing the correct answer at all!

Schwartz and Metcalfe (1992) manipulated both cue and response term accessibility in a paired-associate recall task. Targets were either generated or read during learning, and cue words were either preexposed in a previous pleasantness-rating task or not. Their results demonstrated that only cue priming (affecting perceptual fluency) and not target retrievability affected FOK judgments. Reder and Ritter (1992) found a similar effect using arithmetic problems as stimuli—prior exposure to the terms (but not necessarily the operand!) in a problem increased estimates of the retrievability of the answer from memory.

These examples illustrate that using perceptual fluency as a basis for judgments about the objective nature of perceptual events, or about the objective state of one's knowledge, is subject to inferential errors. Because we often fail to understand that prior exposure facilitates perception, we misattribute such perceptual fluency to other factors, such as physical aspects of the stimulus (e.g., loudness or duration) or knowledge that we do not actually have. The remainder of this chapter focuses on how *retrieval fluency*—the ease with which information is accessed from memory—affects metamemory in similar ways. Attributing retrieval fluency to one's state of knowledge when, in fact, that fluency arises from sources unrelated to one's knowledge state, can be at least as insidious—and in applied settings, at least as dangerous (Jacoby et al., 1994).

Retrieval Fluency

From a phenomenological perspective, we are all aware that some things seem to "come to mind" more easily than others. We are inclined to relate this ease to our level of knowledge—we know our own phone number better (usually) than we know our friends' numbers; thus its retrieval is marked by greater facility. Not surprisingly, this relationship appears in controlled experiments: Overlearned information is retrieved more quickly and with greater accuracy than less well-learned information (e.g., Nelson, Leonesio, Shimamura, Landwehr, & Narens, 1982).

As stated earlier, one goal of the remainder of this analysis is to outline cases in which humans seem to use retrieval fluency as a metacognitive index. A parallel goal is to consider those cases in which monitoring the dynamics of retrieval provides the metacognizer with misinformation. Using one index to predict another illustrates a failure to appreciate differences between the predictive task and the to-be-predicted behavior and illuminates aspects of human memory, the complexities of which are clearly often misunderstood by its users.

First, however, it is important for the purposes of the present analysis to more precisely define what we mean by *retrieval fluency*. Moreover, we review some important *objective* determinants of retrieval fluency.

THE DEFINITION AND DETERMINANTS OF RETRIEVAL FLUENCY

Aspects of Fluent Retrieval

When we speak of "fluent" retrieval of information in response to a cue, three characteristics of access are relevant.

Latency. First, we can speak of how quickly information is accessed by a certain cue. Given the cue *early American presidents*, for example, we typically experience greater fluency of access for George Washington and Thomas Jefferson than for John Quincy Adams and Andrew Jackson. The latter names can indeed be recalled, but typically only after a greater delay than their more accessible counterparts.

Persistence. Second is the persistence of the information that does come to mind. When asked to recall wars in which the United States has been involved in the current century, a Vietnam veteran may find that particular war coming to mind more often than would a veteran of the Second World War. We would thus infer greater fluency of access to the Vietnam War for the Vietnam vet than by a World War II vet.

Amount. Third, retrieval fluency involves the raw amount of information accessed by a given retrieval cue. A teenager may thus have greater retrieval fluency for rock-and-roll artists than composers of baroque music, whereas that relationship might reverse for one or both of his or her parents.

High retrieval fluency thus generally refers to retrieval which is quick, persistent, abundant with information, or any combination of those three effects. We turn now to a cursory discussion of the determinants of retrieval fluency.

Objective Determinants of Fluent Retrieval

We began our discussion of the retrieval-fluency heuristic by noting that reliance on such an index is, in general, not a bad idea. In fact, the ease with which we retrieve information is often closely related to the levels of knowledge and surety appropriate for metamnemonic judgments and the selection and execution of control processes. The following paragraphs delineate some of the major determinants of retrievability and retrieval fluency.

Degree of Learning. In general, speed and the reliability of access to information will, indeed, be correlated with levels of learning. How elaborated a learned representation is in terms of linkage to other concepts and schemas will also influence the reliability of access to that representation and the amount of information retrieved.

Frequency and Recency of Usage. The act of retrieval itself makes the retrieved information more retrievable in the future, as we stress later in this chapter. Information that is accessed frequently, especially in multiple contexts, will tend to be retrieved fluently in the future. The current fluency of access to information in memory will also be influenced by the recency of prior access.

Episodic Distinctiveness. A factor that influences ease of access to episodic traces is episodic distinctiveness. Uniqueness, salience, emotionality, temporal isolation, and other factors all play a role in the extent to which an event is "distinct." The relatively ready access to "flashbulb memories," such as where one was and what one was doing when one heard that the space shuttle Challenger exploded, is one example of the influence of such episodic distinctiveness.

Cue Sufficiency. Retrieval processes are driven by cues, and fluency of access to information is heavily influenced by the effectiveness of those cues. The effectiveness of a cue or configuration of cues depends, in turn, on such factors as strength of association of the target information to the cue(s) in question, and the extent to which that information is uniquely associated to that (those) cue(s). When there is competition; that is, when cues are associated to multiple items in memory, retrieval of any given item is slower and less reliable. This principle is consistent with the notion of *cue overload* (see e.g., Watkins & Watkins, 1975; cf. fan effect, Anderson,

1974)—that a cue loses its potency in evoking any given response when associated with a greater number of potential responses.

Priming. Finally, prior presentation of some target item, even if that presentation occurs in a context nominally unrelated to a current task of some kind, has been shown to increase the speed and frequency with which that item, among other possible items, is accessed in response to a cue that is part of the task in question.

It is clear that many of the characteristics which make retrieval fluent are ones that are entirely appropriate to rely on as an index of what we know, or how well we know it. Because, however, spurious factors do influence retrieval fluency, it is also possible that metacognitive predictions which are driven by subjective assessments of retrieval fluency can be misled. The following section reviews evidence which appears to support the proposition that retrieval fluency is used as a heuristic tool—and that it often fails in circumstances where retrieval fluency derives from a confluence of factors, some of which are related to degree of learning, and some of which are not.

RETRIEVAL FLUENCY AS A HEURISTIC

Confidence in Retrieved Answers

Costermans, Lories, and Ansay (1992, Experiment 1) provide evidence for a strong relationship between the latency to answer a question and the confidence one has in that answer. Subjects in their experiment answered a series of general-information questions and rated their confidence in those answers. Costermans et al. found a strongly negative gamma correlation (G) between response latency and confidence (G = ~ −.5). Open to interpretation, of course, is the nature of the relationship: Are response speed and judged confidence *both* a function of actual accuracy of the answer, are we more confident in answers *because* we produce them quickly, or are we just more quick to provide answers in which we have high confidence? Several pieces of evidence bear on this question.

First, Costermans et al. (1992) found that the relationship between response latency and confidence held for both correct and incorrect answers. If, indeed, a third variable, such as response accuracy, wholly mediated the observed correlation, then we would expect a greatly attenuated effect for incorrect answers. In fact, in their data, Costermans et al. found the relationship to be somewhat stronger for incorrect answers.

Even more convincing is a demonstration by Kelley and Lindsay (1993). They had subjects answer questions such as "What was Buffalo Bill's last name?" For each such question, during a prior phase of the experiment, subjects were preexposed to either a correct answer (Cody), a plausible but incorrect answer (Hickock), or an unrelated term (Letterman). With respect to the former two conditions, they found that subjects who provided the primed name were more confident than if they had not been primed—*regardless of whether that answer was correct.* In other words, increasing the retrieval fluency for an answer via priming increased confidence in that answer independent of the correctness of that answer. In a subsequent experiment, the authors actually made explicit that the preexposed words contained answers, some correct, some incorrect, to the questions to be asked. Alerting subjects to that fact did not change the basic pattern of results. Such demonstrations clearly indicate that subjects use the speed of retrieving an answer to a question as a basis for confidence in the accuracy of that answer.

A further demonstration by Shaw (1996) illustrates the manner in which such misguided confidence may have real-world consequences. Subjects in Shaw's experiment were exposed to the aftermath of a mock crime presented on a series of slides. After viewing the "crime scene," they were questioned about objects present or absent in the scene. In the interval separating the two questioning sessions, half of the subjects were asked to think about the event and carefully consider the answers they had previously provided and whether or not those answers were indeed correct. Both those subjects and the control subjects (who engaged in various unrelated distractor tasks during the same period) were then asked the same questions again. Both groups chose the same answers again most of the time, but the subjects asked to "mull over" their answers were more confident in those answers at the time of the second test, even though the actual accuracy of those answers was not different. We argue that the "mere thought" manipulation increased the retrieval fluency of the answers chosen earlier, thereby increasing confidence. The similarities between Shaw's mere-thought condition and the common experience of an actual crime eyewitness who is typically subjected over and over to interrogations and discussions about a crime further substantiates the importance of understanding the heuristic inferential nature of such metacognitions.

Koriat, Lichtenstein, and Fischhoff (1980) provided a theory for the basis of confidence that is relevant to such findings. They attempt to explain the perpetual overconfidence subjects exhibit (a) in the accuracy of their beliefs (e.g., Fischhoff, Slovic, & Lichtenstein, 1977) and (b) the degree to which those beliefs are representative of the beliefs of others (as in the *false consensus effect,* e.g., Marks & Miller, 1985). In their theory, people are overconfident because they selectively come up with reasons consistent with the answer they have provided. Support for such an interpretation derives from several findings that forcing subjects to provide an equal number of reasons for and against a proposition attenuates the overconfidence bias. By the present reasoning, we would argue that reasons that support answers that had been provided are retrieved more fluently than reasons to the contrary. Whether such fluency is the basis for confidence, or arises as a function of committing oneself to a decision, is unclear.

Estimation Biases

In their seminal analysis of probability estimation, Tversky and Kahneman (1974) documented a number of ways in which such assessments may go awry. One oft-cited bias lies in the use of the *availability heuristic*. This heuristic involves using the ease with which an instance of an event comes to mind as a basis for estimating the probability of that event. Consider a case in which subjects are asked, for each of the following, to judge the number of words present in a typical four-page segment of a novel which would satisfy the fragment constraints provided (from Tversky & Kahneman, 1983):

(a) -----n- (b) -----ing

The first fragment conjures up little, if anything, in the way of specific completions. After some effort, one may generate a few instances, but their retrieval is marked by considerable difficulty. The second example, however, evokes a great number of immediate candidates. It does so probably because it somewhat constrains the potential response set to familiar gerunds, such as *running* or *playing*. However, because the set of completions for fragment (b) is a logical subset of the set of completions for (a), it is obvious that fragment (a) allows for a greater number of completions. The merits of logical reasoning notwithstanding, subjects typically estimate a larger number of word responses for (b), thus exhibiting a preference for a suboptimal decision strategy that utilizes retrieval fluency over an infallible one that involves syllogistic reasoning.

Such misestimation is also evident in the evaluation of accident probabilities. Subjects are quite likely to underestimate the probability of being in an automobile accident; however, they typically overestimate the probability of being in a plane crash. The explanation provided by Tversky and Kahneman lies in the differential salience of the events: Plane crashes receive more media attention and are a more "glamorous" event. These kinds of events "pop to mind" more quickly and, by the present analysis, are misinterpreted on that basis as being more frequent.

Predicting Future Performance

Feeling-of-Knowing Phenomena. The feeling-of-knowing (FOK) phenomenon was first documented by Hart (1965). In his experiments, the procedure of which is quite similar to the more recent studies discussed later, subjects first attempted to answer a number of general-information questions. For those cases in which they were unsuccessful (when they provided either an incorrect answer or no answer at all), they then indicated whether they felt that they would or would not be able to recognize the correct answer among four alternatives. In fact, subjects were quite able to predict their own later recognition performance.

Explanations of the FOK effect have typically fallen into two major categories: *trace-access* theories and *inferential* theories (Nelson, Gerler, & Narens, 1984). Trace-access theories view the metacognizer as having some access to the object of judgment (i.e., the memory trace under evaluation) that serves as a basis for prediction. Such theories posit a monitor that has access to aspects of memory that cannot be accessed via conventional attempts to recall. Trace-access explanations have historically been invoked (e.g., Hart, 1965) to explain why, in the absence of recall, subjects can nonetheless discriminate between cases where they will and will not be able to recognize an answer.

Inferential theories involve the overt stipulation that no such privileged access exists. They posit, instead, an inferential basis for metamnemonic judgments. An example is the idea that retrieval-cue familiarity affects subjects' decisions about the impending retrievability of an associated target (Reder & Ritter, 1992; Schwartz & Metcalfe, 1992). Central to such theories is the heuristic nature of such judgments; because predictions are *inferred*, they are fallible and open to being misled.

It is not the goal of the present chapter to argue the relative merits of trace-access and inferential theories, but we take as a working assumption that metacognitive judgments are inferential in nature. In that context, the question of interest to us is a paradox of sorts: How is the claim to be made that retrieval fluency serves as the basis for FOK judgments when there is, by definition, no retrieval of the to-be-judged answer prior to those judgments?

One argument has been that the FOK derives from partial information retrieval. Presumably, in a paradigm like the one of Hart (1965), enough information relevant to the answer comes to mind to support a FOK judgment, but not enough to form a coherent answer. Support for such an idea was presented by Blake (1973) in his analysis of partial response production in the retrieval of nonsense trigrams. He found that higher FOK ratings were given to nonrecalled trigrams for which one or more of the correct letters could be provided. Similar results were reported by Schacter and Worling (1985) using less abstract stimuli. In their study, subjects studied unrelated paired associates, the targets for which were of either a "good" (e.g., *happy*) or a "bad" (e.g., *terrible*) connotation. Schacter and Worling found that FOK ratings were higher for those unrecalled targets for which the affective connotation could be produced.

Several other experiments provide results consistent with the proposal of Blake and Schacter and Worling. Nelson et al. (1982) showed that items learned to a higher criterion (4 correct recalls) evoked greater FOKs when unrecalled than other items learned to a lower criterion (1 correct recall). The difference between the two sets of items is not apparent in the actual production of an intact answer, but those item sets are likely to differ in the extent to which partial information is retrieved. Another example that "better" processing leads to higher FOK judgments is provided by Lupker, Harbluk, and Patrick (1991), who demonstrated that deeper levels of processing resulted in higher FOK judgments than did more shallow levels. Also consistent with the notion of partial retrieval serving FOK judgments is the finding that errors of *commission* evoke greater FOKs than errors of *omission*, even when subjects are informed of the incorrectness of their answer (Krinsky & Nelson, 1985).

A potential problem with the notion that partial information retrieval underlies FOK judgments is that it seems to blur the distinction between trace-access and inferential theories. If the partial information that does come to mind cannot contribute to the selection of an answer, how does the monitor "know" that such information is related to the answer? Do we need to posit a monitoring homunculus that has access to retrieval information that the response-production homunculus does not? A resolution of this sticky issue is provided by Koriat (1993, 1995).

Koriat's answer, put simply, is that the monitor does not, in fact, "know" anything about the relationship between the partial information retrieved and the currently unproducible correct answer. In his theory, FOK judgments are supported by the raw amount of information that comes to mind in response to a cue—whether that information is correct or incorrect. The following experiment supports this notion convincingly.

As material for his experiments, Koriat (1995) developed a series of questions that varied on two dimensions: *accessibility* (ACC) and *output-bound accuracy* (OBA). Accessibility refers to the number of responses that the questions evoked; some questions elicited many responses and others few. Output-bound accuracy refers to the proportion of answers to a given question that were correct; questions which were most often answered correctly when they were answered at all were said to have high OBA; questions principally answered falsely when an answer was given were said to have low OBA. Koriat's results are reproduced in Fig. 14.1.

As shown in Fig. 14.1, items that differ in ACC levels evoke very different FOK judgments. In general, high ACC translates into high FOK judgments. Items that have high ACC and high OBA (*consensually correct*, or CC, items) provide for accurate FOK judgments: High predicted accuracy translates into actual success on the to-be-predicted recognition test. However, items that are high ACC but low OBA (*consensually wrong*, or CW, items) yield

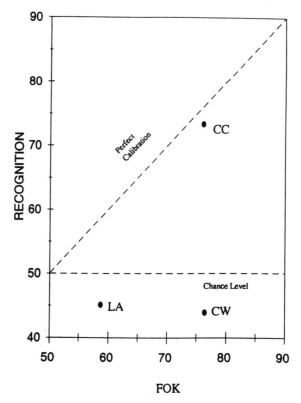

FIG. 14.1. Recognition scores and FOK ratings for consensually correct (CC), consensually wrong (CW), and low accessibility (LA) items. Adapted from Koriat (1995). Reproduced with permission.

judgments of future performance that are wild overestimates. In fact, recognition accuracy is not above chance for such items. Koriat uses such a demonstration to support the idea that the feeling of knowing derives from sources different than actual knowing. Namely, it is argued that FOK arises as a result of ready recall of some information, right or wrong.

Judgments of Learning. Judgments of learning (JOLs) involve having the subject evaluate the level of his or her knowledge during the course of learning. In a typical paradigm, subjects might cycle through a list of words and, after studying each word, estimate their probability of being able to free recall that word at some future time. Subjects do so with above-chance accuracy (e.g., Lovelace, 1984), and their predictions seem to take into account more than the current recallability of the item (Mazzoni & Nelson, 1995).

Again, however, it appears as though retrieval fluency serves as a potent cue for such judgments. Lee, Narens, and Nelson (1993, as cited in Narens,

Jameson, & Lee, 1994) demonstrated a case in which a temporary enhancement of retrieval fluency misleads JOLs. In their experiment, subjects studied paired associates and, 3–5 minutes after the presentation of a particular pair, engaged in the prediction task. In that task, they were presented with just the cue word and asked to estimate their probability of being able to recall the target. The clever twist in the Lee et al. experiment, however, involved a subthreshold presentation of some of the correct target words immediately prior to the prediction. In those cases, Lee et al. hypothesized that the priming would influence target retrieval in such a manner as to temporarily inflate JOLs. In fact, their results bore this idea out: JOLs were indeed higher for the primed items, yet the "transitory nature of this kind of priming effect" left the final-recall rates unaltered. Clearly, potent but fleeting changes in retrieval fluency profoundly affect JOLs.

The conceptualization of retrieval fluency as a basis for the JOL also suggests an interpretation of a phenomenon that has been seen somewhat as an enigma in the JOL literature. Dunlosky and Nelson (1992, see also Nelson & Dunlosky, 1991) described what has been called the "delayed-JOL" effect. This "effect" refers to the fact that JOLs are (a) more accurate when the subject is presented with only the cue and not the target when making their prediction and (b) more accurate at a delay than immediately after study.

An evaluation of these circumstances makes it clear that, for the prediction to be accurate, two sources of information have to be intact. First, there must be *retrieval.* When subjects are presented with the entire cue–target pair, the necessity of retrieval and thus its diagnostic value are obviated. Subjects are thus deprived of the intact subjective experience that would inform their JOL. Second, there must be a degree of *fluency* that matches the degree on the impending test. That is, immediate predictions are clouded by recency and other factors that attenuate the diagnosticity of the retrieval. If subjects are in a situation in which their retrieval fluency is in fact predictive of later retrieval probability (as is more likely to be true in the cue-only, delayed prediction case), their predictions will be more accurate. Conversely, experimentally making retrieval fluency non-diagnostic leads to poorer predictions.

USING CURRENT FLUENCY AS A PREDICTOR OF LATER FLUENCY

Clearly, it makes sense to use retrieval fluency as an indicator of what we know. More often than not, the factors that currently support retrieval will act to support retrieval in the future as well. Using such a heuristic in a given situation, however, reflects the tacit belief that certain assumptions have been met. Those assumptions include:

1. That the retrieval cues at the to-be-predicted time, and the retrieval task itself, will not differ substantially from the current cues and task, OR that any such differences will not measurably affect performance.
2. That events and the passage of time between now and the later task of interest will not alter the relative accessibility of competing representations in memory.
3. That the act of retrieval during prediction does not appreciably affect the relative ease of access to competing representations at the later time of interest.

In any predictive task, these assumptions may or may not hold; when they do, current retrieval fluency will be a good index of later performance. There is, however, considerable evidence that *none* of the preceding assumptions are always valid, and, in fact, that their being true simultaneously may be the exception rather than the rule. The following sections treat each of these assumptions in turn.

Conditions Now Versus Conditions Later

In general, our performance on a given task at a given time will be sensitive to the variety of cues available to us at that time, including environmental, social, body-state, and mood-state cues, as well as task-specific cues. The first assumption may fail to hold because the later task setting, although nominally the same as the current setting, may actually differ significantly in the cues that are or are not available. That assumption may also fail because the task itself, although nominally the same or similar to the current retrieval task, may actually differ in ways that fundamentally alter the nature of the retrieval process.

Overlap of Cues. It has been pointed out by a number of writers (for a recent example, see Christina & Bjork, 1991) that every test of retention is actually a test of transfer. The point is that the conditions at the time of any later test will necessarily differ from present conditions, if for no other reason than that the performer himself or herself will not be exactly the "same" person in terms of body state, mood state, and mental set. In addition, superficial and not-so-superficial cues may also differ. A retention test therefore becomes a test of whether performance will transfer to a situation that is functionally new, at least to some extent, even if nominally the same.

From a research standpoint, we have known for decades that the ability to retrieve learned information is sensitive to the overlap of cues between a current learning or test environment and some later criterion time. McGeogh (1932), for example, cited "altered stimulating conditions" as one factor in his three-factor theory of forgetting. He argued that one factor responsible for forgetting is the extent to which the stimulus conditions at test differ from those present at learning. The experimental findings that gave rise to Tulving and Thomson's (1973) *encoding specificity principle* are one clear illustration of such effects.

From the standpoint of our own experience, however, there are indications that we fail to appreciate the extent to which our access to skills and knowledge may falter as conditions change. In real-world training environments, it is a continuing surprise and frustration to training personnel that their trainees, who may have passed every criterion test with ease at the end of training, frequently make on-the-job errors under new or unanticipated conditions, even when those conditions seem to differ only superficially from the conditions of training (for a discussion of such training issues, see Christina & Bjork, 1991, and Reder & Klatzky, 1994). Trainees themselves—with hindsight—are often in fact dismayed that they were unable to access the appropriate procedure or knowledge in some new situation. In effect, as metacognizers, we do not fully realize the extent to which our present performance is tied to present cues.

Overlap of Tasks. We may also fail to realize the extent to which some current task—our performance, which serves as the basis for predicting our future performance—may differ from some later task in the demands it places, or does not place, on our memories. In general, when using current retrieval fluency as an index, we are subject to a certain misconception about memory—namely, that performance on different tasks derive from the same underlying memory traces, which vary in strength on a unidimensional continuum.

Contemporary memory research has produced a variety of results that discredit any such construct of strength unidimensionality. Associationist notions of "strength" fail to explain important phenomena in both human and animal learning (e.g., blocking, Kamin, 1969). The following phenomena are among those that demonstrate the multidimensionality of human memory.

The *word-frequency paradox* is one such result. When subjects study a list of both high- and low-frequency words, they are more able to produce the high-frequency items on a test of free recall. On a recognition test, however, low-frequency words are better recognized than high-frequency words. If recall and recognition both reflect the strength of a unidimensional trace, such a pattern could not obtain.

More recently, much interest has been devoted to understanding dissociations between *explicit* and *implicit* tests of memory. Explicit tests, such as
recall or recognition, overtly stipulate that subjects should access their
memory for a given prior episode. Implicit tasks involve the measurement
of performance on a task that is nominally unrelated to some prior episode
of interest. For example, subjects may be asked to resolve a lexically
ambiguous sentence. The measure of "performance" is the degree to which
the "primed" group—the group that was exposed to a study episode of some
sort—has a greater proclivity than a control group to disambiguate the
sentence in a manner influenced by their prior study. Such influences
typically happen in the absence of the subject recognizing any overt
contingency between the study and test episodes; in fact, often, in such
experiments, the two phases are deliberately contrived so as to appear
unrelated.

Clear dissociations have been found in which manipulations affect performance on an explicit test in one way and, on an implicit test, in an
opposite way. For example, the *generation effect* (Slamecka & Graf, 1978)—
that recall or recognition is typically better for items that are generated
rather than read—may turn to a real advantage on indirect tests such as
perceptual identification (Jacoby, 1983).

It is outside the mission of this chapter to document in any detail the
variety of dissociations that have been demonstrated on direct and indirect
tests of memory. The important point is that there is abundant evidence
that memory is multidimensional. Although there is no clear consensus
on the number of dimensions necessary to fully explain the wealth of data
on memory, estimates of such a number have ranged as high as 50 (Tulving,
1983). It should suffice to say that performance on one test does not
necessarily predict performance on another.

Changes in Fluency With Time and Intervening Events

To argue that we *forget* is to engage in egregious understatement. A
fundamental quality of human memory (and potentially an adaptive one;
see Bjork, 1989) is that the ease with which we access information from
long-term memory decreases with disuse of that information over time. As
is evident from Ebbinghaus' classic work on nonsense syllable learning,
our ability to retrieve learned information can drop dramatically with the
passage of time. Classic work on interference processes, and more recent
work on retrieval dynamics, make it clear, however, that time itself is not
the crucial factor responsible for changes in retrieval access over time.

Unlearning and Spontaneous Recovery. The research of Postman, Underwood, and others using paired-associate paradigms, such as the A–B, A–C
paradigm, demonstrates the importance of cue uniqueness in the elicita-

tion of a paired target term (for a review, see Postman, 1971). The pairing of a cue with a new target term impairs cued recall of the original response, thus producing retroactive interference. Clearly, however, memory does not work so simply as to "overwrite" the old information—with the passage of time and the forgetting of more newly paired responses, *spontaneous recovery* of the original target terms is evident. Thus, any completely accurate prospective evaluation of the retrievability of a target memory must incorporate information about interfering learning and the retrievability of that learning—a tall order for any metamnemonist, particularly when the learning has yet to take place!

Retrieval-Induced Forgetting. Recent work by Anderson, Bjork, and Bjork (1994) demonstrates that retrieving some information in response to a given cue can inhibit retrieval access to other information associated with that cue. Competitive dynamics at any point in time influence the retrievability of a target memory, even when the ongoing activity may bear little superficial relation to the original encoding episode. These dynamics may be predictable at the time of metamnemonic evaluation, as they may be intrinsic to the task on which performance is to be predicted. Incorporation of such information into metamnemonic judgments is hardly an obvious strategy, but it is—at least in principle—available at the time of prediction. For example, knowledge of these competitive dynamics might allow a subject to predict lowered recall of remaining-list items when half of the members of an originally studied list are presented as "cues" at the time of test (as in the *part-list cuing* effect, cf. Brown, 1968).

Shifts From Recency to Primacy. Other changes in the retrieval environment from assessment to test may violate the assumption that the relative accessibility of different items will remain the same across the retention interval. Some such changes require the subject to recognize that short-term influences are affecting current performance (during prediction), but that those influences are likely to be absent at the later time in question. For example, the *recency* effect in traditional serial-position curves of immediate list recall has been shown to disappear if the test is delayed even by 30 seconds, whereas recall of the primacy and middle portions of the list is essentially unchanged (Glanzer & Cunitz, 1966; Postman & Phillips, 1965). Figure 14.2 demonstrates an even more striking change from positive recency in immediate free recall to "negative recency" in end-of-experiment free recall (Bjork, 1975; Craik, 1970).

The top curve in the top panel of Fig. 14.2 shows the probability of recall of a word as a function of the position of that word in its original input list, averaged over a series of lists presented in succession. Note that immediate recall exhibits the typical primacy and recency effects. The

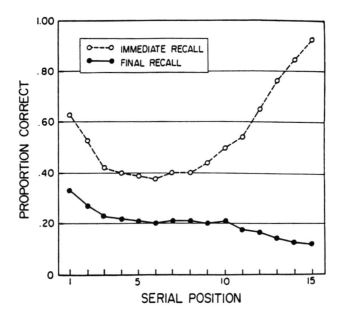

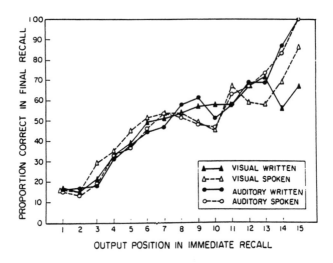

FIG. 14.2. Top panel: Probability of recall on immediate and delayed tests of retention as a function of initial input position. Bottom panel: Probability of recall on an end-of-experiment test as a function of an item's original output position on an immediate test of recall. Adapted from Craik (1970). Reproduced with permission.

bottom curve in the top panel shows the probability of recall of a word as a function of its initial input position when subjects are asked, at the end of the experiment, to free recall any and all words that they can from any of the prior lists. Note that words that were at the beginnings of lists are still recalled with greater frequency, but words that came at the ends of lists are now suppressed as compared to their original recall levels. Thus, subjects who, at the time of immediate free recall, are asked to predict their own later recall performance on individual items must evaluate not only the temporary accessibility of a particular word in that list (i.e., retrieval fluency), but also adjust such estimates for the misleading effects of short-term memory.

Episodic distinctiveness, another factor cited earlier as a determinant of retrieval fluency, can also change with time. With the continuous-distractor method, for example, in which the presentations of successive to-be-remembered items are separated in time by interpolated periods of a distracting activity of some type, there are recency effects that extend well beyond the range of short-term memory. Such "long-term recency effects" were interpreted by Bjork and Whitten (1974; see also Glenberg & Swanson, 1986; Hitch, Rejman, & Turner, 1980, as reported in Baddeley, 1990) in terms of temporal distinctiveness. To the extent that the presentation of a given set of items remains temporally distinct in memory at the time of recall, defined by whether the temporal interval that separated that set of items from adjacent sets is above some fraction of the current retention interval, retrieval of that set of items will be facilitated. As the retention interval increases, however, the functional separation of successive sets of items in memory becomes insignificant, and such recency effects disappear.

In general, as memories become more and more distant, the less episodically distinct they become in memory, other factors being held constant. To predict future access reliably, then, requires not only an understanding that retrieval currently facilitated by short-term memory will not be supported by short-term memory in the future, but also that items that are now readily accessible because they are temporally distinct in memory will not necessarily enjoy that same advantage in the future.

In the most general sense, cues change from one point in time to another. Aspects of retrieval that are cue-driven are thus highly variable, and unless one has knowledge of future cues, some portion of that variance is unpredictable. In some simple cases, such knowledge is indeed available and potentially highly useful in metamnemonic prediction. For example, one might expect to see different assessments of the recallability of the target "kiwi" between a retrieval circumstance with no cues, one with the cue "fruit," and one with the cue "fruit–k___." However, the momentary incidental cues available during encoding, the reoccurrence of which may facilitate later recall (see Richardson-Klavehn & Bjork, 1988), are often not consciously perceived and are thus not available to the predictive apparatus. Recapitulating a particular bowel state similar to one experienced during learning may facilitate recall, but it is unlikely that subjects perceive such a tangential variable to be an important cue.

Retrieval as a Memory Modifier

The act of retrieving a memory has been shown to be a potent influence in increasing later accessibility of that memory (e.g., Bjork, 1975). Thus, to the degree that a predictive task involves retrieval, covert or otherwise, one must adjust one's estimates of how retrieval fluency at the time of prediction maps onto retrieval fluency at the time of interest. In fact, dissociations have already been noted between predictive tasks that incorporate retrieval and those that discourage it. Dunlosky and Nelson (1992, 1994) found that cue-only prompts were more effective in promoting JOL accuracy than intact cue-target prompts. One clear explanation is that retrieval fluency in the cue-only case was more diagnostic of later retrieval. Furthermore, it has been argued that the necessary retrieval in that case affected future recall to the degree that the act of retrieval during prediction made the prediction serendipitously accurate (Spellman & Bjork, 1992).

Moreover, not all retrievals are created equal. In fact, it appears as though a more difficult retrieval facilitates later accessibility to a greater degree than does an easy one (Bjork & Bjork, 1992). One corollary of such a hypothesis is that a successful retrieval that is delayed by an amount of time t will be more effective in fostering future retrievability than will a successful retrieval at time t_2, $t_2 < t$. Such a relationship appears to hold and is evident in the phenomena of spacing effects and the efficacy of expanding retrieval practice (Landauer & Bjork, 1978). Successful metamnemonic prediction must thus adjust for the beneficial effects of retrieval, but in a counterintuitive manner—those traces that are difficult to retrieve will become *relatively more accessible* as a result of that retrieval than will traces which are initially easy to retrieve. In order to adjust appropriately, then, retrieval fluency must thus be used in a manner counter to the way in which it has been argued to be used here!

WHEN RETRIEVAL FLUENCY IS COUNTERDIAGNOSTIC: TWO EXAMPLES

As we have argued at some length in the preceding sections, retrieval fluency on one task at one time may prove to be a misleading index of retrieval fluency at a later time on a different task, or even on the same task. Benjamin, Bjork, and Schwartz (1996) set out to examine the extent to which subjects understand some of the dynamics summarized earlier. The first experiment to be discussed here examined whether subjects understand that fluent access to items in immediate free recall may not be accompanied by fluent access to those same items in delayed free recall. The second experiment examined whether subjects understand that the fluency of access to information from semantic memory may or may not predict the later access to that information from episodic memory.

The Recency-to-Primacy Shift

Earlier in this chapter we discussed the manner in which end-of-list (recency) items tend to be recalled with high probability on an immediate test of retention, but "suffer" more than items from the remainder of the list over a delay (again, see the top panel of Fig. 14.2). Another way in which such a result can be characterized is in the change in the makeup of the recall protocol from an immediate test to a delayed test. This change has been called the "recency-to-primacy shift," reflecting the fact that, whereas recency items are recalled very well immediately, only the primacy items show such enhanced end-of-experiment recall. This result presumably reflects two major contributing factors:

1. Because recency items are so easy to recall immediately after learning, they are typically provided before other items (middle or primacy) in the recall protocol. In that sense, they are privy to greater retrieval fluency than other items, yet this fluency is short-lived. Because such easy retrieval owes to the items' immediate availability and not to particularly good long-term memory, later recall of those same items suffers relative to the rest of the list. Again, this relationship is expressed in the serial position curves displayed in the top panel of Fig. 14.2.

2. Those items that are produced with some difficulty on an initial recall derive more benefit than easily produced items in terms of later retrievability. Thus, those items that are produced quickly, with ease, on an initial recall (i.e., recency items) enjoy less retrieval enhancement as a function of that recall than items produced later in the recall protocol. This relationship is shown in the bottom panel of Fig. 14.2, which plots the probability of end-of-experiment recall as a function of the serial *output* position of a word on an immediate test of retention. It is apparent that items which are produced later, with difficulty, on an immediate test of retention are more likely to be recalled at a delay than items which are produced on the immediate retention test with ease (i.e., earlier in the output). The data from Craik (1970) demonstrate this relationship, but are subject to a possible subject selection bias; namely, items constituting the data plotted at the higher serial positions come from increasingly few

subjects, and, in fact, from a particular subset of subjects who are demonstrably better at recall than the average subject! However, Bjork (1970) demonstrated that this relationship holds even when each individual subject's output is normalized into quartiles, and the analysis is performed on output quartile and later recall probability.

If, as hypothesized here, subjects rely principally on current retrieval fluency as an index for later retrieval ability, we might expect them to make gross errors in their estimates of what they are likely to remember at a delay when the predictions are made after an immediate (misleading) test. In fact, such mispredictions would be the strongest evidence possible for the retrieval fluency heuristic presented here—not only would subjects fail to predict their later recall qualitatively, their predictions would be opposite to their eventual recall!

In fact, such errors are made. Benjamin et al. (1996, Experiment 2) showed that subjects engage in such backwards prediction in the following paradigm. As in the experiment described earlier, subjects studied a series of six lists of 13 words each and recalled each list immediately after study. After studying and recalling all six, they were given a final free-recall test for all of the items on all of their lists.

In addition, however, subjects were asked to make a prediction for each word as they recalled it on the immediate test. In fact, subjects only made such predictions for half of the lists, in order to ascertain that the prediction had no qualitative effect on the nature of the items recalled, either at immediate or final test. In fact, the prediction making had no deleterious effects whatsoever on either test. They were asked to give their estimate of the probability of being able to recall that word again in approximately 10 minutes.

As noted earlier, subjects typically recall recency items first when tested immediately. Because these items are exactly those ones that will suffer maximally at later test, items which are produced in the latter portion of each individual immediate recall protocol tend to be recalled again with higher probability than those items recalled in the first half. Furthermore, because those items produced with ease on the initial test "gain" less in terms of later retrievability from this initial recall, we expect the relationship between immediate-recall output position and later-recall probability to be magnified.

This relationship does indeed hold, and is presented in the top half of Fig. 14.3. Items which are produced later on each immediate recall test are re-recalled with higher frequency than those items which are produced earlier.

Correct prediction must thus entail the assignment of lower estimates of final free recall to items "first-out" (high retrieval fluency) and higher

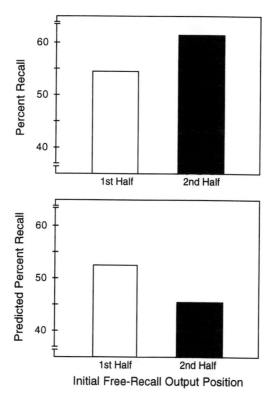

FIG. 14.3.   Top panel: Probability of final recall as a function of initial recall output half. Bottom panel: Predictions of free recall as a function of initial recall output half. Adapted from Benjamin et al. (1996). Reproduced with permission.

estimates for items that are produced later on the initial-recall test (low retrieval fluency). As hinted at, however, subjects' predictions follow the opposite pattern. This relationship is depicted in the bottom half of Fig. 14.3.

Clearly, these mispredictions reflect the tacit use of the assumption dictating intact ordinal relations of retrieval fluency over time (Assumption 2, cited earlier). Because these relations do vary and predictors have no access to the nature of such change, we see predictions severely misled.

Furthermore, we have some evidence that subjects are unable to recognize when Assumption 3 may be validly applied. With respect to this experiment, the laws of retrieval practice delineated earlier dictate that the items that are more difficult to retrieve "gain" more in terms of later recallability. By this argument, the relative increase in final recall capacity as a function of the initial retrieval should increase with the serial position of an item in the output protocol. Recency items, which are typically output first, should thus be attributed lesser beneficial effects of retrieval practice than those items that come out later. Again, there is no evidence that subjects appreciate such a relationship—predictions tend to decrease with output position, not increase. For a thorough treatment of the failure to recognize effects of retrieval practice in the judgment-of-learning paradigm, see Spellman and Bjork (1992).

Distinctions Between Episodic and Semantic Memory

In another experiment, Benjamin et al. (1996, Experiment 1) examined whether subjects could appreciate the relationship between initial ease of access to the answer to a general-information question and the probability of free recalling that answer again later. Gardiner, Craik, and Bleasdale (1973) demonstrated that the probability of free recall varied positively with the latency to answer the general-information question. In the Benjamin et al. task, subjects answered a series of general-information questions that were designed to be answerable, but varied somewhat in their difficulty. After providing an answer, they made a prediction as to the future free recallability of that answer. It was emphasized to the subjects that the future task would be different from the present one, in that no recall cues would be provided. After answering and predicting for 20 such questions, and engaging in 10 minutes of distractor activity, subjects were given a blank sheet of paper and asked to recall as many of the provided answers as possible.

As noted previously, earlier work has shown that the probability of free recalling any answer is positively related to the original latency taken to provide that answer to a question. This relationship is consistent with the following perspective on the task: The longer it takes to answer the question, the more a distinctive retrieval episode is created, thus maximizing the probability of remembering that episode during the free-recall task. In other words, questions that are answered very quickly and easily do not leave much to be remembered at time of free recall. Benjamin et al. replicated this relationship, which is presented in the top panel of Fig. 14.4.

Such a conceptualization rests on a popular distinction between *semantic* and *episodic* memory (Tulving, 1983). Semantic memory contains abstract factual and relational information stored in an associative manner. Such an architecture makes the conjecture plausible that answers to questions that are provided slowly or with some difficulty are in some sense not well known.

Episodic memory, on the other hand, stores events and autobiographical experiences from a first-person perspective and does not represent information abstractly. In fact, the free-recall task described earlier is a paradigmatic example of an episodically based task—target memories are not cued by or associated to probes presented at time of retrieval; rather, retrieval is of the episode in which the to-be-recalled information was learned. From this perspective, again, the words which took longer to

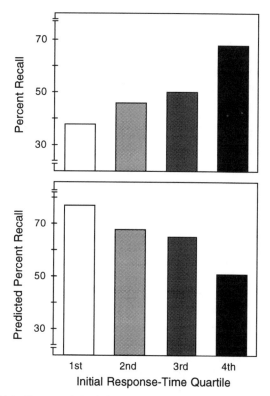

FIG. 14.4. Top panel: Probability of free recall as a function of initial response time quartile. Bottom panel: Predictions of free recall as a function of initial response time quartile. Adapted from Benjamin et al. (1996). Reproduced with permission.

produce provide more of an episode to be recalled. It is for this reason that original response latency in the Gardiner et al. (1973) task is positively related to later probability of free recall, despite the superficial counterintuitive nature of such a relationship.

If, however, subjects fail to recognize such a dissociation of memory types (semantic vs. episodic), and instead rely on retrieval fluency as a predictor of later performance, their estimates of future recallability will again be misled. Specifically, those questions that take a long time to respond to should evoke low predictions of later recall of the answer, predicated on a phenomenological sense of "not knowing the answer well." Conversely, those answers that subjects feel they know well (i.e., answer quickly) should be assigned high estimates of later free recallability.

The bottom panel of Fig. 14.4 shows that subjects do in fact mistakenly rely on initial retrieval fluency as an indicant of later recallability, despite the fact initial retrieval fluency in the Gardiner et al. (1973) paradigm predicted *poorer* later recall. Subjects predict greater recallability for those items that are initially produced quickly and less recallability for those produced slowly.

This circumstance violates another assumption tacit within the global use of retrieval fluency as a predictive index. In particular, Assumption 1 dictating the homogeneity of tasks and their sources of retrieval fluency is violated. That is, the Gardiner et al. (1973) paradigm provides a case where retrieval fluency on different tasks clearly draws on two separate sources in memory. Because subjects fail to recognize this episodic–semantic distinction, they are subscribing to the assumption that different tasks derive retrieval fluency from the same source. This is the fallacy alluded to in Assumption 1.

MISCONCEPTIONS ABOUT OURSELVES
AS LEARNERS AND REMEMBERERS

Several ways in which naive notions of memory appear to be misguided are apparent within the discussion presented here. For example, we discussed early in this analysis the fact that subjects demonstrate a failure to understand the transitory nature of priming effects, and instead attribute them as enhanced confidence (Kelley & Lindsay, 1993) or even enhanced knowing (Lee et al., 1993, cited in Narens et al., 1994).

More importantly, however, we have provided a set of three assumptions inherent within the indiscriminant use of retrieval fluency as a metacognitive index. Although these assumptions may, in practice, be met, they most definitely represent an oversimplified and incorrect view of the nature of human memory. By demonstrating that these assumptions guide predictive behavior—even when such guidance misleads metacognition in a direction opposite to true performance—we hope to have convinced the reader of several fundamental failures of the implicit models of memory held by humans:

1. The failure to appreciate the multidimensionality of memory.
2. The failure to fully appreciate the role of time and context in the preservation of memory and the manner in which they interact with the multiple dimensions of memory.
3. The failure to recognize and understand either the existence or qualitative nature of retrieval practice.

These fallacies follow directly from the assumptions listed earlier—assumptions, the truth of which in any given situation, either apparently cannot be or simply is not assessed.

Subjects demonstrate an acute unawareness of the marked difference between memory tasks, performance on which derives from semantic memory and those in which it derives from episodic memory (Benjamin et al., 1996, Experiment 1). This has been referred to as the "fallacy of homogeneous memory" and manifests itself in paradigms in which the predictive task and the to-be-predicted behavior stem from different sources in memory.

There is also a failure to understand the effects of time on memory. Specifically, Benjamin et al. (1996, Experiment 2) have shown that the differential decay processes underlying recency and primacy recall are not incorporated into metamnemonic evaluation. This inability is also reflected in the examples alluded to earlier (e.g., Narens et al., 1994) in which predictions subject to temporary priming effects do not reflect the transitory nature of such effects.

Finally, Benjamin et al. (1996, Experiment 2) and Spellman and Bjork (1992) show that subjects do not duly utilize information concerning the nature of retrieval practice when making metamnemonic predictions.

CONCLUDING COMMENT

The appearance of metacognition as a viable topic of scientific inquiry reflects a return to a central issue in psychology. Early "experimental" psychologies sought to illuminate the nature of immediate experience via trained introspection. It was of particular importance that the subjects be well trained—the idea being that only after extensive practice could a phenomenological report serve as an accurate metric for the underlying mental processes. Thus, the subject matter of psychology concerned the *objective* nature of smelling a rose or imagining a wild beast with five limbs.

In the modern era, the approach is somewhat different. A general rejection of a dualist conception of mind means that the verbal report no longer holds an untarnished image. In fact, the use of verbal reports in experimental psychology fell into such disfavor as to evoke claims of uselessness—that such reports bear essentially no relation to cognitive processes (Nisbett & Wilson, 1977).

Indeed, the resurgence of introspection within psychology is marked by a fundamental difference from its usage in the era of Wilhelm Wundt. The verbal report, like signal detection ability, sleeping behavior, or bar pressing in the rat, is viewed as a behavioral product to be explained. It is not seen as a vehicle with explanatory power for greater deeper mysteries of the human psyche—its predictive capacity, as well as its fallibility and unreliability, are all aspects to be explained much in the way that any cognitive process might be.

Toward that end, it is crucial to identify systematic biases people have in the production of introspections (see, e.g., Ericsson & Simon, 1984).

The goal of the current chapter has been to outline one such bias. It has been argued that such an undertaking has not only theoretical, but also practical value.

It might be argued that the education of metamemory is, by definition, more important than the improvement of memorial processes per se. Memory has evolved to be a highly adaptive, but fallible organ of human cognition (cf. Bjork, 1989). Metamemory, which has been considered as a sort of "system manager" for the incredible complexity of memory, serves in one sense the paramount role in cognition—as a determiner of when and how to use memory. Such a metaphor, although smacking of the problem of homunculi-driven cognition and the infinite regress problem, does emphasize an important point: Assessment of how and what we know drives what we believe we can and cannot do and, furthermore, what we do and do not continue to try to learn. Perhaps, then, one underrepresented key to enhancing human performance and learning is to redirect our focus from how to improve the system to how to use the system we have with maximal efficiency.

REFERENCES

Anderson, J. R. (1974). Retrieval of propositional information from long-term memory. *Cognitive Psychology, 6,* 451–474.

Anderson, M. C., Bjork, R. A., & Bjork, E. L. (1994). Remembering can cause forgetting: Retrieval dynamics in long-term memory. *Journal of Experimental Psychology: Learning, Memory, and Cognition, 20,* 1063–1087.

Baddeley, A. (1990). *Human memory: Theory and practice.* Boston, MA: Allyn and Bacon.

Benjamin, A. S., Bjork, R. A., & Schwarz, B. L. (1996). *The mismeasure of memory: When retrieval fluency is misleading.* Manuscript submitted for publication.

Bjork, R. A. (1970, September). *Control processes and serial position effects in free recall.* Symposium on Memory, Mathematical Psychology Meetings, Miami Beach, FL.

Bjork, R. A. (1975). Retrieval as a memory modifier. In R. Solso (Ed.), *Information processing and cognition: The Loyola Symposium* (pp. 123–144). Hillsdale, NJ: Lawrence Erlbaum Associates.

Bjork, R. A. (1989). Retrieval inhibition as an adaptive mechanism in human memory. In H. L. Roediger & F. I. M. Craik (Eds.), *Varieties of memory and consciousness: Essays in honor of Endel Tulving* (pp. 309–330). Hillsdale, NJ: Lawrence Erlbaum Associates.

Bjork, R. A., & Bjork, E. L. (1992). A new theory of disuse and an old theory of stimulus fluctuation. In A. Healy, S. Kosslyn, & R. Shiffrin (Eds.), *From learning processes to cognitive processes: Essays in honor of William K. Estes* (Vol. 2, pp. 35–67). Hillsdale, NJ: Lawrence Erlbaum Associates.

Blake, M. (1973). Prediction of recall when recognition fails: Exploring the feeling-of-knowing phenomenon. *Journal of Verbal Learning and Verbal Behavior, 12,* 311–319.

Brown, J. (1968). Reciprocal facilitation and impairment in free recall. *Psychonomic Science, 10,* 41–42.

Christina, R. W., & Bjork, R. A. (1991). Optimizing long-term retention and transfer. In D. Druckman & R. A. Bjork (Eds.), *In the mind's eye: Enhancing human performance* (pp. 23–56). Washington, DC: National Academy Press.

Costermans, J., Lories, G., & Ansay, C. (1992). Confidence level and feeling of knowing in question answering: The weight of inferential processes. *Journal of Experimental Psychology: Learning, Memory, and Cognition, 18,* 142–150.

Craik, F. I. M. (1970). The fate of primary memory items in free recall. *Journal of Verbal Learning and Verbal Behavior, 9,* 143–148.

Dunlosky, J., & Nelson, T. O. (1992). Importance of the kind of cue for judgments of learning (JOL) and the delayed-JOL effect. *Memory & Cognition, 20,* 374–380.

Dunlosky, J., & Nelson, T. O. (1994). Does the sensitivity of judgments of learning (JOLs) to the effects of various study activities depend on when the JOLs occur? *Journal of Memory and Language, 33,* 545–565.

Ericsson, K. A., & Simon, H. A. (1984). *Verbal reports as data.* Cambridge, MA: MIT Press.

Gardiner, J. M., Craik, F. I. M., & Bleasdale, F. A. (1973). Retrieval difficulty and subsequent recall. *Memory & Cognition, 1,* 213–216.

Glanzer, M., & Cunitz, A. R. (1966). Two storage mechanisms in free recall. *Journal of Verbal Learning and Verbal Behavior, 55,* 351–360.

Hart, J. T. (1965). Memory and the feeling-of-knowing experience. *Journal of Educational Psychology, 56,* 208–216.

Jacoby, L. L. (1983). Remembering the data: Analyzing interactive processes in reading. *Journal of Verbal Learning and Verbal Behavior, 22,* 485–508.

Jacoby, L. L., Allan, L. G., Collins, J. C., & Larwill, L. K. (1988). Memory influences subjective experience: Noise judgments. *Journal of Experimental Psychology: Learning, Memory, and Cognition, 14,* 240–247.

Jacoby, L. L., Bjork, R. A., & Kelley, C. M. (1994). Illusions of comprehension, competence, and remembering. In D. Druckman & R. A. Bjork (Eds.), *Learning, remembering, believing: Enhancing human performance* (pp. 57–81). Washington, DC: National Academy Press.

Jacoby, L. L., & Kelley, C. M. (1987). Unconscious influences of memory for a prior event. *Personality and Social Psychology Bulletin, 13,* 314–336.

Kamin, L. J. (1969). Predictability, surprise, attention and conditioning. In B. A. Campbell & R. M. Church (Eds.), *Punishment and aversive behavior* (pp. 279–296). New York: Appleton-Century-Crofts.

Kelley, C. M., & Lindsay, D. S. (1993). Remembering mistaken for knowing: Ease of retrieval as a basis for confidence in answers to general knowledge questions. *Journal of Memory and Language, 32,* 1–24.

Koriat, A. (1993). How do we know that we know? The accessibility model of the feeling of knowing. *Psychological Review, 100,* 609–639.

Koriat, A. (1995). Dissociating knowing and the feeling of knowing: Further evidence for the accessibility model. *Journal of Experimental Psychology: General, 124,* 311–333.

Koriat, A., Lichtenstein, S., & Fischhoff, B. (1980). Reasons for confidence. *Journal of Experimental Psychology: Human Learning and Memory, 6,* 107–118.

Krinsky, R., & Nelson, T. O. (1985). The feeling of knowing for different types of retrieval failure. *Acta Psychologica, 58,* 141–158.

Landauer, T. K., & Bjork, R. A. (1978). Optimum rehearsal patterns and name learning. In M. M. Gruneberg, P. E. Morris, & R. N. Sykes (Eds.), *Practical aspects of memory* (pp. 625–632). London: Academic Press.

Lee, V. A., Narens, L., & Nelson, T. O. (1993). *Subthreshold priming and the judgment of learning.* Manuscript submitted for publication.

Lovelace, E. A. (1984). Metamemory: Monitoring future recallability during study. *Journal of Experimental Psychology: Learning, Memory, and Cognition, 10,* 756–766.

Lupker, S. J., Harbluk, J. L., & Patrick, A. S. (1991). Memory for things forgotten. *Journal of Experimental Psychology: Learning, Memory, and Cognition, 17,* 897–907.

Marks, G., & Miller, N. (1985). The effect of certainty on consensus judgments. *Personality and Social Psychology Bulletin, 11,* 165–177.

Mazzoni, G., & Nelson, T. O. (1995). Judgments of learning are affected by the kind of encoding in ways that cannot be attributed to level of recall. *Journal of Experimental Psychology: Learning, Memory, and Cognition, 21*, 1263–1274.

McGeogh, J. A. (1932). Forgetting and the law of disuse. *Psychological Review, 39*, 352–370.

Narens, L., Jameson, K. A., & Lee, V. A. (1994). Subthreshold priming and memory monitoring. In J. Metcalfe & A. P. Shimamura (Eds.), *Metacognition: Knowing about knowing* (pp. 71–92). Cambridge, MA: MIT Press.

Nelson, T. O., & Dunlosky, J. (1992). How shall we explain the delayed judgment-of-learning effect? *Psychological Science, 3*, 317–318.

Nelson, T. O., Gerler, D., & Narens, L. (1984). Accuracy of feeling-of-knowing judgments for predicting perceptual identification and relearning. *Journal of Experimental Psychology: General, 113*, 282–300.

Nelson, T. O., Leonesio, R. J., Shimamura, A. P., Landwehr, R. F., & Narens, L. (1982). Overlearning and the feeling of knowing. *Journal of Experimental Psychology: Learning, Memory, and Cognition, 8*, 279–288.

Nisbett, R. E., & Wilson, T. D. (1977). Telling more than we can know: Verbal reports on mental processes. *Psychological Review, 84*, 231–259.

Postman, L. (1971). Organization and interference. *Psychological Review, 78*, 290–302.

Postman, L., & Phillips, L. W. (1965). Short term temporal changes in free recall. *Quarterly Journal of Experimental Psychology, 17*, 132–138.

Reder, L. M. (1987). Strategy selection in question answering. *Cognitive Psychology, 19*, 111–138.

Reder, L. M., & Klatzky, R. L. (1994). Transfer: Training for performance. In D. Druckman & R. A. Bjork (Eds.), *Learning, remembering, believing: Enhancing human performance* (pp. 25–56). Washington, DC: National Academy Press.

Reder, L. M., & Ritter, F. E. (1992). What determines initial feeling of knowing? Familiarity with question terms, not with the answer. *Journal of Experimental Psychology: Learning, Memory, and Cognition, 13*, 435–451.

Richardson-Klavehn, A., & Bjork, R. A. (1988). Measures of memory. *Annual Review of Psychology, 39*, 475–543.

Schwartz, B. L., & Metcalfe, J. (1992). Cue familiarity but not target retrievability enhances feeling-of-knowing judgments. *Journal of Experimental Psychology: Learning, Memory, and Cognition, 18*, 1074–1083.

Schacter, D. L., & Worling, J. R. (1985). Attribute information and the feeling-of-knowing. *Canadian Journal of Psychology, 39*, 467–475.

Shaw, J. (1996). Increases in eyewitness confidence resulting from postevent questioning. *Journal of Experimental Psychology: Applied, 2*, 126–146.

Slamecka, N. J., & Graf, P. (1978). The generation effect: Delineation of a phenomenon. *Journal of Experimental Psychology: Human Learning and Memory, 4*, 592–604.

Spellman, B. A., & Bjork, R. A. (1992). When predictions create reality: Judgments of learning may alter what they are intended to assess. *Psychological Science, 3*, 315–316.

Tulving, E. (1983). *Elements of episodic memory.* New York: Oxford University Press.

Tulving, E., & Thomson, D. M. (1973). Encoding specificity and retrieval processes in episodic memory. *Psychological Review, 80*, 352–373.

Tversky, A., & Kahneman, D. (1974). Judgment under uncertainty: Heuristics and biases. *Science, 185*, 124–131.

Tversky, A., & Kahneman, D. (1983). Extensional versus intuitive reasoning: The conjunction fallacy in probability judgment. *Psychological Review, 90*, 293–315.

Watkins, O. C., & Watkins, M. J. (1975). Buildup of proactive inhibition as a cue-overload effect. *Journal of Experimental Psychology: Human Learning and Memory, 104*, 442–452.

Witherspoon, D., & Allan, L. G. (1985). The effects of a prior presentation on temporal judgments in a perceptual identification task. *Memory & Cognition, 13*, 103–111.

Chapter 15

Closing Remarks

Herbert A. Simon
Carnegie Mellon University

I am glad that my responsibility in this symposium is limited to providing "closing remarks" and does not require me to provide commentaries on all of the 14 impressive papers heard over the three days of the symposium and presented here. We have learned about a large number of interesting experiments and observations aimed at elucidating the phenomena of implicit memory and metacognition as well as hypotheses for explaining the phenomena that were reported. I draw on these works to illustrate some of my points, but I do not feel obligated to comment on each and all of them; and I make no pretense of dealing with the whole range of issues that have been raised and discussed here. In particular, I restrict my remarks almost entirely to the information-processing level and avoid comments on the evidence about the locations of knowledge and processes in the brain. That is an important topic, but one distinct from the one I feel best qualified to address.

Two terms are central to the symposium: *implicit memory* and *metacognition.* As there has been essential consistency in the meanings that the speakers have assigned to these terms (far more, I think, than we experienced at a previous symposium on consciousness), we have been able to focus on substantive phenomena rather than terminology. However, let me preface my own substantive remarks by some comments on how we observe and measure implicit memory and metacognition.

OBSERVING IMPLICIT MEMORY

Explicit and Implicit

When someone asks us the name of the capital of Oregon and we answer "Salem," we have provided evidence by our behavior that the name was stored in our memory and was accessible on the cue provided by the question. We then call the memory explicit. If, instead, we respond that we know the answer (i.e., we know that it is stored in our memory) but cannot just now retrieve it, we call the memory implicit.

More generally, we call memory explicit if, in response to a question calling for specific knowledge, the respondent provides that knowledge. We call memory implicit if the respondent's behavior contains any kind of evidence, other than the specific knowledge in question, indicating that he or she holds the knowledge in memory. One form, but only one form, of implicit memory are assertions of respondents, when asked whether they possess certain knowledge, that they do. They may actually have the knowledge (and even access it); alternatively, the evidence that they have it (i.e., the evidence available to them internally) may be only some kind of reportable "feeling" that it is there. Sometimes (an intermediate case), they cannot produce a piece of knowledge but can describe (correctly or incorrectly) some of its characteristics (e.g., that the name of the capital of Oregon begins with an "S"—or with an "A").

In all cases, explicit knowledge is attributed to someone if and only if the knowledge can be reported. By contrast, attributing implicit knowledge to someone entails various kinds of inferences from behavior (inferences that may make use of a model of the mind). Such attributions cannot be entirely atheoretical; they both presuppose some properties of memory and allow us to test these presuppositions.

In his commentary, John Anderson (Chapter 5, this volume) emphasized that information processing models of memory are models of both explicit and implicit memory, and do not generally make an overt distinction between them, just as they do not make an overt distinction between processes that are "logical" and those that are "illogical," or those that are "conscious" and those that are "subconscious" or "unconscious." To make these distinctions, we must look at the structures and processes of the models, and decide where we wish to draw these boundaries. In what follows, I call knowledge explicit if (in terms of the model of memory we are using) it can be accessed and brought into short-term memory (STM). The external evidence that it is explicit is that it can be produced verbally or by some other behavioral means (e.g., by pointing). The central theoretical presupposition that connects the behavioral definition of "explicit" with the model is that what we are conscious of is essentially the contents of STM.

Processes for Explicit Recall

The basic symbolic processes required for explicit memory responses are reasonably well understood and even agreed on by cognitive psychologists. Here I describe them in terms of the particular theory that is embodied in the EPAM program (Richman, Staszewski, & Simon, 1995). Alternatively, many of the same phenomena are captured by theories like Act*, or currently popular PDP theories. (For a review of some contemporary memory architectures see VanLehn, 1991.) For our purposes, we are concerned mostly with the common parts of these theories and not with the details in which they differ.

For behaviors that demonstrate explicit memory, we require a means for recognizing a cue (the question), and an association from the recognized cue to the information, stored in long-term memory (LTM), that constitutes the response. Whether the cue is recognized and evokes the answer may depend on the level of activation of the access path. In order to produce the response after accessing the answer, a pointer to the answer must be held in STM long enough to generate the oral, written, or other behavioral response. In the EPAM model, the recognition mechanism is a discrimination net that accesses an image containing the desired information, and places a pointer to the image in STM. The image is accessed by sorting the cue through the discrimination net.

The discrimination net is highly redundant so that there will generally be multiple paths leading to any particular piece of well-learned knowledge, with the consequences that partial cues may achieve recognition and that the system will have substantial resistance to forgetting on the loss of single nodes or links. Nodes and links in the net may have various levels of activation so that priming is possible.

The EPAM model, and others like it, also gives us a clear explanation of the relation between recall and recognition (the latter sometimes being regarded as a form of implicit memory). In the case of recall, the cue (e.g., "What is the capital of Oregon?") is adequate to access the knowledge in memory. In the case of recognition without recall, this cue fails, for there is no route in the discrimination net from "capital of Oregon" to "Salem." However, when we are given additional information (e.g., asked whether the answer is Salem or Eugene), we access directly an appropriate memory node (e.g., the node for Salem) and obtain the information stored there that Salem is the capital of Oregon. (An association from A to B does not imply an association from B to A.) It appears that the distinctions that Jacoby emphasizes in his experiments between "remember" and "know" responses can be understood along the lines I have just indicated for the "recall" and "recognition" distinction.

Implicit memory is inferred from explicit memory. Contemporary theory on the nature and validity of verbal protocols holds that explicit memory is limited to things that can be held in STM, and that these things are essentially the inputs and outputs to cognitive processes, not the processes themselves (Ericsson & Simon, 1993). Hence, my memory that a moment ago I added two numbers is implicit, inferred from the explicit memory that I had inputs, 4 and 3, in STM, followed by the output, 7. If I am asked, however, "What is the sum of 4 and 3?," and answer, "7," I have demonstrated explicit memory of the sum.

Goals (intentions) can also be symbolized as outputs of processes and inputs to other processes, and in that form may be remembered explicitly. So, perhaps I remember that I added two numbers because I remember the goal of doing so. In this case, the memory of the goal is explicit whereas the memory of adding is implicit, inferred from the temporary presence in STM of the goal (and/or of the inputs and outputs to the addition process).

The inferences that enable implicit memory responses may be far more complex and indirect than those just illustrated. I can "know" implicitly that I know the capital of Oregon (or "feel" that I know it) if I know that State capitals are cities and that I know the names of many cities; or if I know the names of many capitals, and by experience know that, having recalled a capital, I can generally remember the name of its state; or if, on sorting the cues, "Oregon" and "capital," down my EPAM net, I do not reach a city name but do reach a terminal node with an incomplete symbol with two syllables whose initial letter is "S."

The Tip of the Tongue

We come in this way to the "tip-of-the-tongue" phenomenon that Kelley and Jacoby (Chapter 13, this volume) take as paradigmatic for implicit knowledge. The phenomenon is well described in the classic paper of Brown and McNeill (1966), who provided an explanation for it within the EPAM framework I have just sketched. Partial cues about the answer are the source of the feeling that we know it (the "fringe of consciousness" that Jacoby speaks of, quoting William James), and may lead us to additional cues that, in turn, finally lead to the answer itself.

The Brown and McNeill paper still provides a rich stock of data about implicit memory and the mechanisms that underlie it. Instead of discussing that paper in detail (although I encourage you to review it at your earliest opportunity), let me turn to the evidence of similar inferential processes in Funnel, Metcalf, and Tsapkini's description (Chapter 7, this volume) and striking TV film of the responses of an anomic patient. The patient responded to certain questions, not to others. One response provided clear evidence that his memory contained knowledge (explicit knowledge) of what a door looked like, for when he was (unsuccessfully) searching for the word "door," he could point to one in the room in order to communicate what word he was seeking. The analogy with aspects of the tip-of-the-tongue phenomenon is direct. Just as Brown and McNeill's subjects, unable to find a word in memory when given its definition, sometimes responded (inaccurately) with a semantically related term ("astrolabe" for "sextant"), so the anomic patient replaced the desired word (correctly in this case) with the visual stimulus that represented its meaning.

The patient's response also could be viewed as expressing his implicit knowledge of information in his LTM. It showed (implicitly) that he had intact processes for understanding the verbal question that had been put to him, that he had a mental representation (probably visual) of the meaning of the answer, and that an intact motor process (pointing) could provide a surrogate for the verbal answer by showing an alternate path to the meaning. The film showed that he could use his own inference processes to indicate that he knew (implicitly) what word he was seeking even though the word was unavailable to him. Moreover, he recognized the word (explicit knowledge, as evidenced by a nod) when he was asked whether that was the one he was seeking.

There is nothing mysterious about this: We observe the patient's explicit responses, and these, combined with our theory of memory structure, gives clues to many of his implicit "feelings of knowing" (the unreachable word) and control processes. The patient himself uses these same kinds of inferences to give evidence of his knowledge of meanings.

METACOGNITION

This brings me to the topic of metacognition. We already observe, from the examples I have used, that much implicit knowledge is concerned with the processes that control and monitor the course of thought. It is this control and monitoring knowledge that is designated by the term metacognition. A first answer to the question implied by the title of this symposium, "What is the relation of implicit memory to metacognition?," is simply that part of implicit memory consists of inferences about the control and monitoring processes. Cognition is rich in processes, both "substantive" processes and those that control and monitor the others. Knowledge of them can be inferred from knowledge of their immediate inputs and outputs or by inferences along more indirect routes.

However, we must be a little careful with terminology here. If "metacognition" is to refer to all memory of control and monitoring, not all metacognition is implicit. Goals may appear as inputs in STM, and consequently can be (and frequently are) reported explicitly in verbal protocols. For this reason metacognitive elements can appear in both explicit and implicit memory.

Metacognitive processes, as they take the form of productions, are knowable only implicitly, when they reveal themselves through their inputs and outputs or by means of longer chains of inferences. For example, if we regard the act of recognition as a metacognitive process (it presumably depends on the focus of attention and results in accessing a particular LTM image), we see that the cues employed for recognition are known only implicitly, through the presence in STM of the item recognized. We cannot report veridically what cues were actually used in making the discrimination, as the intermediate steps in the discrimination process do not appear in STM. Furthermore, although we have seen that goals may be reportable, hence may constitute explicit metacognitive knowledge, the motives that played a key role in establishing the goals do not appear in STM, hence constitute implicit knowledge which can only be inferred, often unreliably, from behavior and from goals of which the actor is aware (Ericsson & Simon, 1993; Nisbett & Ross, 1980; Nisbett & Wilson, 1977).

However, there is quite another connection between metacognition and implicit memory that was brought out both in the work by Narens, Graf, and Nelson (Chapter 6, this volume), and in the work by Benjamin and Bjork (Chapter 14, this volume). Control of task performance may depend to an important degree on the actors themselves being able to note and record the ease or difficulty of particular steps in their performance, which may be translated, for example, into judgments of the probability of correctness of the steps and the need for checking (confidence judgments, judgments of retrieval fluency). It is not clear to what extent this information is stored in such a manner as to be available to explicit recall, or to what extent recall is inferential, hence, according to our definitions, involves implicit memory. The experiments reported in these chapters are aimed at discovering how implicit cognition like judgments of retrieval fluency are achieved, and the conditions under which they are or are not likely to be accurate. Again, an explicit memory model could be used profitably to guide such analysis, and its employment for this purpose could cast specific light on the parameters associated with priming and activation processes.

IMPLICIT COGNITION IN PROBLEM SOLVING

Kihlstrom, Shames, and Dorfman (Chapter 1, this volume) suggest that the notion of implicit cognition can be extended beyond memory tasks to problem solving, and they point in particular to the phenomena of intuition, incubation, and insight. In what sense can we assert that these involve "implicit" processes? If we find the behavior involving intuition, incubation, or insight to imply that knowledge has been present but cannot be recalled, then this knowledge fits our definition of implicit memory. Let us consider each of the three kinds of phenomena in turn.

Intuition

The usual operational definition of intuition is that a question is answered or a problem solved quite rapidly and without the respondent being able to recall just how the answer or solution was obtained. The response clearly depended on the availability of knowledge, but there is no awareness of that knowledge at the moment that the answer is given. Intuition, so defined, is an extremely common characteristic of expert behavior when experts are confronted with tasks of a kind that they encounter repeatedly in practice; for example, a rapid medical diagnosis by an experienced medical specialist. Of course, the answers are not always correct, but they are right in a great majority of cases.

The phenomenon is not hard to explain within the EPAM model. In the task situation, the expert encounters cues (e.g., medical symptoms) that are highly familiar from past experience, and that immediately lead to recognition and access to such information as possible diagnosis, additional diagnostic tests needed for verification, prognosis, methods of treatment, and so on. In EPAM, STM only records the final result of a series of discriminations—that is, the thing recognized—and the respondent has no awareness of the specific tests performed by the discrimination net that led up to the recognition. Hence, we do not need to hypothesize a special process of "intuition": What we call intuition is simply the familiar process of recognition, readily modeled in a system like EPAM.

Incubation

As the authors point out, the evidence for unconscious incubation during problem solving is quite inconsistent, and we must take care not to explain phenomena that do not exist. However, let us, for present purposes, posit that there are sometimes indications that progress was made toward a problem solution while the solver was asleep or attending to quite different matters. On the basis of the evidence available in the literature today, most, and perhaps all, of the phenomena described under the heading of "incubation" are still explainable by the forgetting mechanism discussed by Kihlstrom, Dorfman, and Shames, which was proposed by Woodworth (1938). If that is so, then the differences in forgetting rates for STM and LTM in models like EPAM can account for incubation.

Insight

If intuition is explainable in terms of immediate recognition, what about the so-called "insight" problems, where a solution arrives suddenly (or at least rapidly) but only after a shorter or longer period of striving, and sometimes frustration? There is no doubt about the reality of the "aha!" phenomenon in these situations. What distinguishes them from other occasions of expert recognition is that the solution is not recognizable when the problem is represented in one way, but the path to it is recognizable when the problem representation is changed (Kaplan & Simon, 1990). Discovery of the new representation leads to the "aha," followed by rapidly increasing confidence that the problem will be solved, as it usually soon is.

In the mutilated checkerboard problem, which has been studied in detail, the "natural" or direct representation of the problem, which almost all subjects adopt, does not provide the cues that would permit recognition of the solution path. Some subjects, after a long struggle, or after being given simple hints, change their problem representations and then find the solution within a matter of minutes—that is, by recognition. Implicit metacognitive processes take part in the process as evaluators of search progress and as controls that ultimately shift attention from the original problem to the problem space of alternative representations. As with intuition and incubation, it does not appear that we need additional mechanisms to account for the phenomena, which are explicable within standard memory models.

ROLE OF MEMORY MODELS

We see from these examples that a model of memory structures and processes can make strong predictions about what memories are explicit and implicit, and about the levels of accuracy that can be expected in making various kinds of responses to questions about memories. Conversely, ability or inability to make responses and the accuracy of the responses provides a powerful tool for developing and testing models of memory.

While presenting their paper at the symposium, Graf and Birt made a case for employing a checklist of constraints on memory as a framework for memory research. By a constraint, they meant "any factor whose presence or absence influences and shapes memory performance in a particular situation." I would see such a checklist as a potential aid to building a specific memory model, but not as a substitute for the model, for we need not only a knowledge of the constraints, but also clear hypotheses about how, singly and in interaction, these constraints influence the memory processes in each task environment. The distinction, as I see it, is between, on the one hand, having a list of variables, and, on the other, having a set of equations that describes the interaction of these variables in controlling system behavior.

A memory model, to the extent that we have independent evidence for its structure, can be a powerful tool for understanding the vexatious problem, discussed by Loftus, Coan, and Pickrell in Chapter 8, of reported memories of childhood abuse. The model cannot, of course, tell us which particular reports are veridical and which are not, but it can provide us with alternative hypotheses about the mental processes that can lead to such reports, and thereby help define what "beyond reasonable doubt" might mean in such situations.

CONCLUSION

That there should be implicit as well as explicit memory is not surprising or mysterious as long as we recognize that not everything about memory structure and process is reportable. The subject must use indirect means to infer much of it. We label as "implicit memory" the responses to task demands that provide clues to the more indirectly available components of this system. This statement holds whether we are talking of EPAM, ACT–R, Cohen and Servan-Schreiber's connectionist net, a schematic neural net, or any other model of memory that is valid for the phenomena under consideration (VanLehn, 1991).

Research on implicit memory requires us to invent tasks that give us cues to the indirectly observable components and processes of LTM and to draw inferences from the observed behavior that enable us to develop and test models of the system. In such research, experimenting and model building must go hand in hand.

The human memory system is far too complex to be understood through informal verbal arguments that lack the discipline of a formal, computationally effective model for inferring interactions and other indirect consequences of the operation of components. At this symposium, Anderson gave us one simple example of how to employ a model for understanding explicit and implicit memory, using ACT–R; McClelland another, using a PDP net; Shimamura, using a neural net; I another, using EPAM. Although much remains to be done before we reach consensus about the properties that should be incorporated in a memory model, these examples provide a considerable range of illustrations of the strategy to be followed. Modeling, in combination with the careful and ingenious experimentation that is typified by the papers of this symposium, will broaden and deepen our understanding both of those elements in memory that can be reported explicitly and those about which we must learn through indirect paths of inference.

REFERENCES

Brown, R., & McNeill, D. (1966). The "tip of the tongue" phenomenon. *Journal of Verbal Learning and Verbal Behavior, 5*, 325–337.

Ericsson, K. A., & Simon, H. A. (1993). *Protocol analysis.* Cambridge, MA: MIT Press.

Kaplan, C., & Simon, H. A. (1990). In search of insight. *Cognitive Psychology, 22,* 374–419.

Nisbett, R. E., & Ross, L. (1980). *Human inference: Strategies and shortcomings of social judgment.* Englewood Cliffs, NJ: Prentice-Hall.

Nisbett, R. E., & Wilson, T. D. (1977). Telling more than we can know: Verbal reports on mental processes. *Psychological Review, 84,* 231–259.

Richman, H., Staszewski, J., & Simon, H. A. (1995). Simulations of expert memory using EPAM IV. *Psychological Review, 102,* 305–330.

VanLehn, K. (Ed.). (1991). *Architectures for intelligence.* Hillsdale, NJ: Lawrence Erlbaum Associates.

Woodworth, R. S. (1938). *Experimental psychology.* New York: Henry Holt.

Author Index

Subject Index